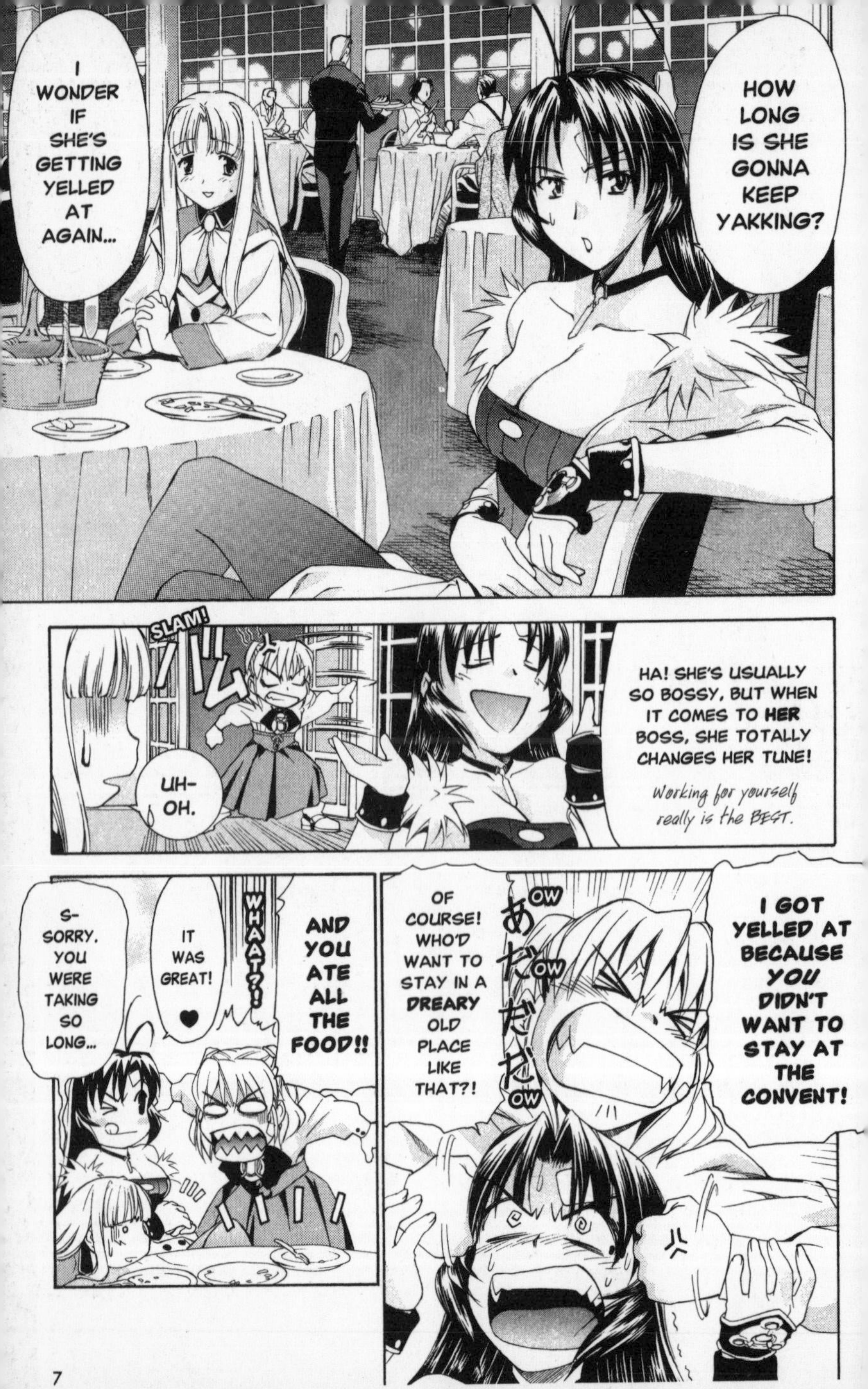
HOW LONG IS SHE GONNA KEEP YAKKING?
I WONDER IF SHE'S GETTING YELLED AT AGAIN...
HA! SHE'S USUALLY SO BOSSY, BUT WHEN IT COMES TO HER BOSS, SHE TOTALLY CHANGES HER TUNE!
SLAM!
Working for yourself really is the BEST.
UH-OH.
I GOT YELLED AT BECAUSE YOU DIDN'T WANT TO STAY AT THE CONVENT!
あだだだ
OW OW OW
OF COURSE! WHO'D WANT TO STAY IN A DREARY OLD PLACE LIKE THAT?!
AND YOU ATE ALL THE FOOD!!
WHAAAT?!
IT WAS GREAT! ♥
S-SORRY. YOU WERE TAKING SO LONG...

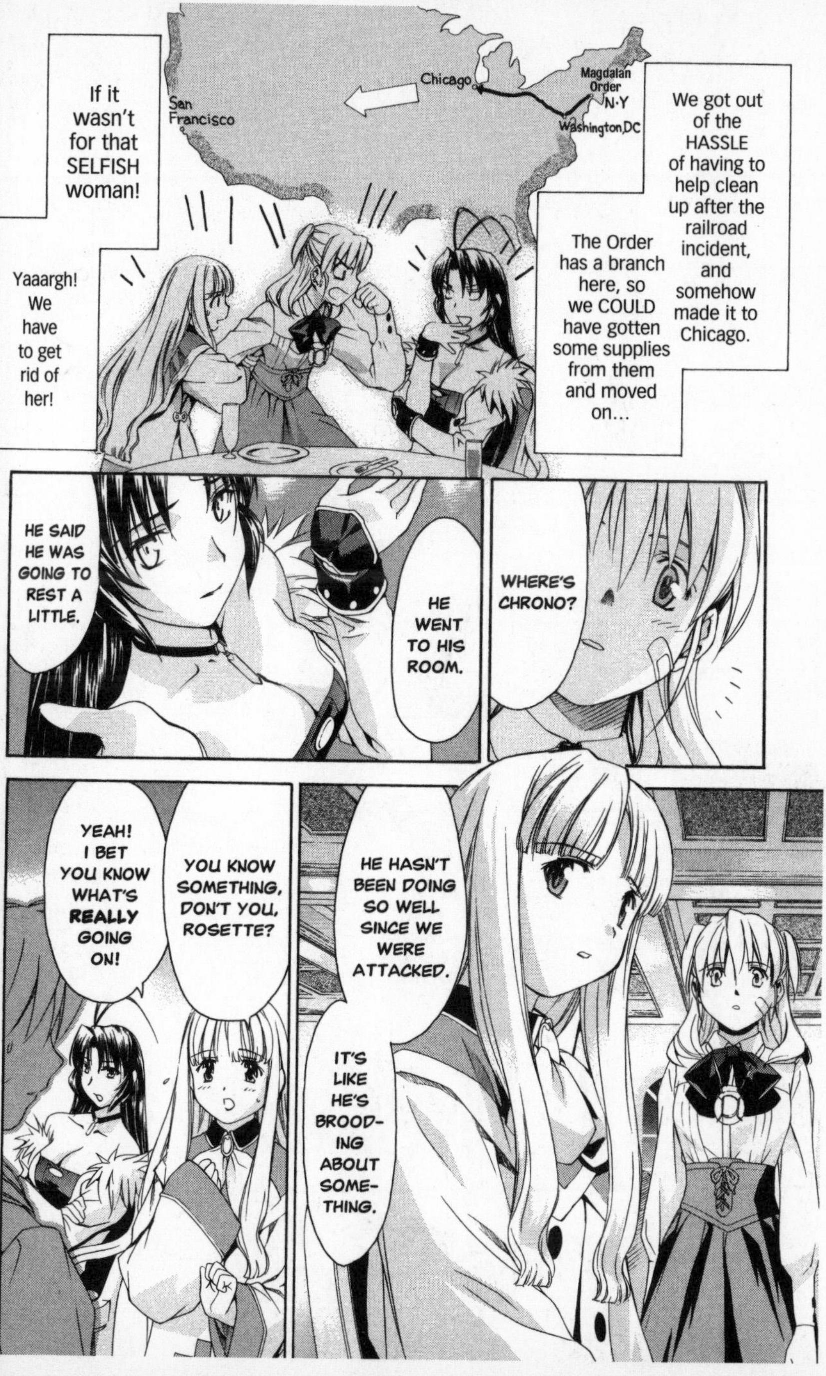

Chicago
Magdalan Order
N·Y
Washington,DC
San Francisco
We got out of the HASSLE of having to help clean up after the railroad incident, and somehow made it to Chicago.
The Order has a branch here, so we COULD have gotten some supplies from them and moved on...
If it wasn't for that SELFISH woman!
Yaaargh! We have to get rid of her!
WHERE'S CHRONO?
HE WENT TO HIS ROOM.
HE SAID HE WAS GOING TO REST A LITTLE.
HE HASN'T BEEN DOING SO WELL SINCE WE WERE ATTACKED.
IT'S LIKE HE'S BROOD-ING ABOUT SOME-THING.
YOU KNOW SOMETHING, DON'T YOU, ROSETTE?
YEAH! I BET YOU KNOW WHAT'S **REALLY** GOING ON!

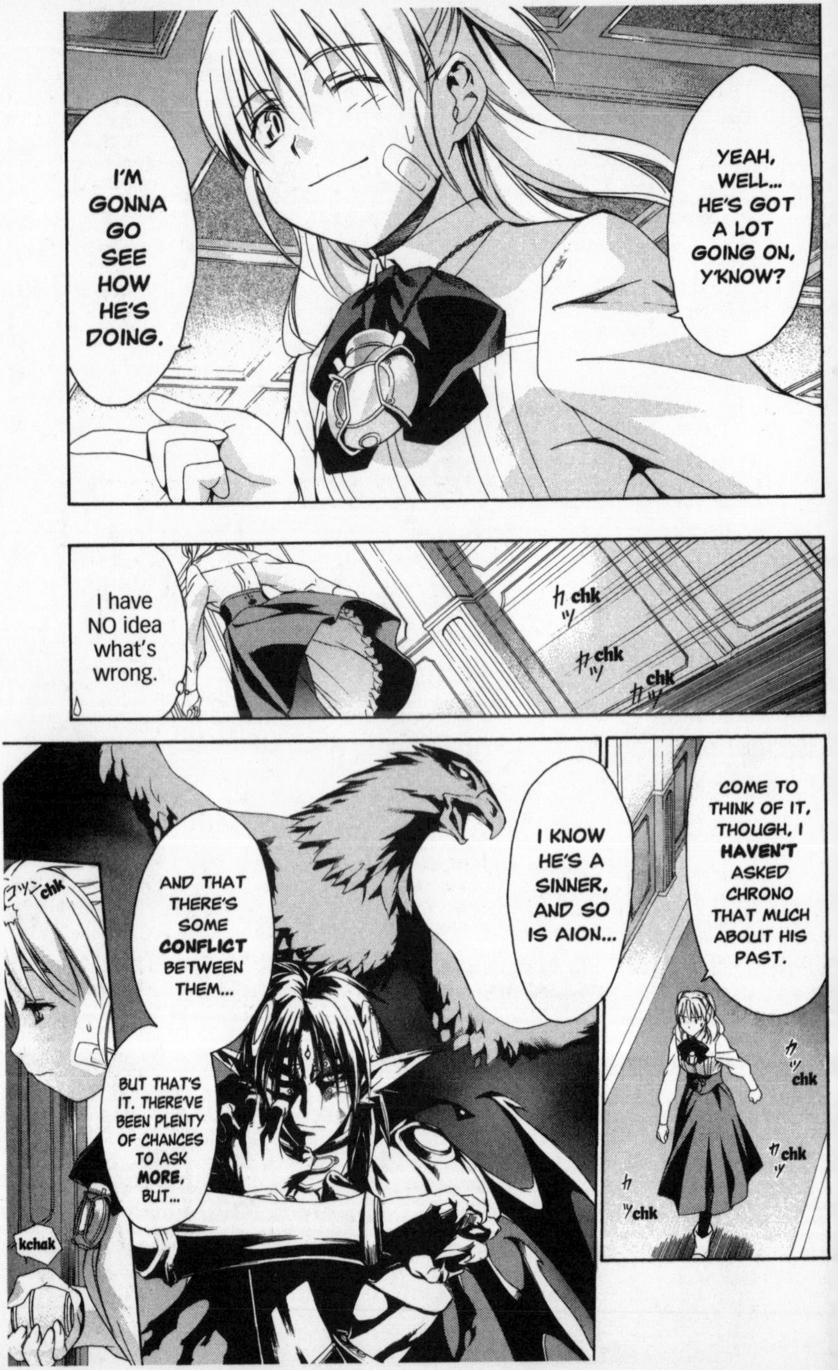
YEAH, WELL... HE'S GOT A LOT GOING ON, Y'KNOW?
I'M GONNA GO SEE HOW HE'S DOING.
chk
chk
chk
I have NO idea what's wrong.
COME TO THINK OF IT, THOUGH, I HAVEN'T ASKED CHRONO THAT MUCH ABOUT HIS PAST.
chk
chk
chk
I KNOW HE'S A SINNER, AND SO IS AION...
AND THAT THERE'S SOME CONFLICT BETWEEN THEM...
chk
BUT THAT'S IT. THERE'VE BEEN PLENTY OF CHANCES TO ASK MORE, BUT...
kchak

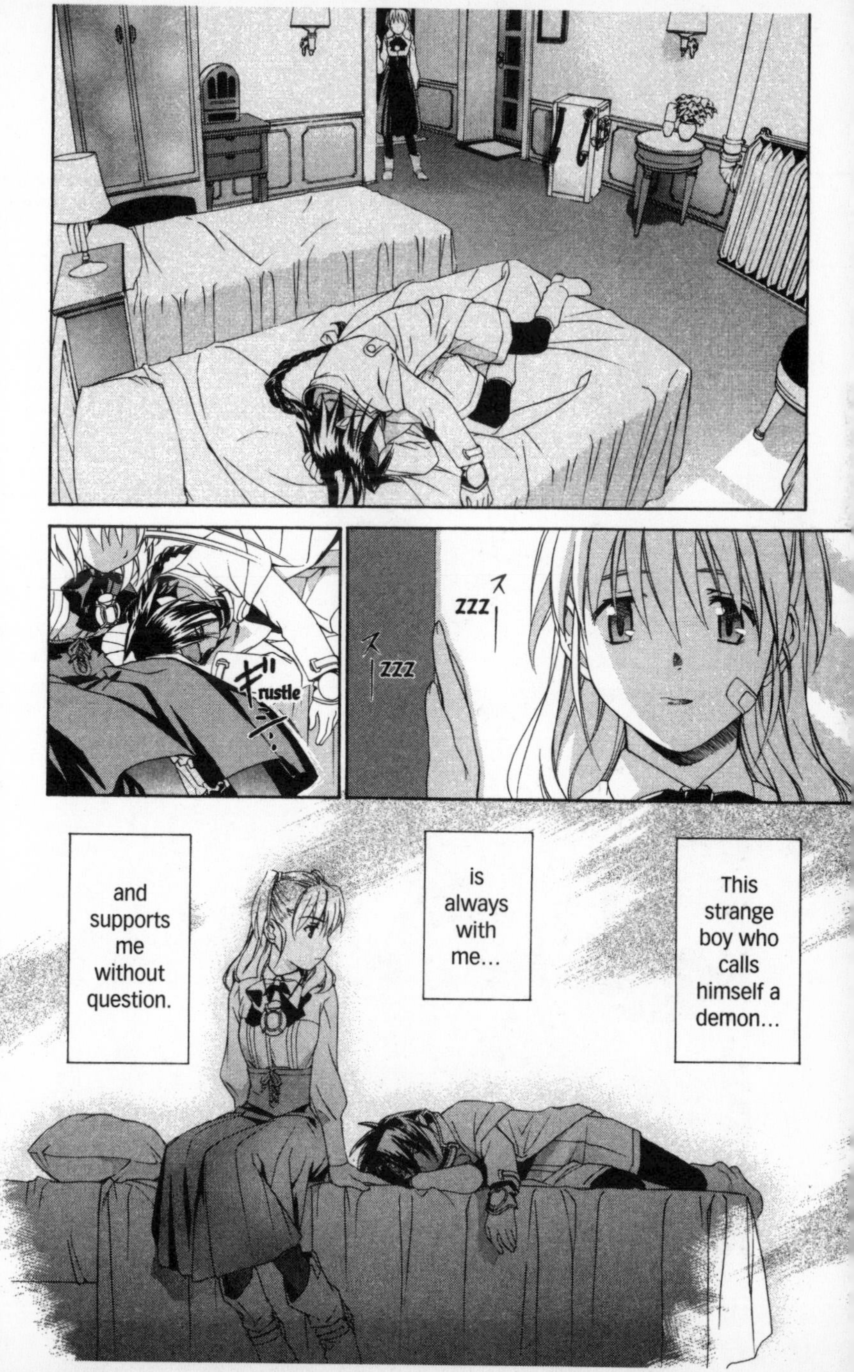

ス
ZZZ
ス
ZZZ
ギ
rustle
This strange boy who calls himself a demon...
is always with me...
and supports me without question.

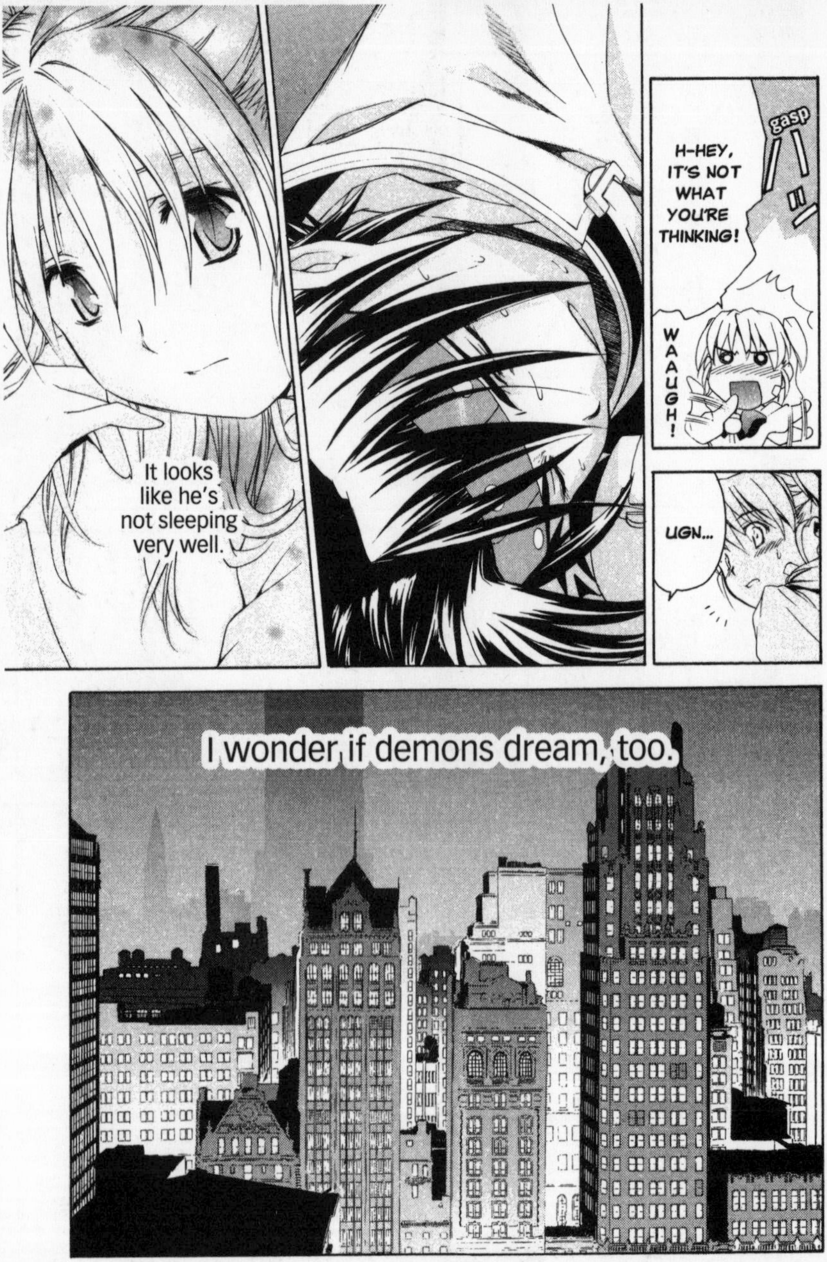
gasp
H-HEY, IT'S NOT WHAT YOU'RE THINKING!
WAAUGH!
UGN...
It looks like he's not sleeping very well.
I wonder if demons dream, too.

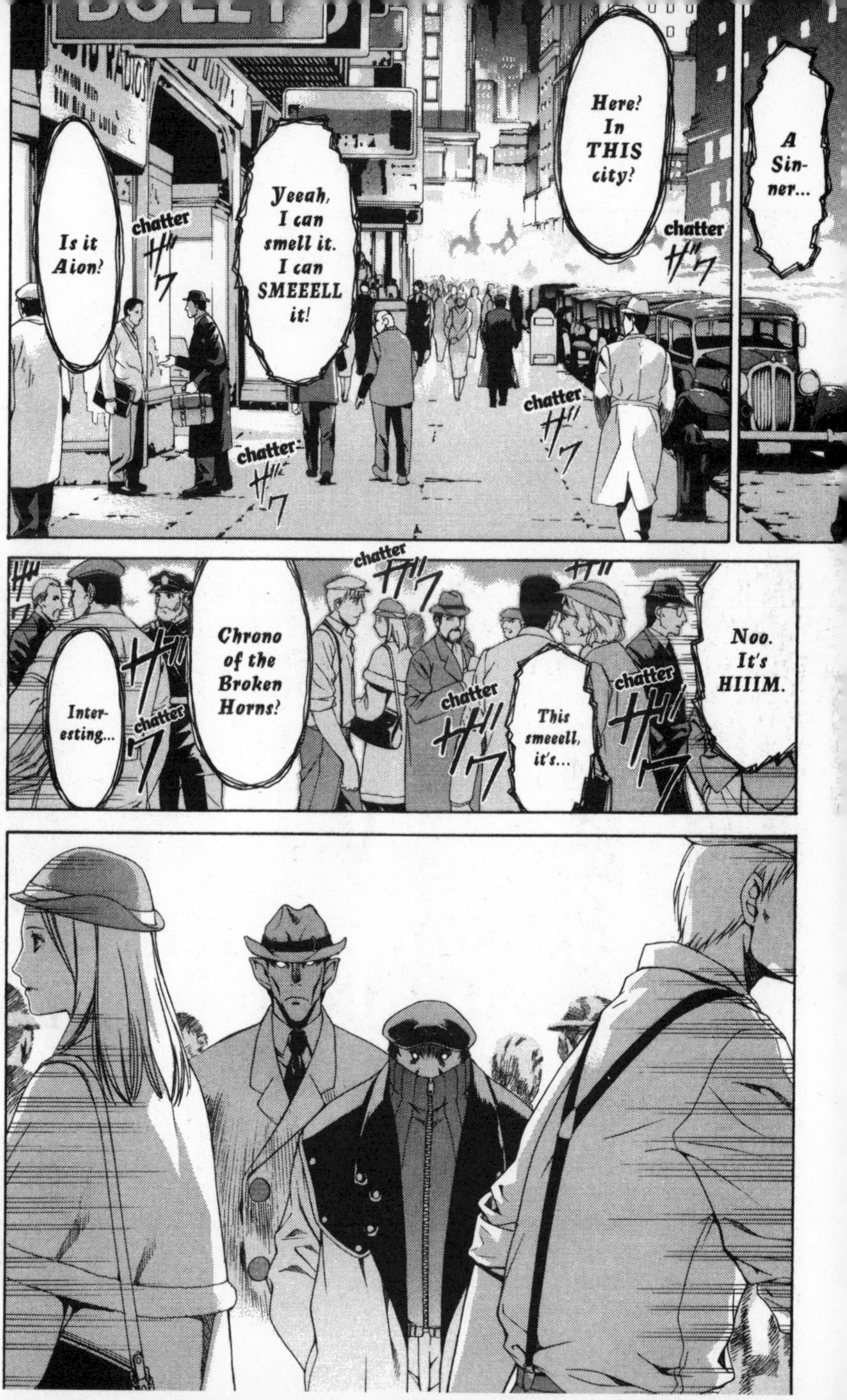
A Sinner...
Here? In THIS city?
chatter
Yeeah, I can smell it. I can SMEEELL it!
chatter
Is it Aion?
chatter
chatter
Noo. It's HIIIM.
chatter
This smeeell, it's...
chatter
chatter
Chrono of the Broken Horns?
chatter
Interesting...

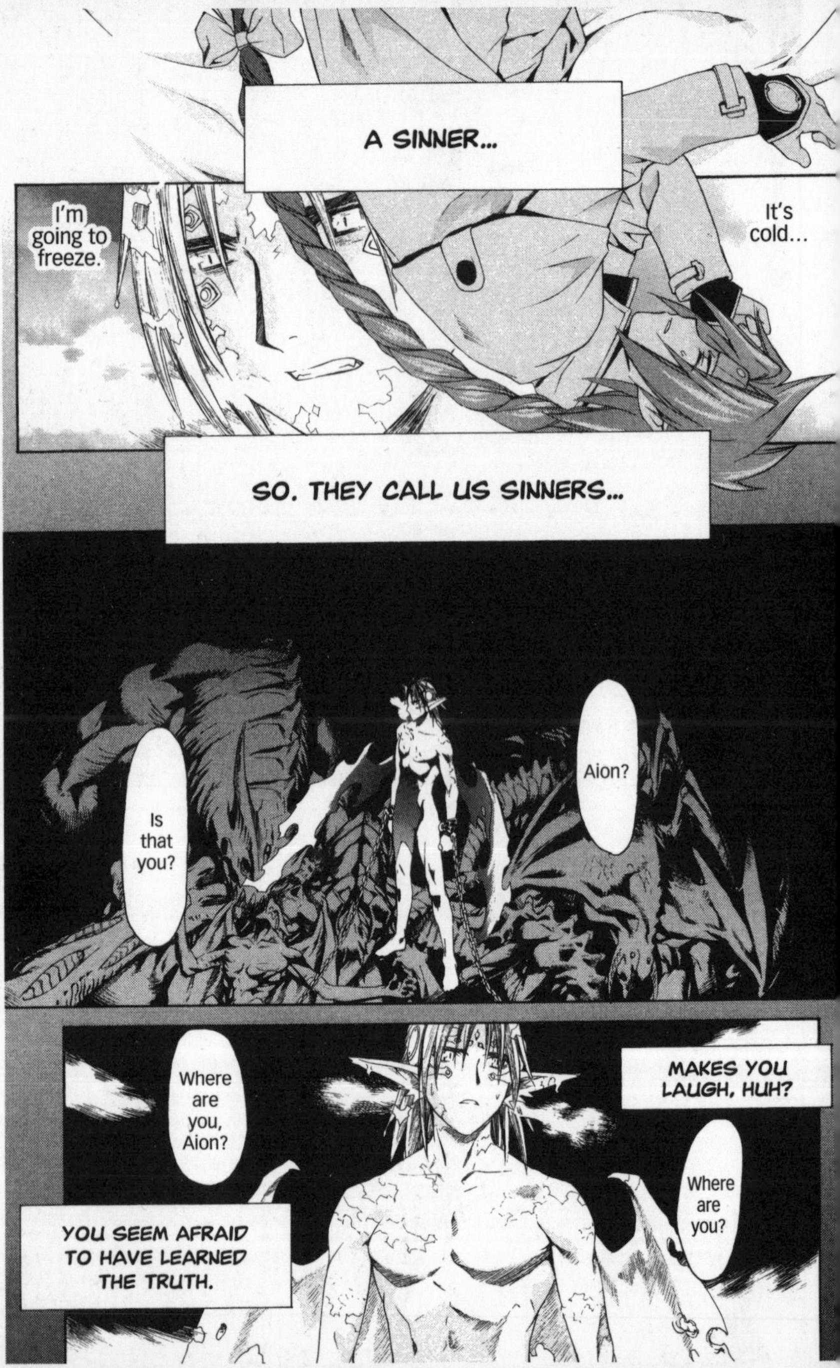
A SINNER...
It's cold...
I'm going to freeze.
SO. THEY CALL US SINNERS...
Aion?
Is that you?
MAKES YOU LAUGH, HUH?
Where are you?
Where are you, Aion?
YOU SEEM AFRAID TO HAVE LEARNED THE TRUTH.

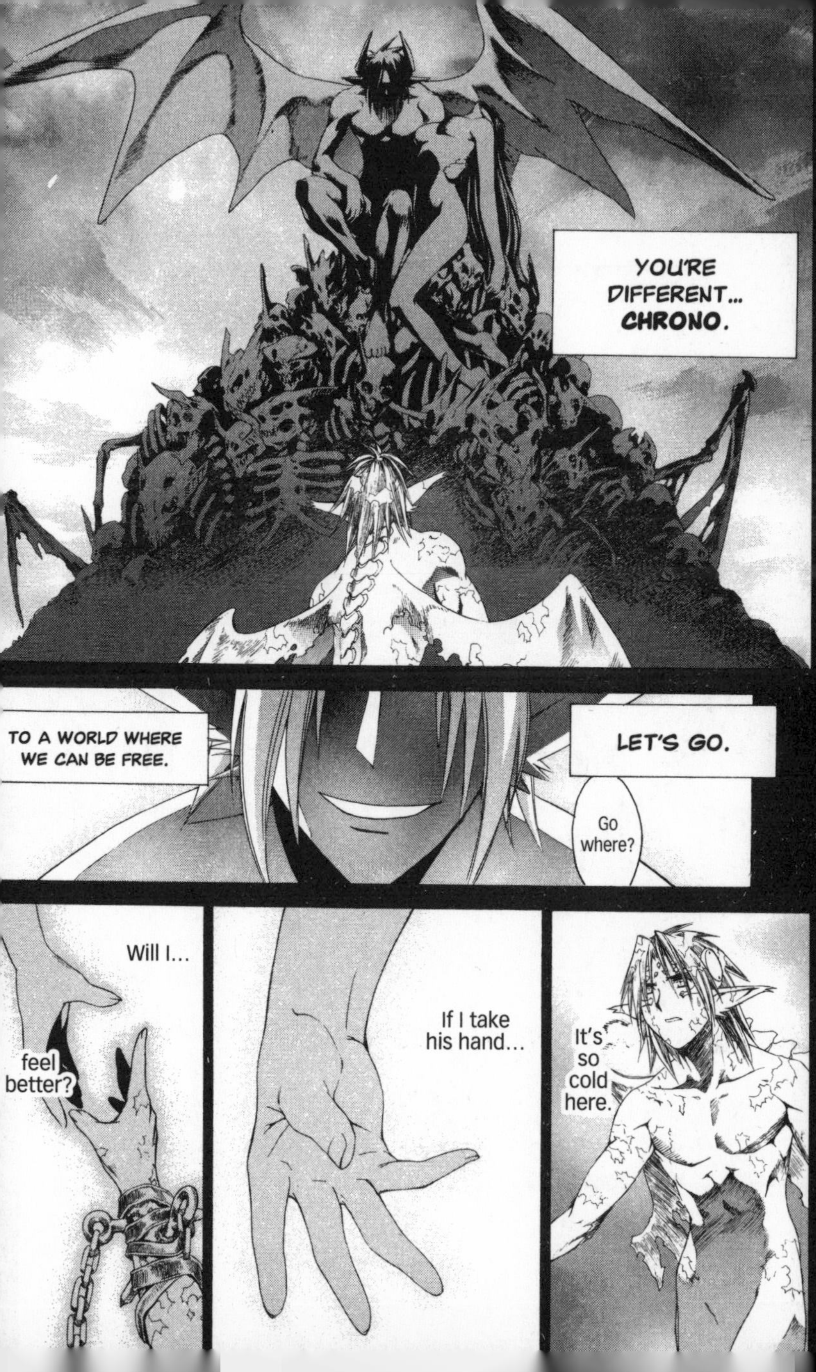
YOU'RE DIFFERENT... CHRONO.
LET'S GO.
Go where?
TO A WORLD WHERE WE CAN BE FREE.
It's so cold here.
If I take his hand...
Will I...
feel better?

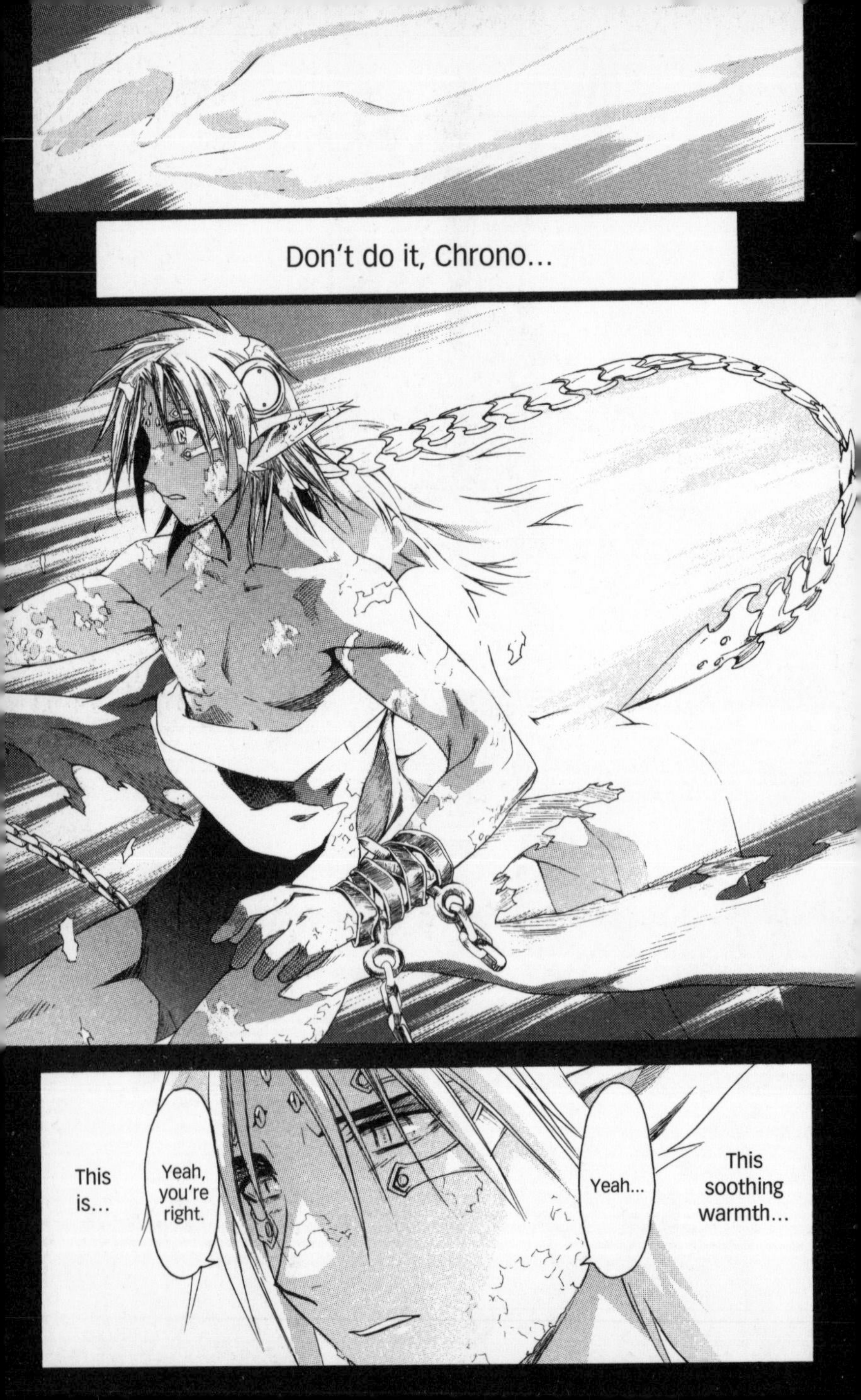
Don't do it, Chrono...
This soothing warmth...
Yeah...
Yeah, you're right.
This is...

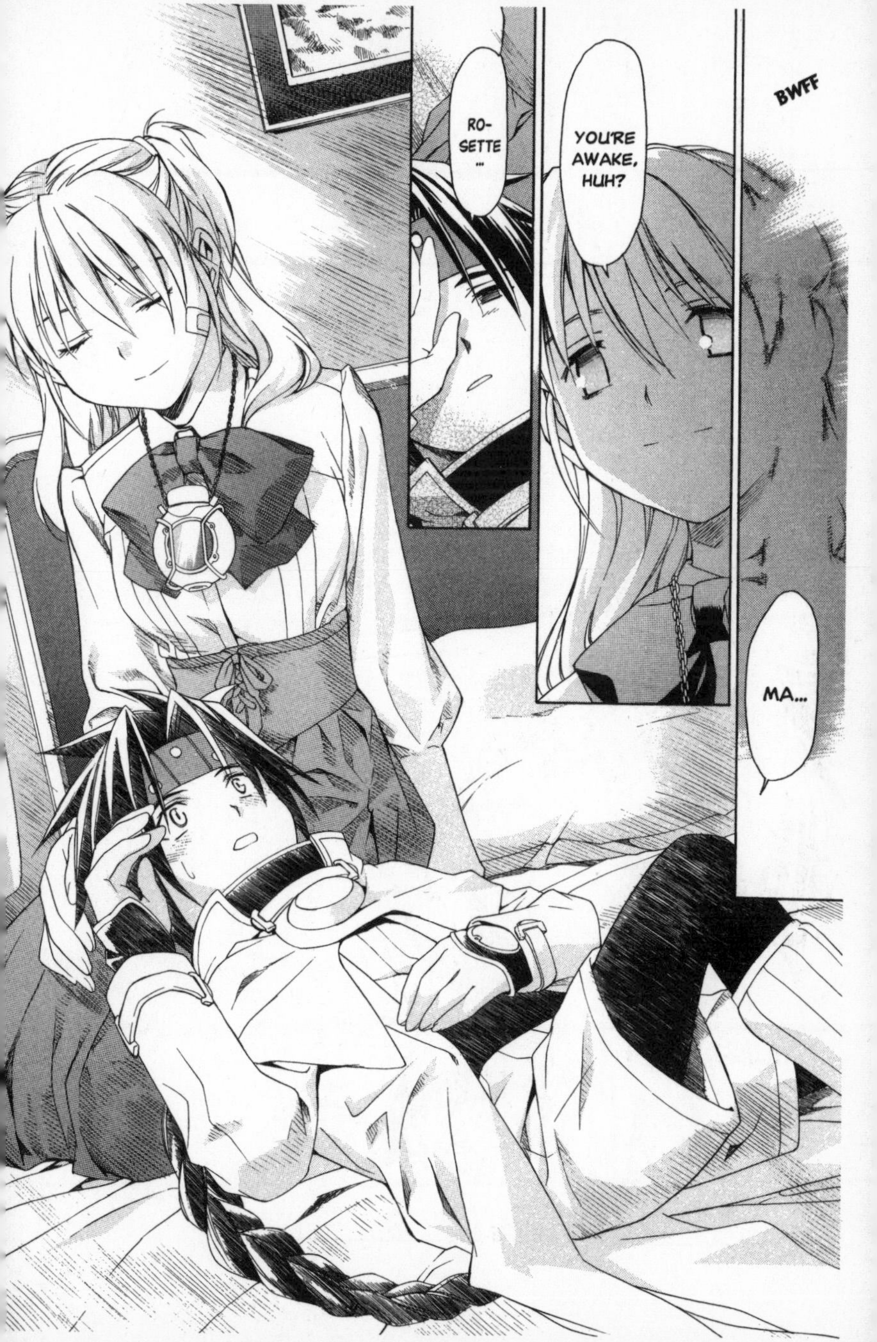
BWFF
YOU'RE AWAKE, HUH?
RO-SETTE ...
MA...

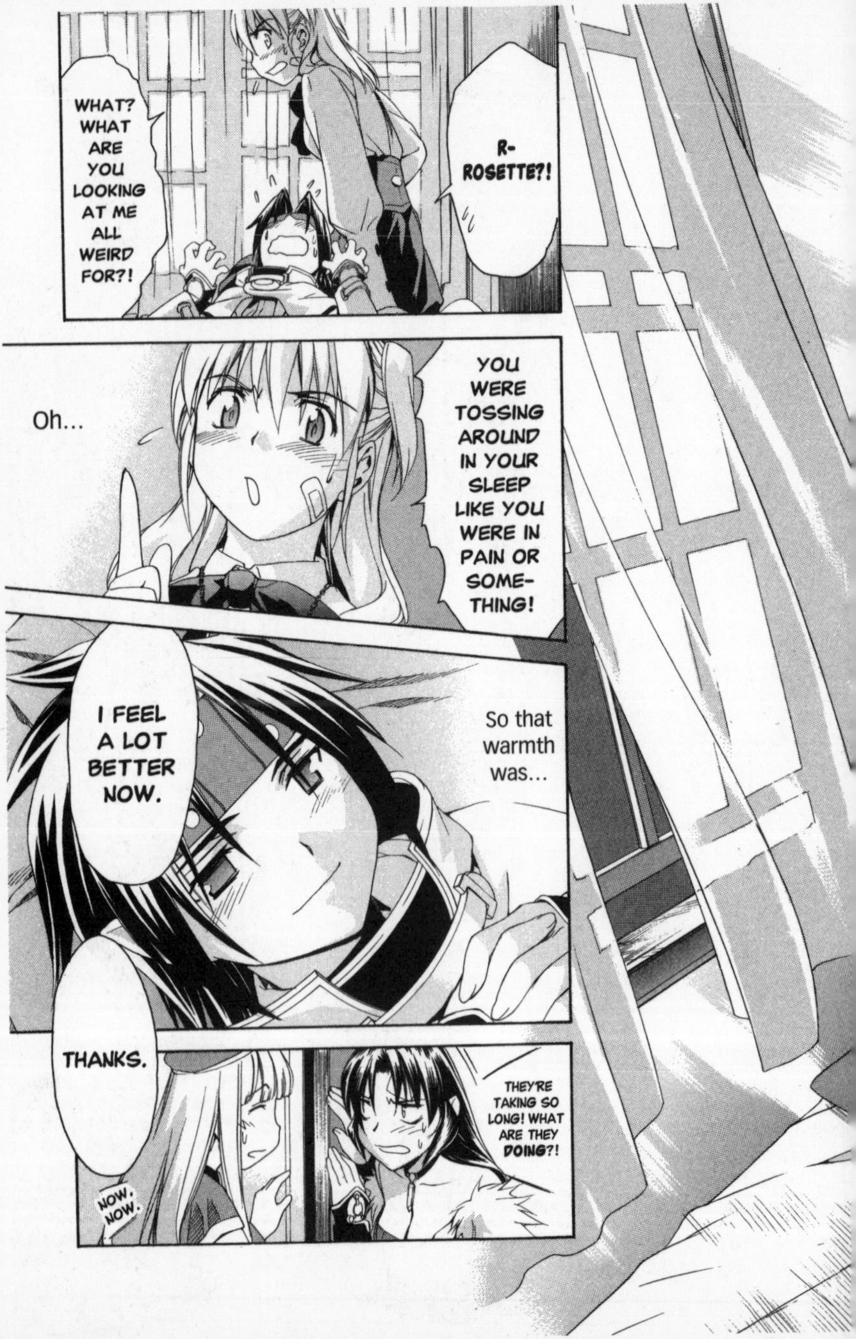
R-ROSETTE?!
WHAT? WHAT ARE YOU LOOKING AT ME ALL WEIRD FOR?!
YOU WERE TOSSING AROUND IN YOUR SLEEP LIKE YOU WERE IN PAIN OR SOME-THING!
Oh...
So that warmth was...
I FEEL A LOT BETTER NOW.
THANKS.
THEY'RE TAKING SO LONG! WHAT ARE THEY DOING?!
NOW, NOW.

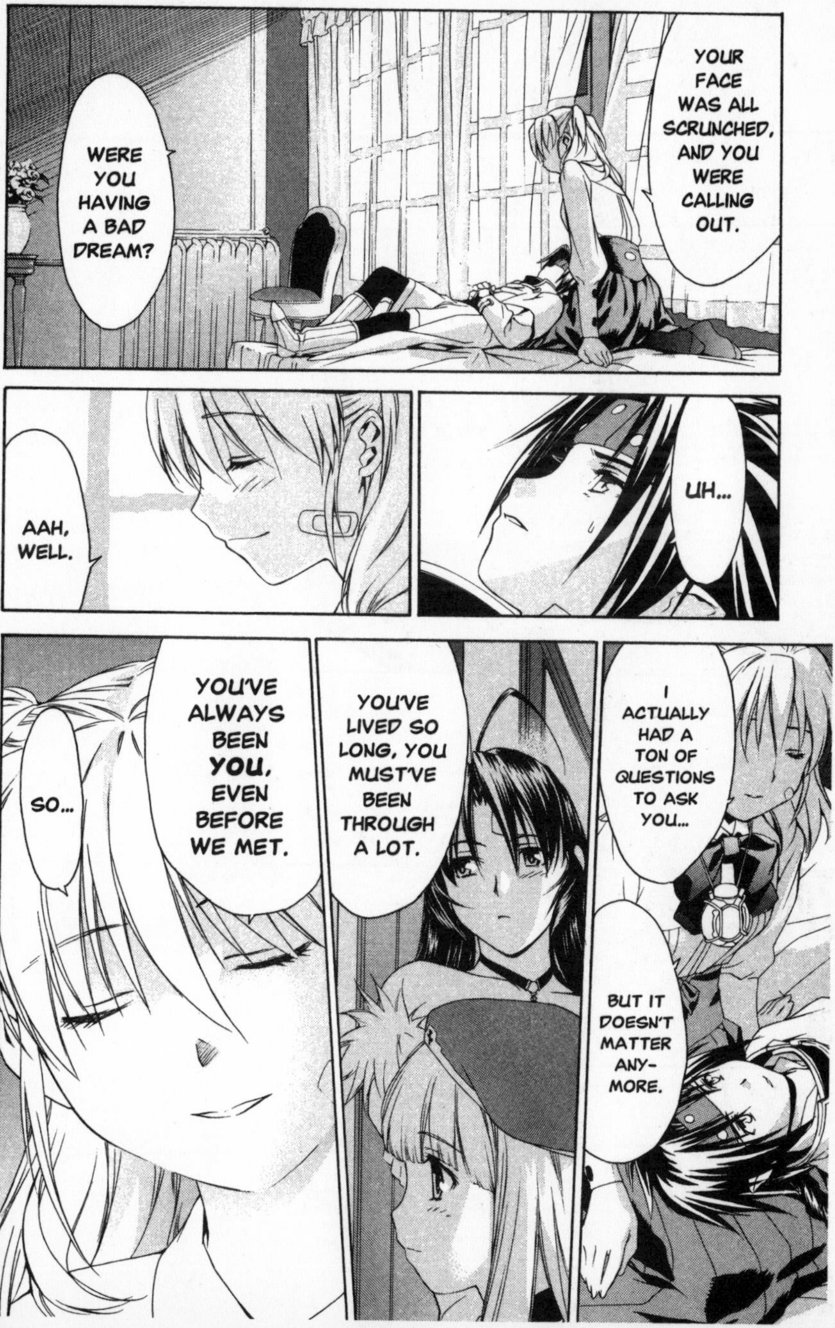
YOUR FACE WAS ALL SCRUNCHED, AND YOU WERE CALLING OUT.
WERE YOU HAVING A BAD DREAM?
UH...
AAH, WELL.
I ACTUALLY HAD A TON OF QUESTIONS TO ASK YOU...
BUT IT DOESN'T MATTER ANYMORE.
YOU'VE LIVED SO LONG, YOU MUST'VE BEEN THROUGH A LOT.
YOU'VE ALWAYS BEEN **YOU**, EVEN BEFORE WE MET.
SO...

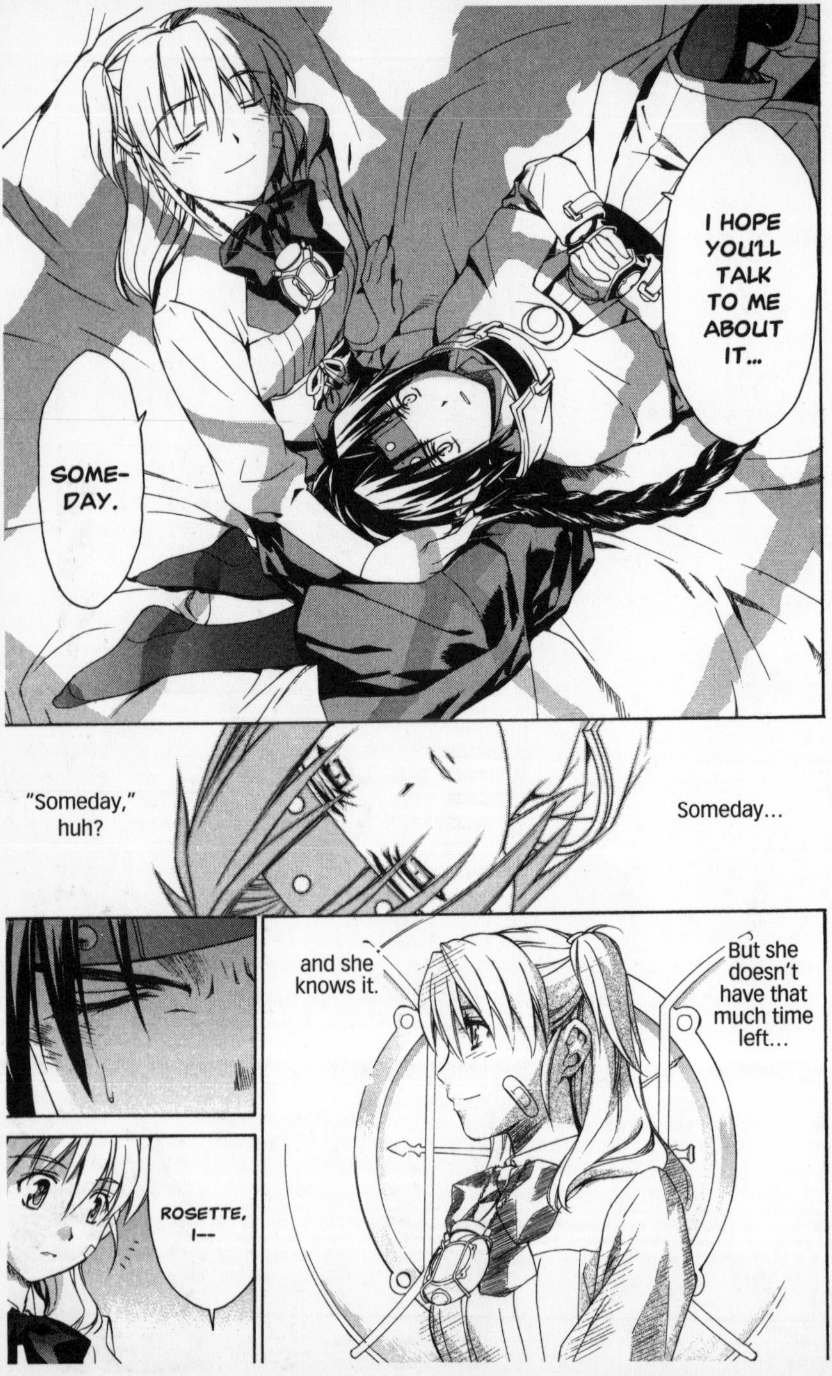
I HOPE YOU'LL TALK TO ME ABOUT IT...
SOME-DAY.
Someday…
"Someday," huh?
But she doesn't have that much time left…
and she knows it.
ROSETTE, I--

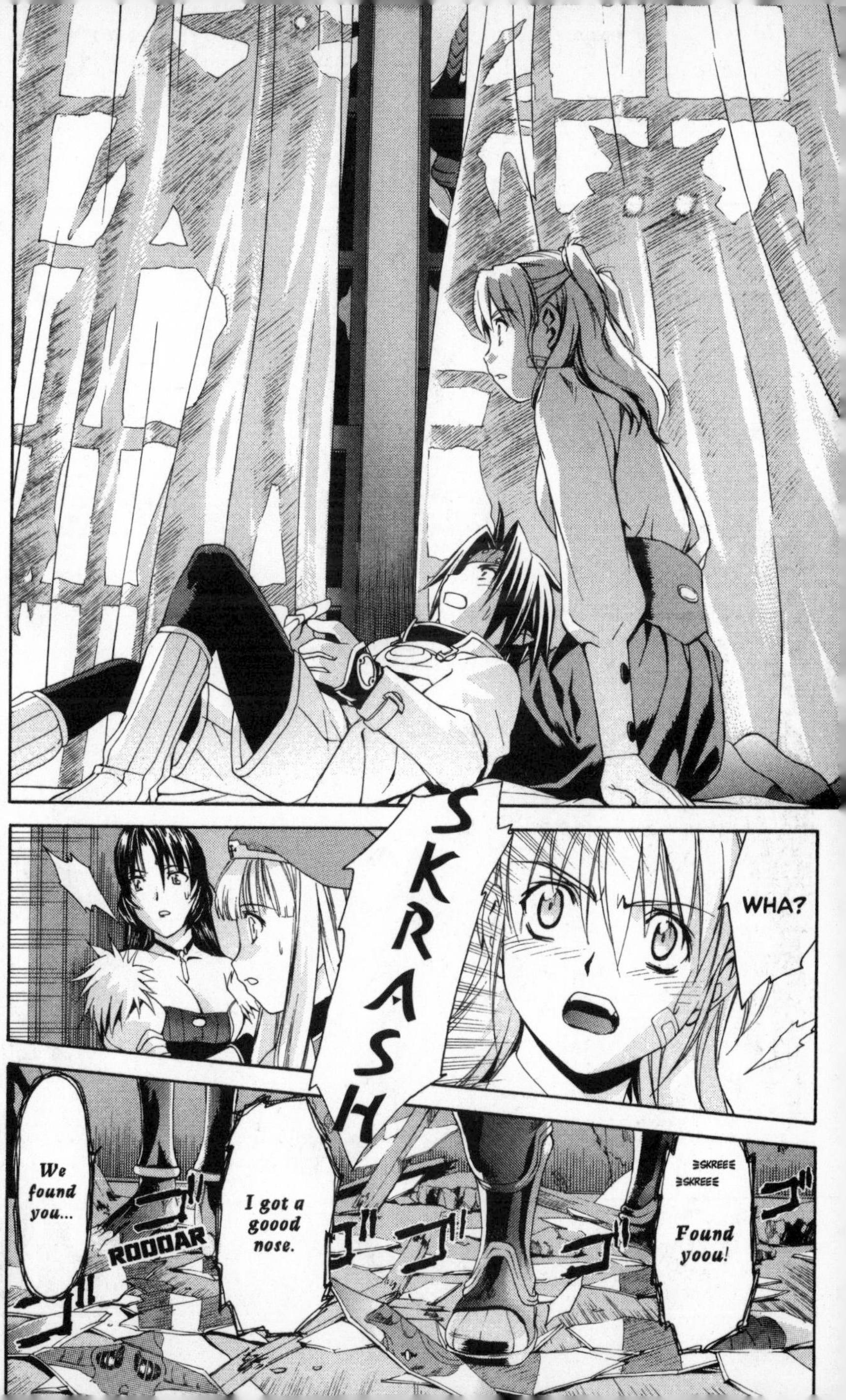
WHA?
SKRASH
SKREE
SKREE
Found yoou!
I got a goood nose.
We found you...
ROOOAR

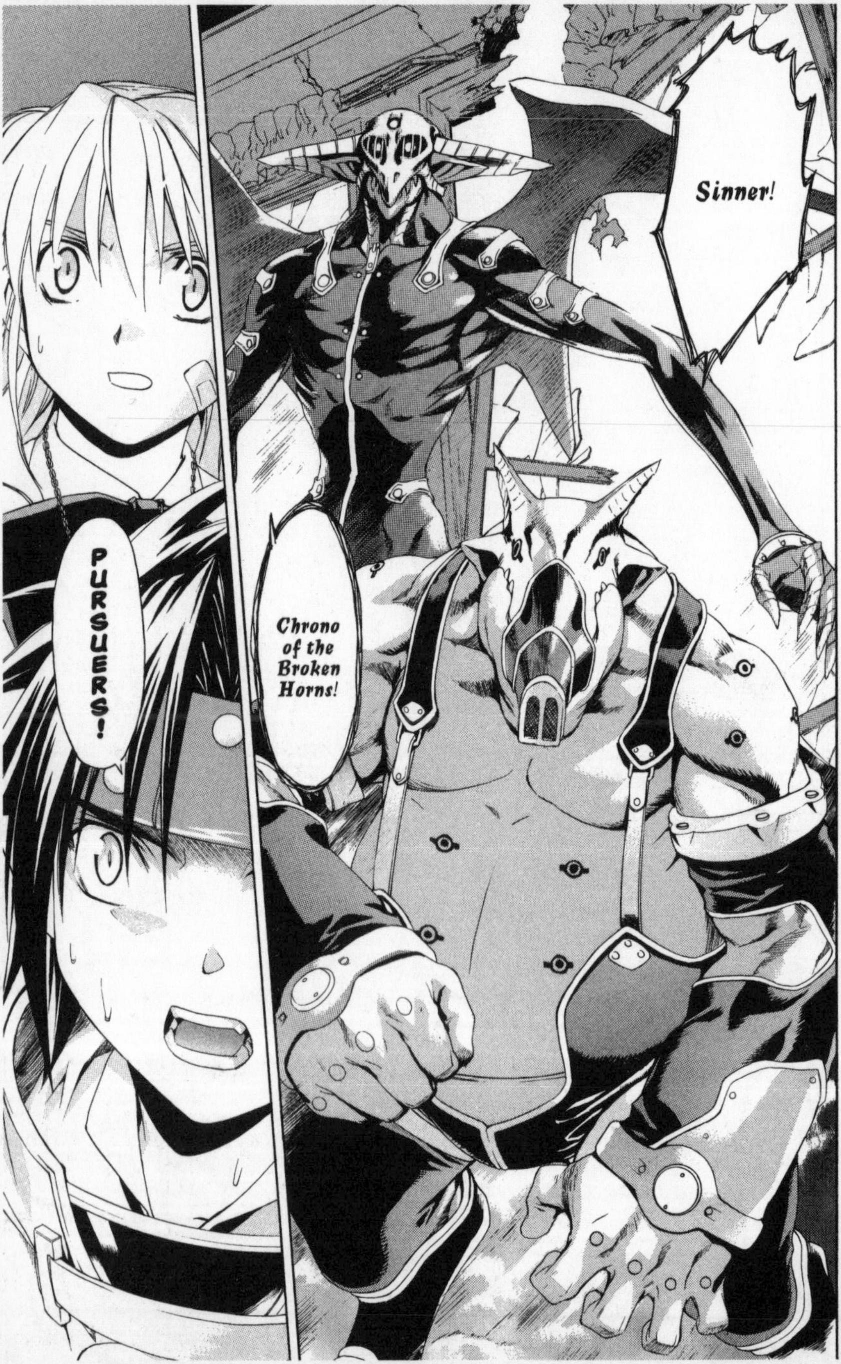
Sinner!
Chrono of the Broken Horns!
PURSUERS!

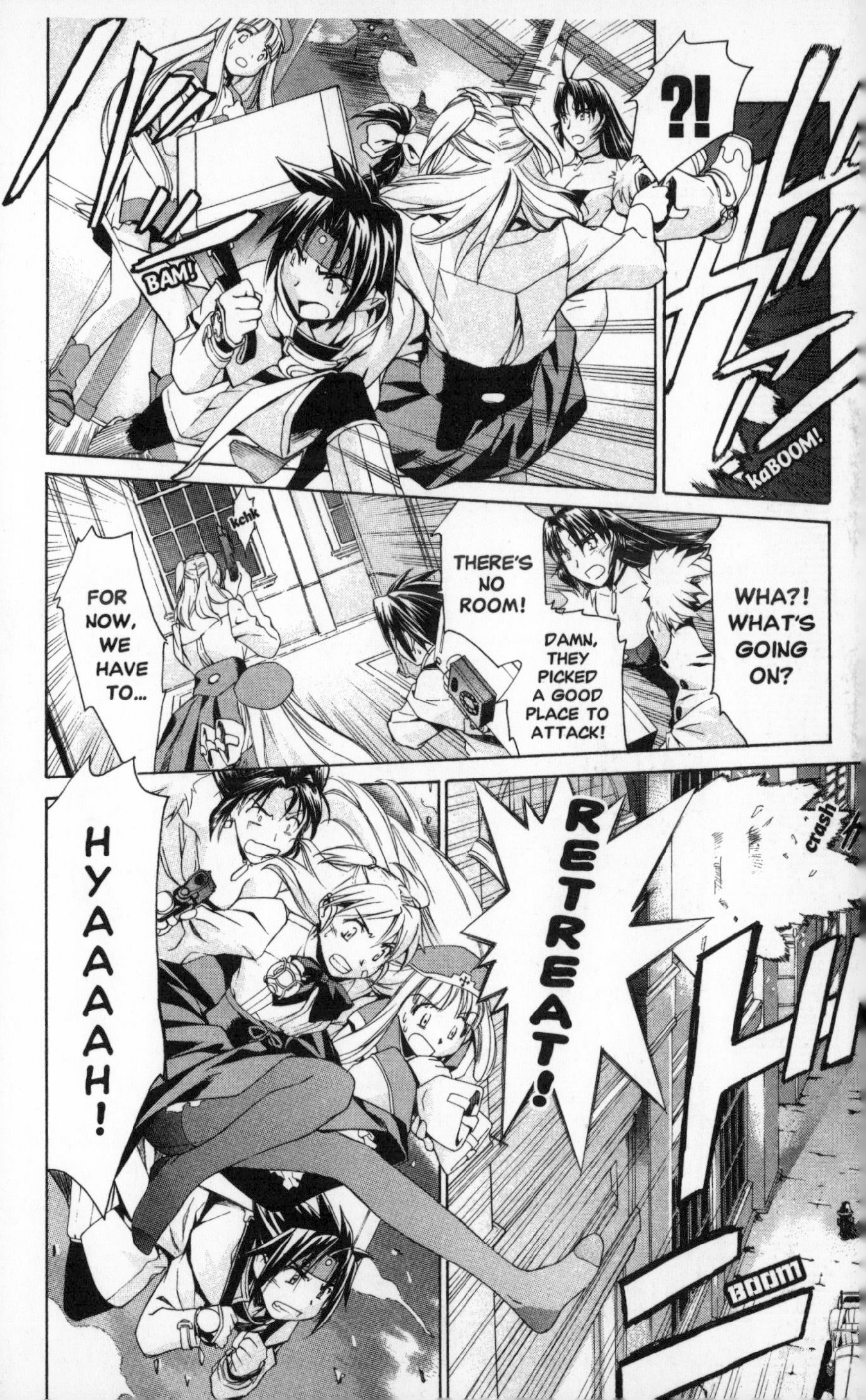
kaBOOM!
?!
BAM!
WHA?! WHAT'S GOING ON?
DAMN, THEY PICKED A GOOD PLACE TO ATTACK!
THERE'S NO ROOM!
kchk
FOR NOW, WE HAVE TO...
crash
BOOM
RETREAT!
HYAAAAH!

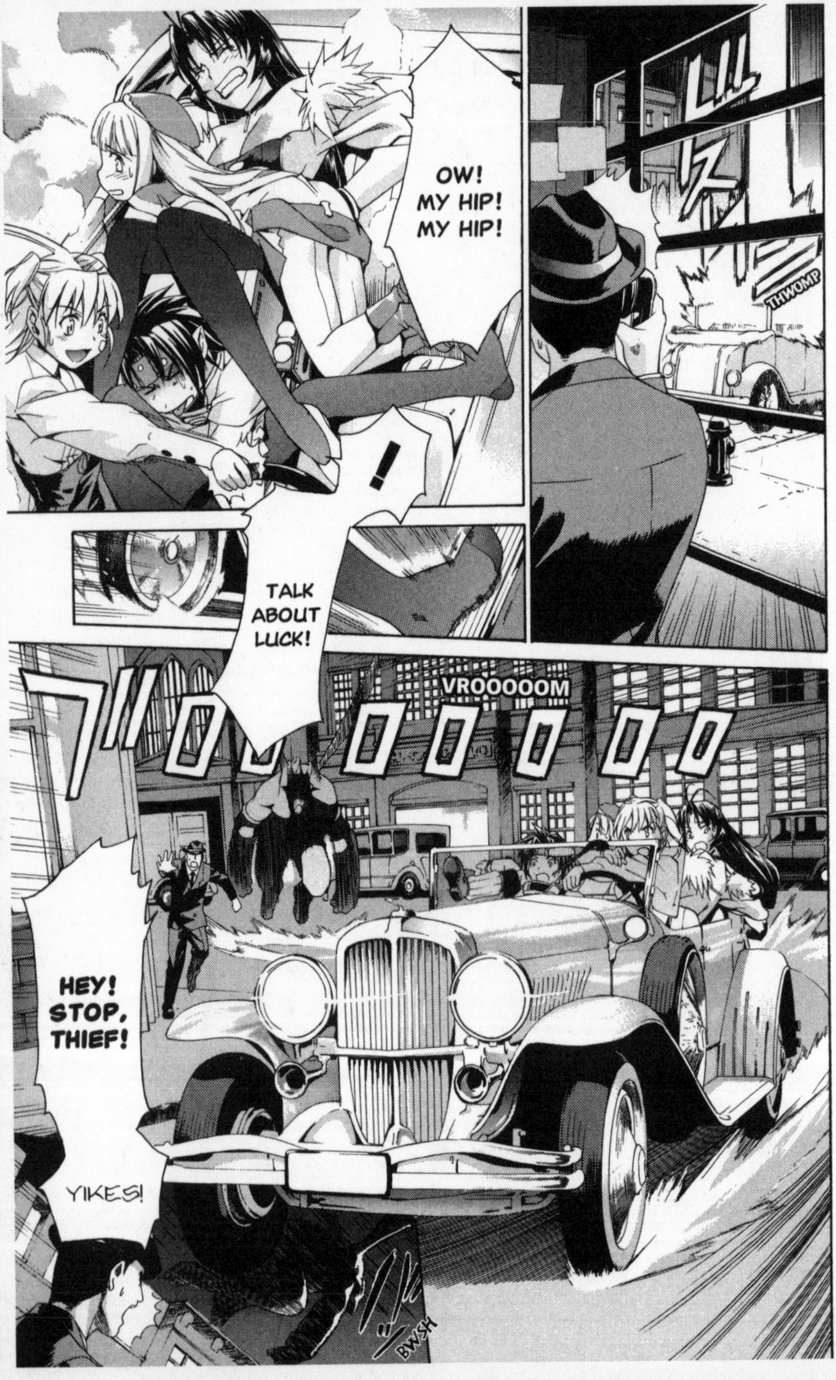
THWOMP
OW! MY HIP! MY HIP!
!
TALK ABOUT LUCK!
VROOOOOM
HEY! STOP, THIEF!
YIKES!
BWSH

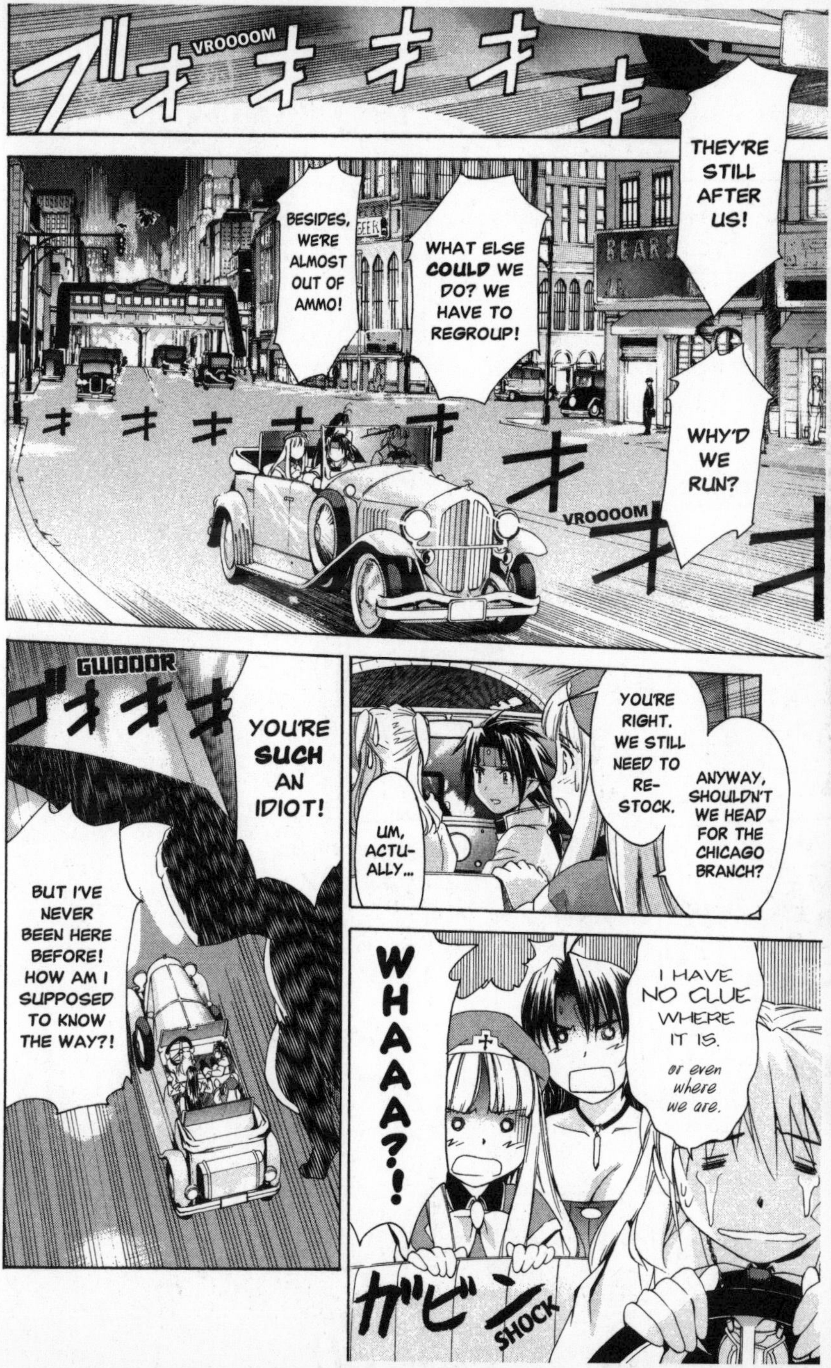
VROOOOM
THEY'RE STILL AFTER US!
WHY'D WE RUN?
WHAT ELSE COULD WE DO? WE HAVE TO REGROUP!
BESIDES, WE'RE ALMOST OUT OF AMMO!
VROOOOM
YOU'RE RIGHT. WE STILL NEED TO RE-STOCK.
ANYWAY, SHOULDN'T WE HEAD FOR THE CHICAGO BRANCH?
UM, ACTUALLY...
I HAVE NO CLUE WHERE IT IS.
or even where we are.
WHAAAA?!
SHOCK
GWOOOR
YOU'RE SUCH AN IDIOT!
BUT I'VE NEVER BEEN HERE BEFORE! HOW AM I SUPPOSED TO KNOW THE WAY?!

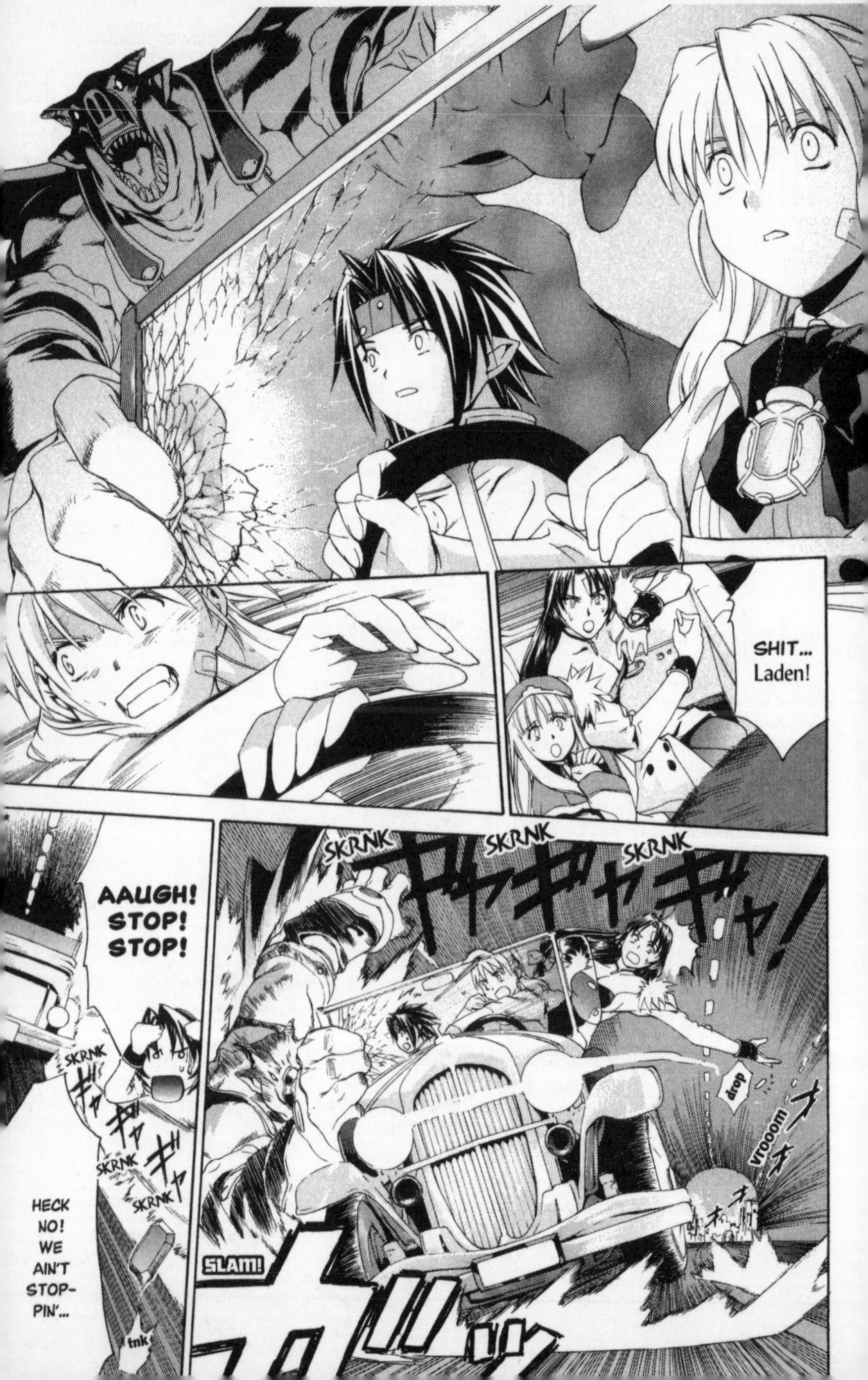
SHIT... Laden!
SKRNK
SKRNK
SKRNK
drop
vrooom
SLAM!
AAUGH! STOP! STOP!
SKRNK
SKRNK
SKRNK
HECK NO! WE AIN'T STOP-PIN'...
tnk

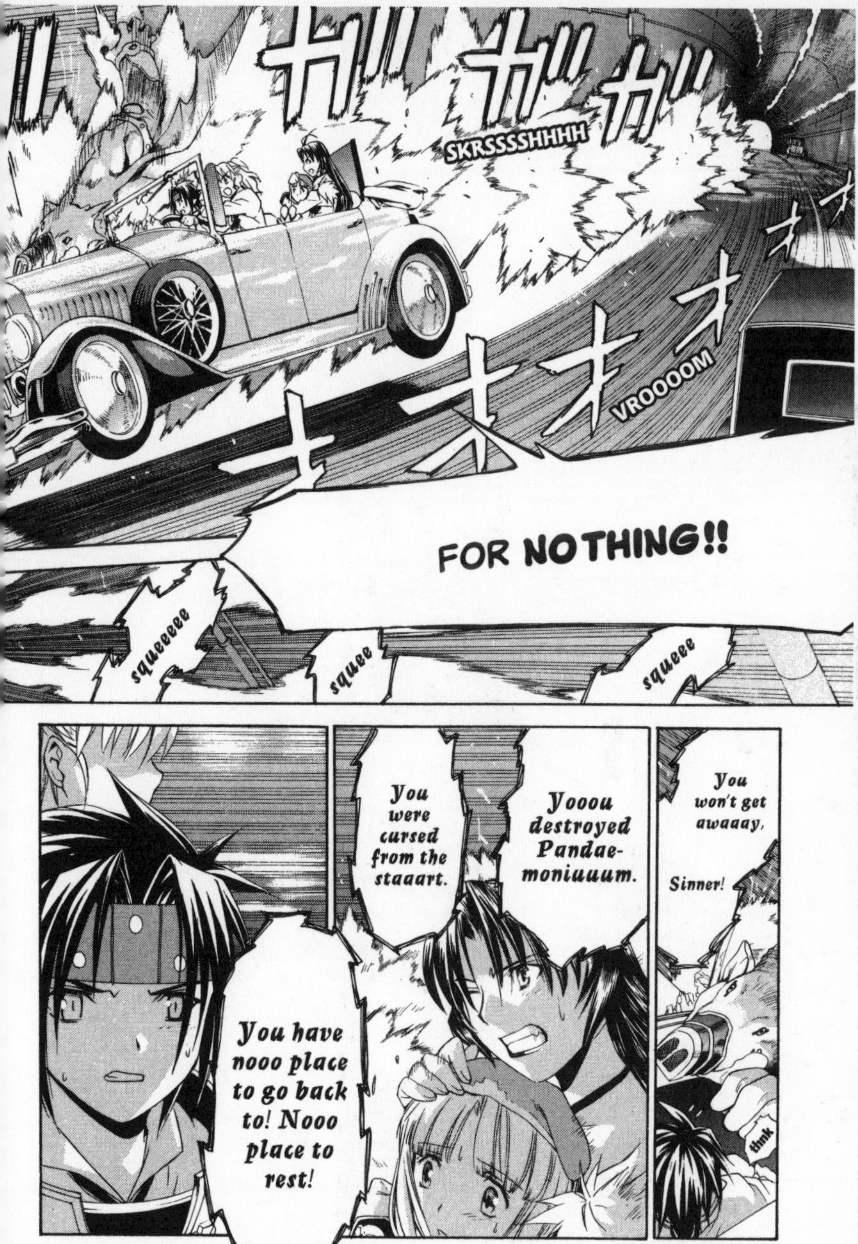
SKRSSSSHHHH
VROOOOM
FOR NOTHING!!
squeeeee
squee
squeee
You won't get awaaay,
Sinner!
think
Yoooou destroyed Pandaemoniuuum.
You were cursed from the staaart.
You have nooo place to go back to! Nooo place to rest!

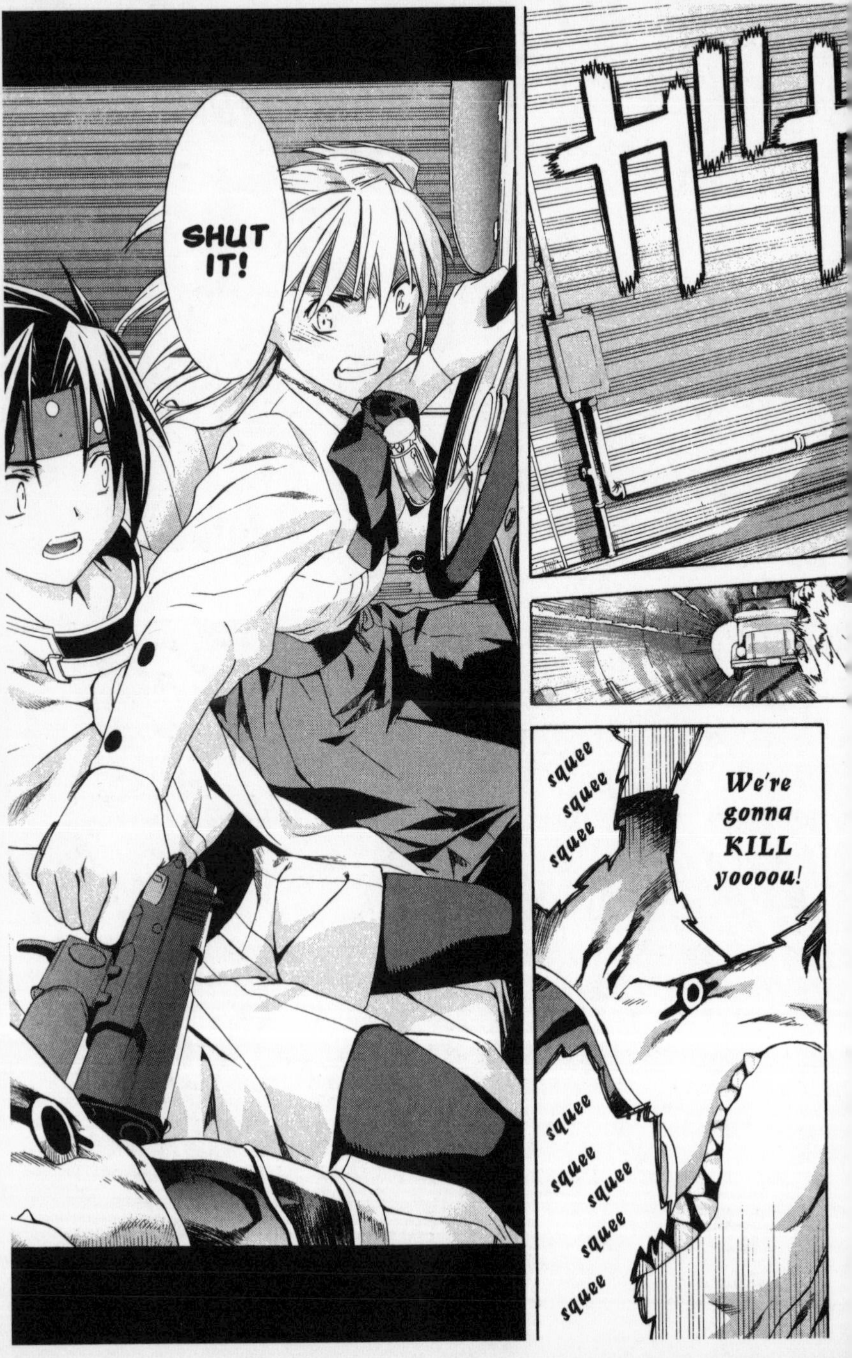
squee
squee
squee
We're gonna KILL yoooou!
squee
squee
squee
squee
squee
SHUT IT!

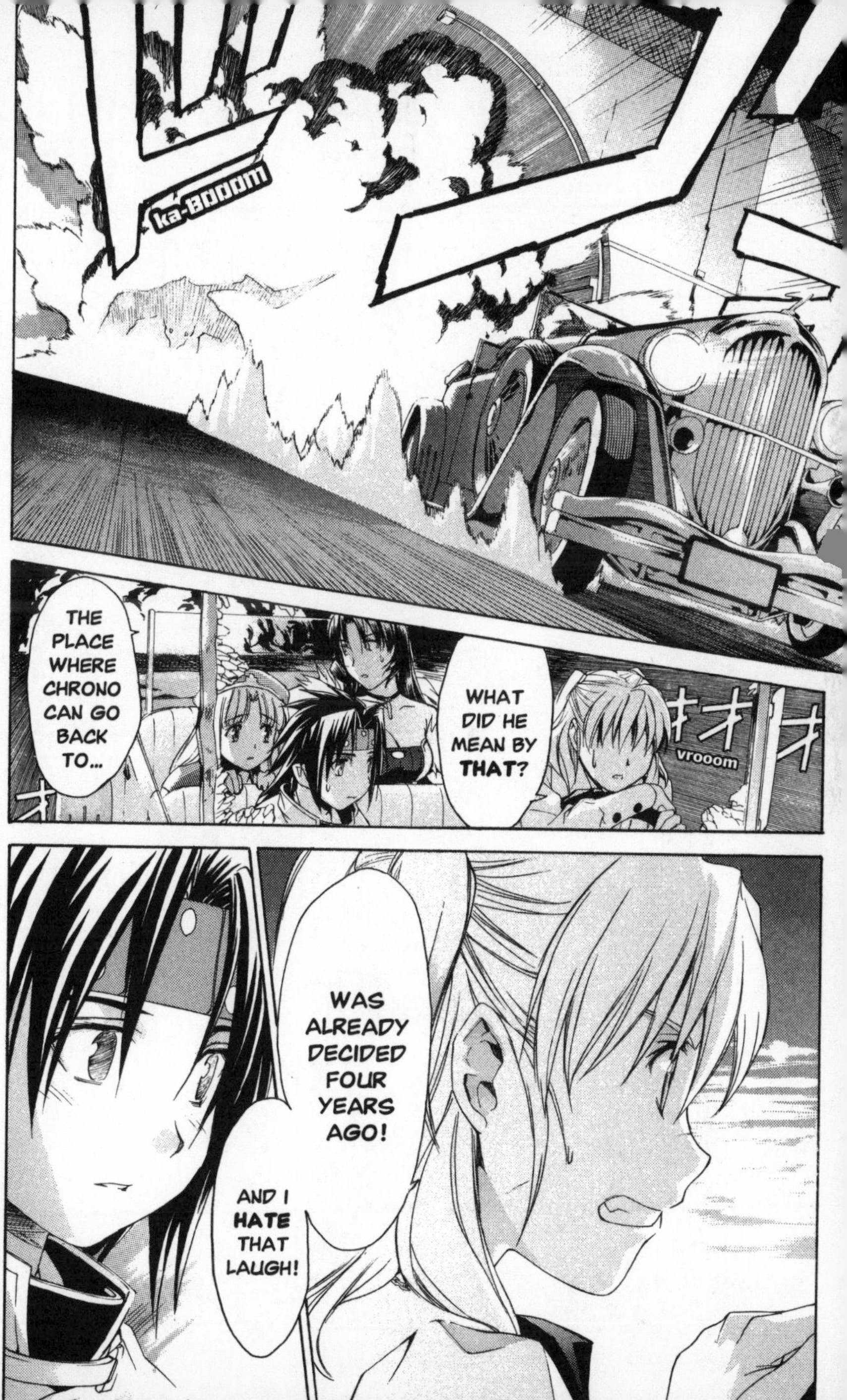
ka-BOOOM
vrooom
WHAT DID HE MEAN BY THAT?
THE PLACE WHERE CHRONO CAN GO BACK TO...
WAS ALREADY DECIDED FOUR YEARS AGO!
AND I HATE THAT LAUGH!

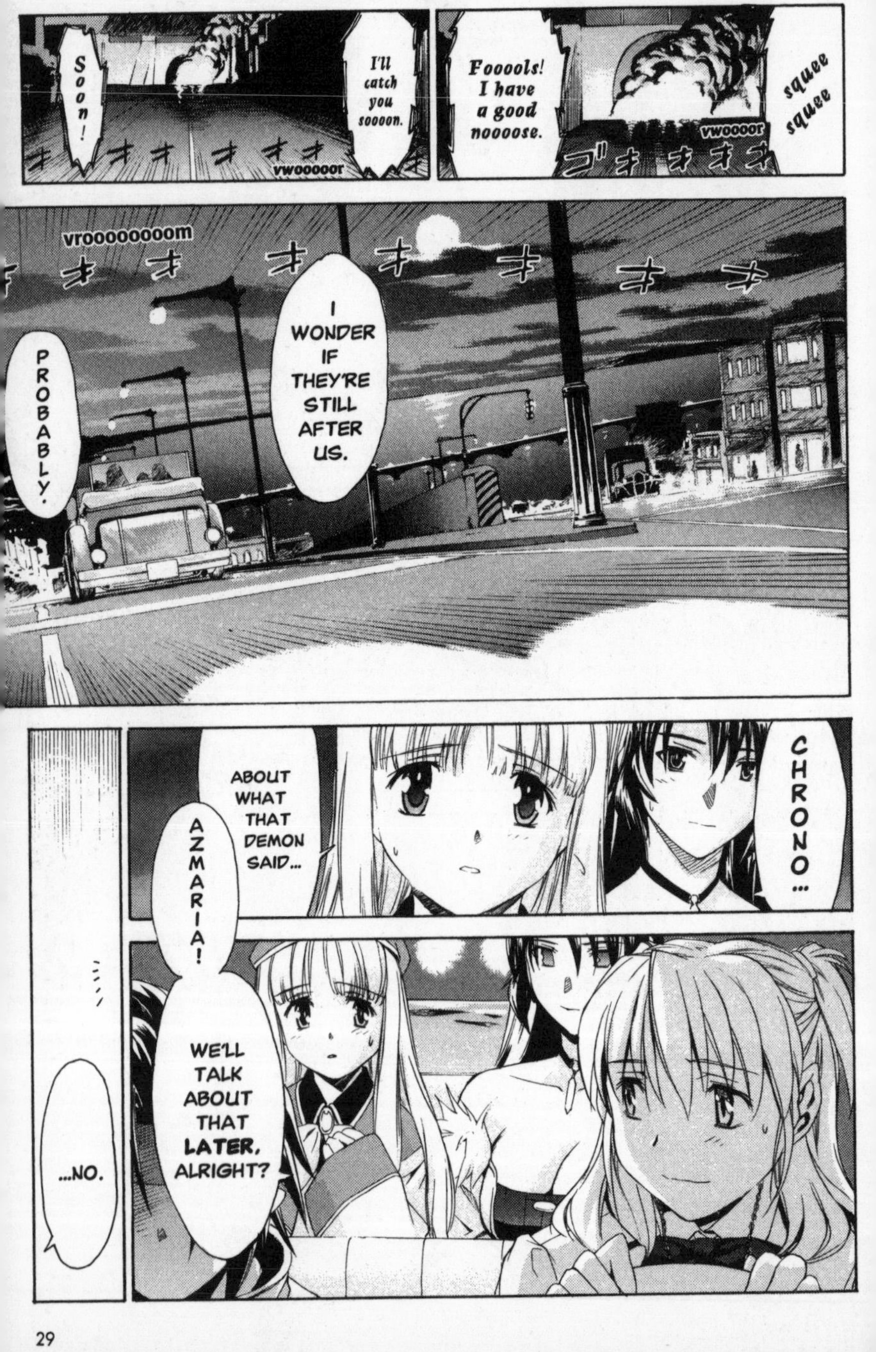

squee squee
Fooools! I have a good nooose.
vwoooor
I'll catch you sooon.
Soon!
vwooooor
vroooooooom
I WONDER IF THEY'RE STILL AFTER US.
PROBABLY.
CHRONO...
ABOUT WHAT THAT DEMON SAID...
AZMARIA!
WE'LL TALK ABOUT THAT LATER, ALRIGHT?
...NO.

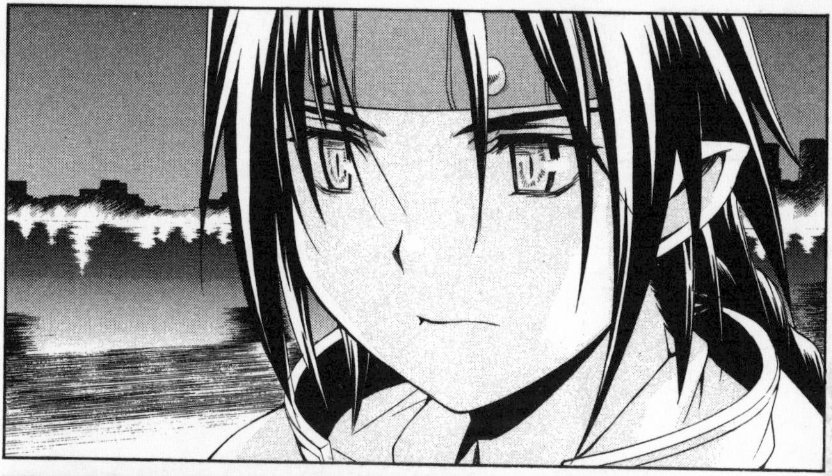
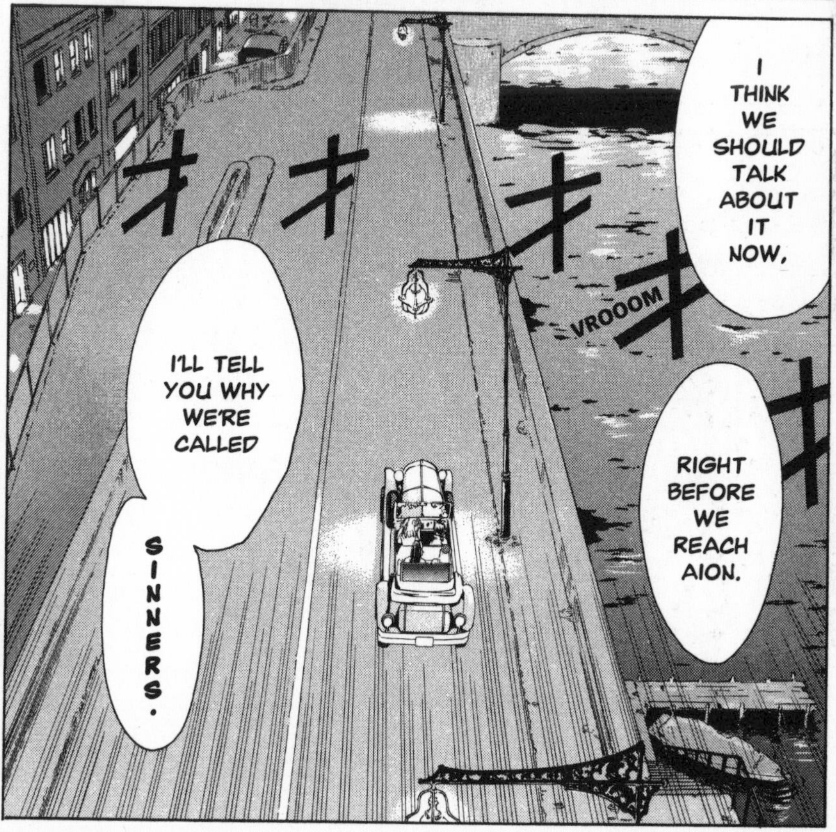
I THINK WE SHOULD TALK ABOUT IT NOW,
VROOOM
RIGHT BEFORE WE REACH AION.
I'LL TELL YOU WHY WE'RE CALLED
SINNERS.

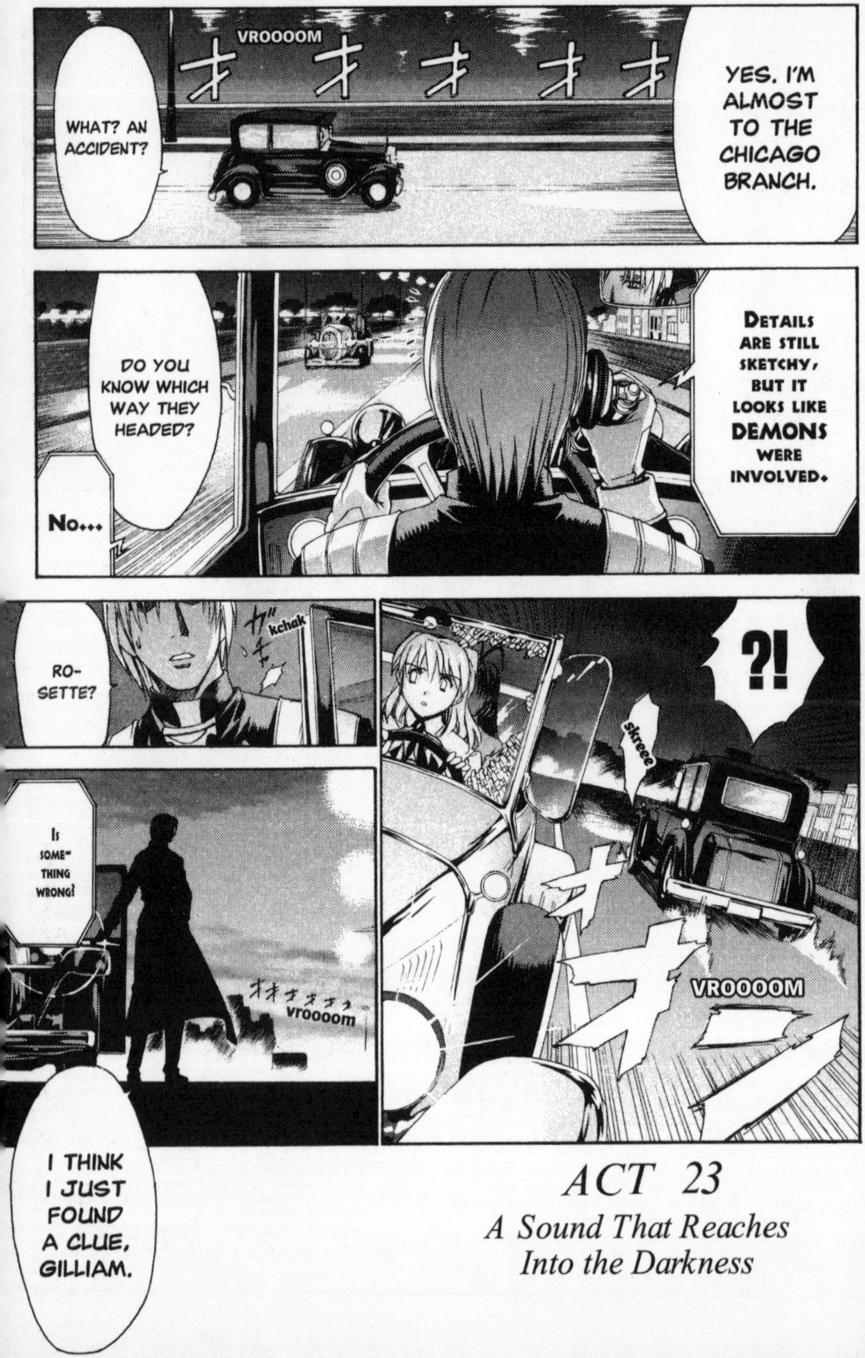
VROOOOM
YES. I'M ALMOST TO THE CHICAGO BRANCH.
WHAT? AN ACCIDENT?
DETAILS ARE STILL SKETCHY, BUT IT LOOKS LIKE DEMONS WERE INVOLVED.
DO YOU KNOW WHICH WAY THEY HEADED?
No...
?!
skreee
VROOOOM
kchak
RO-SETTE?
Is SOME-THING WRONG?
vroooom
I THINK I JUST FOUND A CLUE, GILLIAM.

ACT 23

A Sound That Reaches Into the Darkness

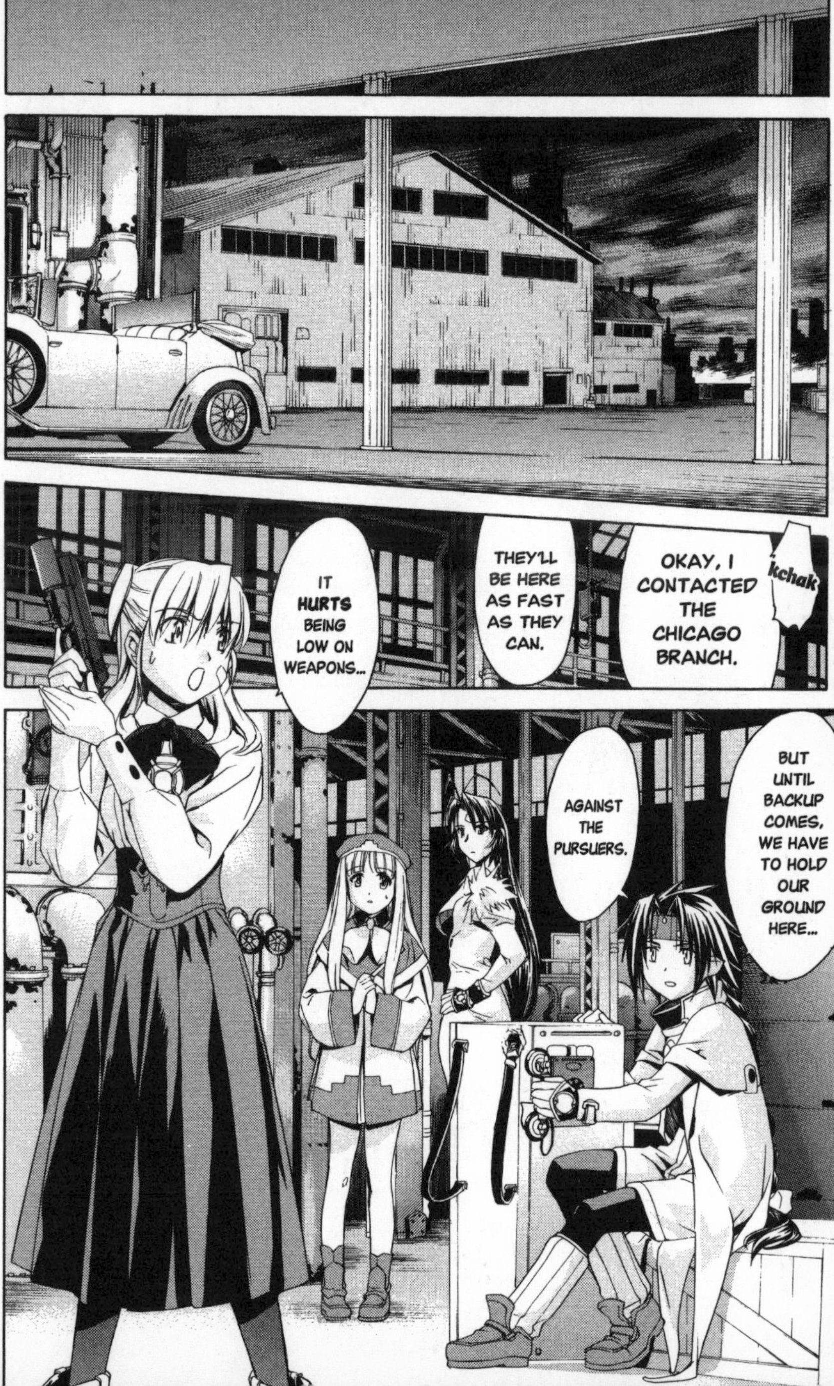
kchak
OKAY, I CONTACTED THE CHICAGO BRANCH.
THEY'LL BE HERE AS FAST AS THEY CAN.
IT **HURTS** BEING LOW ON WEAPONS...
BUT UNTIL BACKUP COMES, WE HAVE TO HOLD OUR GROUND HERE...
AGAINST THE PURSUERS.

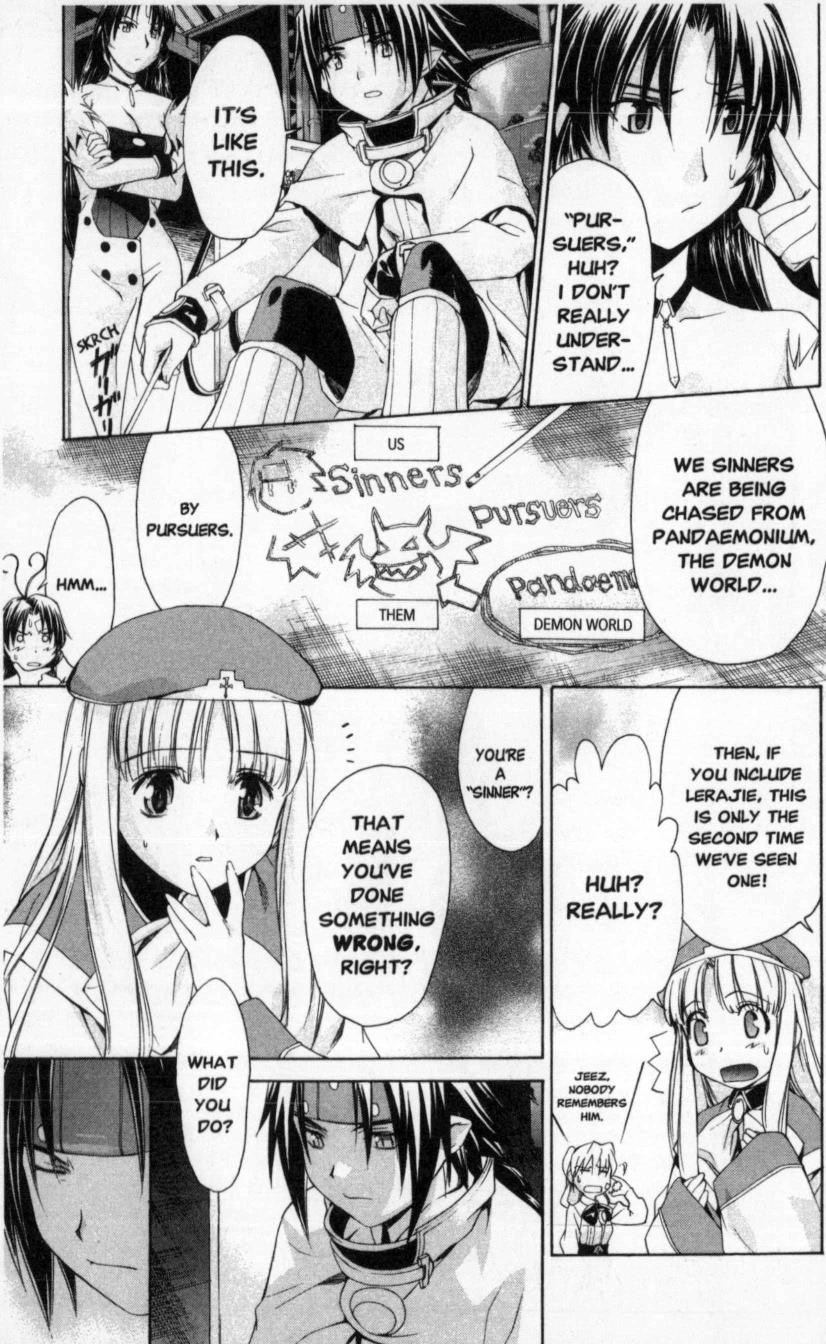

"PUR-SUERS," HUH? I DON'T REALLY UNDER-STAND...
IT'S LIKE THIS.
SKRCH
WE SINNERS ARE BEING CHASED FROM PANDAEMONIUM, THE DEMON WORLD...
US
Sinners
Pursuers
Pandaem
DEMON WORLD
THEM
BY PURSUERS.
HMM...
THEN, IF YOU INCLUDE LERAJIE, THIS IS ONLY THE SECOND TIME WE'VE SEEN ONE!
HUH? REALLY?
JEEZ, NOBODY REMEMBERS HIM.
YOU'RE A "SINNER"?
THAT MEANS YOU'VE DONE SOMETHING **WRONG**, RIGHT?
WHAT DID YOU DO?

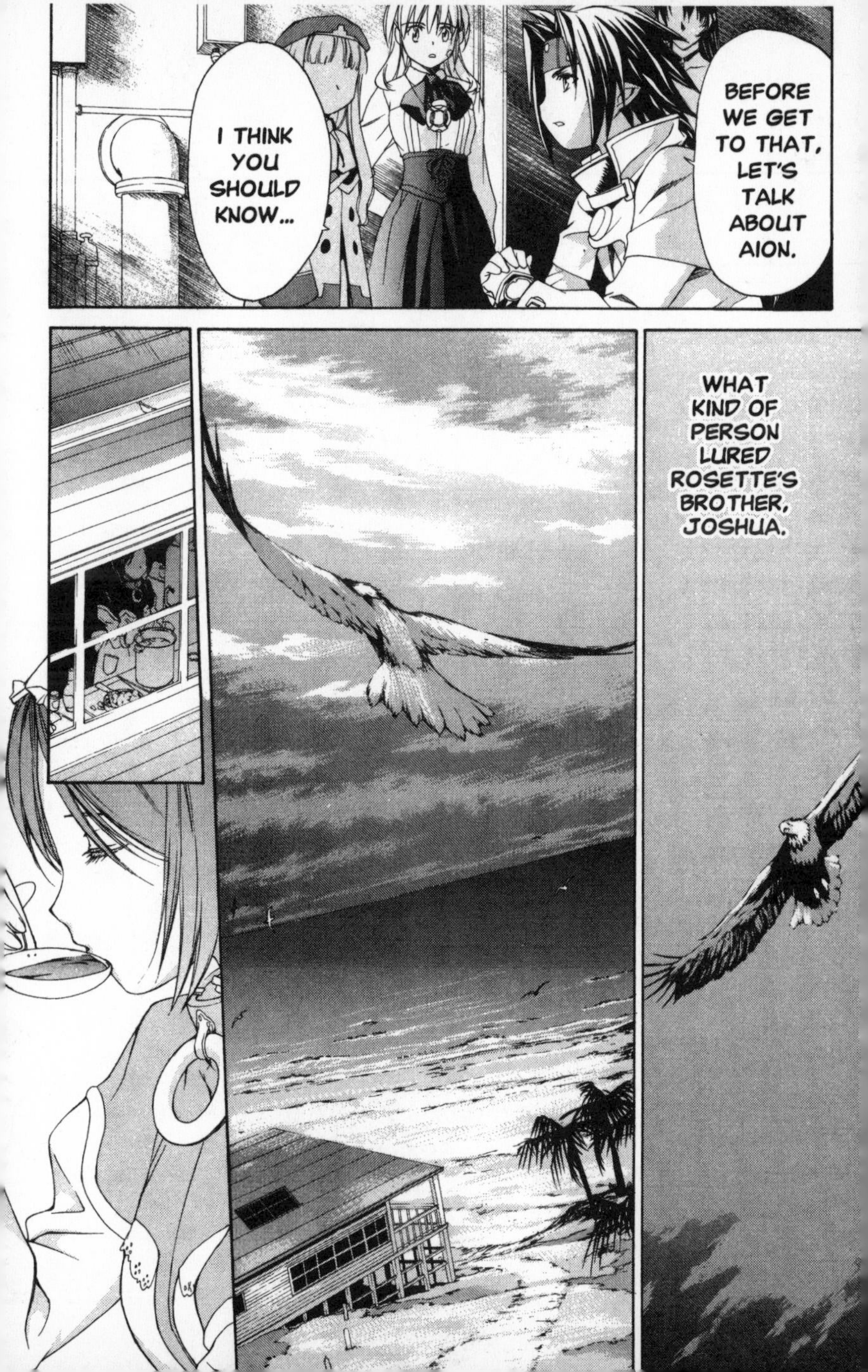
BEFORE WE GET TO THAT, LET'S TALK ABOUT AION.
I THINK YOU SHOULD KNOW...
WHAT KIND OF PERSON LURED ROSETTE'S BROTHER, JOSHUA.

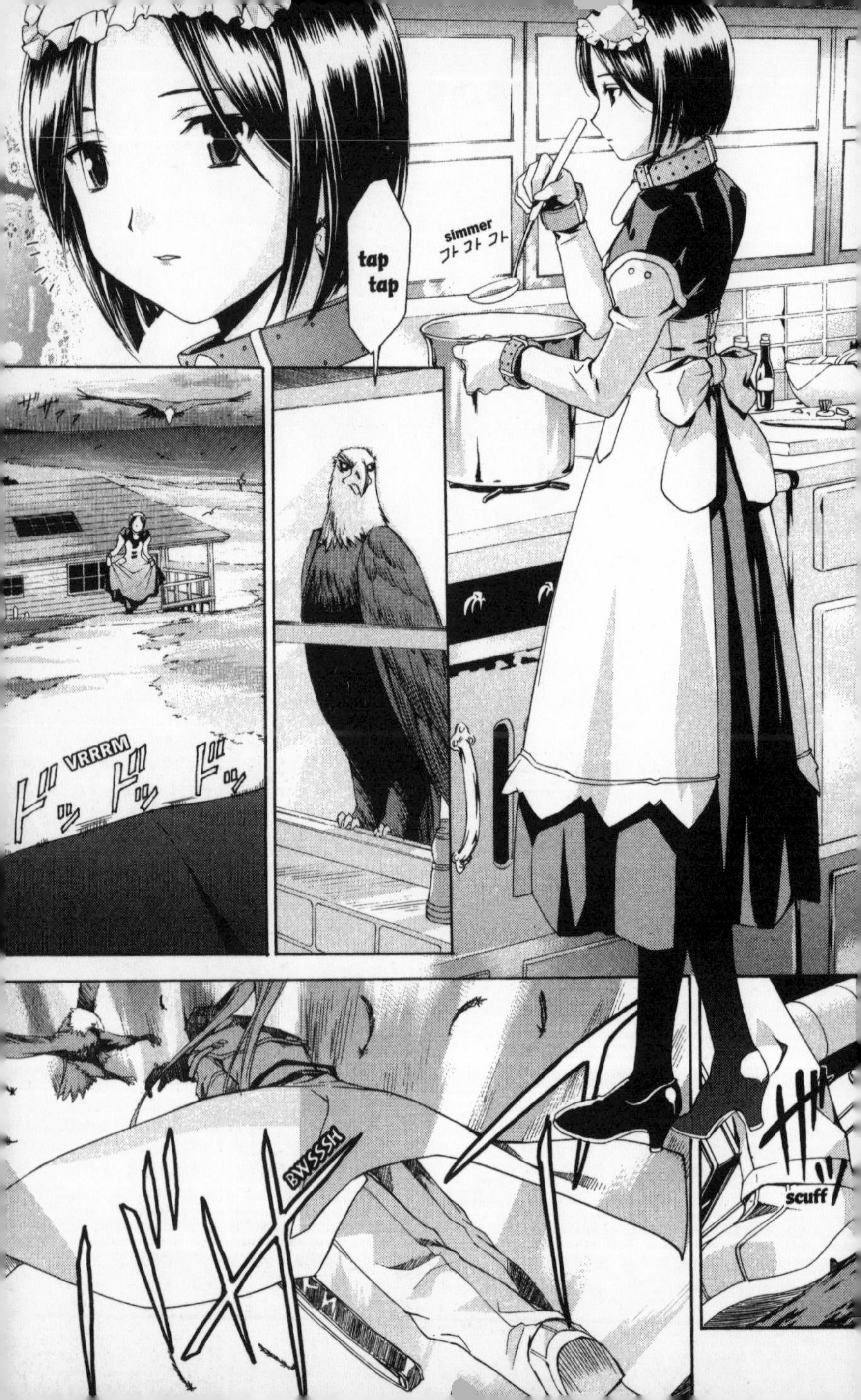
simmer
tap tap
VRRRM
scuff
BWSSSH

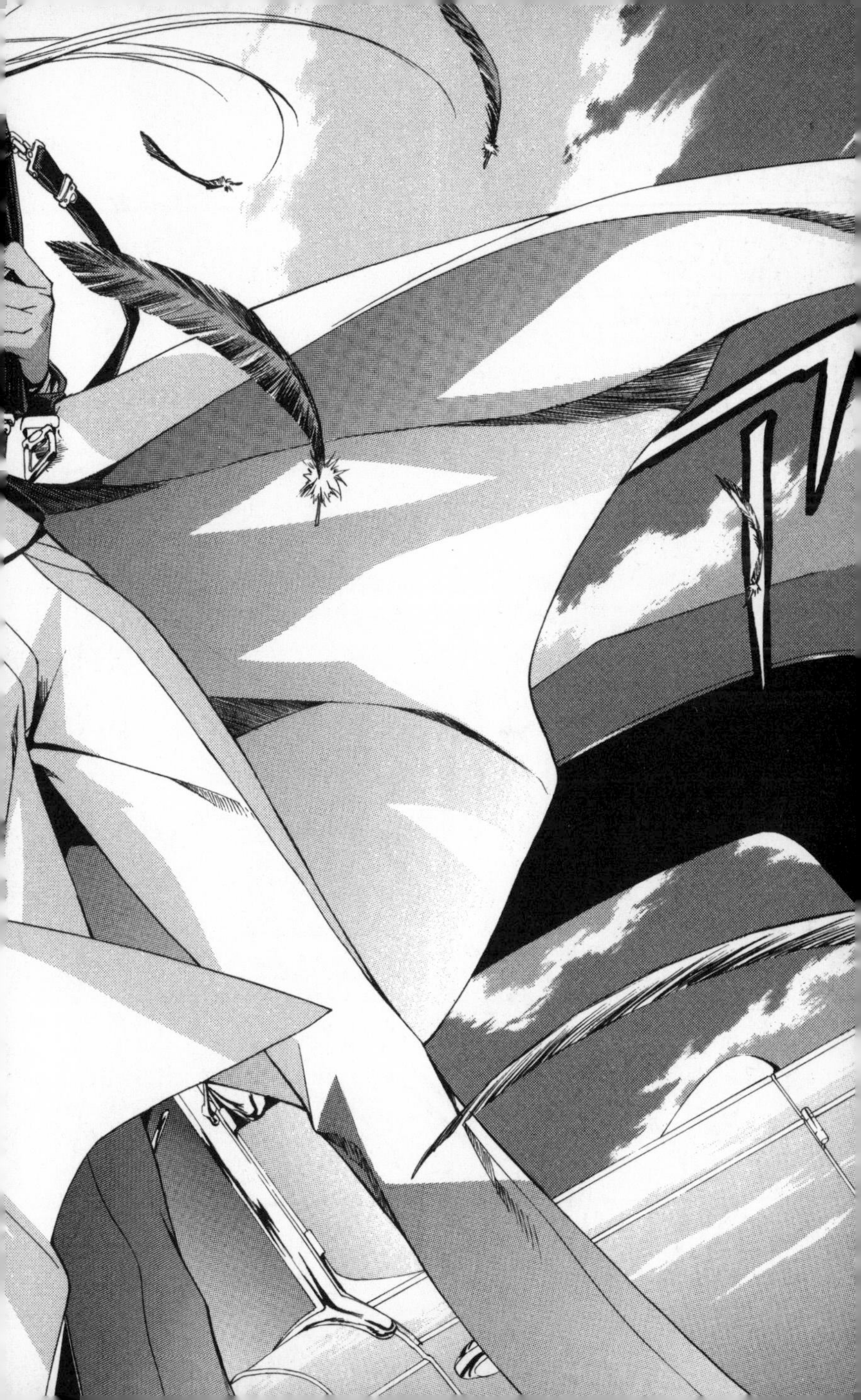

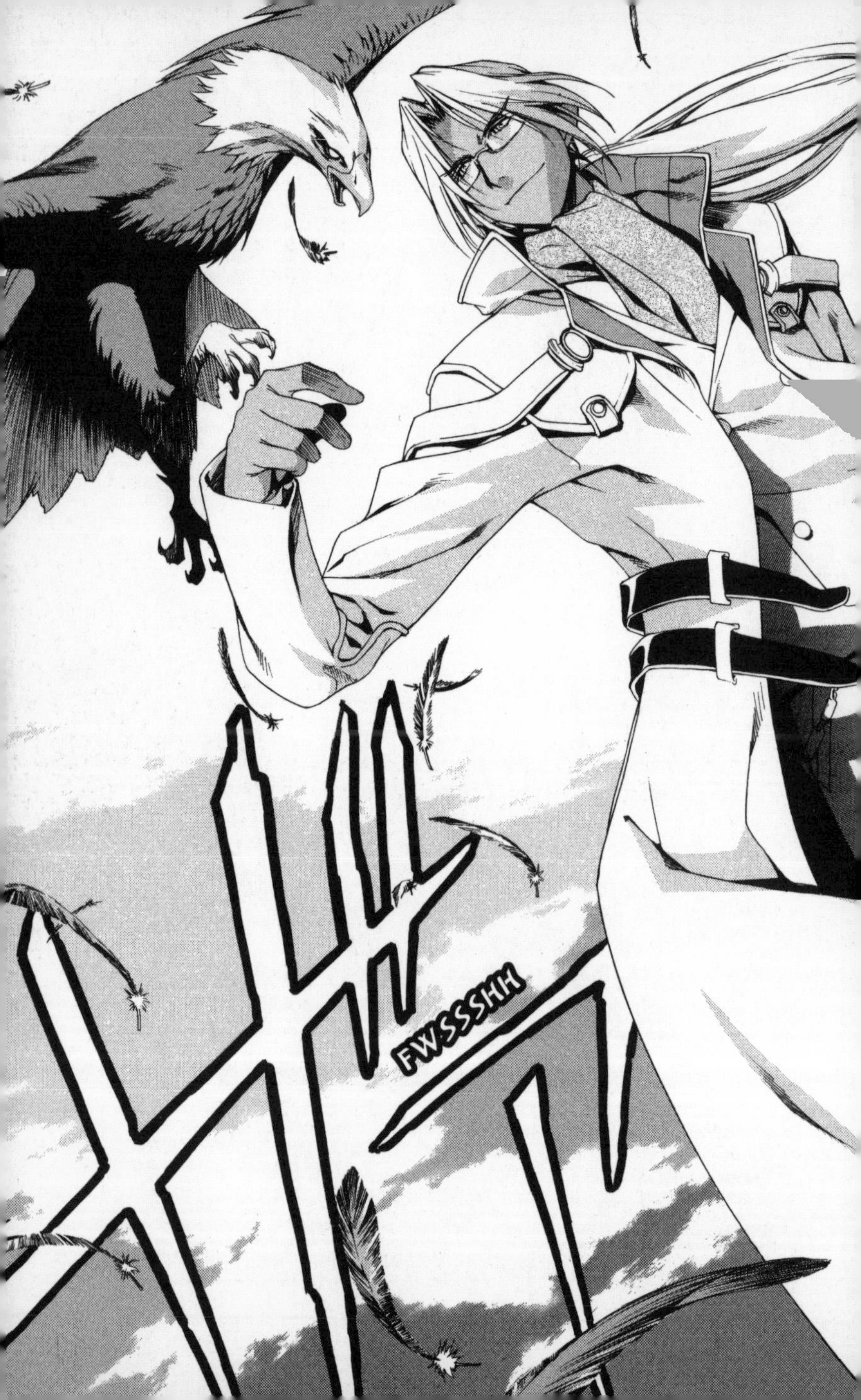
FWSSSHH

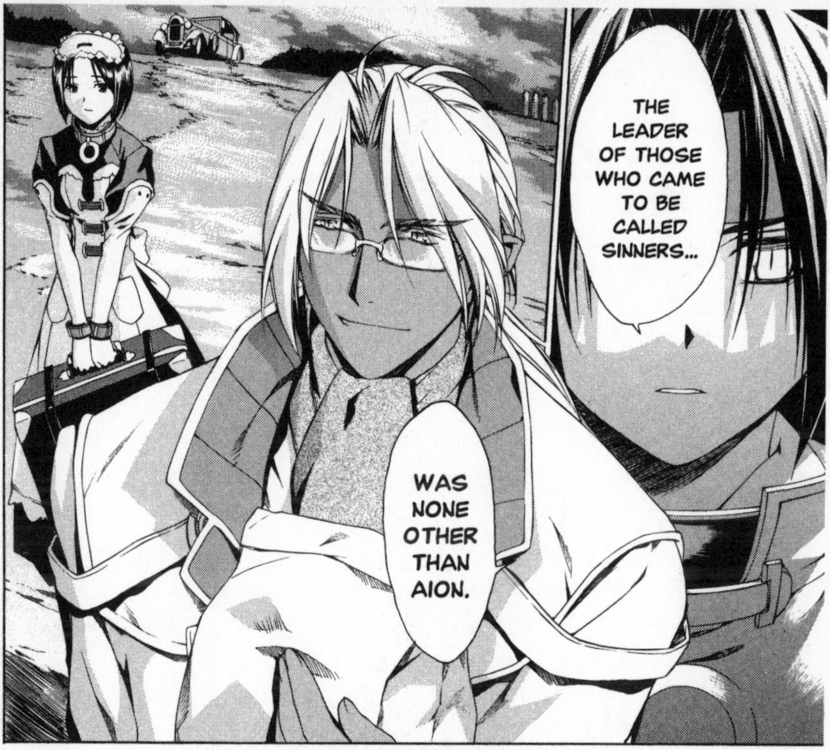
THE LEADER OF THOSE WHO CAME TO BE CALLED SINNERS...
WAS NONE OTHER THAN AION.

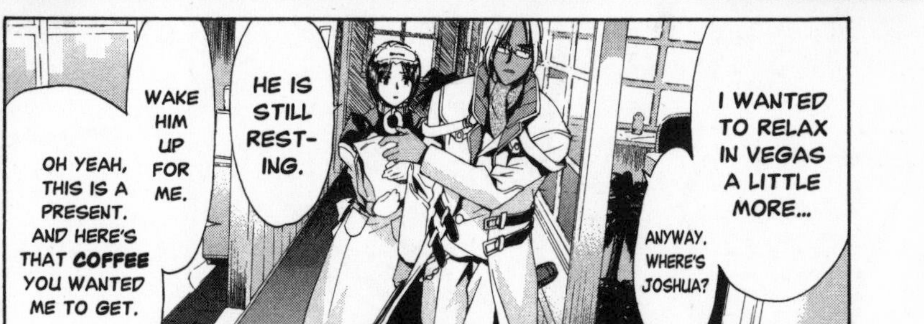
I WANTED TO RELAX IN VEGAS A LITTLE MORE...
ANYWAY, WHERE'S JOSHUA?
HE IS STILL RESTING.
WAKE HIM UP FOR ME.
OH YEAH, THIS IS A PRESENT. AND HERE'S THAT **COFFEE** YOU WANTED ME TO GET.

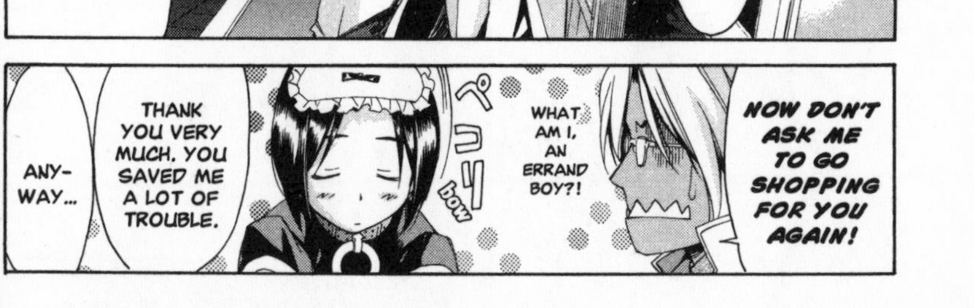
NOW DON'T ASK ME TO GO SHOPPING FOR YOU AGAIN!
WHAT AM I, AN ERRAND BOY?!
ペコリ
bow
THANK YOU VERY MUCH. YOU SAVED ME A LOT OF TROUBLE.
ANYWAY...

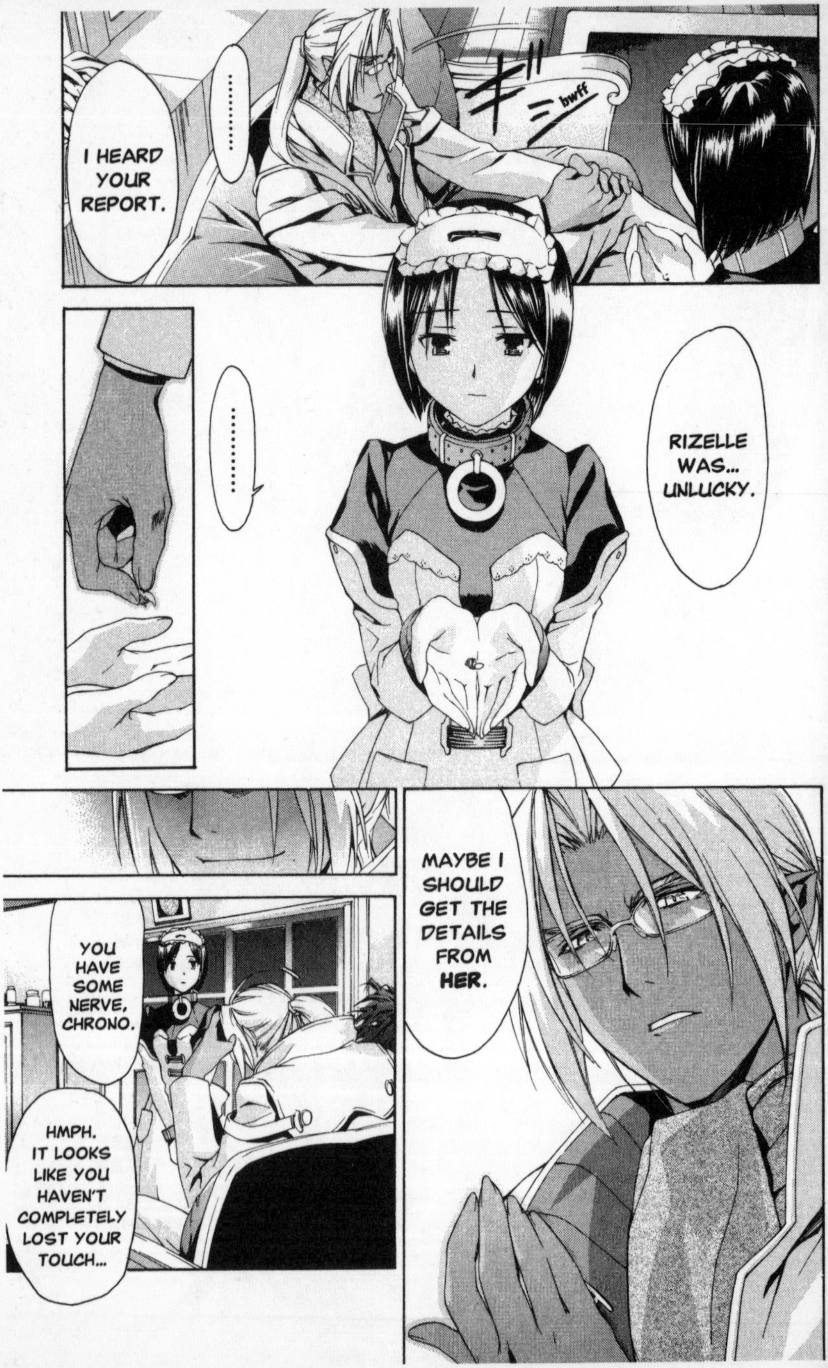
ギシ
bwff
......
I HEARD YOUR REPORT.
RIZELLE WAS... UNLUCKY.
......
MAYBE I SHOULD GET THE DETAILS FROM **HER**.
YOU HAVE SOME NERVE, CHRONO.
HMPH. IT LOOKS LIKE YOU HAVEN'T COMPLETELY LOST YOUR TOUCH...

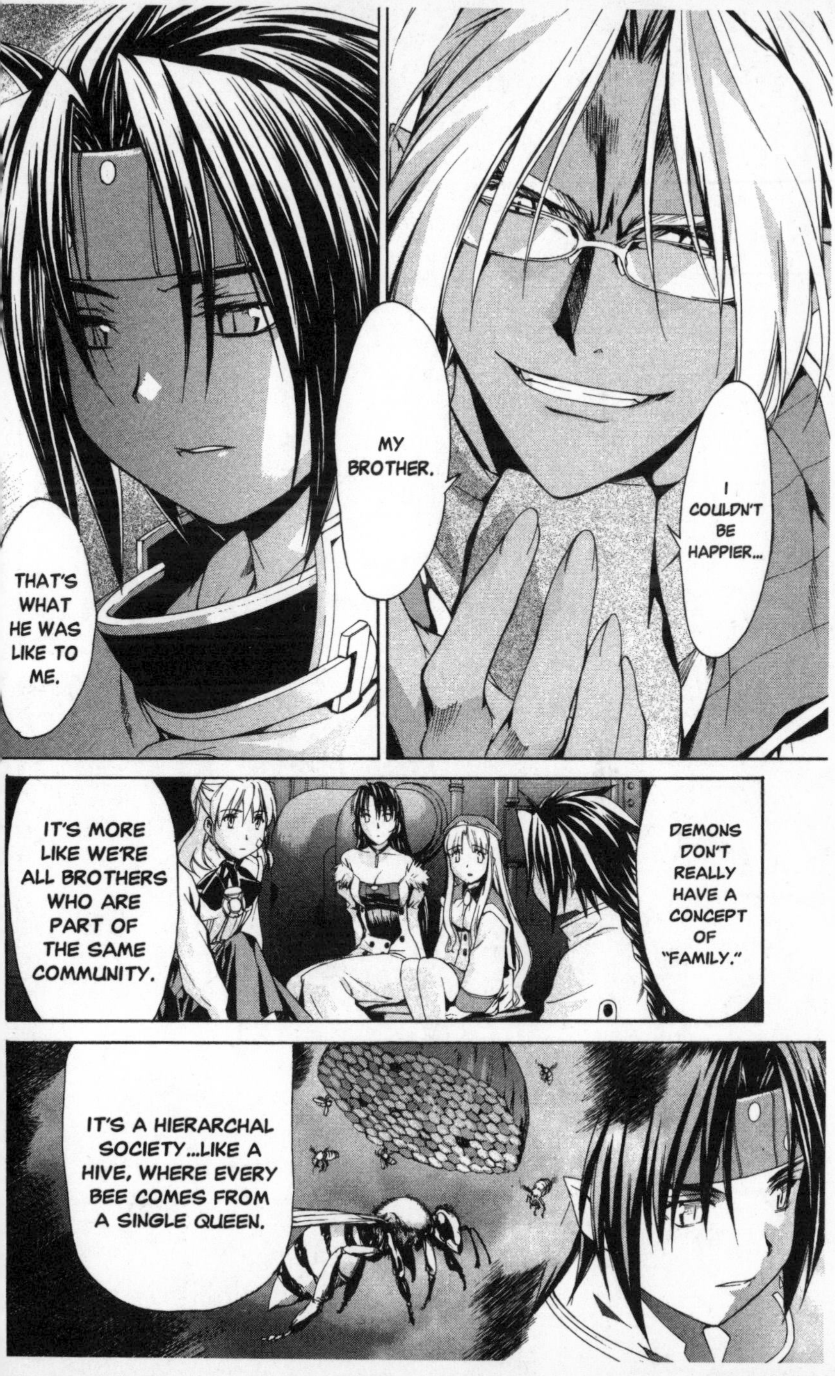
I COULDN'T BE HAPPIER...
MY BROTHER.
THAT'S WHAT HE WAS LIKE TO ME.
DEMONS DON'T REALLY HAVE A CONCEPT OF "FAMILY."
IT'S MORE LIKE WE'RE ALL BROTHERS WHO ARE PART OF THE SAME COMMUNITY.
IT'S A HIERARCHAL SOCIETY...LIKE A HIVE, WHERE EVERY BEE COMES FROM A SINGLE QUEEN.

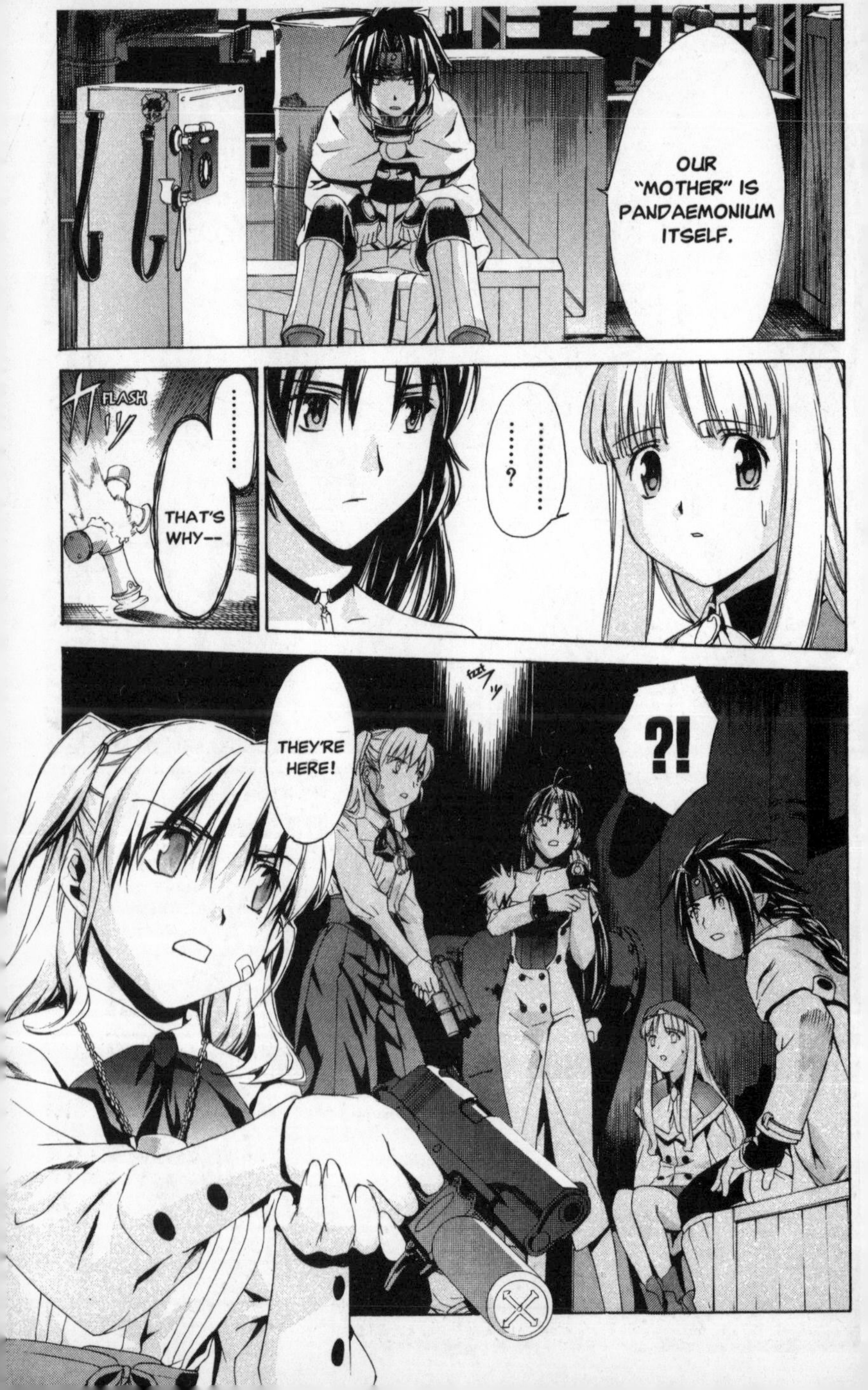
OUR "MOTHER" IS PANDAEMONIUM ITSELF.
......?
FLASH
...... THAT'S WHY--
?!
THEY'RE HERE!

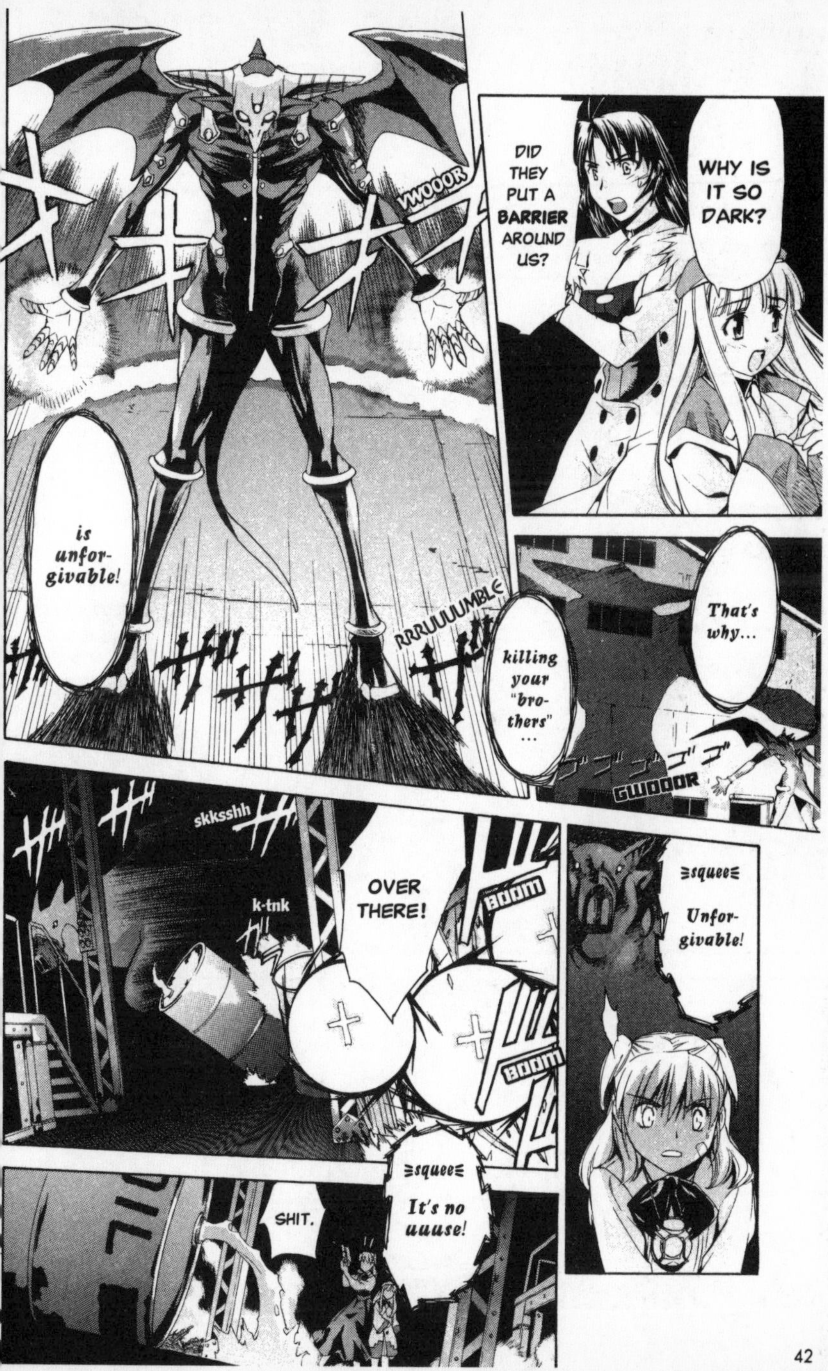
WHY IS IT SO DARK?
DID THEY PUT A BARRIER AROUND US?
That's why...
killing your "brothers"...
GWOOOR
VWOOOR
RRRUUUUMBLE
is unforgivable!
≷squee≶
Unforgivable!
skksshh
k-tnk
OVER THERE!
BOOM
BOOM
≷squee≶
It's no uuuse!
SHIT.

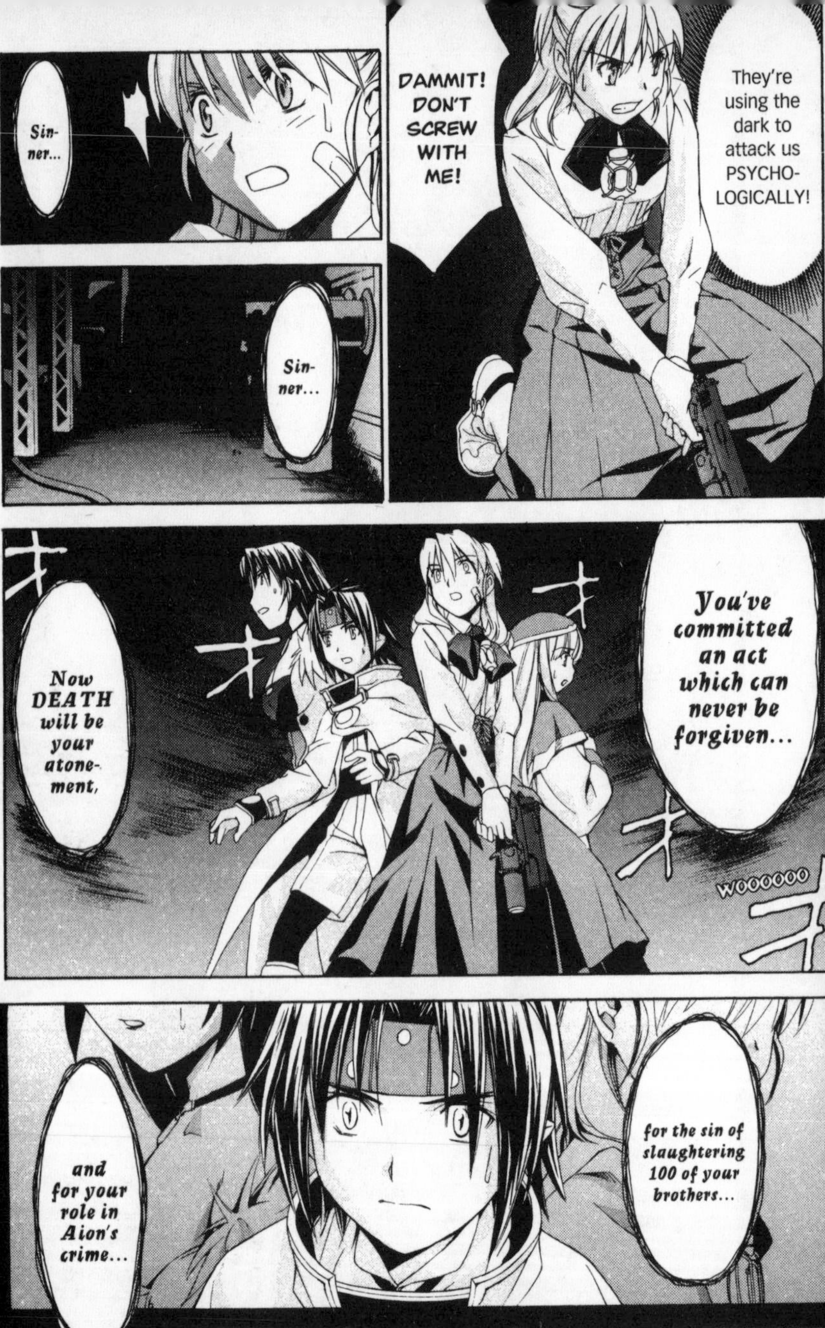
They're using the dark to attack us PSYCHO-LOGICALLY!
DAMMIT! DON'T SCREW WITH ME!
Sin-ner...
Sin-ner...
You've committed an act which can never be forgiven...
WOOOOOO
Now DEATH will be your atone-ment,
for the sin of slaughtering 100 of your brothers...
and for your role in Aion's crime...

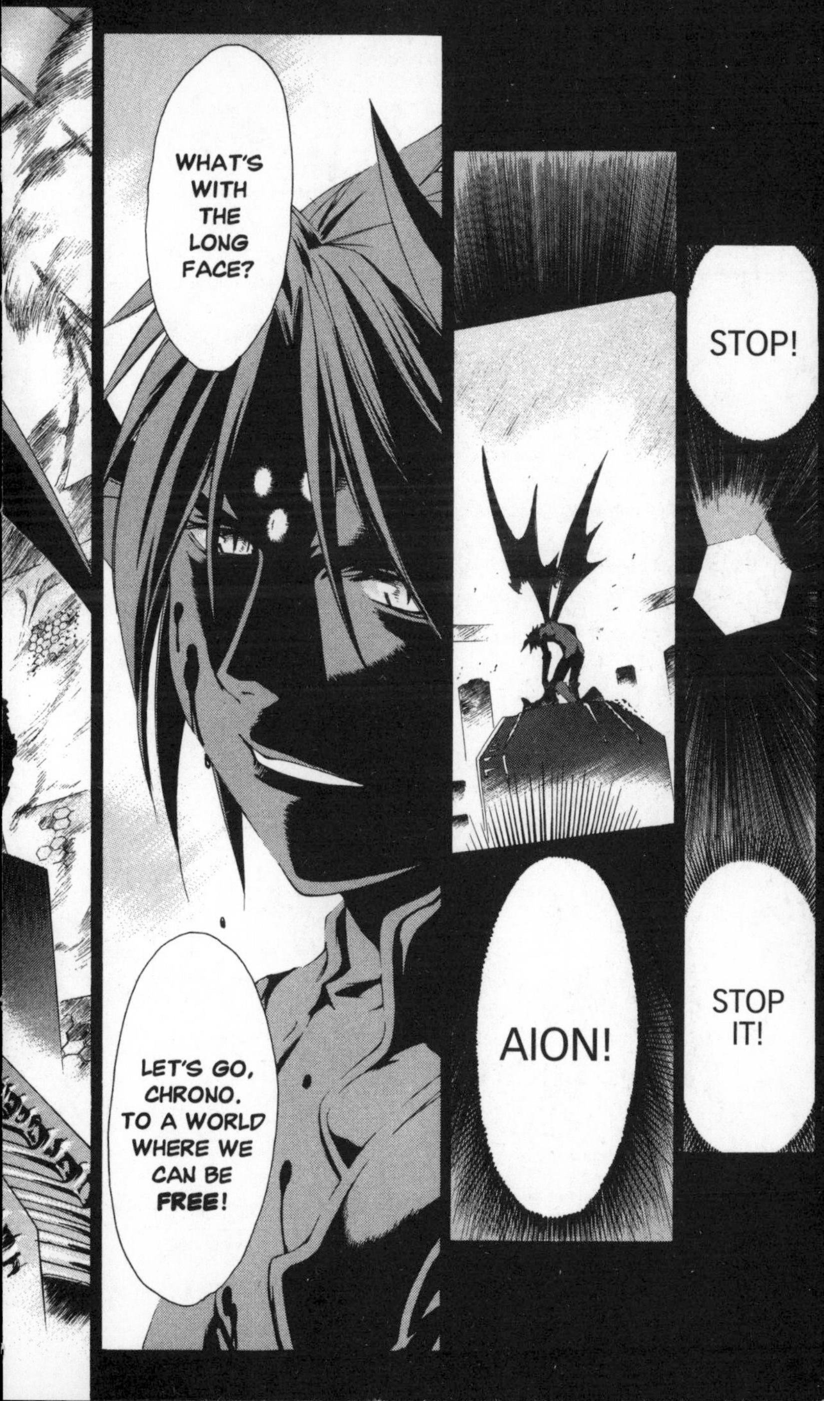
STOP!
STOP IT!
AION!
WHAT'S WITH THE LONG FACE?
LET'S GO, CHRONO. TO A WORLD WHERE WE CAN BE **FREE**!

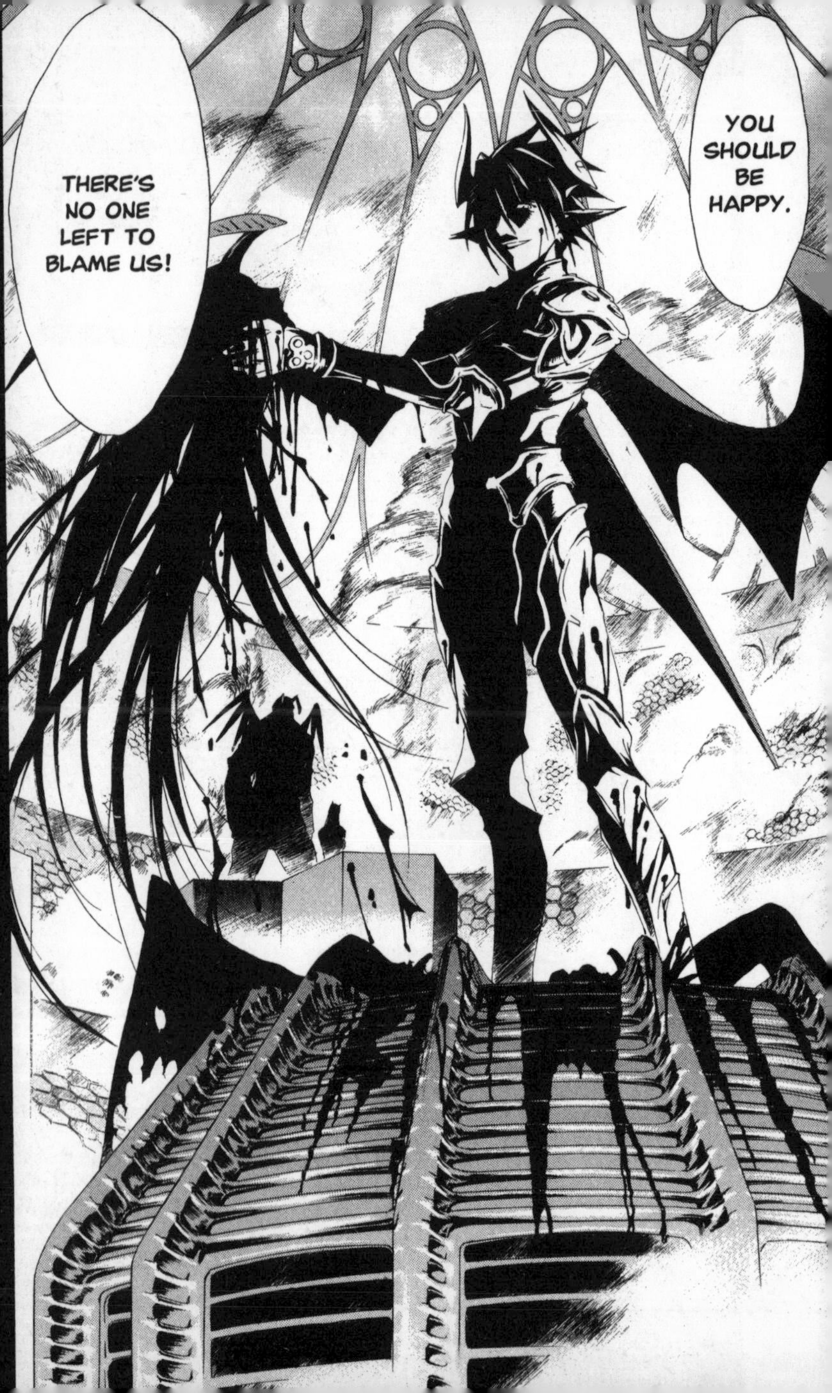
YOU SHOULD BE HAPPY.
THERE'S NO ONE LEFT TO BLAME US!

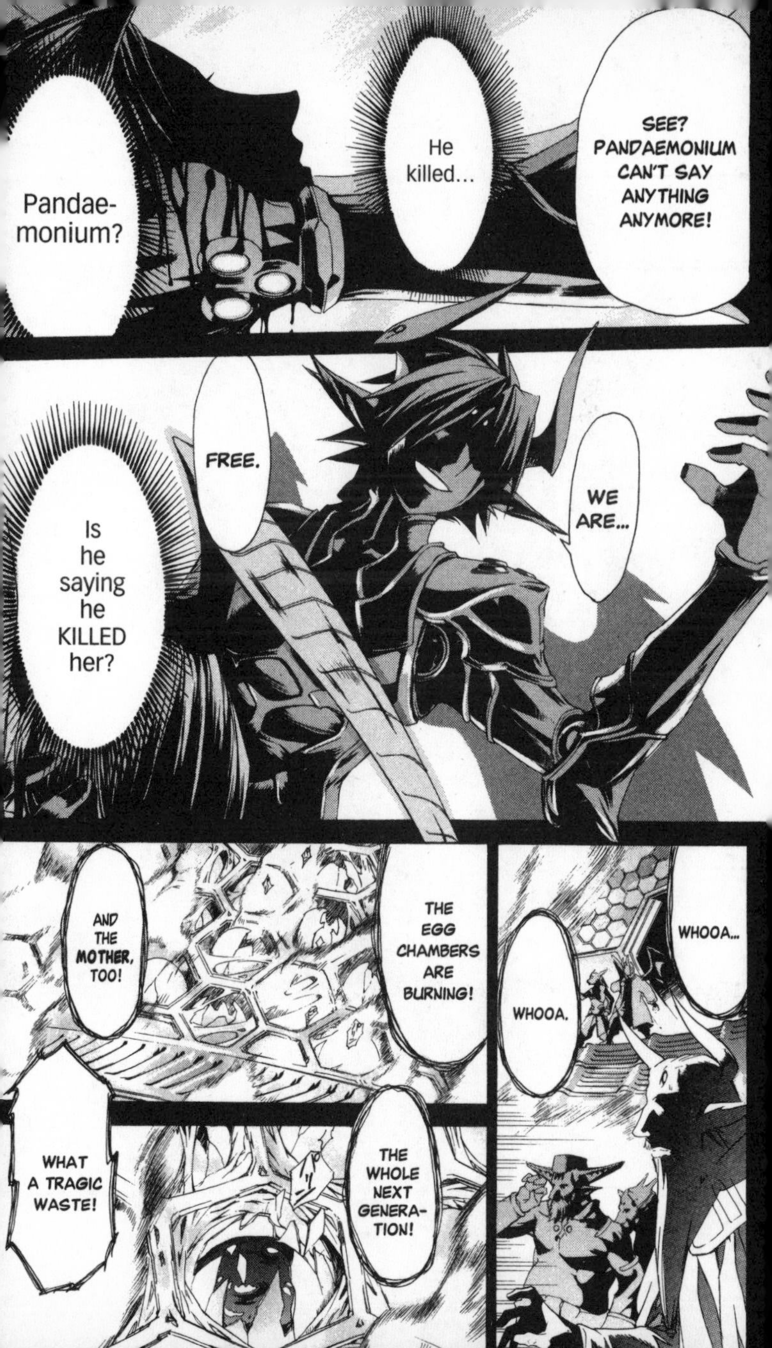
SEE? PANDAEMONIUM CAN'T SAY ANYTHING ANYMORE!
He killed...
Pandae-monium?
WE ARE...
FREE.
Is he saying he KILLED her?
WHOOA...
WHOOA.
THE EGG CHAMBERS ARE BURNING!
AND THE MOTHER, TOO!
THE WHOLE NEXT GENERATION!
WHAT A TRAGIC WASTE!

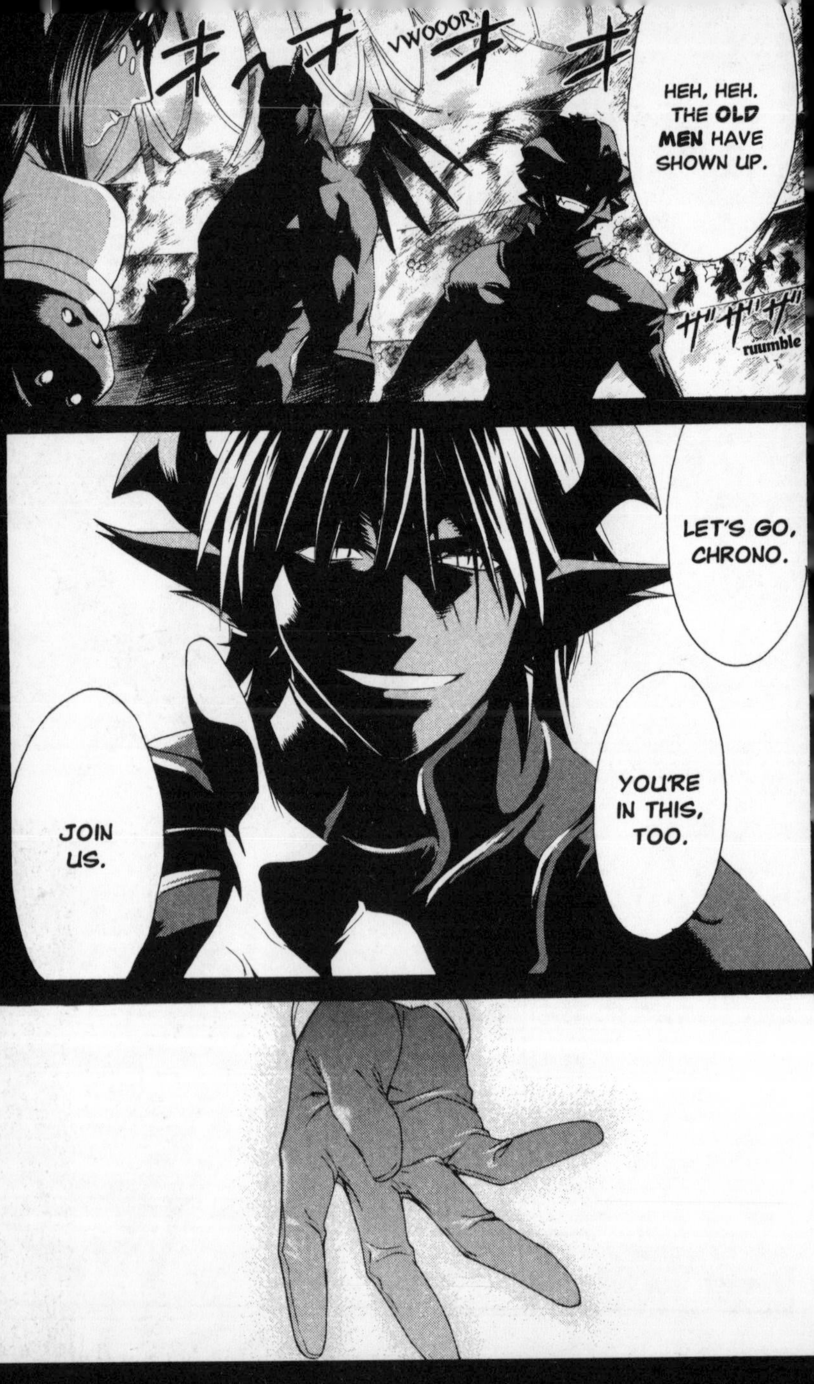
HEH, HEH. THE OLD MEN HAVE SHOWN UP.
VWOOOR
ruumble
LET'S GO, CHRONO.
YOU'RE IN THIS, TOO.
JOIN US.

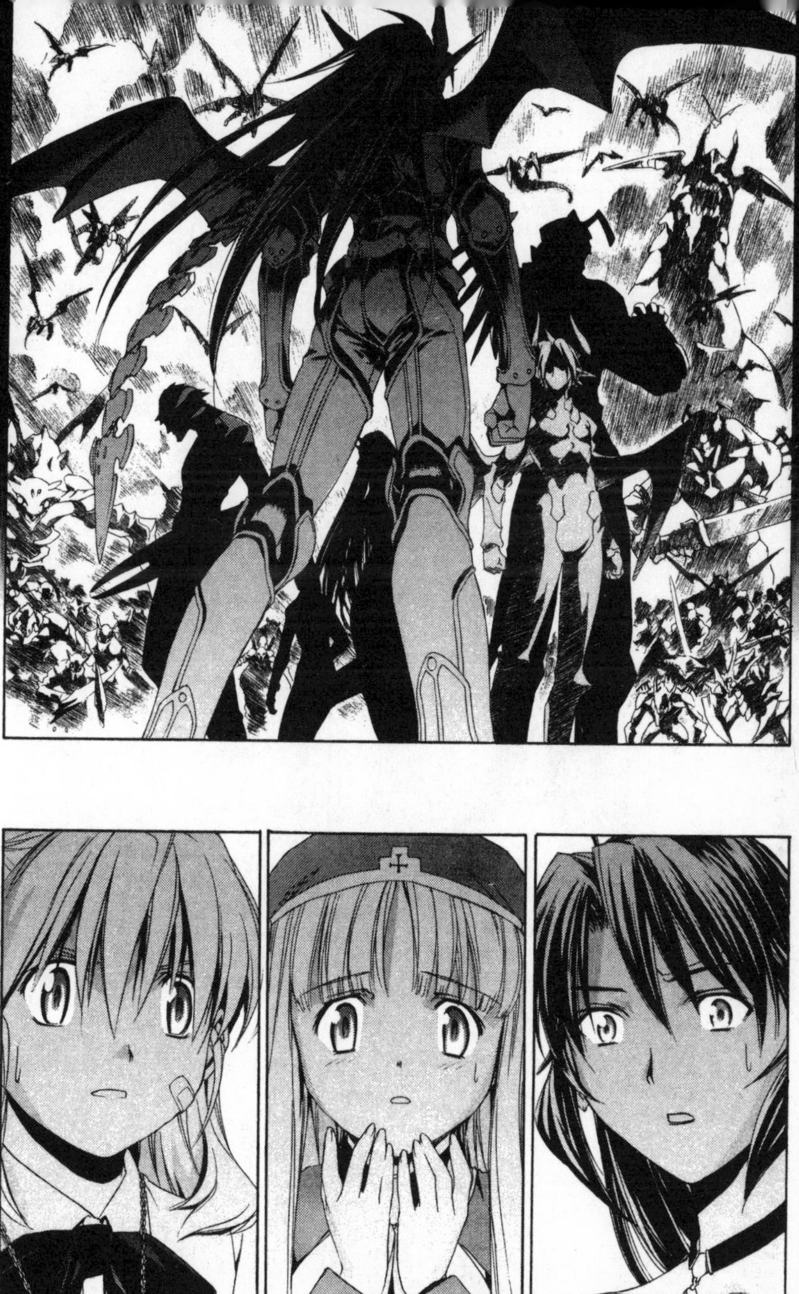

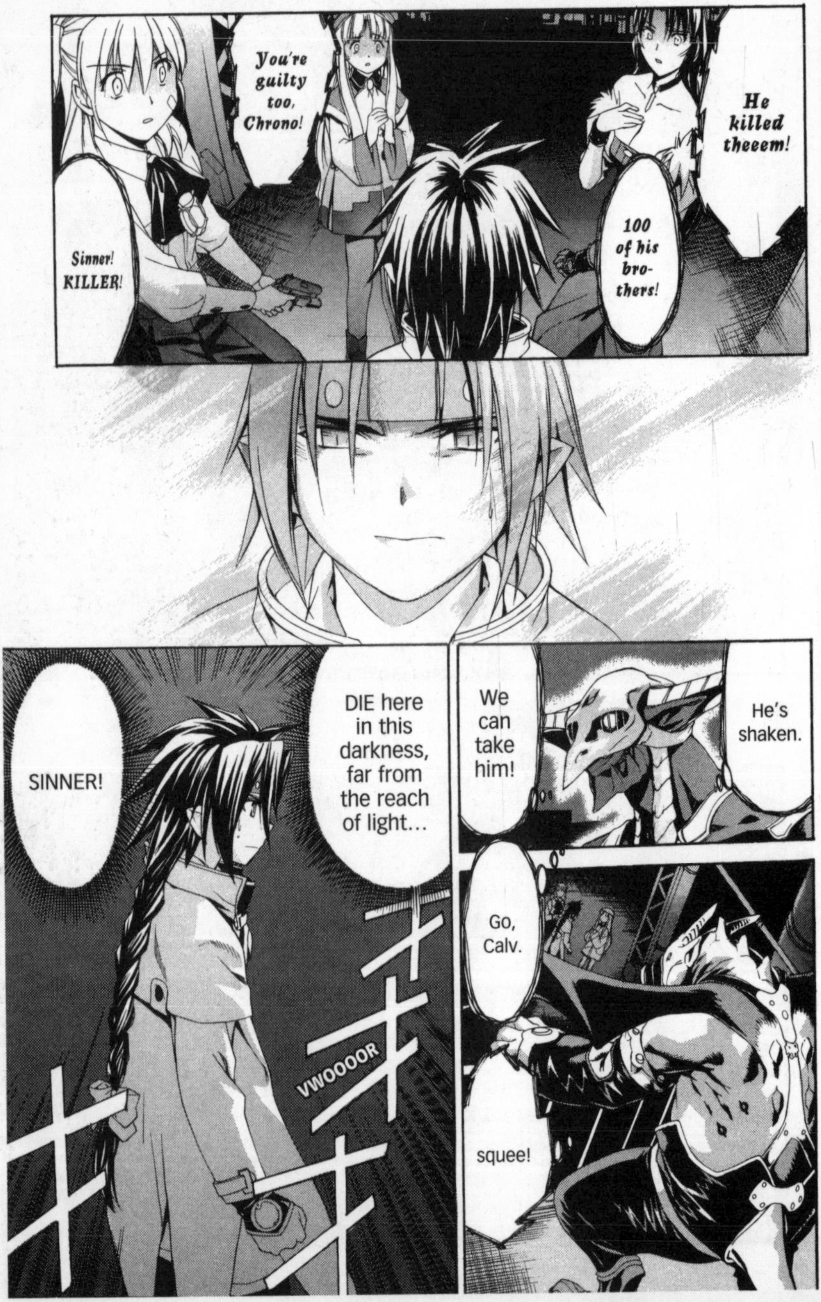
He killed theeem!
100 of his brothers!
You're guilty too, Chrono!
Sinner! KILLER!
He's shaken.
We can take him!
Go, Calv.
squee!
DIE here in this darkness, far from the reach of light...
SINNER!
VWOOOOR

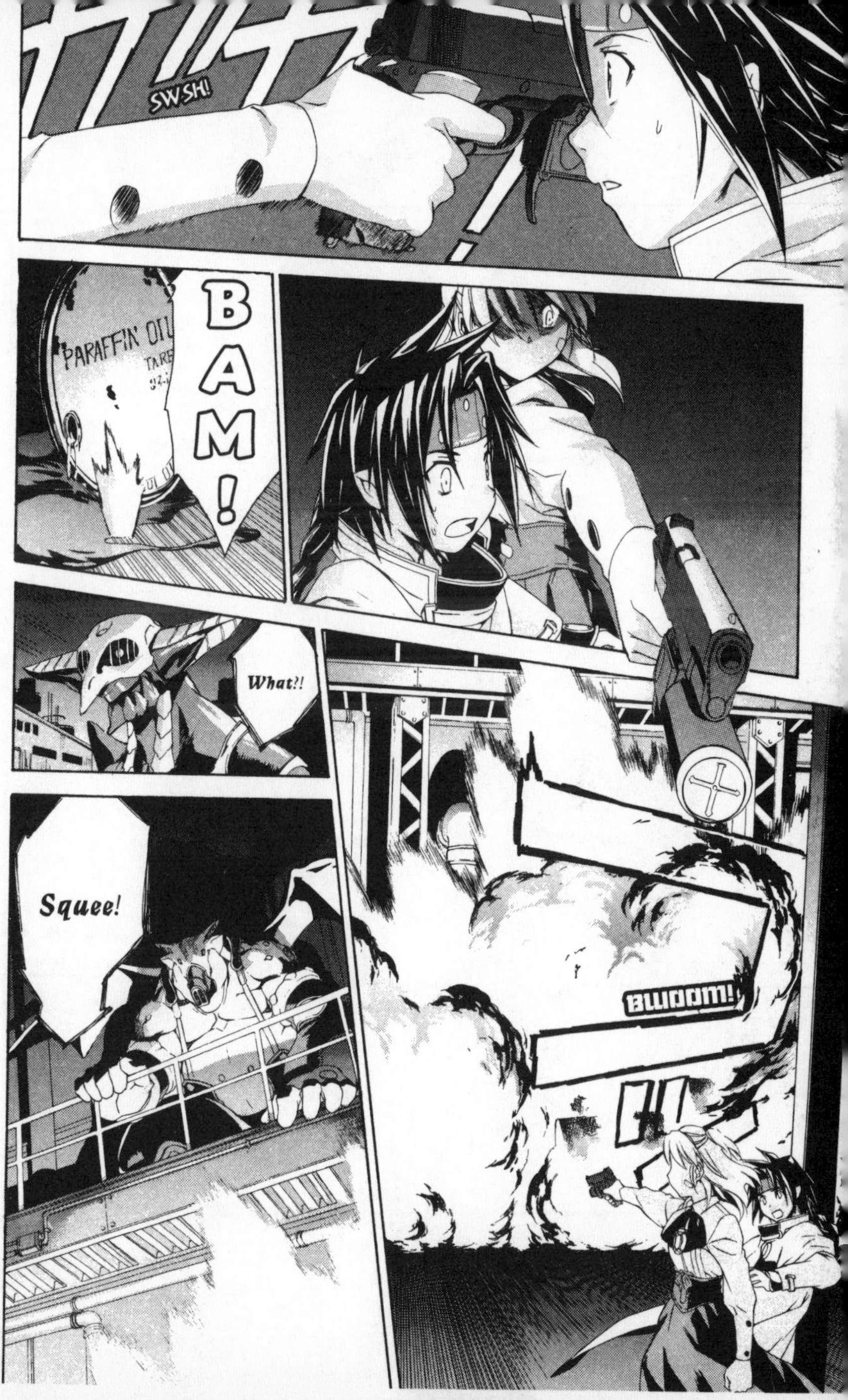
SWSH!
PARAFFIN OI
BAM!
BWOOM!
What?!
Squee!

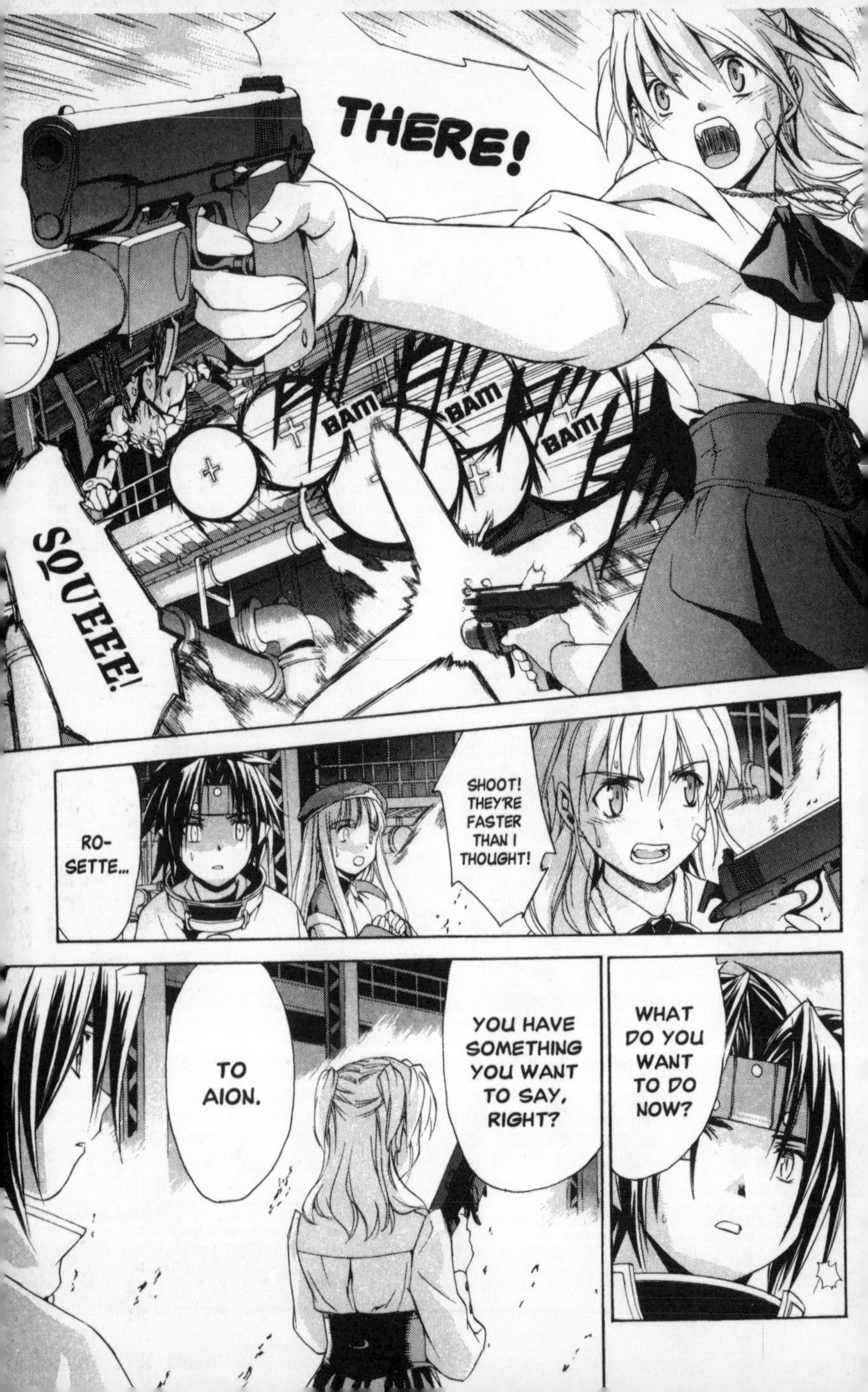
THERE!
BAM
BAM
BAM
BAM
SQUEEE!
SHOOT! THEY'RE FASTER THAN I THOUGHT!
RO-SETTE...
WHAT DO YOU WANT TO DO NOW?
YOU HAVE SOMETHING YOU WANT TO SAY, RIGHT?
TO AION.

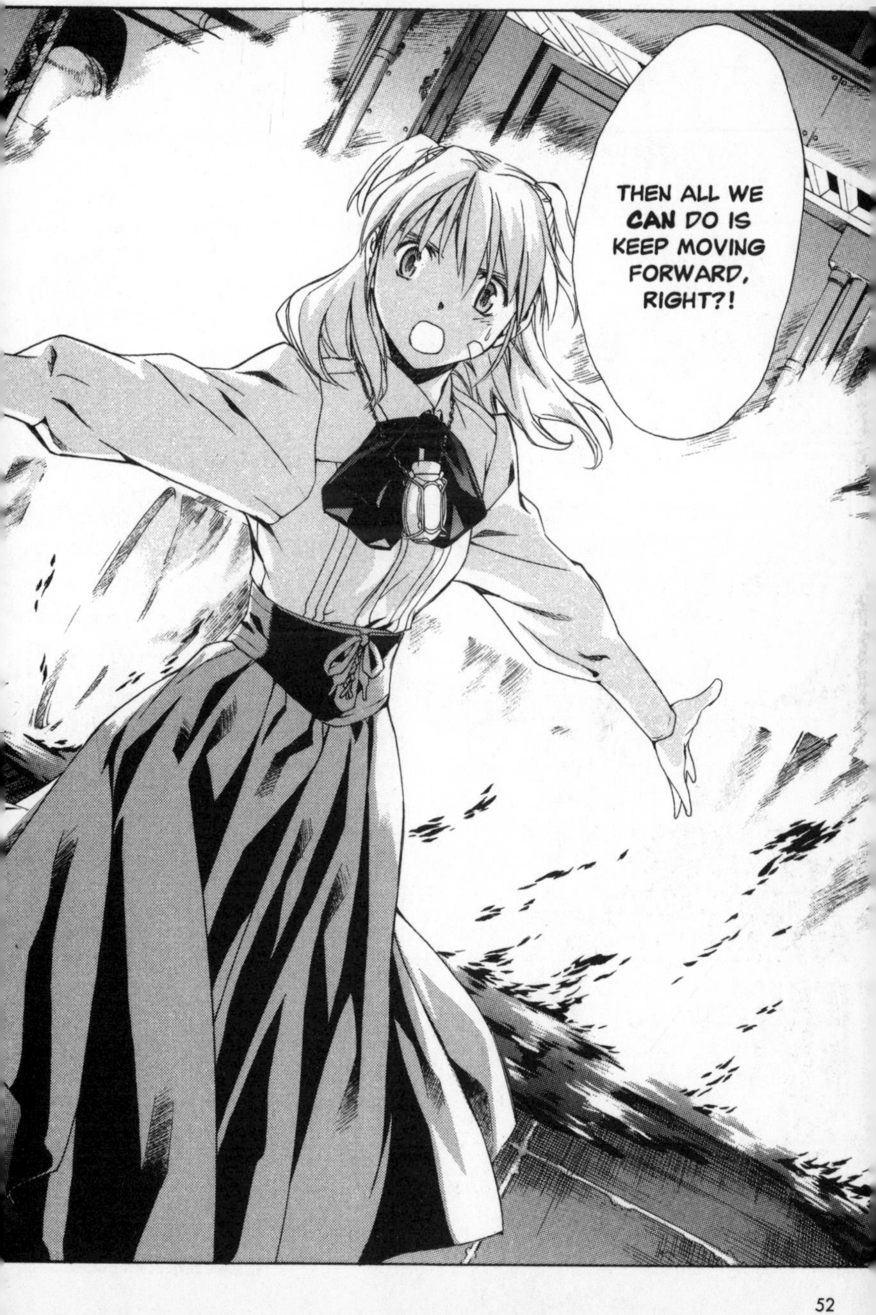
THEN ALL WE **CAN** DO IS KEEP MOVING FORWARD, RIGHT?!

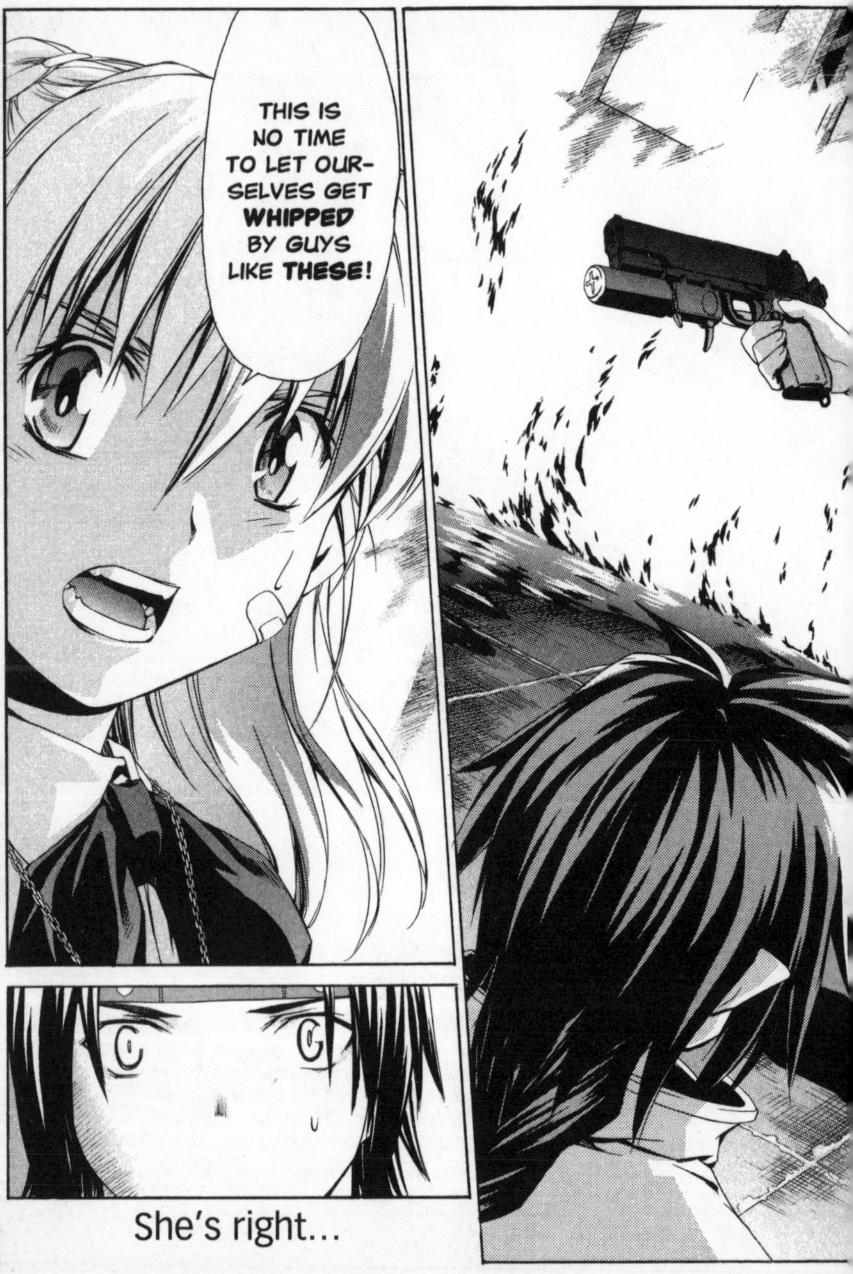
THIS IS NO TIME TO LET OURSELVES GET WHIPPED BY GUYS LIKE THESE!
She's right...

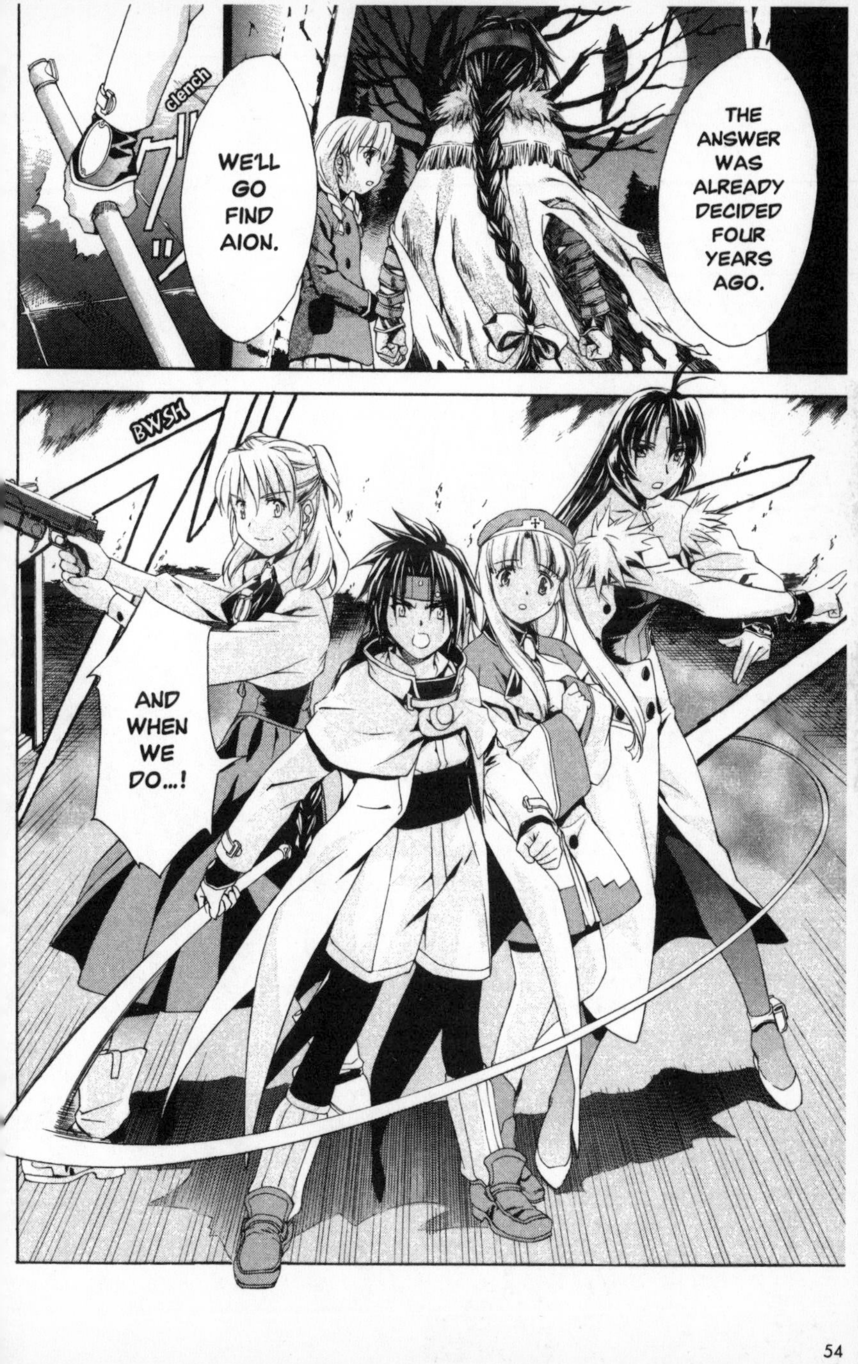
THE ANSWER WAS ALREADY DECIDED FOUR YEARS AGO.
WE'LL GO FIND AION.
clench
BWSH
AND WHEN WE DO...!

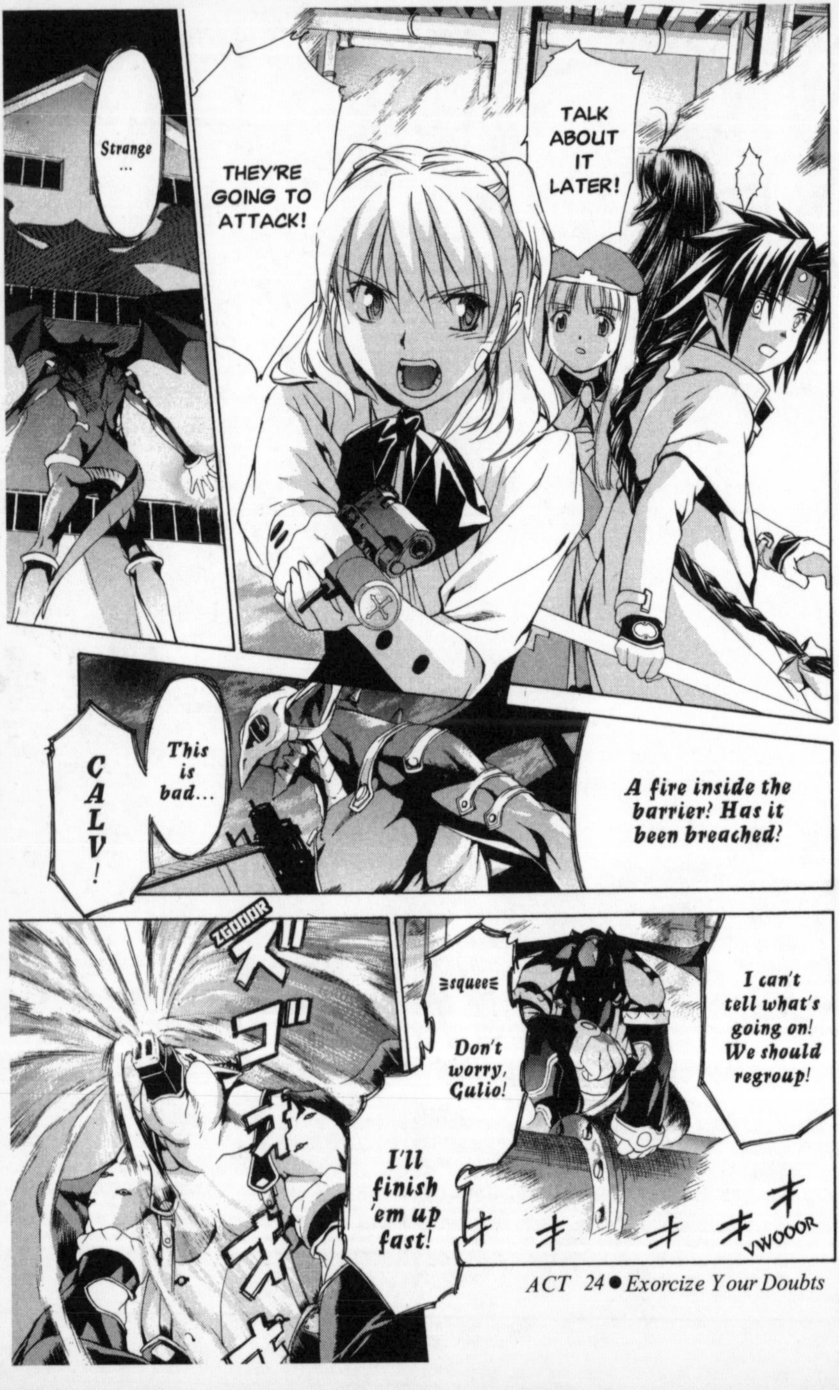
TALK ABOUT IT LATER!
THEY'RE GOING TO ATTACK!
Strange ...
A fire inside the barrier? Has it been breached?
This is bad...
CALV!
I can't tell what's going on! We should regroup!
squee
Don't worry, Gulio!
I'll finish 'em up fast!
VWOOOR
ZGOOOR

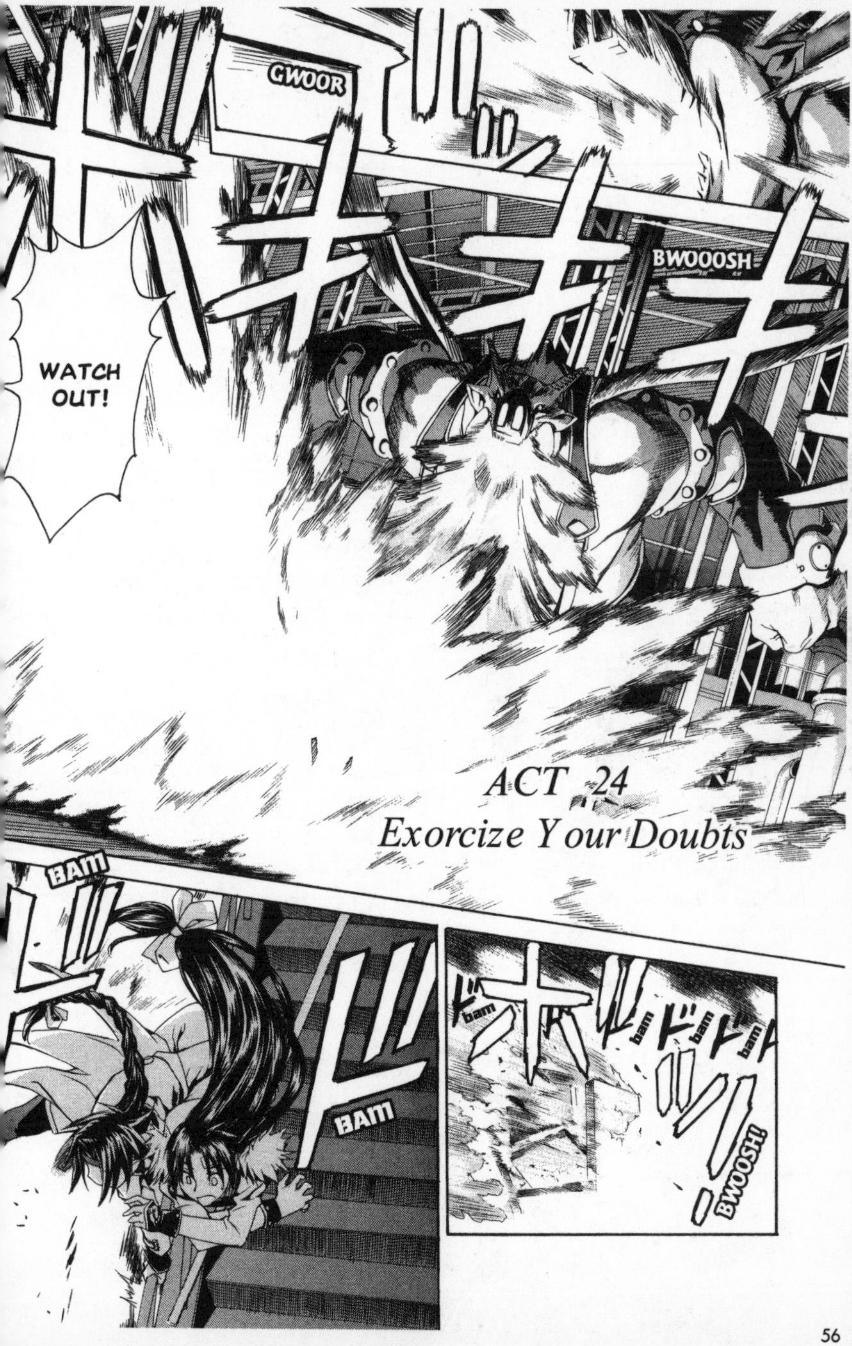
GWOOR
BWOOOSH
WATCH OUT!
ACT 24
Exorcize Your Doubts
bam
bam
bam
bam
BWOOSH!
BAM
BAM

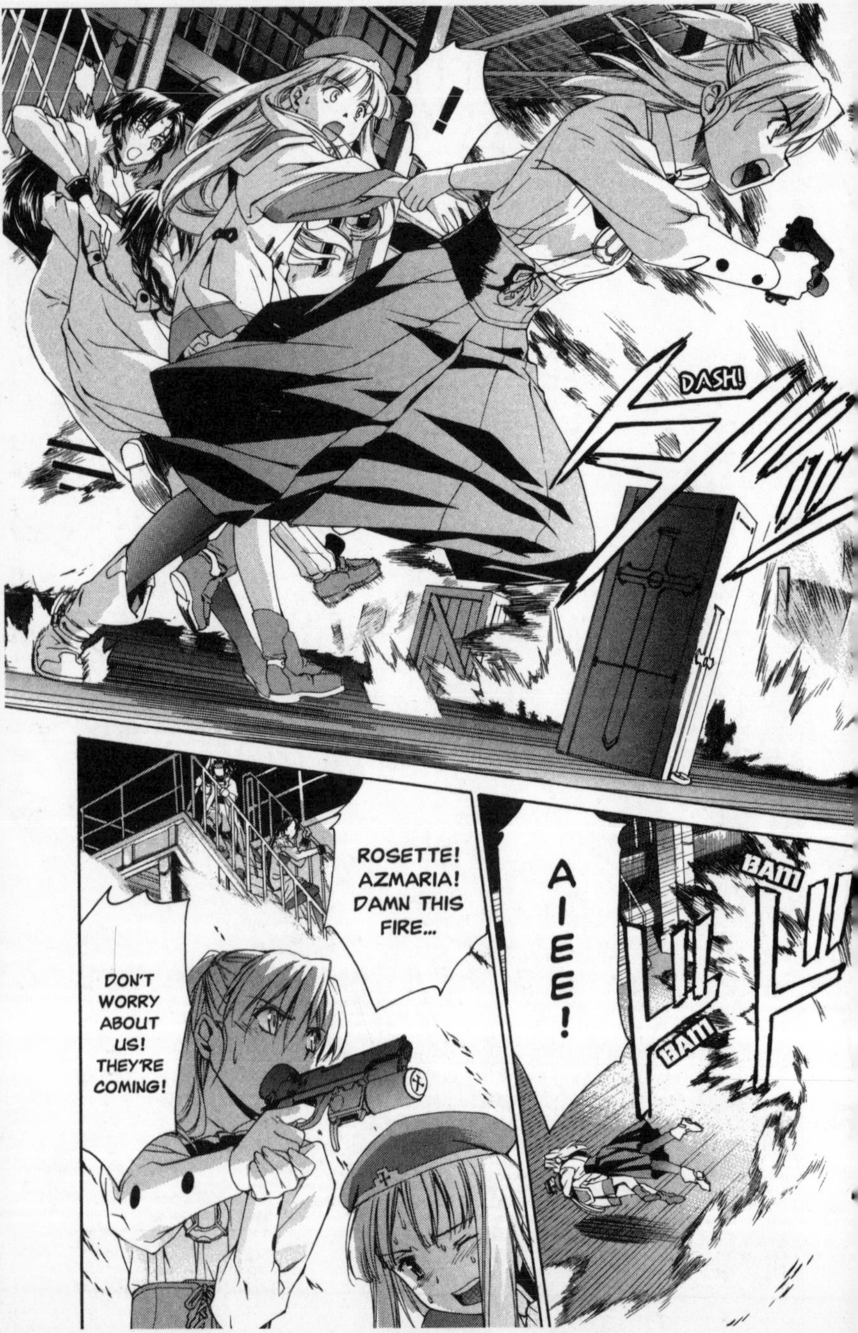
!
DASH!
BAM
BAM
AIEE!
ROSETTE! AZMARIA! DAMN THIS FIRE...
DON'T WORRY ABOUT US! THEY'RE COMING!

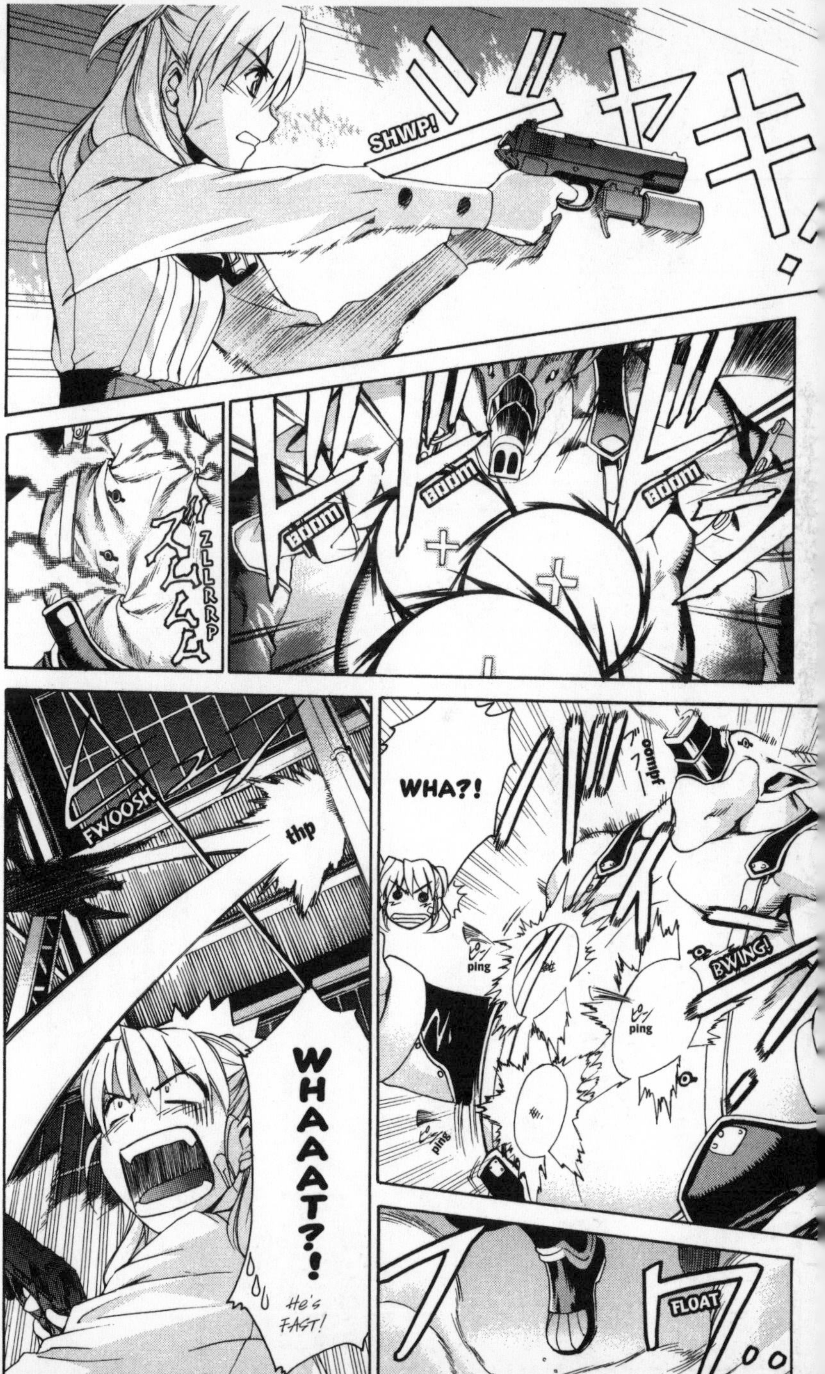
SHWP!
BOOM
BOOM
BOOM
ZLLRRP
WHA?!
oompf
ping
BWING!
ping
ping
FLOAT
FWOOSH
thp
WHAAAT?!
He's FAST!

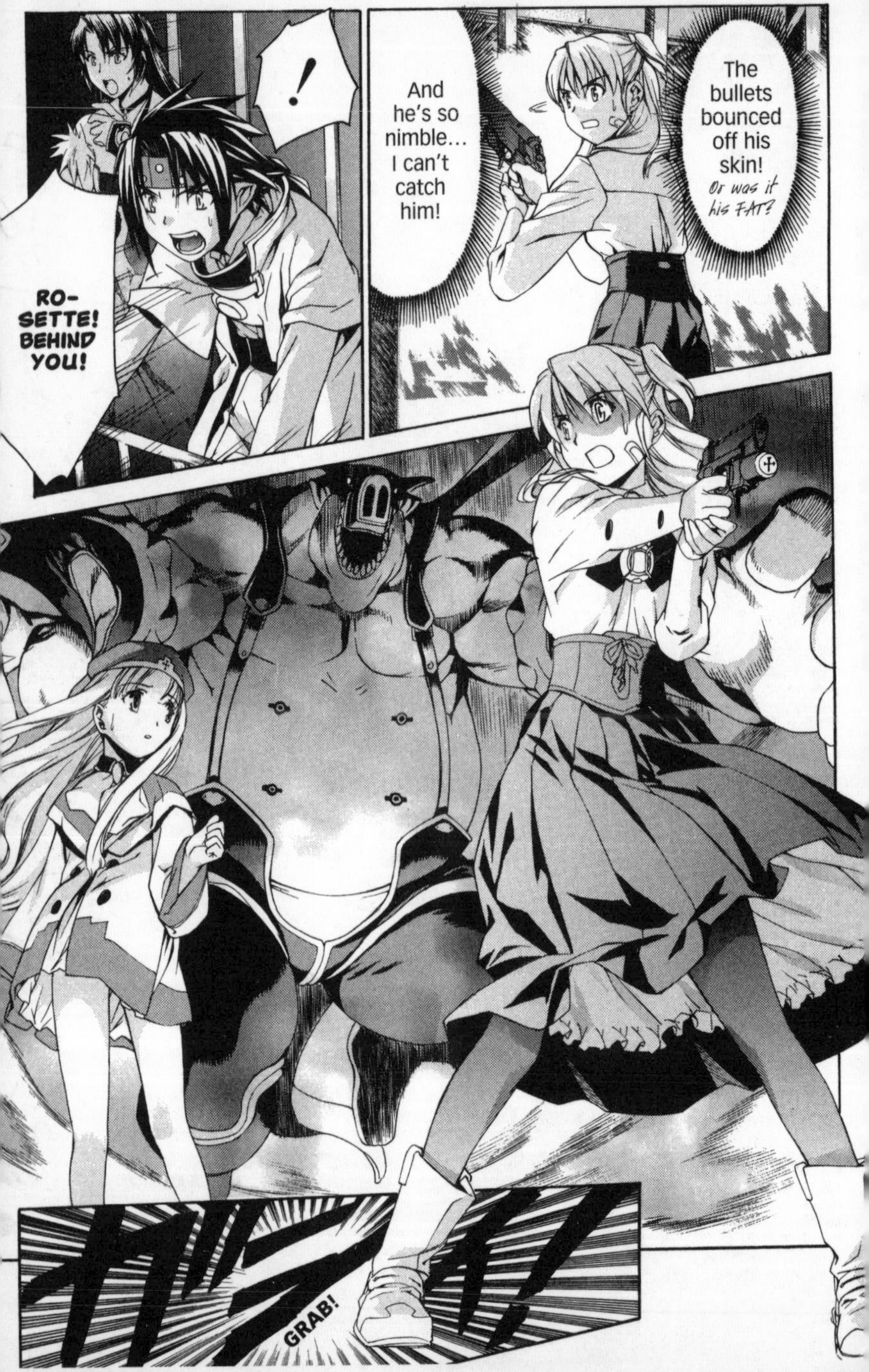
The bullets bounced off his skin!
Or was it his FAT?
And he's so nimble… I can't catch him!
!
RO-SETTE! BEHIND YOU!
GRAB!

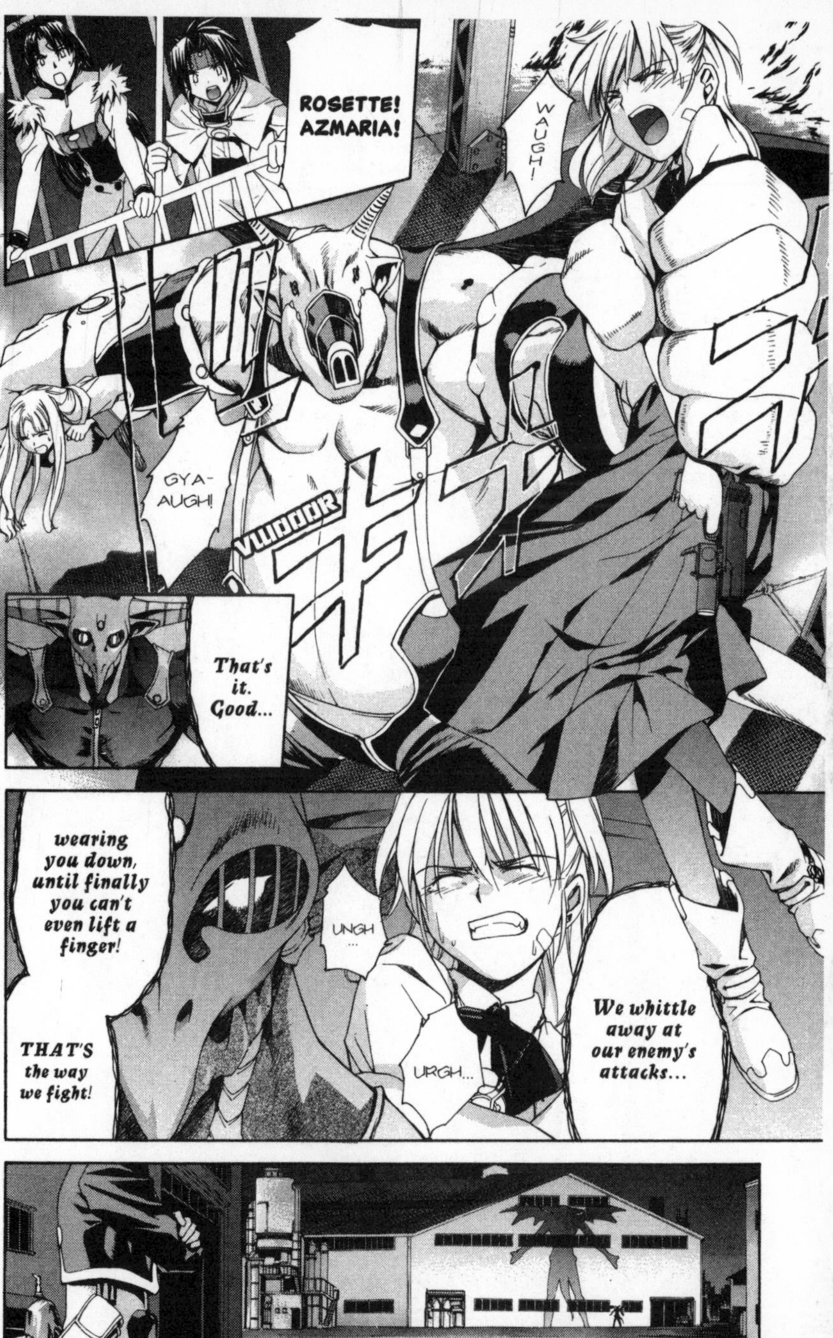
WAUGH!
ROSETTE! AZMARIA!
VWOOOR
GYA-AUGH!
That's it. Good...
We whittle away at our enemy's attacks...
UNGH...
URGH...
wearing you down, until finally you can't even lift a finger!
THAT'S the way we fight!

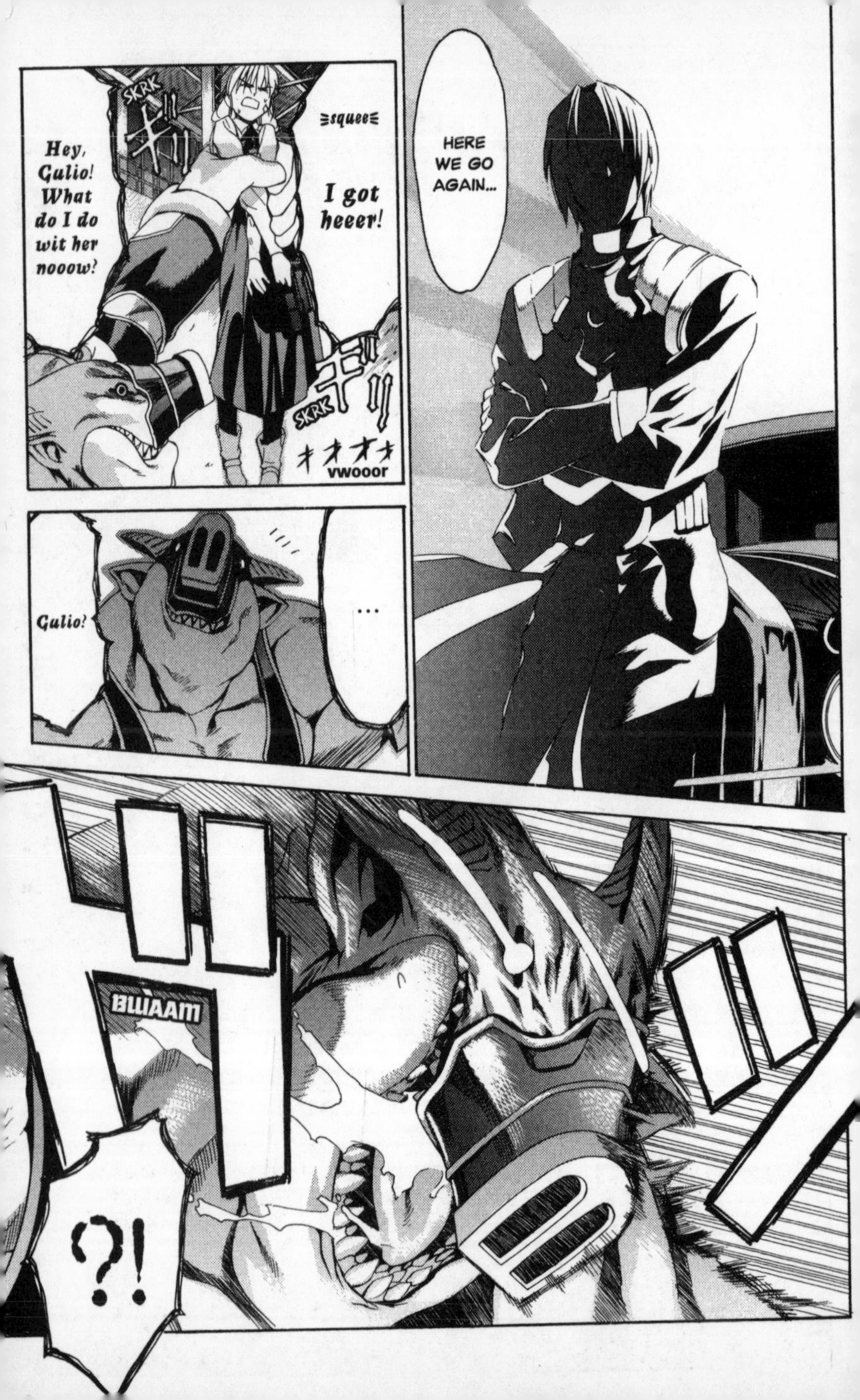
HERE WE GO AGAIN...
≡squee≡
I got heeer!
SKRK
Hey, Gulio! What do I do wit her nooow?
SKRK
vwooor
...
Gulio?
BWAAM
?!

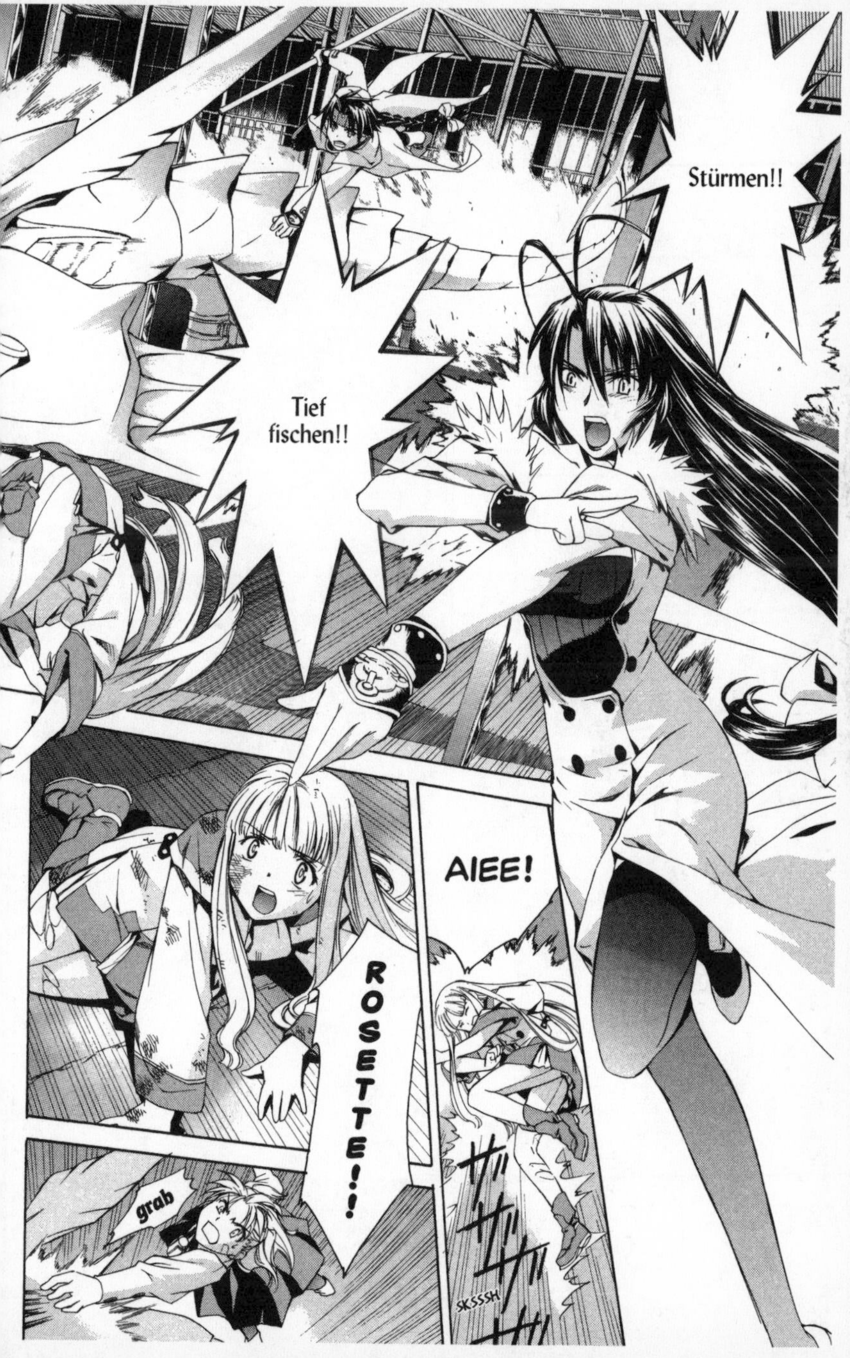

Stürmen!!
Tief fischen!!
AIEE!
SKSSSH
ROSETTE!!!
grab

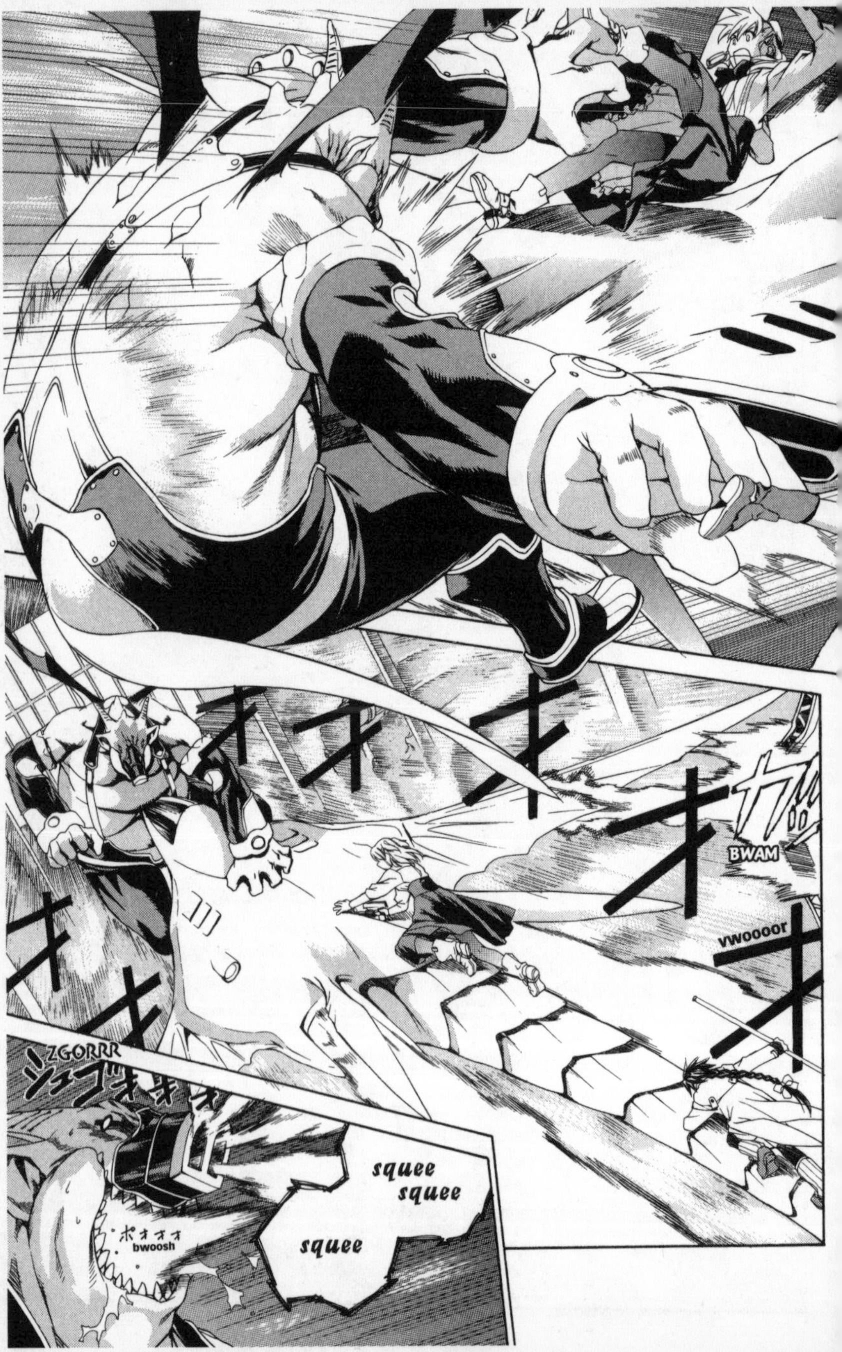
BWAM
vwoooor
ZGORRR
シュゴオオオ
squee
squee
squee
ポオオオ
bwoosh

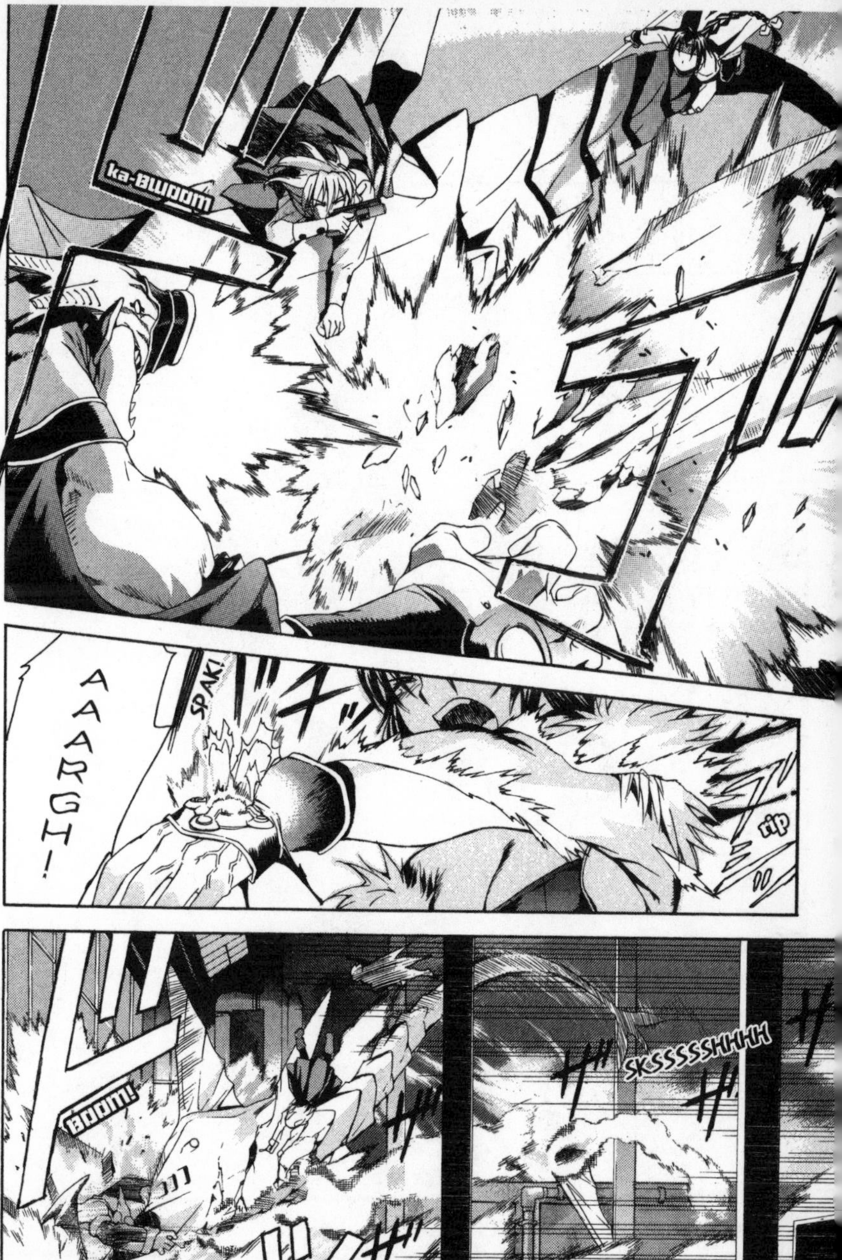
ka-BWOOM
rip
SPAK!
AAAARGH!
SKSSSSSHHHH
BOOM!

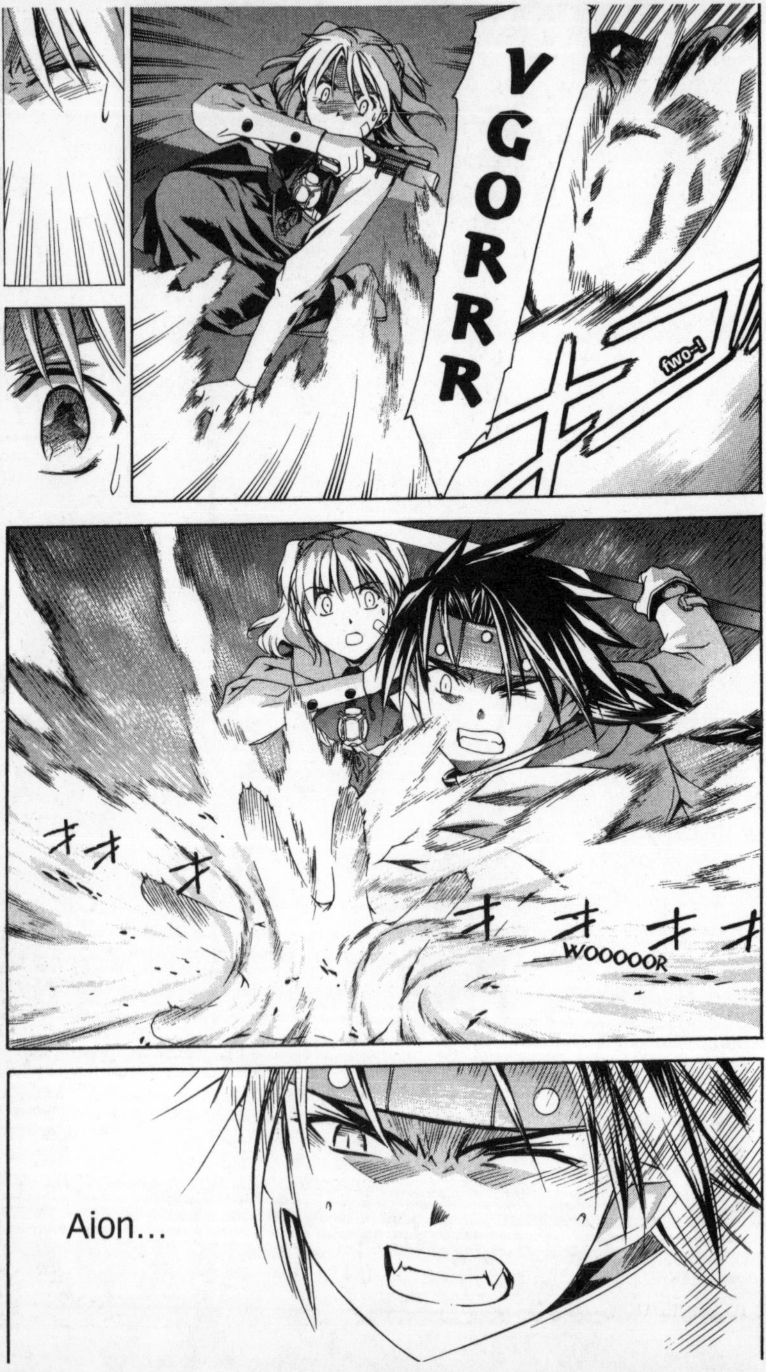
VGORRR
fwo--!
WOOOOOR
Aion...

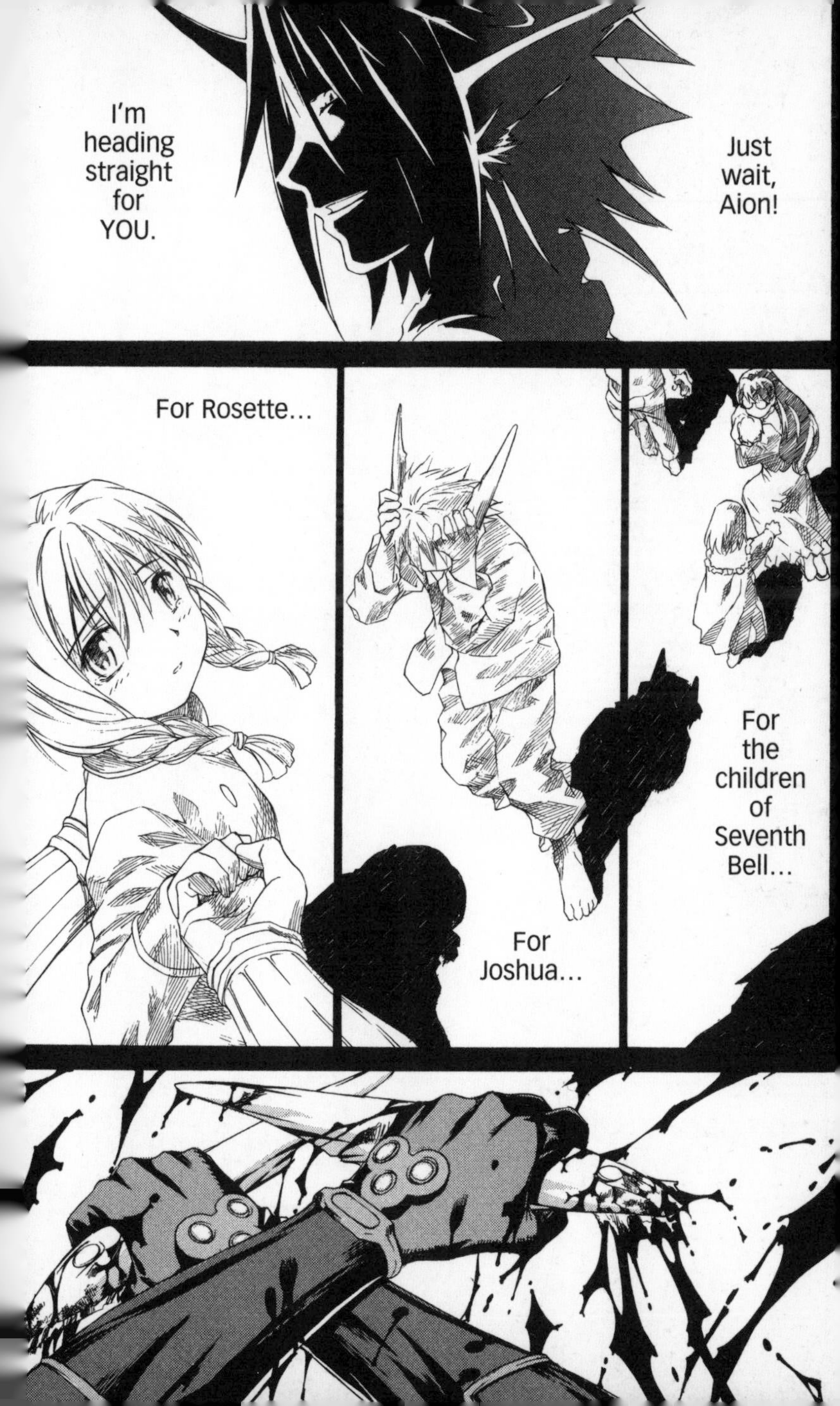
Just wait, Aion!
I'm heading straight for YOU.
For the children of Seventh Bell…
For Joshua…
For Rosette…

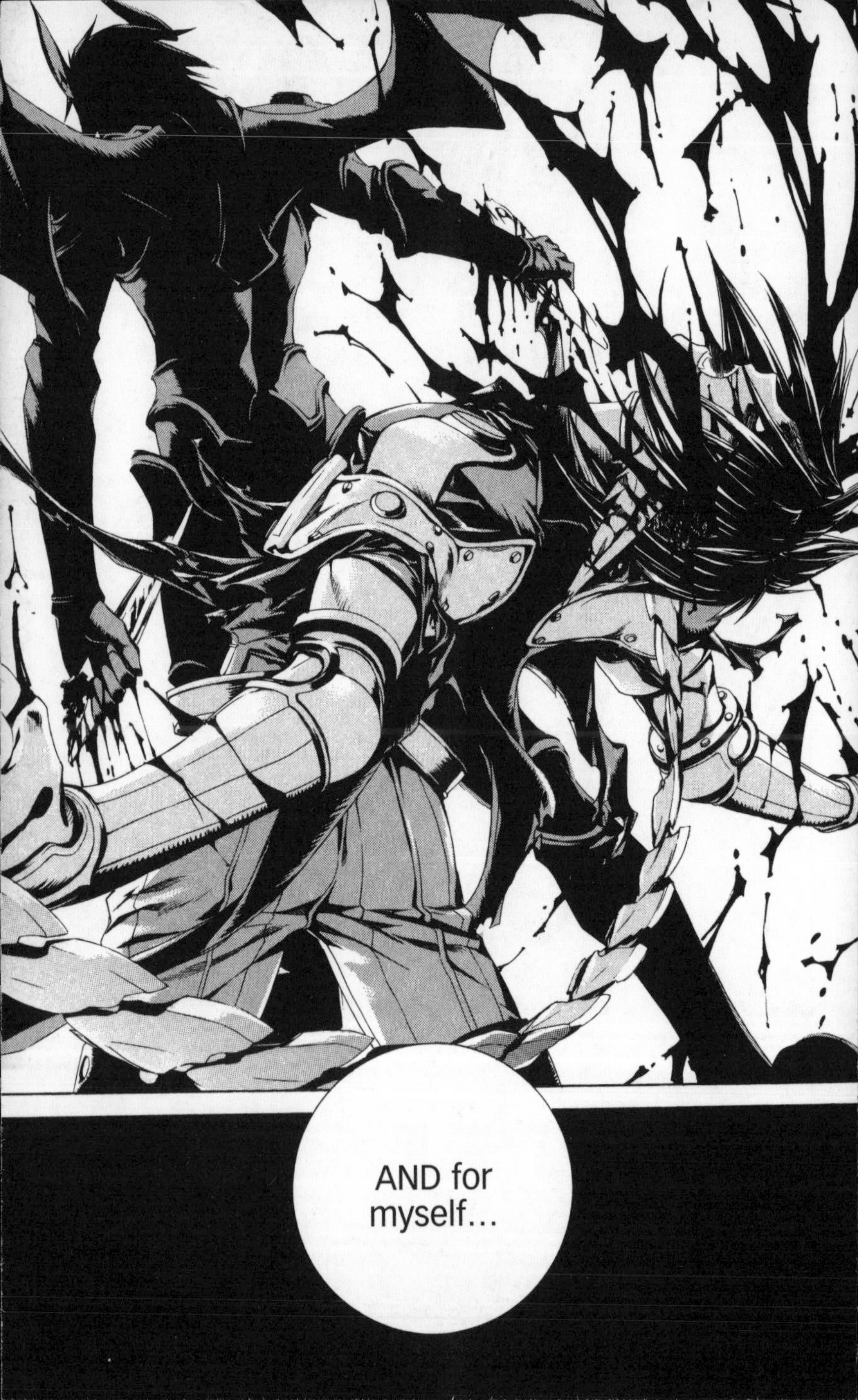
AND for myself...

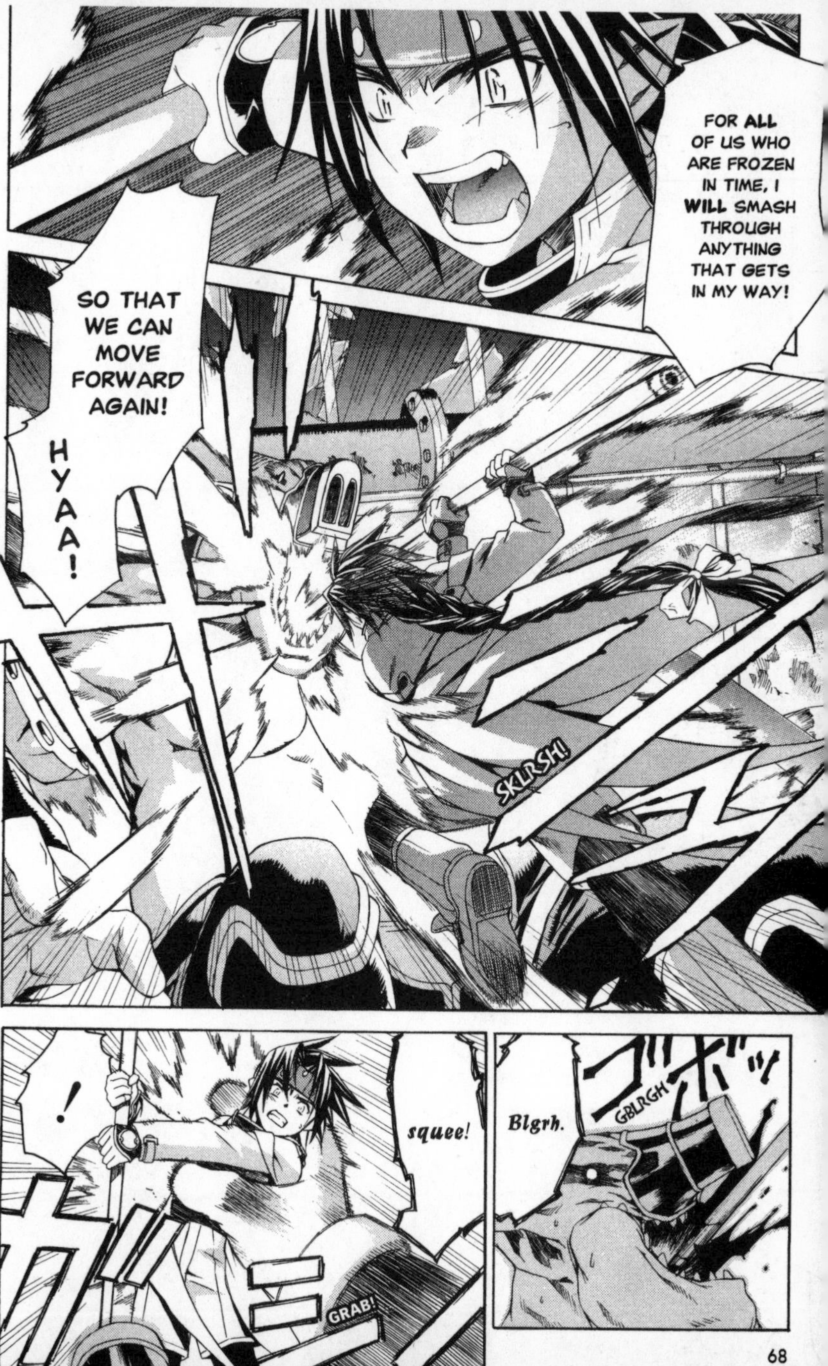
FOR ALL OF US WHO ARE FROZEN IN TIME, I WILL SMASH THROUGH ANYTHING THAT GETS IN MY WAY!
SO THAT WE CAN MOVE FORWARD AGAIN!
HYAA!
SKLRSH!
Blgrh.
GBLRGH
squee!
!
GRAB!

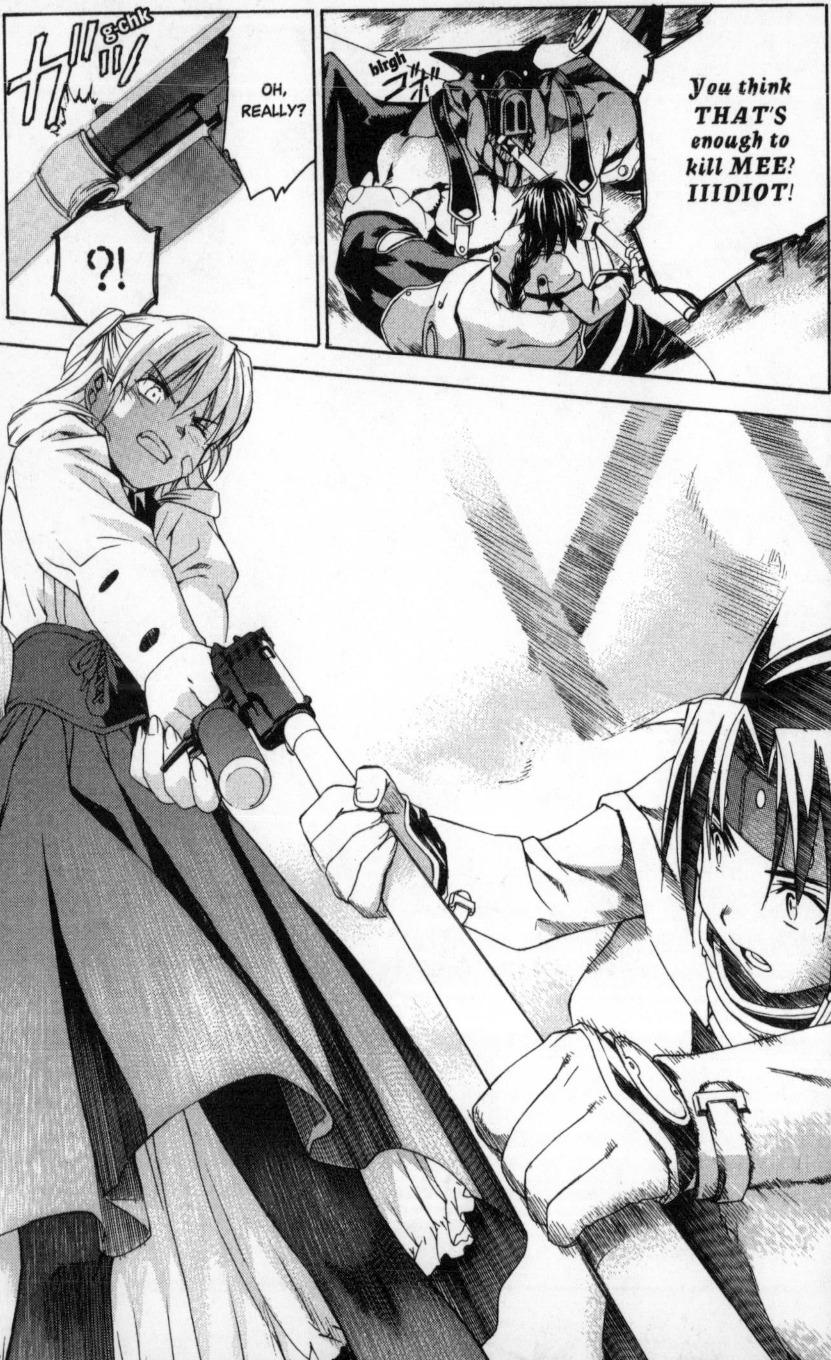
blrgh
ゴボ
You think THAT'S enough to kill MEE? IIIDIOT!
g-chk
ガッ
OH, REALLY?
?!

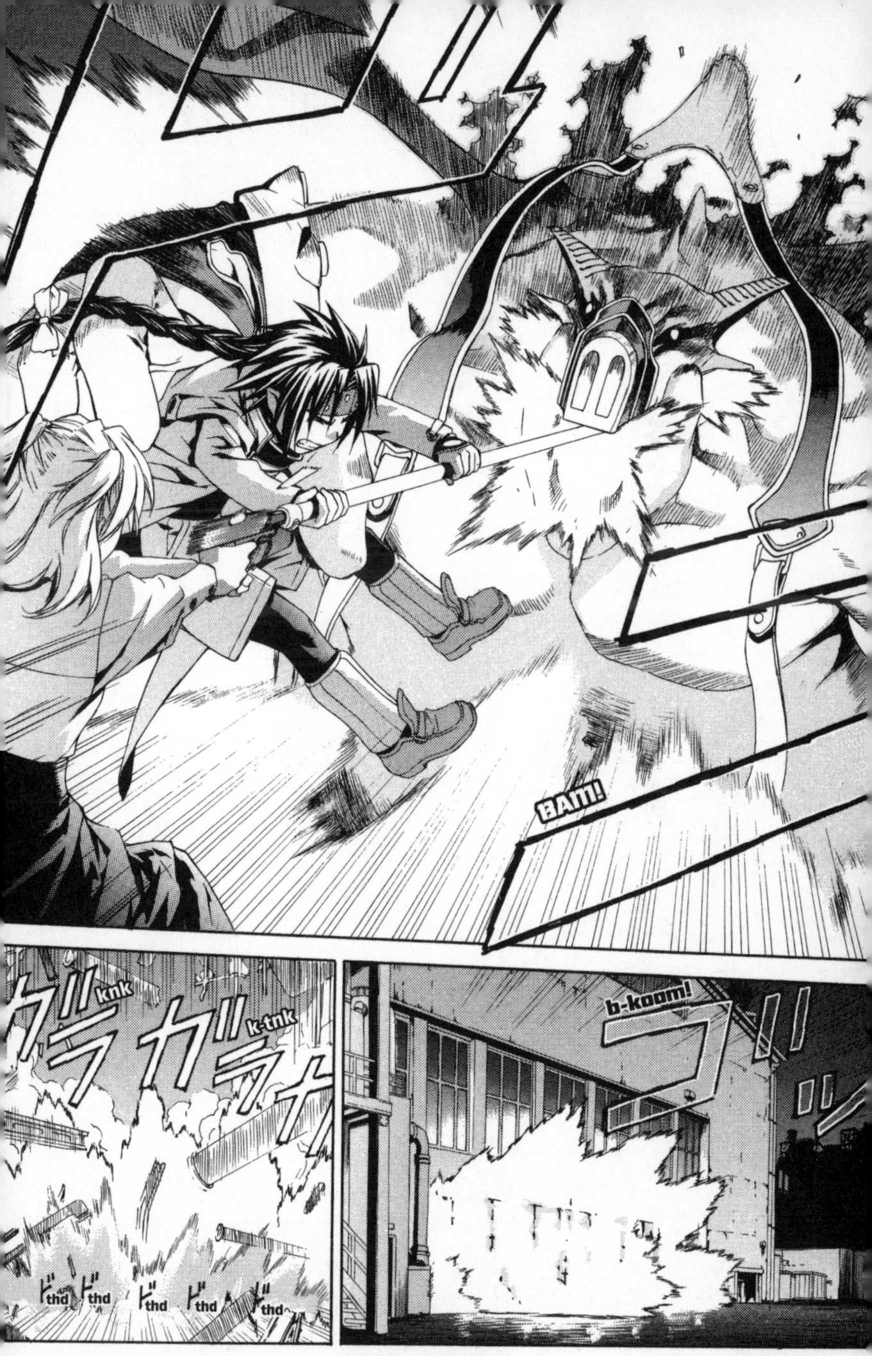
BAM!
b-koom!
knk
k-tnk
thd thd thd thd thd

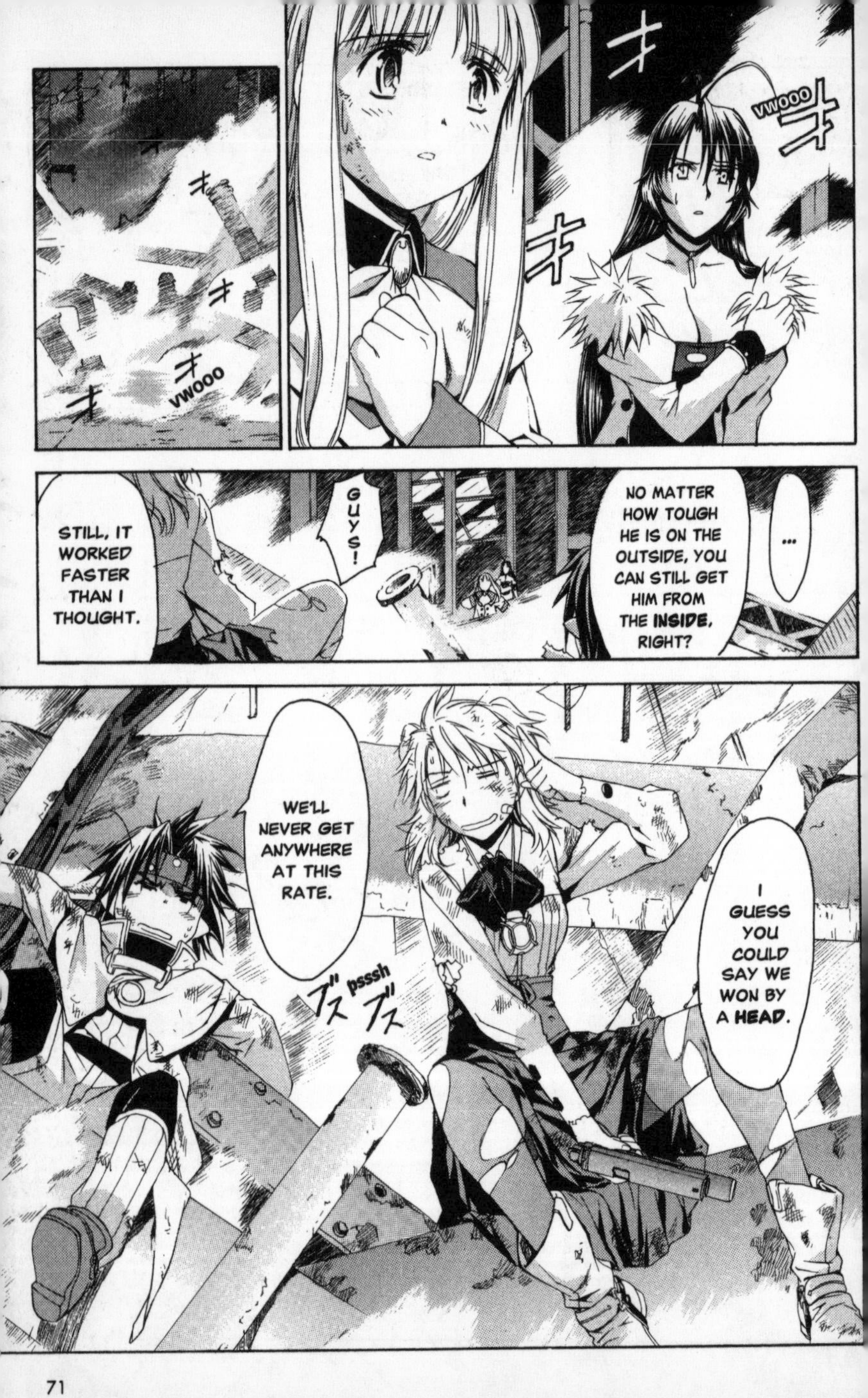
VWOOO
VWOOO
...
NO MATTER HOW TOUGH HE IS ON THE OUTSIDE, YOU CAN STILL GET HIM FROM THE **INSIDE**, RIGHT?
GUYS!
STILL, IT WORKED FASTER THAN I THOUGHT.
I GUESS YOU COULD SAY WE WON BY A **HEAD**.
psssh
WE'LL NEVER GET ANYWHERE AT THIS RATE.

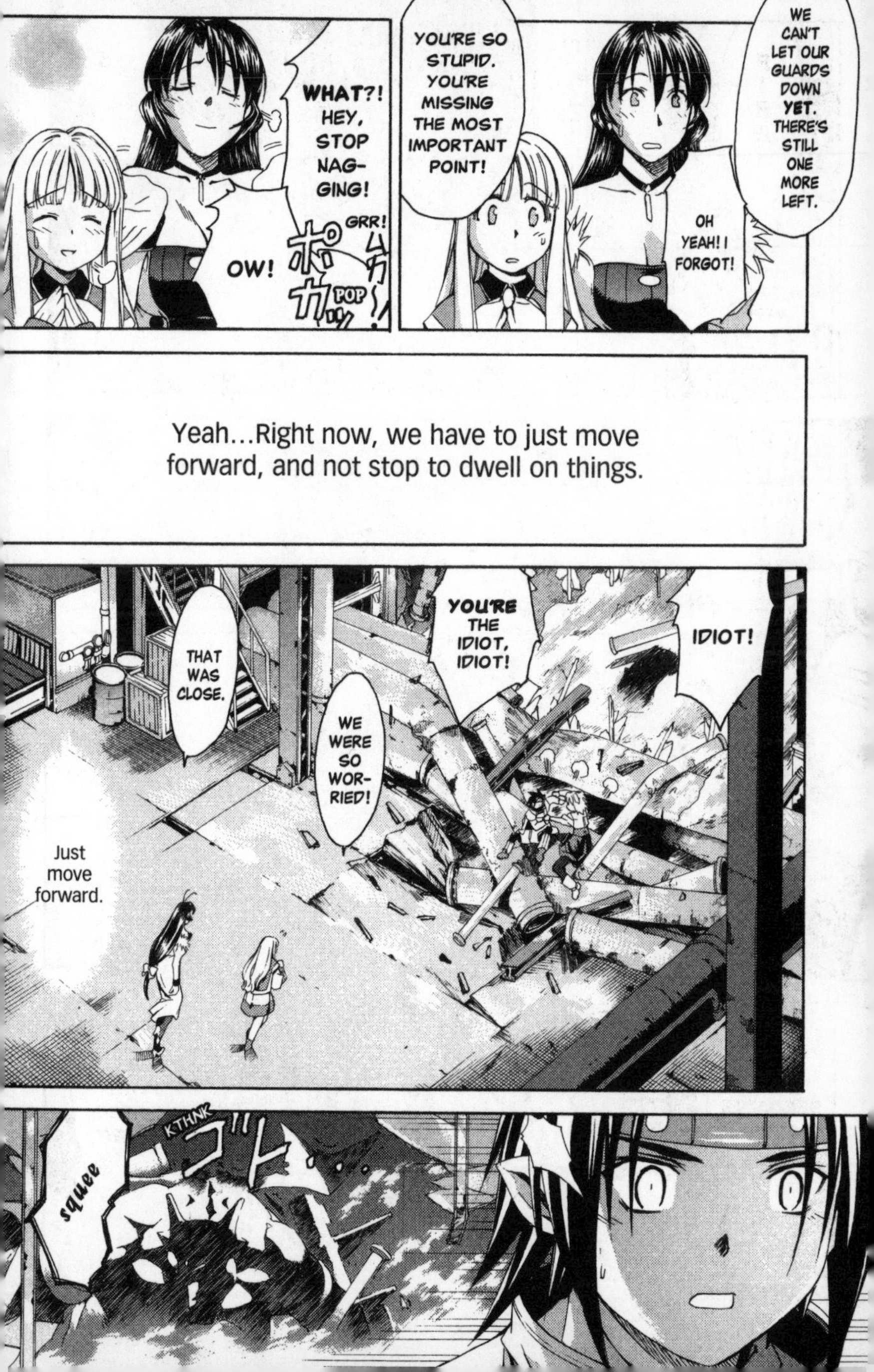
WE CAN'T LET OUR GUARDS DOWN **YET**. THERE'S STILL ONE MORE LEFT.
OH YEAH!! I FORGOT!
YOU'RE SO STUPID. YOU'RE MISSING THE MOST IMPORTANT POINT!
GRR!
POP
WHAT?! HEY, STOP NAG-GING!
OW!
Yeah...Right now, we have to just move forward, and not stop to dwell on things.
IDIOT!
YOU'RE THE IDIOT, IDIOT!
THAT WAS CLOSE.
WE WERE SO WOR-RIED!
Just move forward.
K-THNK
squee

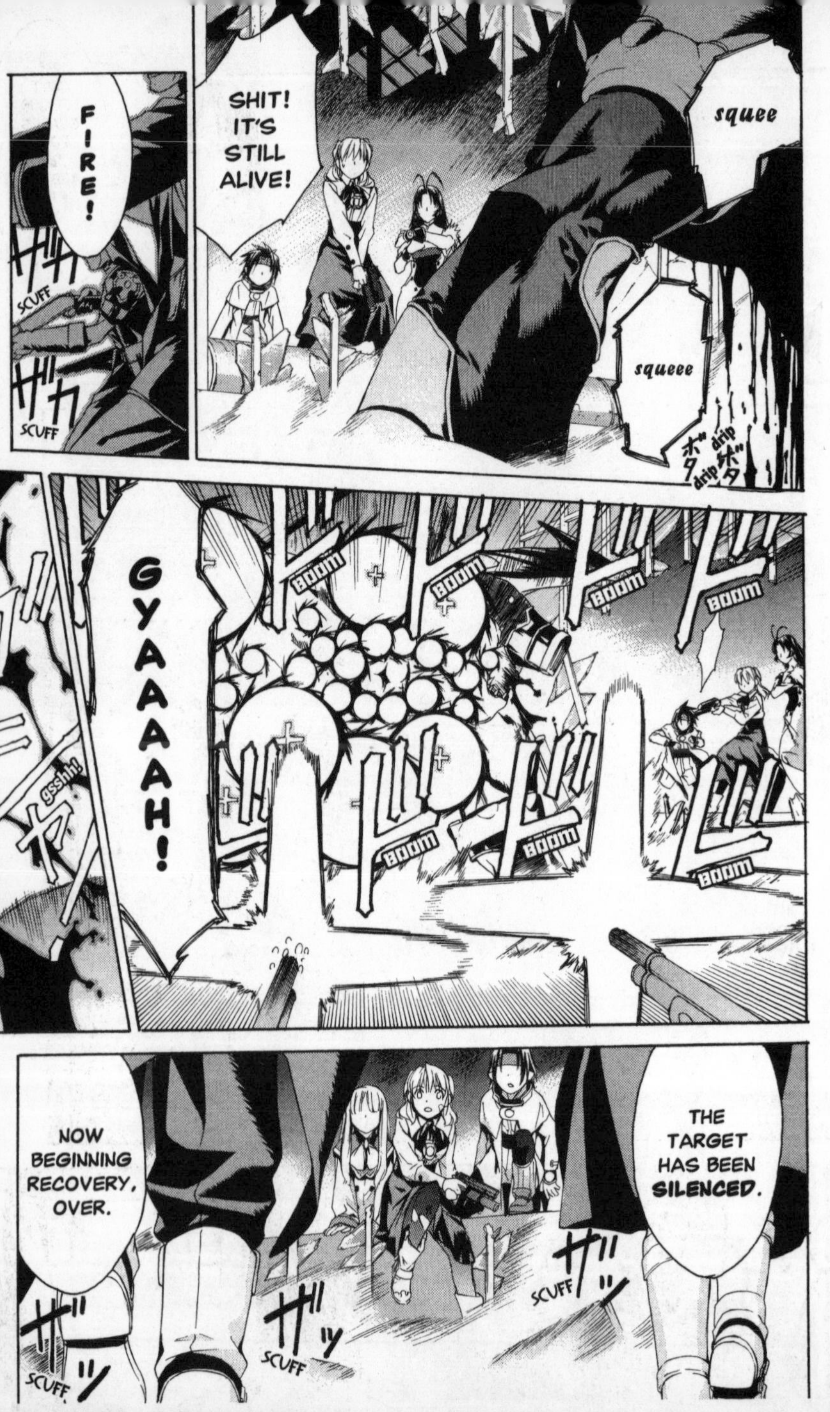
squee
SHIT! IT'S STILL ALIVE!
squeee
drip drip
FIRE!
SCUFF
SCUFF
BOOM
BOOM
BOOM
BOOM
GYAAAAH!
BOOM
BOOM
BOOM
gsshh!
THE TARGET HAS BEEN SILENCED.
SCUFF
NOW BEGINNING RECOVERY, OVER.
SCUFF
SCUFF

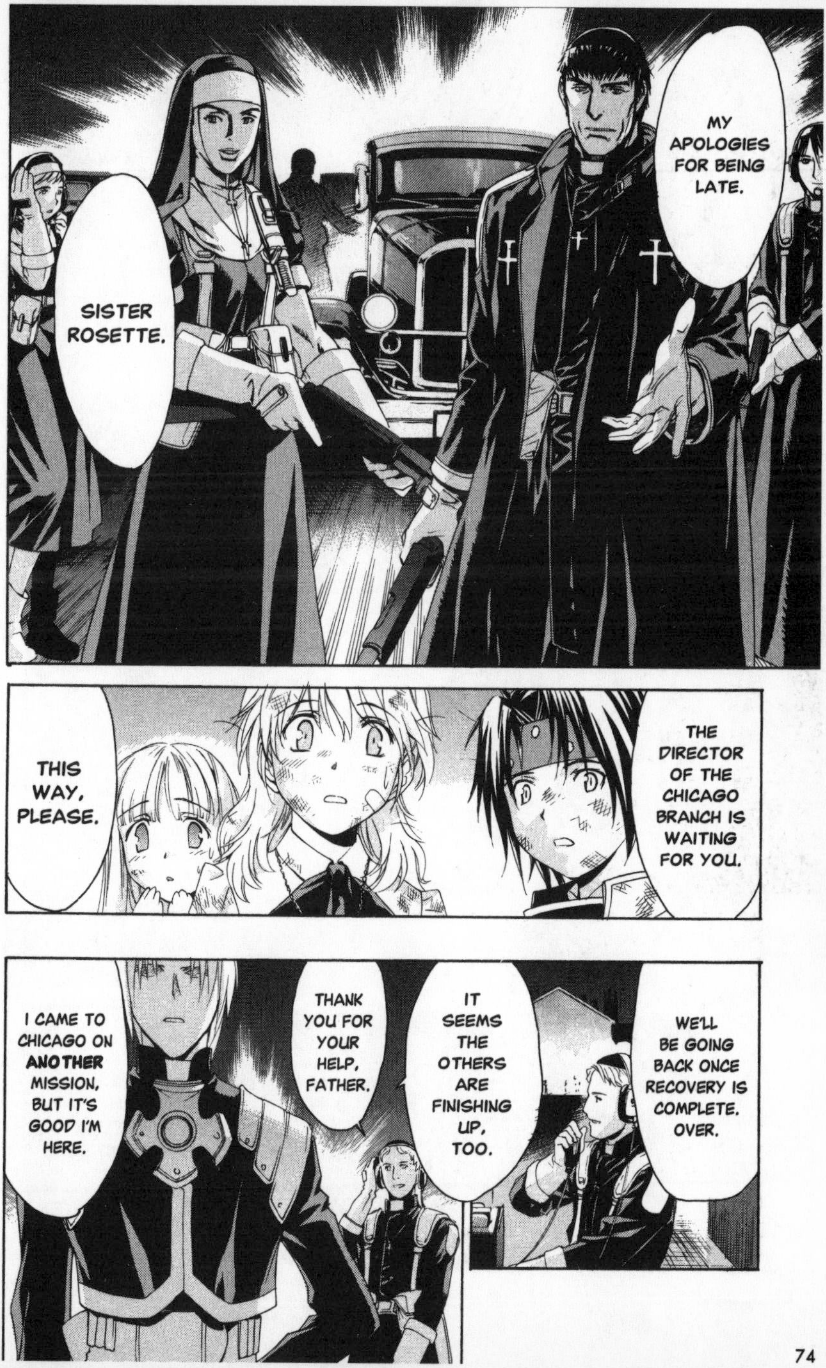
MY APOLOGIES FOR BEING LATE.
SISTER ROSETTE.
THE DIRECTOR OF THE CHICAGO BRANCH IS WAITING FOR YOU.
THIS WAY, PLEASE.
WE'LL BE GOING BACK ONCE RECOVERY IS COMPLETE. OVER.
IT SEEMS THE OTHERS ARE FINISHING UP, TOO.
THANK YOU FOR YOUR HELP, FATHER.
I CAME TO CHICAGO ON **ANOTHER** MISSION, BUT IT'S GOOD I'M HERE.

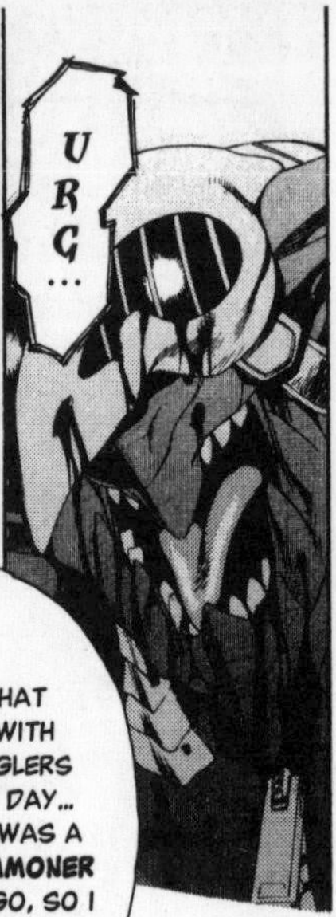
URG...
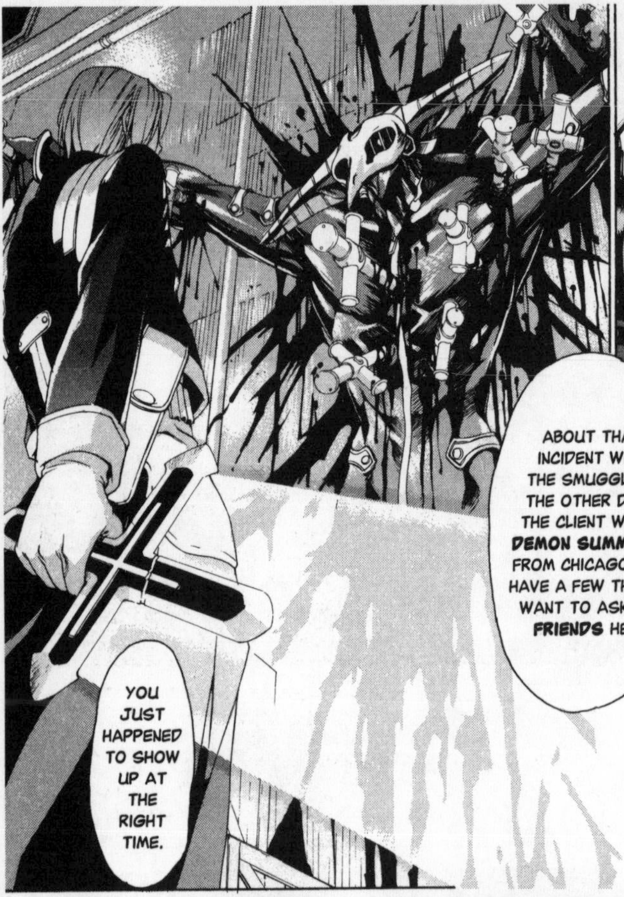
ABOUT THAT INCIDENT WITH THE SMUGGLERS THE OTHER DAY... THE CLIENT WAS A **DEMON SUMMONER** FROM CHICAGO, SO I HAVE A FEW THINGS I WANT TO ASK OUR **FRIENDS** HERE.
YOU JUST HAPPENED TO SHOW UP AT THE RIGHT TIME.
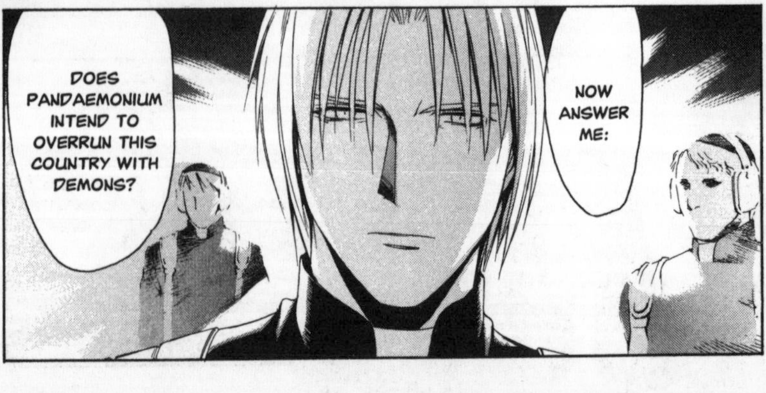
NOW ANSWER ME:
DOES PANDAEMONIUM INTEND TO OVERRUN THIS COUNTRY WITH DEMONS?

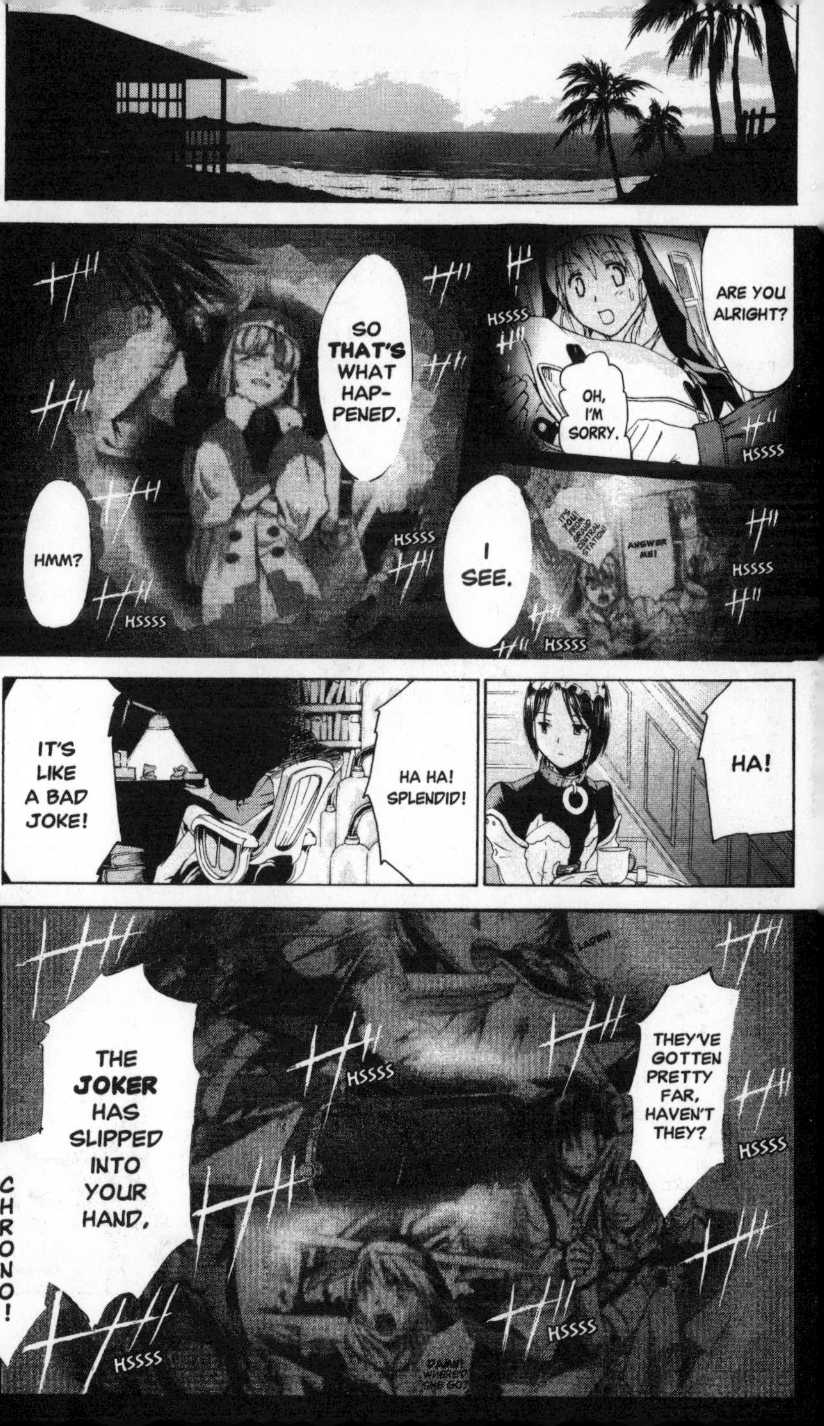
ARE YOU ALRIGHT?
HSSSS
OH, I'M SORRY.
HSSSS
HSSSS
ANSWER ME!
I SEE.
HSSSS
SO THAT'S WHAT HAP-PENED.
HSSSS
HMM?
HSSSS
HA!
HA HA! SPLENDID!
IT'S LIKE A BAD JOKE!
THEY'VE GOTTEN PRETTY FAR, HAVEN'T THEY?
HSSSS
HSSSS
HSSSS
THE JOKER HAS SLIPPED INTO YOUR HAND,
CHRONO!
HSSSS

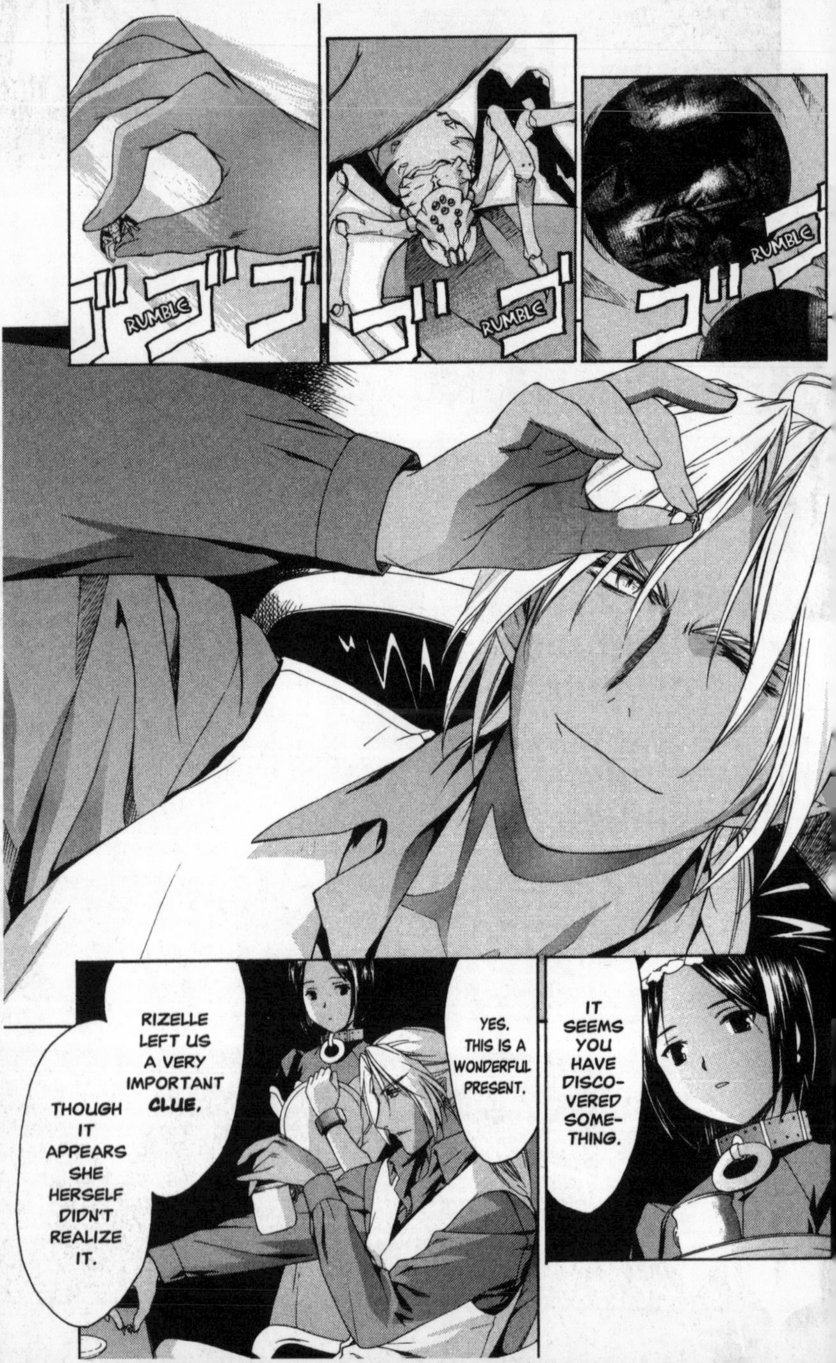
RUMBLE
RUMBLE
RUMBLE
IT SEEMS YOU HAVE DISCOVERED SOMETHING.
YES. THIS IS A WONDERFUL PRESENT.
RIZELLE LEFT US A VERY IMPORTANT **CLUE.**
THOUGH IT APPEARS SHE HERSELF DIDN'T REALIZE IT.

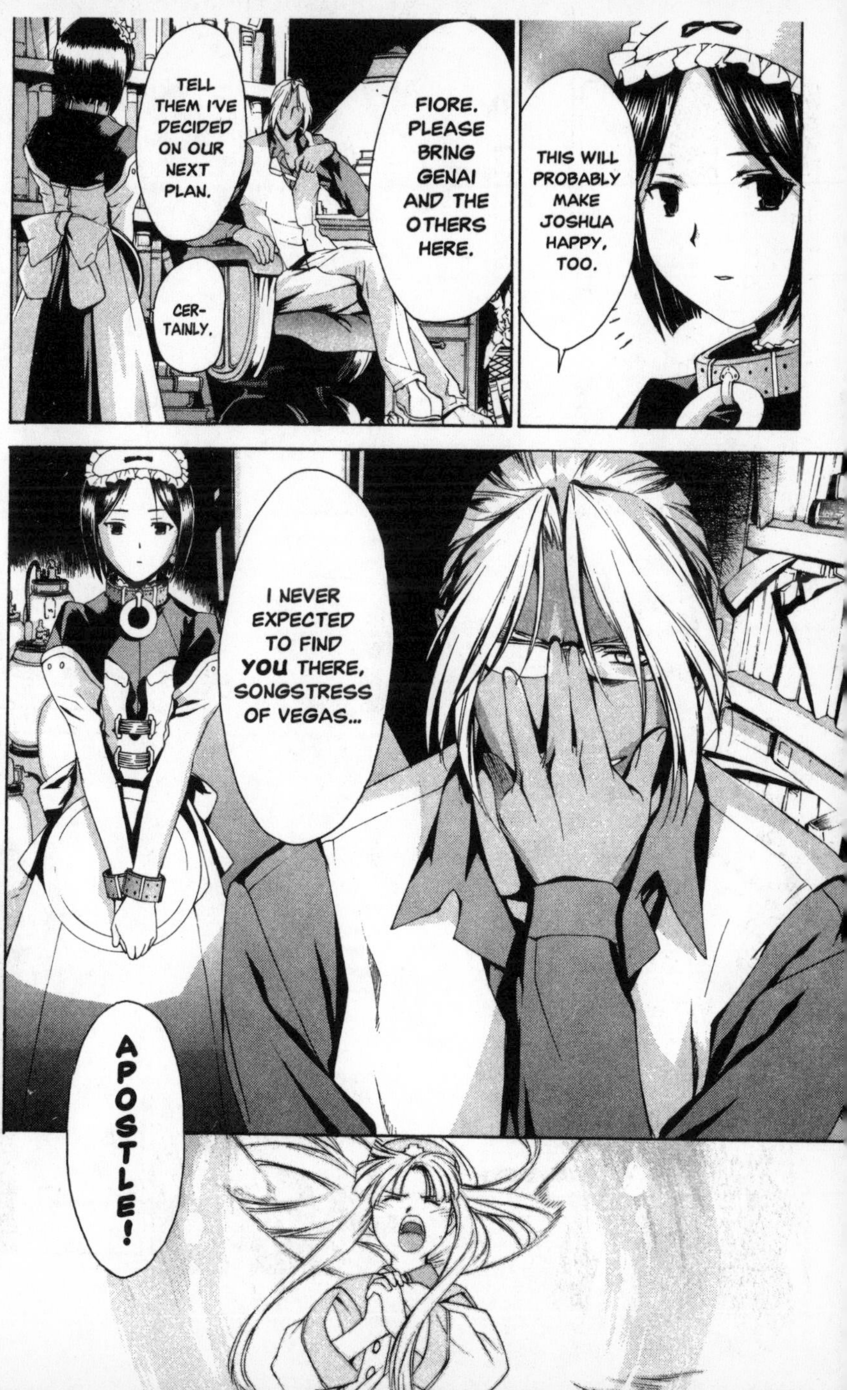
THIS WILL PROBABLY MAKE JOSHUA HAPPY, TOO.
FIORE. PLEASE BRING GENAI AND THE OTHERS HERE.
TELL THEM I'VE DECIDED ON OUR NEXT PLAN.
CER-TAINLY.
I NEVER EXPECTED TO FIND YOU THERE, SONGSTRESS OF VEGAS...
APOSTLE!

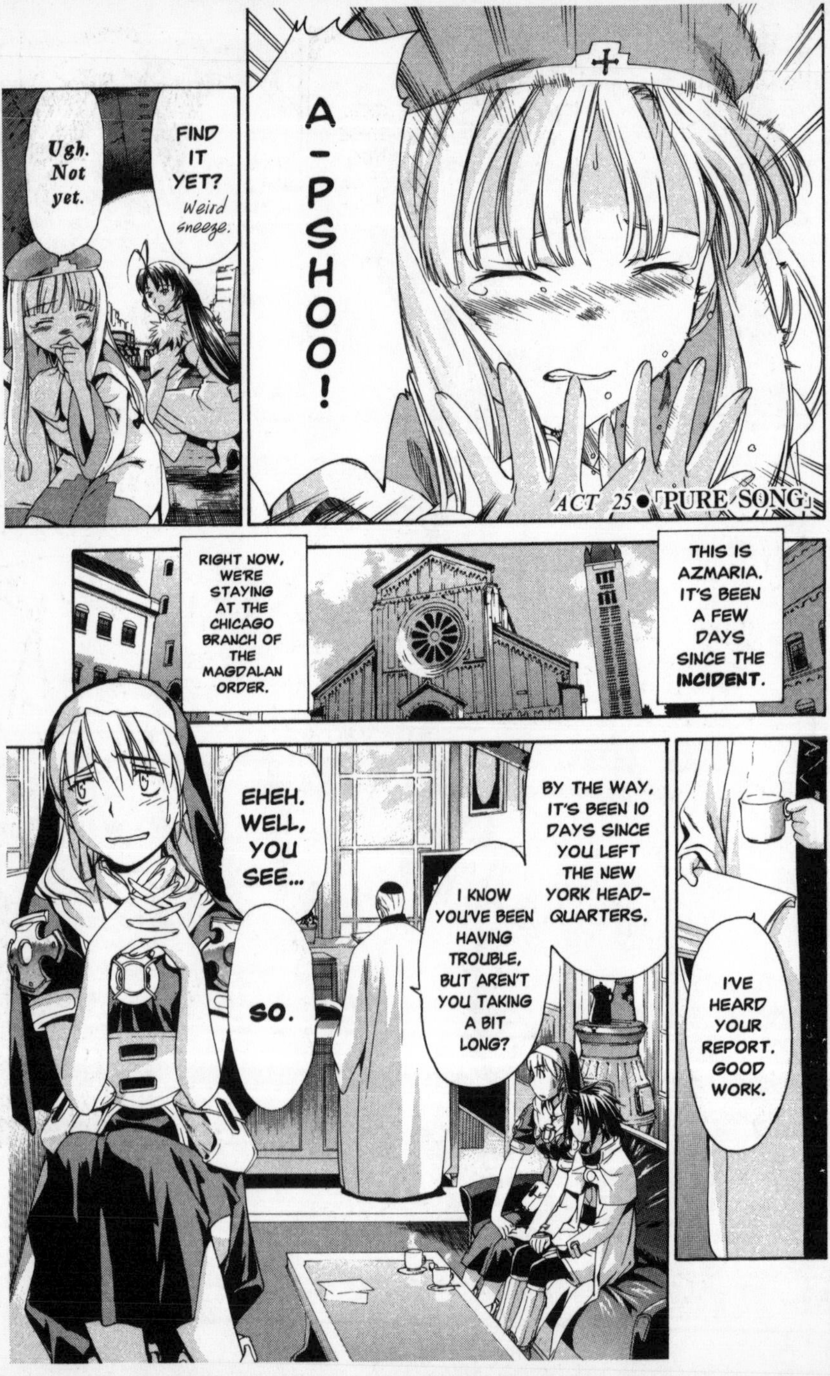
A-PSHOO!
ACT 25●「PURE SONG」
FIND IT YET? Weird sneeze.
Ugh. Not yet.
THIS IS AZMARIA. IT'S BEEN A FEW DAYS SINCE THE **INCIDENT**.
RIGHT NOW, WE'RE STAYING AT THE CHICAGO BRANCH OF THE MAGDALAN ORDER.
I'VE HEARD YOUR REPORT. GOOD WORK.
BY THE WAY, IT'S BEEN 10 DAYS SINCE YOU LEFT THE NEW YORK HEAD-QUARTERS.
I KNOW YOU'VE BEEN HAVING TROUBLE, BUT AREN'T YOU TAKING A BIT LONG?
EHEH. WELL, YOU SEE...
SO.

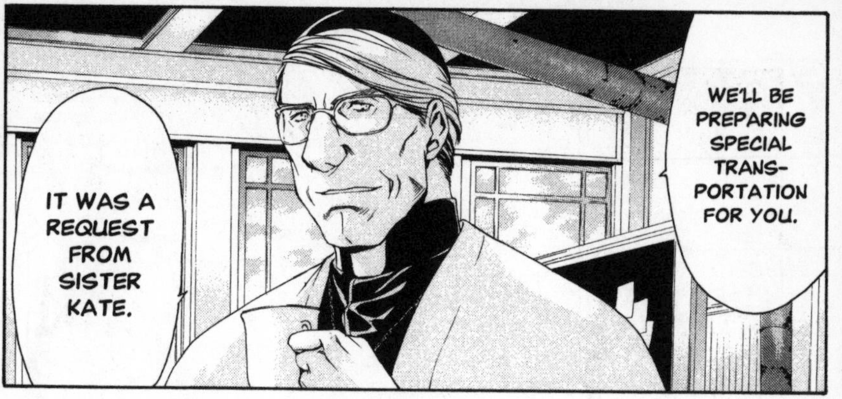
WE'LL BE PREPARING SPECIAL TRANS-PORTATION FOR YOU.
IT WAS A REQUEST FROM SISTER KATE.

ACT 25
「PURE SONG」

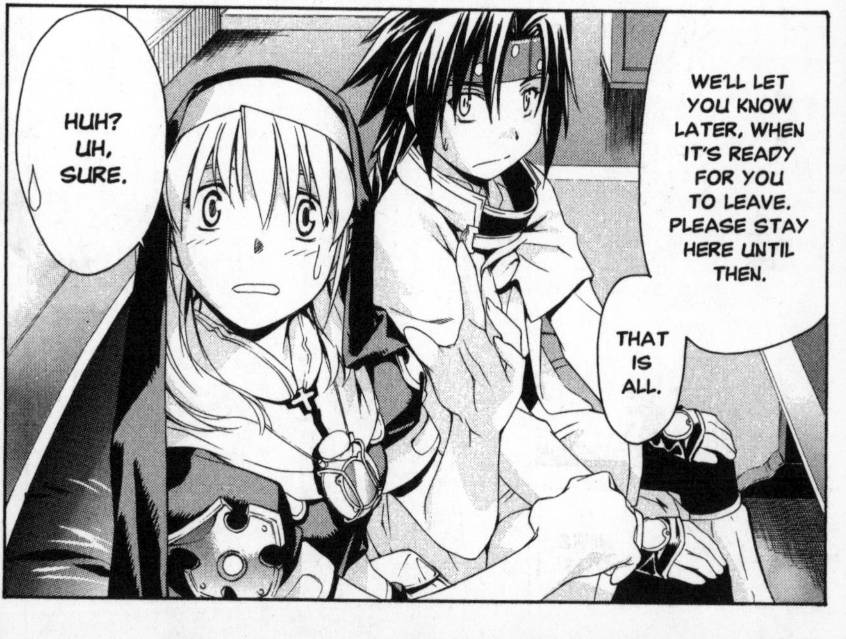
WE'LL LET YOU KNOW LATER, WHEN IT'S READY FOR YOU TO LEAVE. PLEASE STAY HERE UNTIL THEN.
THAT IS ALL.
HUH? UH, SURE.

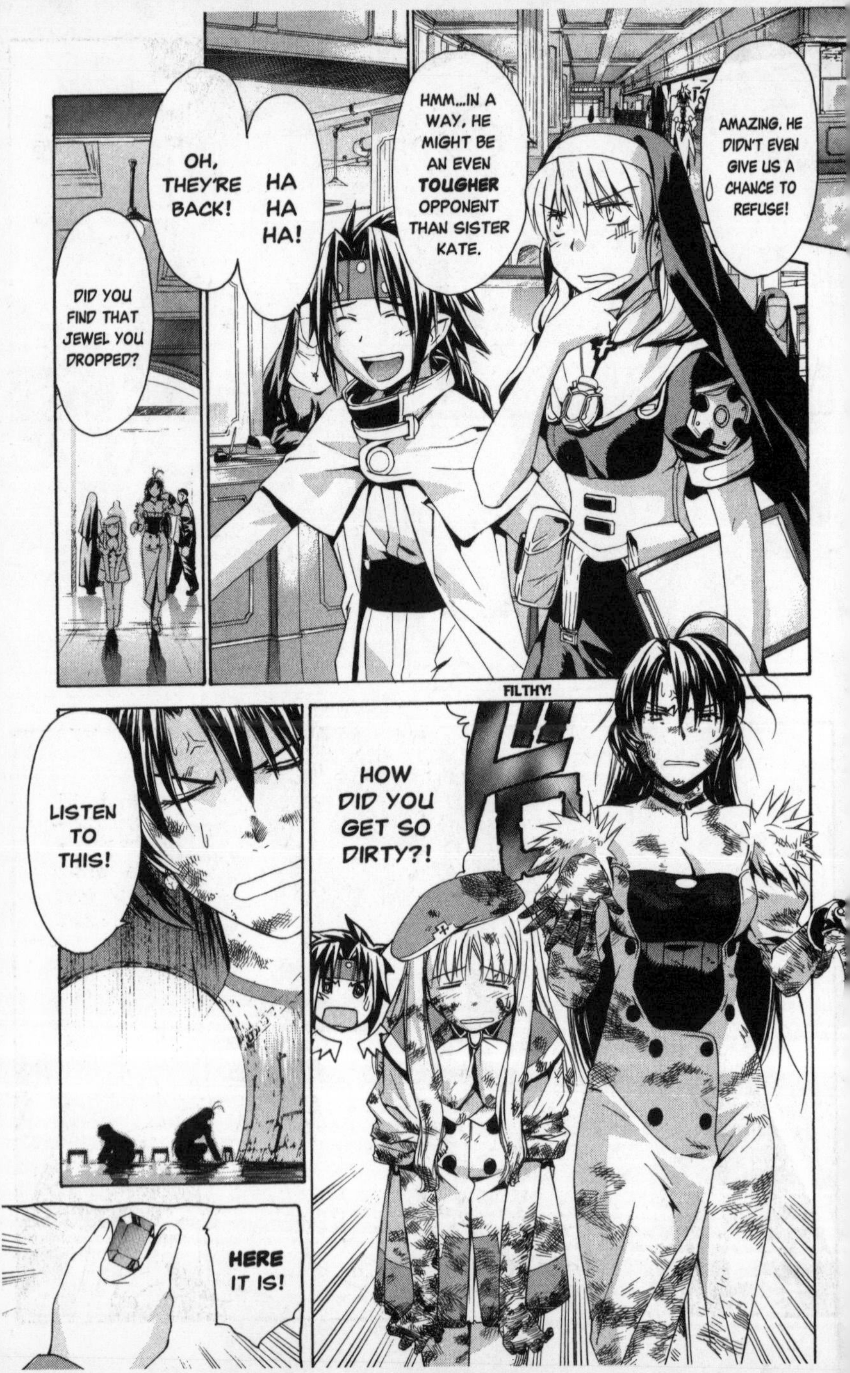
AMAZING. HE DIDN'T EVEN GIVE US A CHANCE TO REFUSE!
HMM...IN A WAY, HE MIGHT BE AN EVEN TOUGHER OPPONENT THAN SISTER KATE.
HA HA HA!
OH, THEY'RE BACK!
DID YOU FIND THAT JEWEL YOU DROPPED?
FILTHY!
HOW DID YOU GET SO DIRTY?!
LISTEN TO THIS!
HERE IT IS!

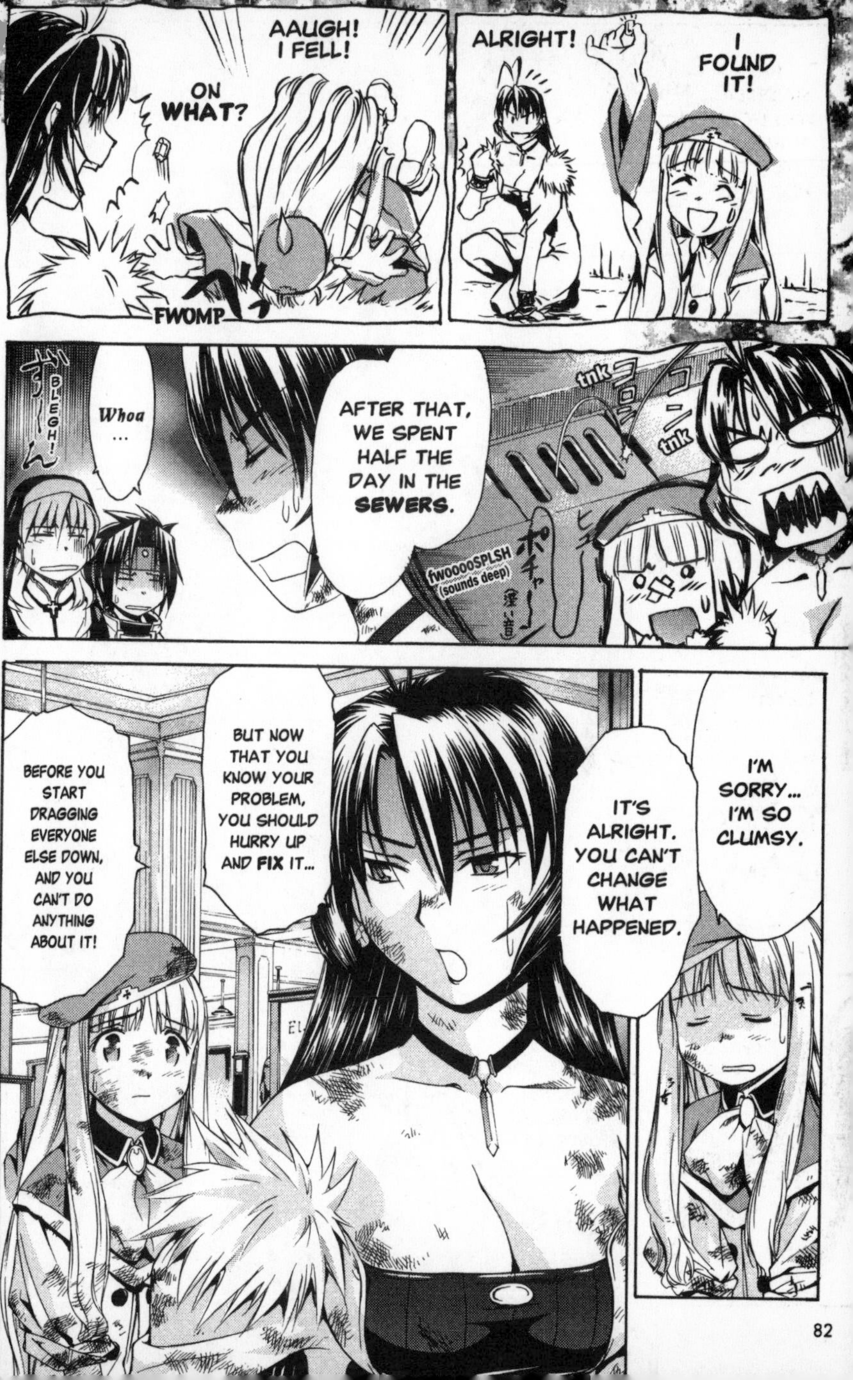
I FOUND IT!
ALRIGHT!
AAUGH! I FELL!
ON WHAT?
FWOMP
tnk
tnk
fwooooSPLSH (sounds deep)
AFTER THAT, WE SPENT HALF THE DAY IN THE SEWERS.
Whoa ...
BLEGH!
I'M SORRY... I'M SO CLUMSY.
IT'S ALRIGHT. YOU CAN'T CHANGE WHAT HAPPENED.
BUT NOW THAT YOU KNOW YOUR PROBLEM, YOU SHOULD HURRY UP AND FIX IT...
BEFORE YOU START DRAGGING EVERYONE ELSE DOWN, AND YOU CAN'T DO ANYTHING ABOUT IT!

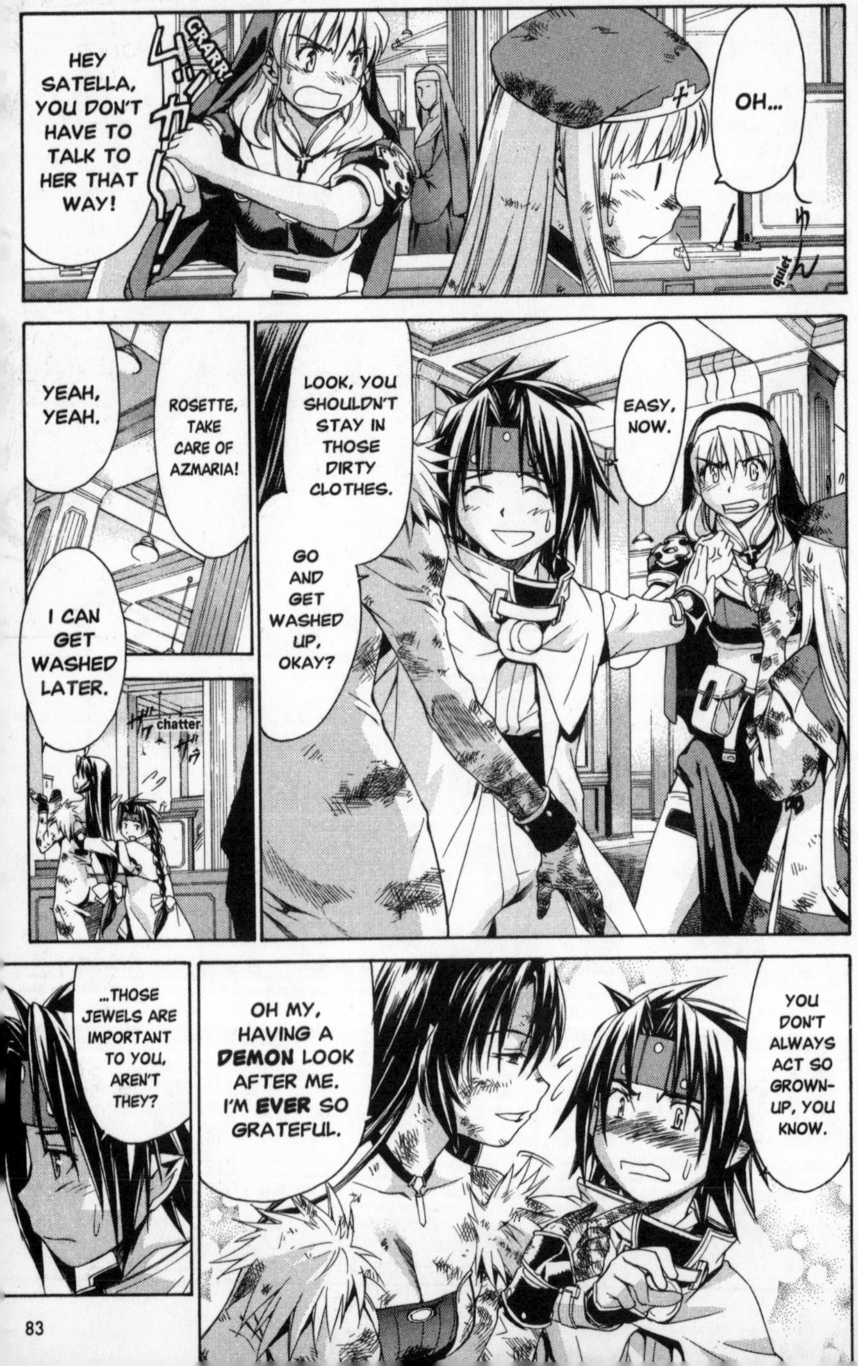
OH...
quiet
HEY SATELLA, YOU DON'T HAVE TO TALK TO HER THAT WAY!
GRARR!
EASY, NOW.
LOOK, YOU SHOULDN'T STAY IN THOSE DIRTY CLOTHES.
GO AND GET WASHED UP, OKAY?
ROSETTE, TAKE CARE OF AZMARIA!
YEAH, YEAH.
I CAN GET WASHED LATER.
chatter
YOU DON'T ALWAYS ACT SO GROWN-UP, YOU KNOW.
OH MY, HAVING A **DEMON** LOOK AFTER ME. I'M **EVER** SO GRATEFUL.
...THOSE JEWELS ARE IMPORTANT TO YOU, AREN'T THEY?

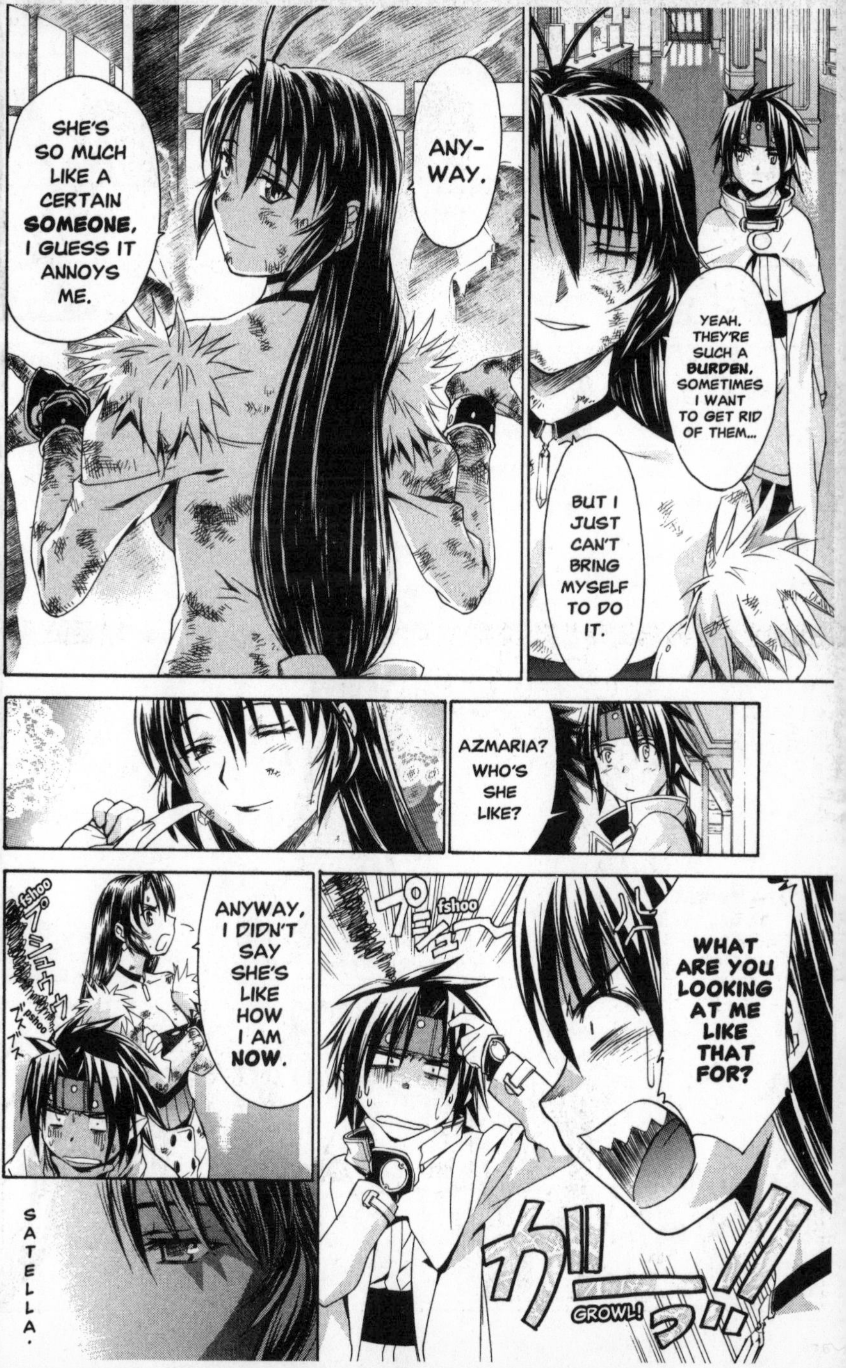
YEAH. THEY'RE SUCH A BURDEN, SOMETIMES I WANT TO GET RID OF THEM...
BUT I JUST CAN'T BRING MYSELF TO DO IT.
ANY-WAY.
SHE'S SO MUCH LIKE A CERTAIN SOMEONE, I GUESS IT ANNOYS ME.
AZMARIA? WHO'S SHE LIKE?
fshoo
WHAT ARE YOU LOOKING AT ME LIKE THAT FOR?
GROWL!
fshoo
ANYWAY, I DIDN'T SAY SHE'S LIKE HOW I AM NOW.
pshoo
SATELLA.

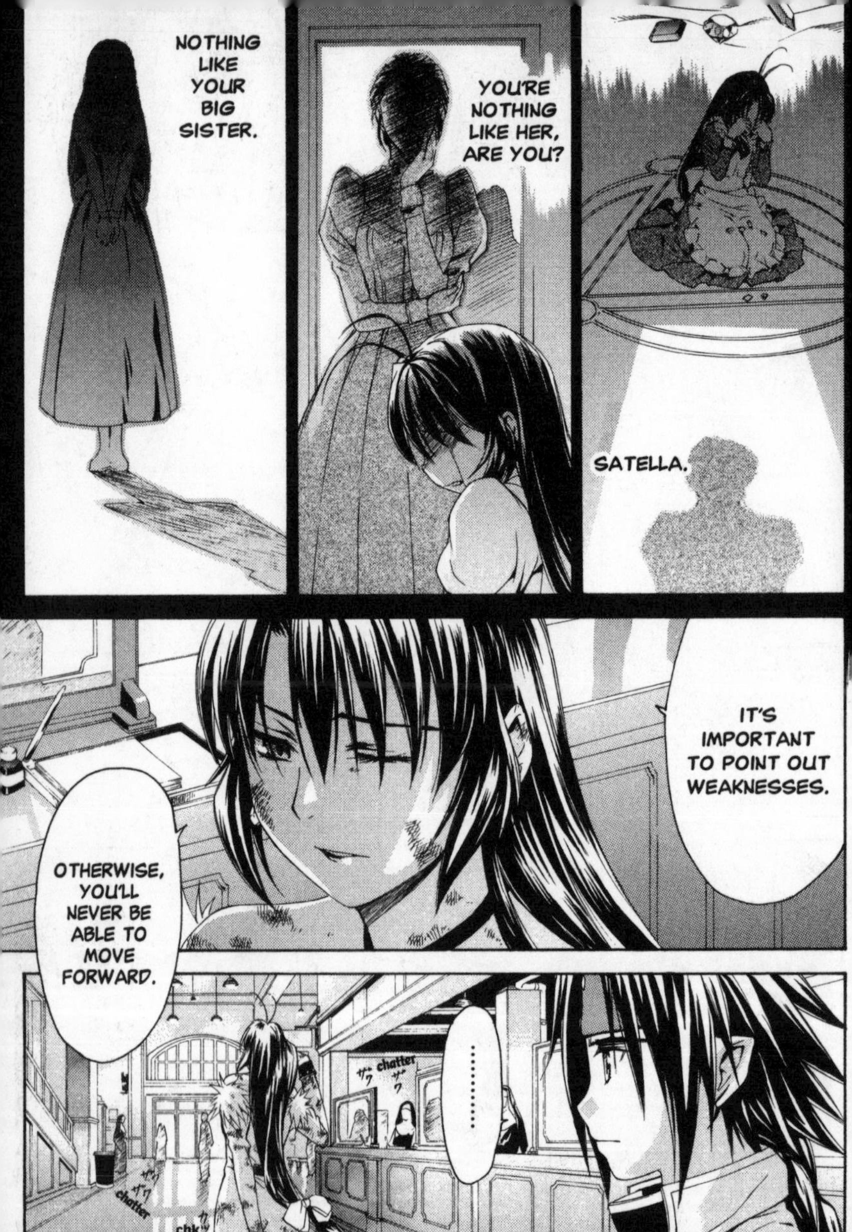
SATELLA.
YOU'RE NOTHING LIKE HER, ARE YOU?
NOTHING LIKE YOUR BIG SISTER.
IT'S IMPORTANT TO POINT OUT WEAKNESSES.
OTHERWISE, YOU'LL NEVER BE ABLE TO MOVE FORWARD.
......
chatter
chatter
chk
chk

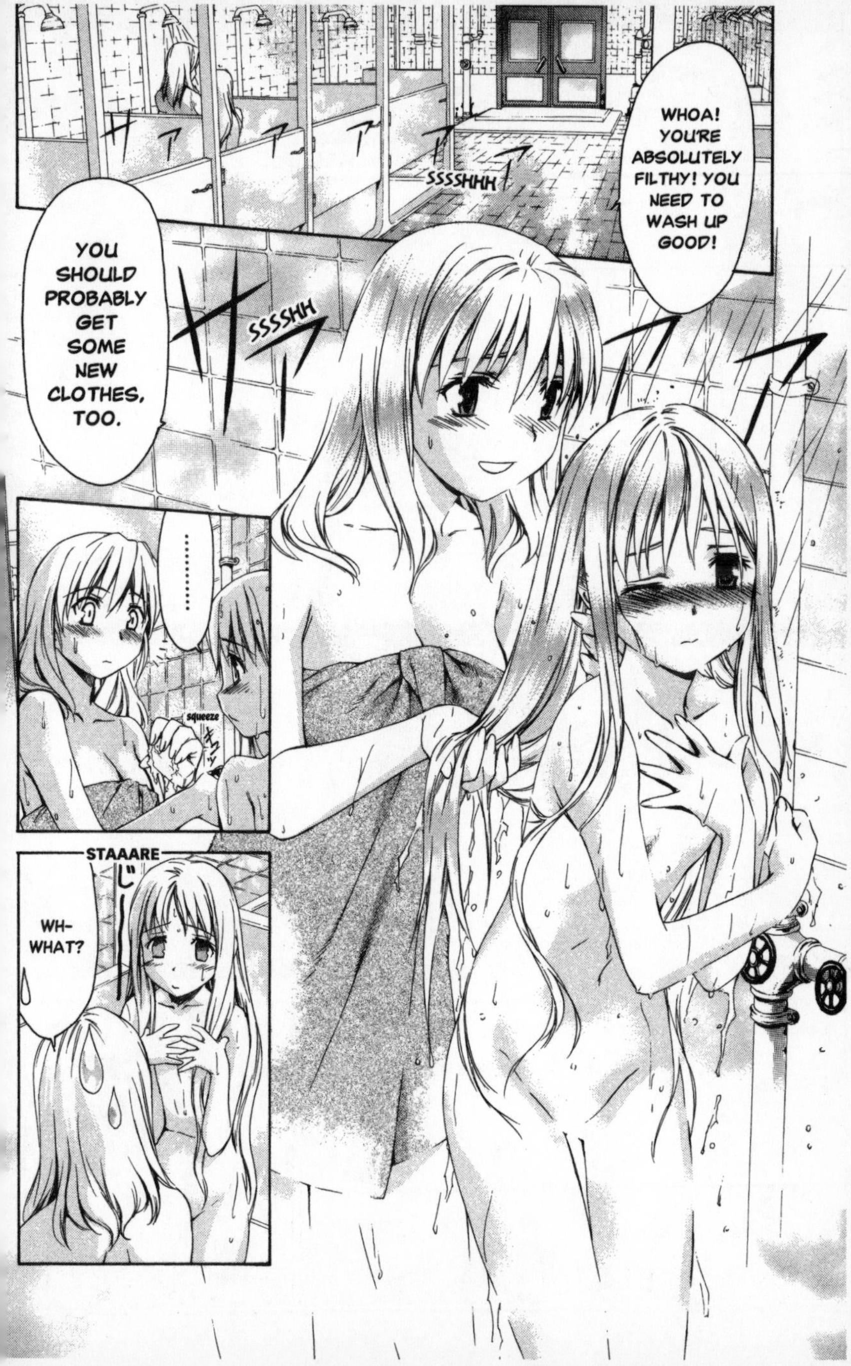
SSSSHHH
WHOA! YOU'RE ABSOLUTELY FILTHY! YOU NEED TO WASH UP GOOD!
SSSSHH
YOU SHOULD PROBABLY GET SOME NEW CLOTHES, TOO.
....
squeeze
STAAARE
WH- WHAT?

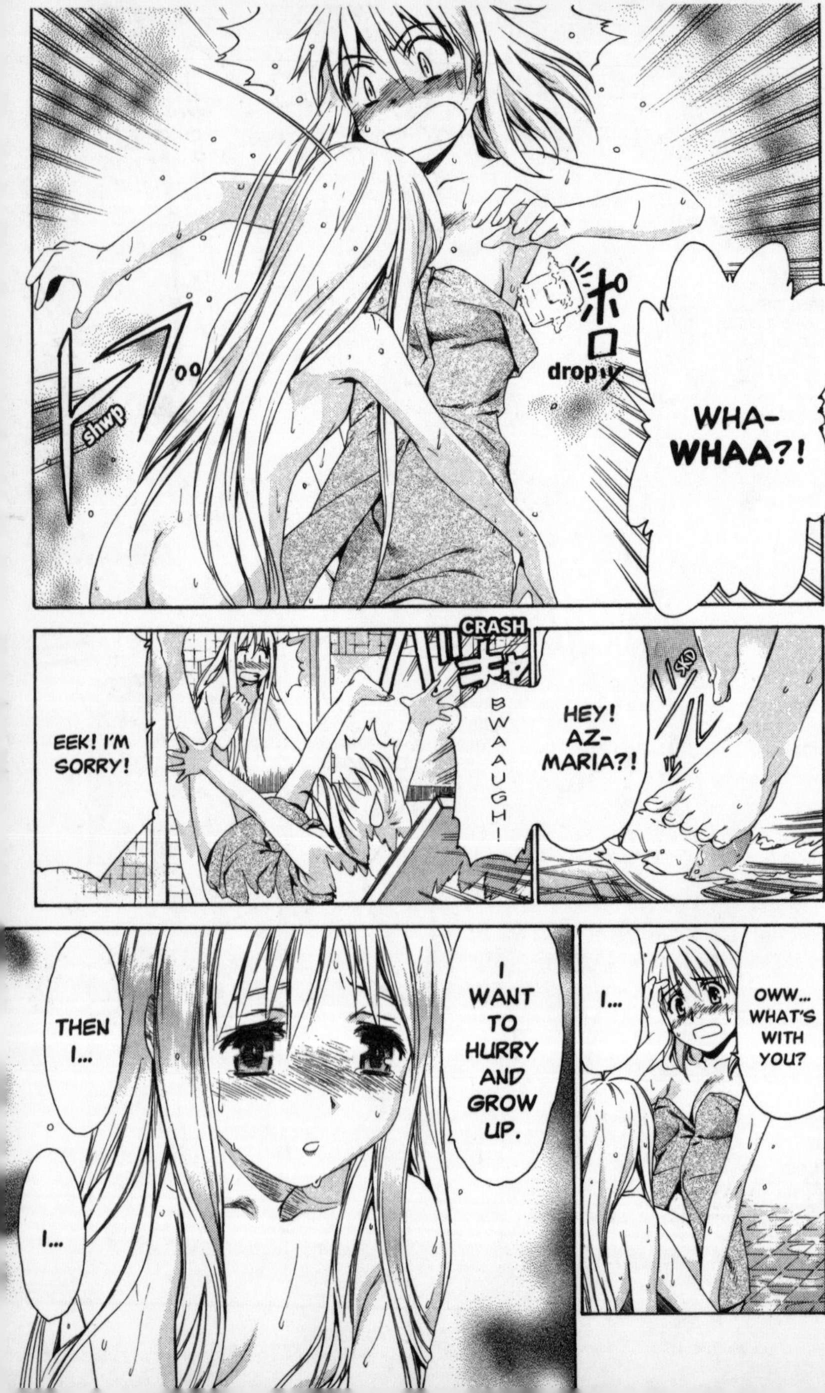
WHA- WHAA?!
ポロ
drop
shwp
skd
HEY! AZ- MARIA?!
CRASH
BWAAAUGH!
EEK! I'M SORRY!
OWW... WHAT'S WITH YOU?
I...
I WANT TO HURRY AND GROW UP.
THEN I...
I...

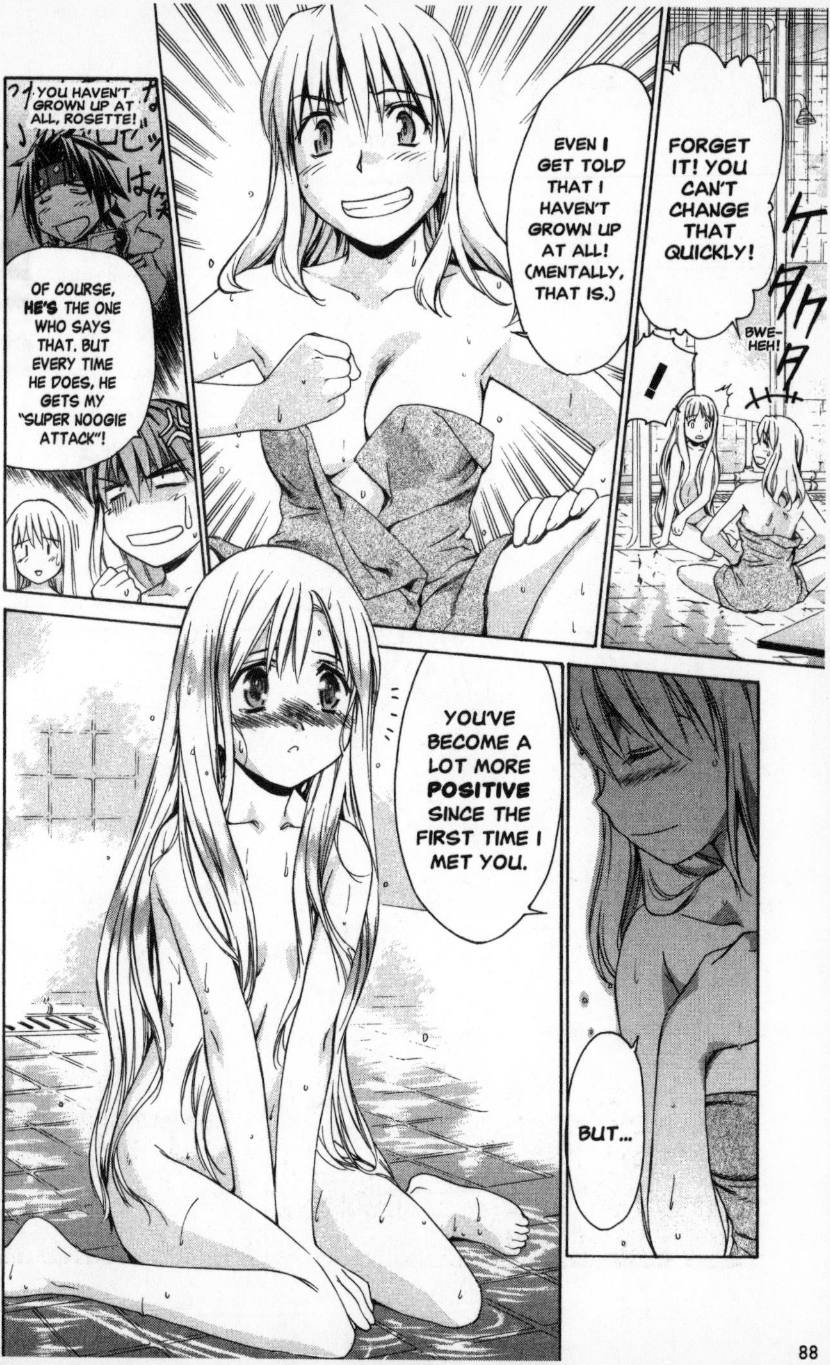
FORGET IT! YOU CAN'T CHANGE THAT QUICKLY!
BWE-HEH!
!
EVEN I GET TOLD THAT I HAVEN'T GROWN UP AT ALL! (MENTALLY, THAT IS.)
YOU HAVEN'T GROWN UP AT ALL, ROSETTE!
OF COURSE, **HE'S** THE ONE WHO SAYS THAT. BUT EVERY TIME HE DOES, HE GETS MY "SUPER NOOGIE ATTACK"!
BUT...
YOU'VE BECOME A LOT MORE **POSITIVE** SINCE THE FIRST TIME I MET YOU.

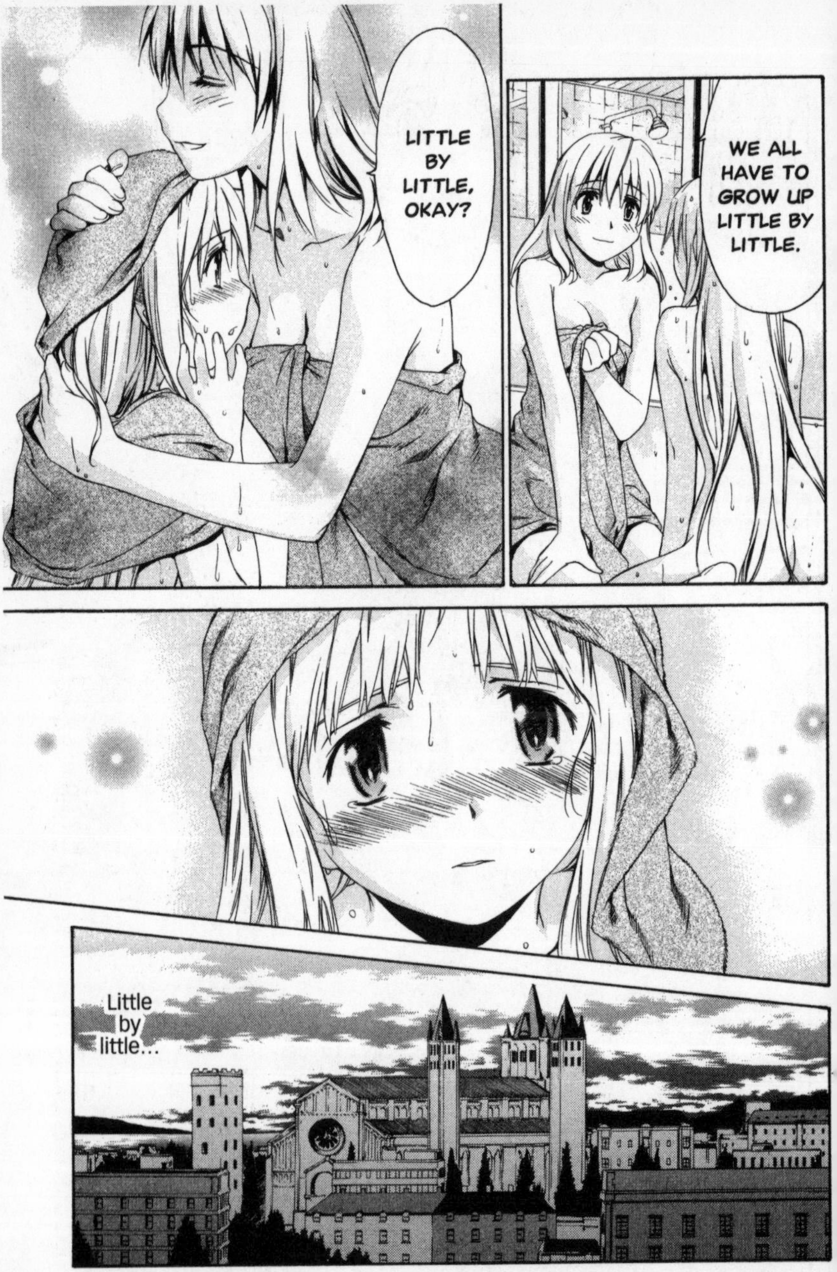
WE ALL HAVE TO GROW UP LITTLE BY LITTLE.
LITTLE BY LITTLE, OKAY?
Little by little...

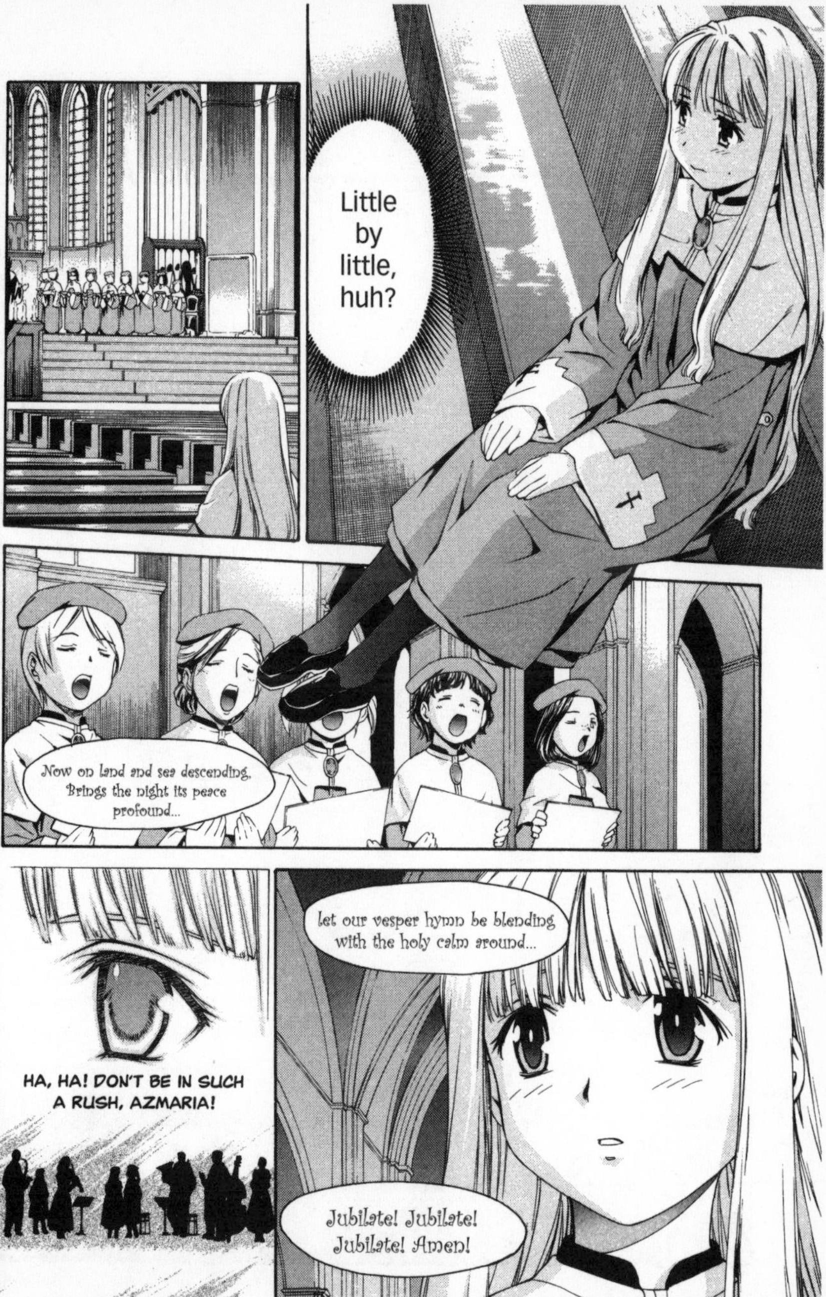
Little by little, huh?
Now on land and sea descending, Brings the night its peace profound...
let our vesper hymn be blending with the holy calm around...
Jubilate! Jubilate! Jubilate! Amen!
HA, HA! DON'T BE IN SUCH A RUSH, AZMARIA!

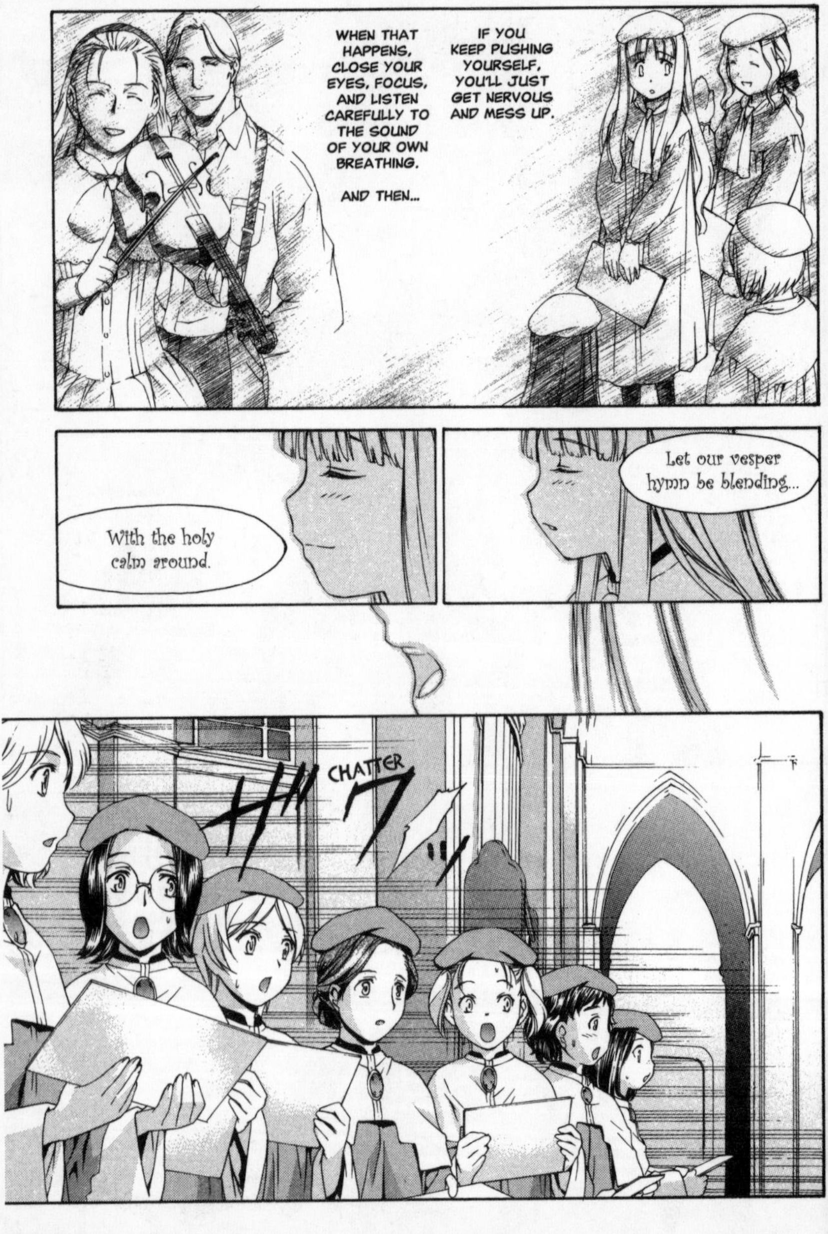
IF YOU KEEP PUSHING YOURSELF, YOU'LL JUST GET NERVOUS AND MESS UP.
WHEN THAT HAPPENS, CLOSE YOUR EYES, FOCUS, AND LISTEN CAREFULLY TO THE SOUND OF YOUR OWN BREATHING.
AND THEN...
Let our vesper hymn be blending...
With the holy calm around.
CHATTER

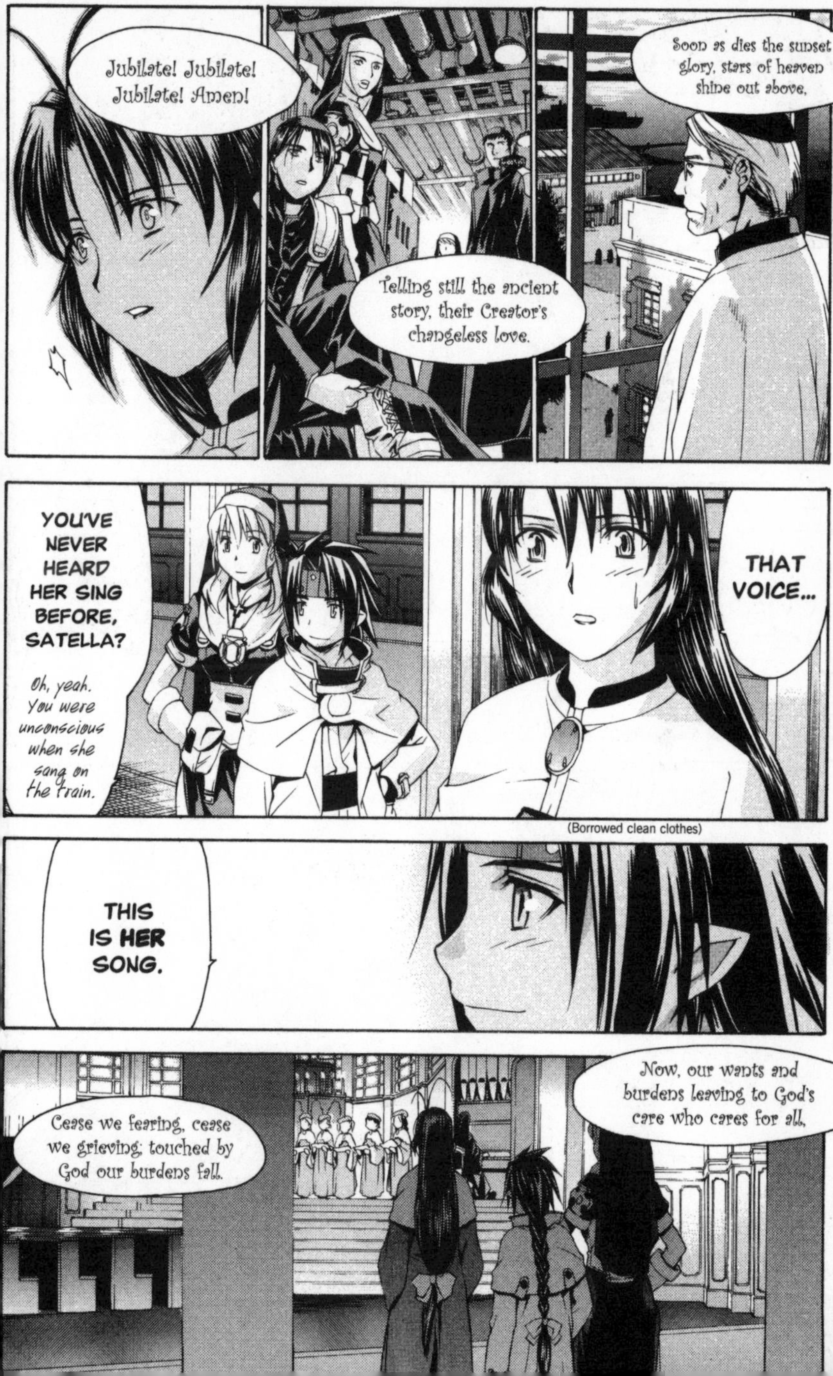
Soon as dies the sunset glory, stars of heaven shine out above,
Telling still the ancient story, their Creator's changeless love.
Jubilate! Jubilate! Jubilate! Amen!
THAT VOICE...
YOU'VE NEVER HEARD HER SING BEFORE, SATELLA?
Oh, yeah. You were unconscious when she sang on the train.
(Borrowed clean clothes)
THIS IS HER SONG.
Now, our wants and burdens leaving to God's care who cares for all,
Cease we fearing, cease we grieving: touched by God our burdens fall.

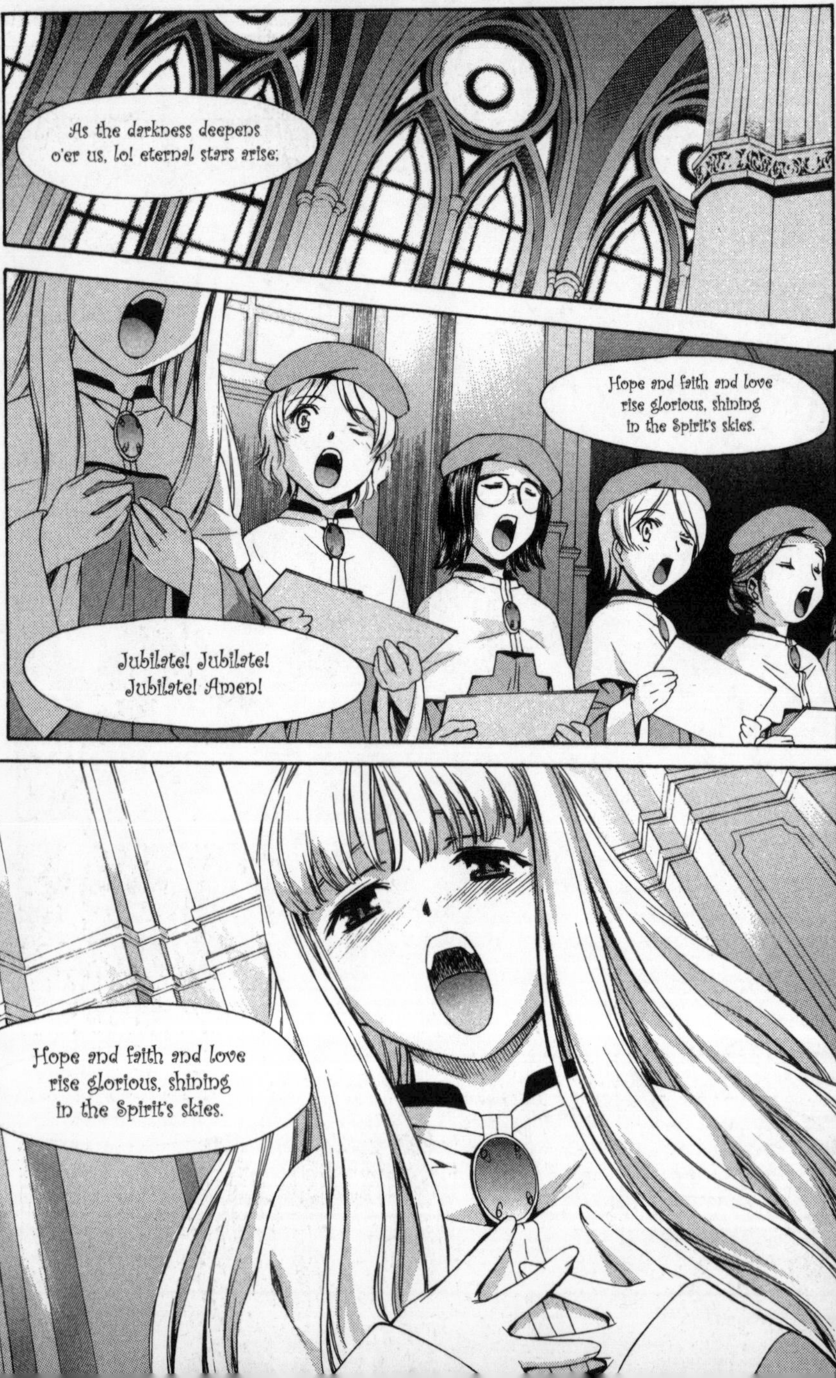
As the darkness deepens o'er us, lo! eternal stars arise;
Hope and faith and love rise glorious, shining in the Spirit's skies.
Jubilate! Jubilate! Jubilate! Amen!
Hope and faith and love rise glorious, shining in the Spirit's skies.

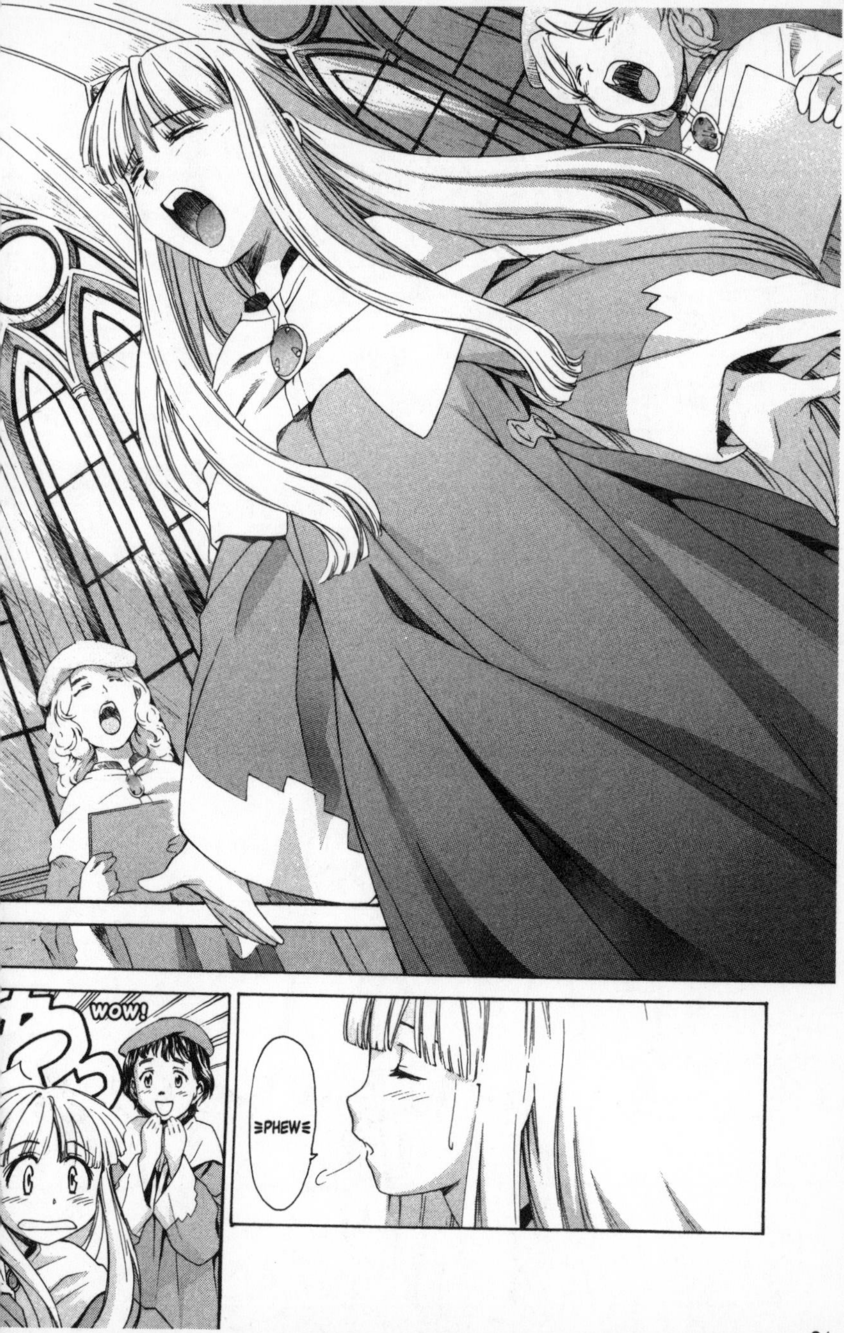
PHEW
WOW!

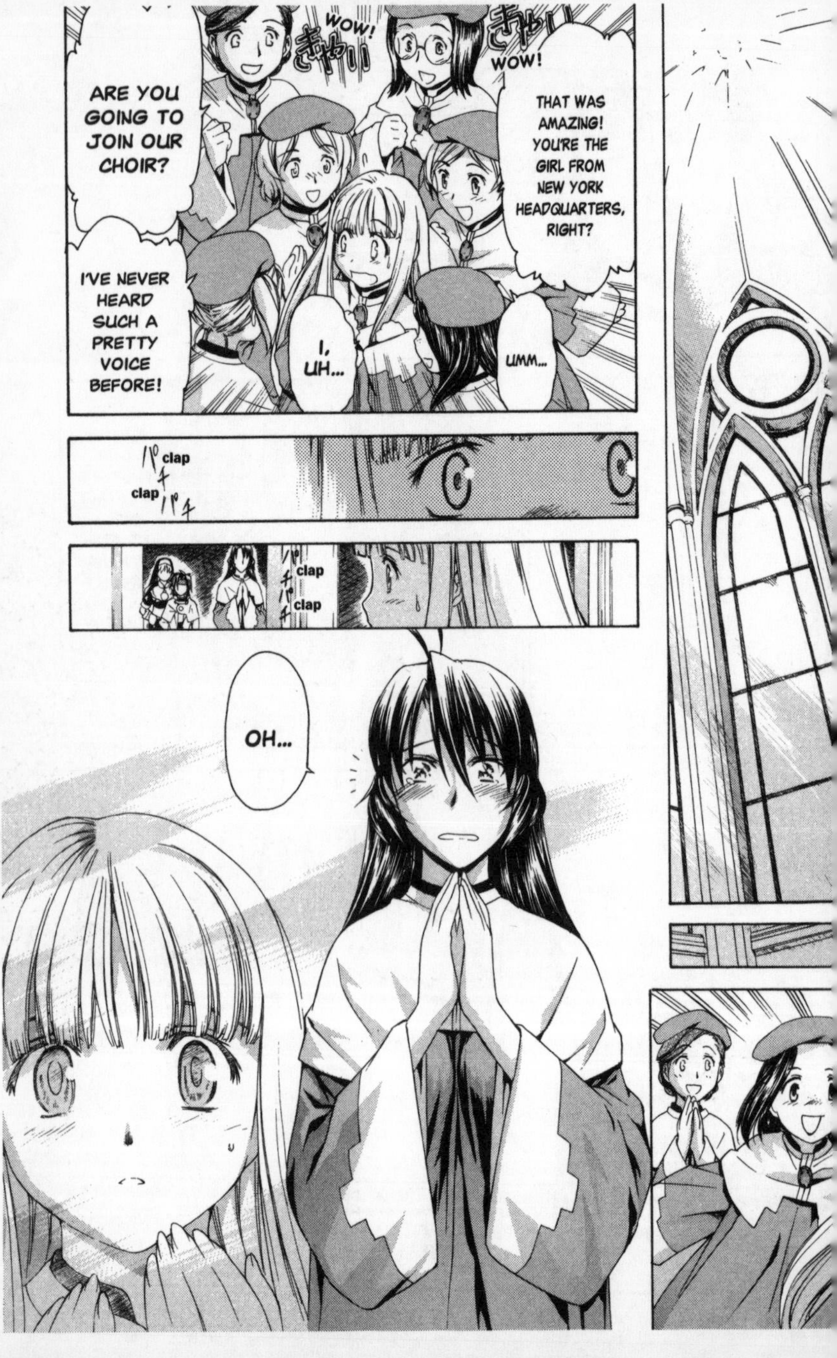
WOW!
THAT WAS AMAZING! YOU'RE THE GIRL FROM NEW YORK HEADQUARTERS, RIGHT?
WOW!
ARE YOU GOING TO JOIN OUR CHOIR?
I'VE NEVER HEARD SUCH A PRETTY VOICE BEFORE!
UMM...
I, UH...
clap
clap
clap
clap
OH...

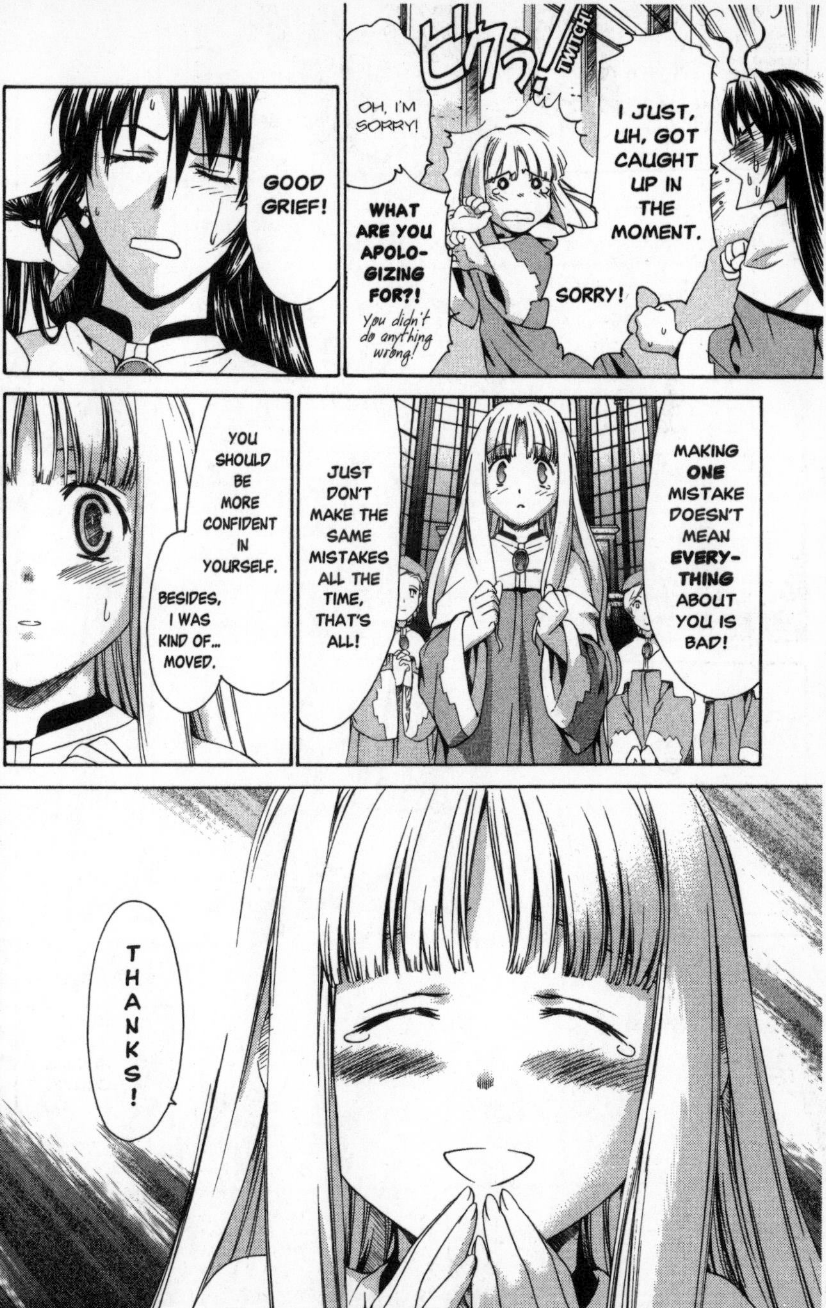
TWITCH!
I JUST, UH, GOT CAUGHT UP IN THE MOMENT.
OH, I'M SORRY!
SORRY!
WHAT ARE YOU APOLOGIZING FOR?!
You didn't do anything wrong!
GOOD GRIEF!
MAKING ONE MISTAKE DOESN'T MEAN EVERYTHING ABOUT YOU IS BAD!
JUST DON'T MAKE THE SAME MISTAKES ALL THE TIME, THAT'S ALL!
YOU SHOULD BE MORE CONFIDENT IN YOURSELF.
BESIDES, I WAS KIND OF... MOVED.
THANKS!

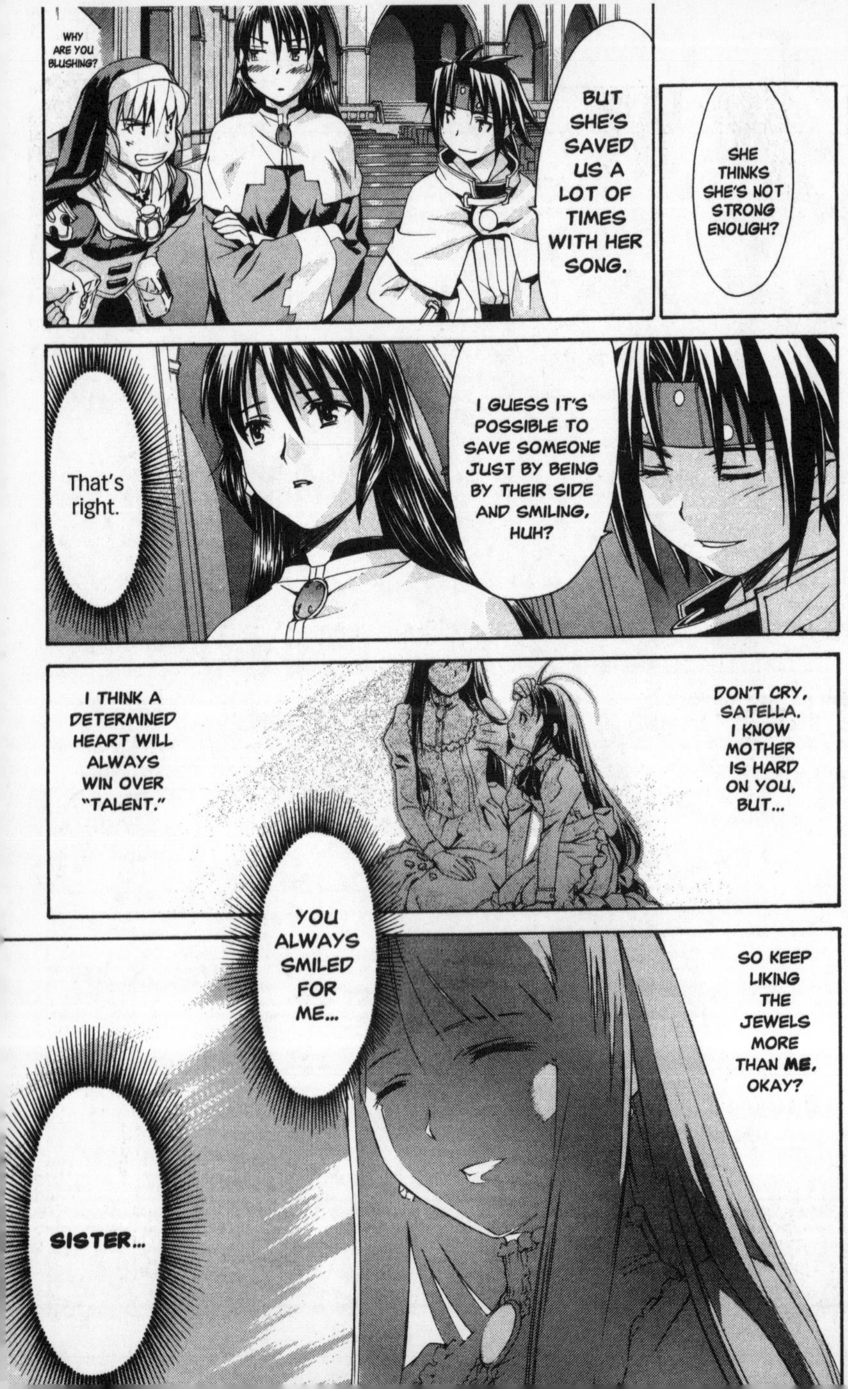
SHE THINKS SHE'S NOT STRONG ENOUGH?
BUT SHE'S SAVED US A LOT OF TIMES WITH HER SONG.
WHY ARE YOU BLUSHING?
I GUESS IT'S POSSIBLE TO SAVE SOMEONE JUST BY BEING BY THEIR SIDE AND SMILING, HUH?
That's right.
DON'T CRY, SATELLA. I KNOW MOTHER IS HARD ON YOU, BUT...
I THINK A DETERMINED HEART WILL ALWAYS WIN OVER "TALENT."
SO KEEP LIKING THE JEWELS MORE THAN ME, OKAY?
YOU ALWAYS SMILED FOR ME...
SISTER...

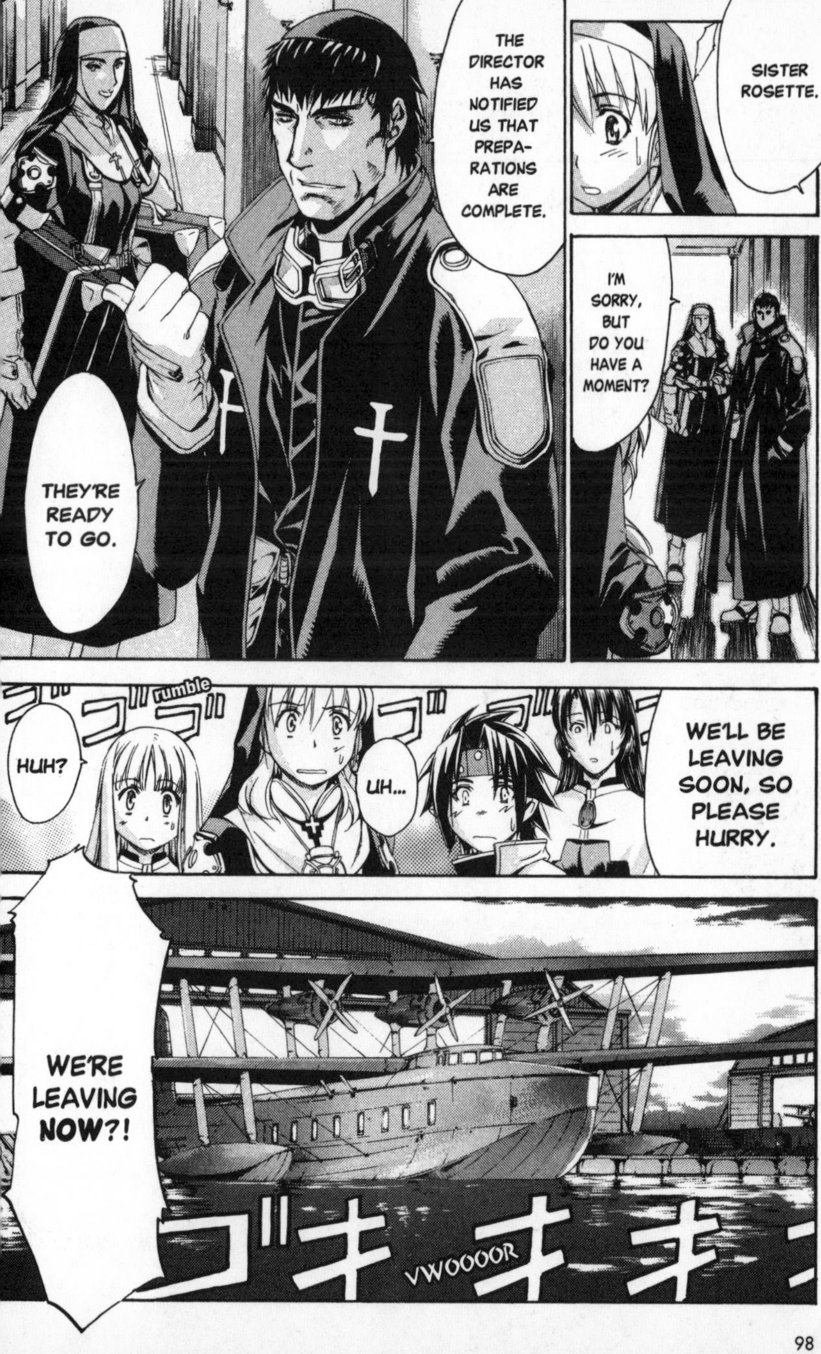
SISTER ROSETTE.
I'M SORRY, BUT DO YOU HAVE A MOMENT?
THE DIRECTOR HAS NOTIFIED US THAT PREPARATIONS ARE COMPLETE.
THEY'RE READY TO GO.
rumble
WE'LL BE LEAVING SOON, SO PLEASE HURRY.
UH...
HUH?
WE'RE LEAVING NOW?!
VWOOOOR

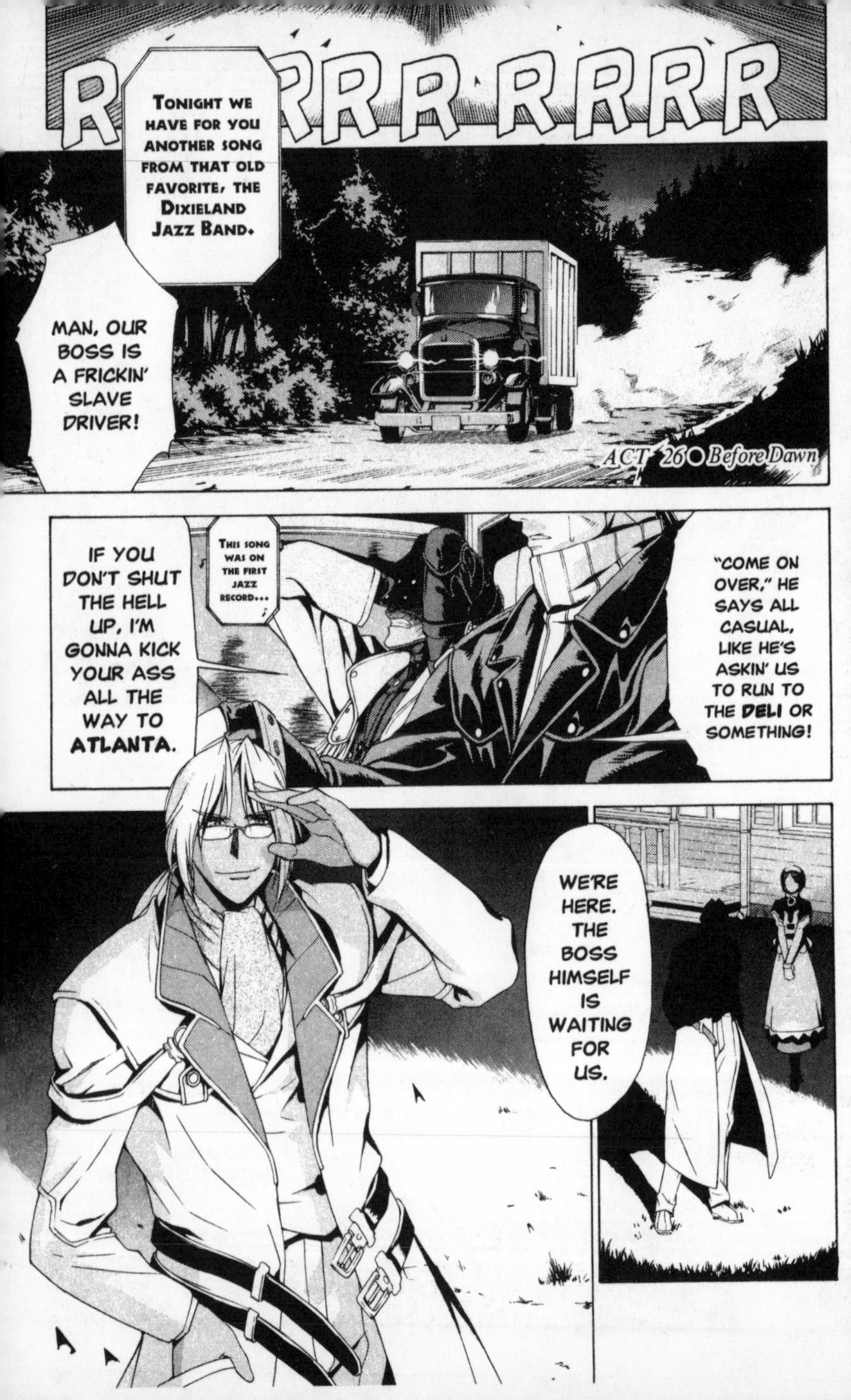
RRRRRRRR
Tonight we have for you another song from that old favorite, the Dixieland Jazz Band.
Man, our boss is a frickin' slave driver!
ACT 26 Before Dawn
"Come on over," he says all casual, like he's askin' us to run to the deli or something!
This song was on the first jazz record...
If you don't shut the hell up, I'm gonna kick your ass all the way to Atlanta.
We're here. The boss himself is waiting for us.

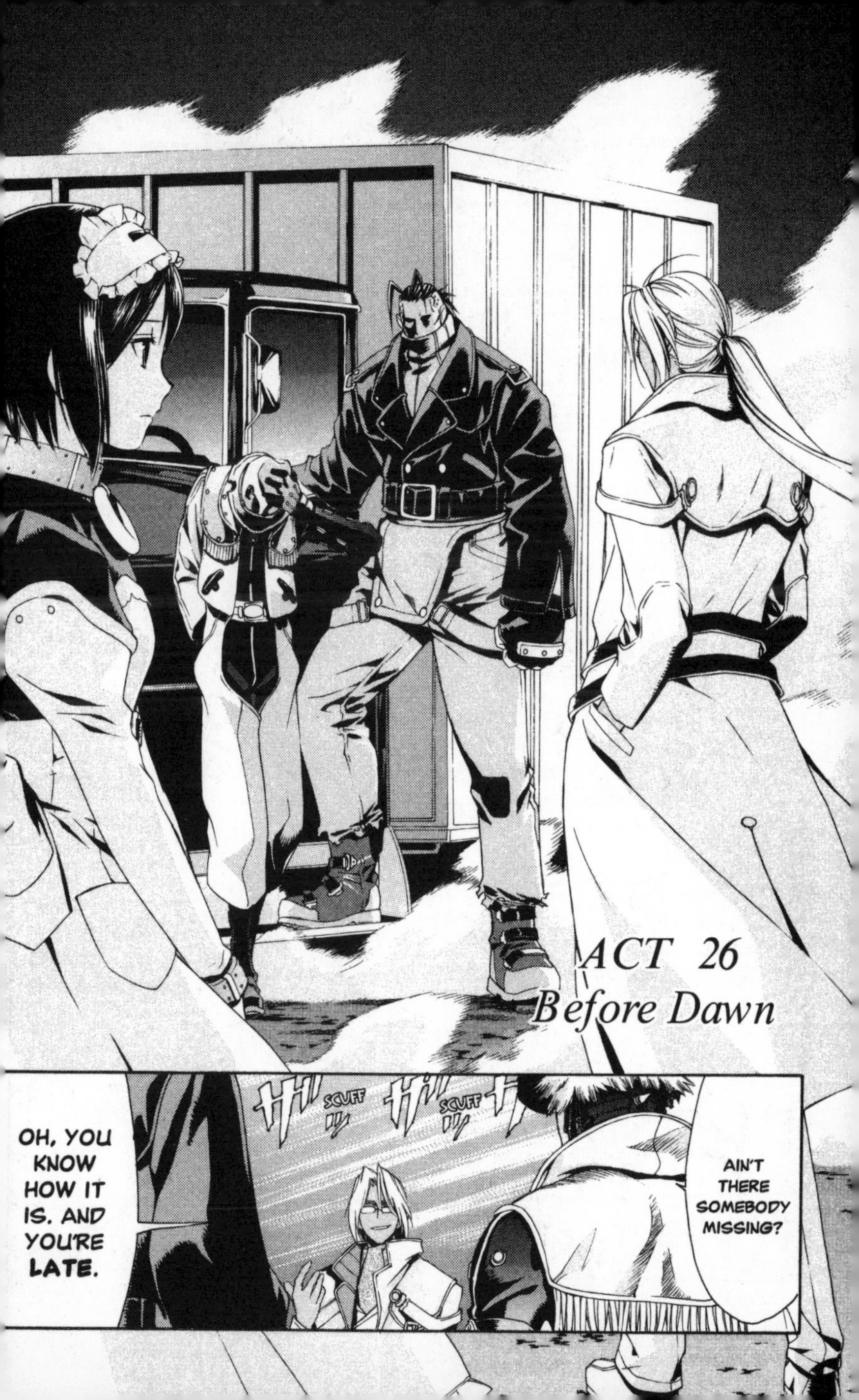
ACT 26
Before Dawn
AIN'T THERE SOMEBODY MISSING?
SCUFF
SCUFF
OH, YOU KNOW HOW IT IS. AND YOU'RE LATE.

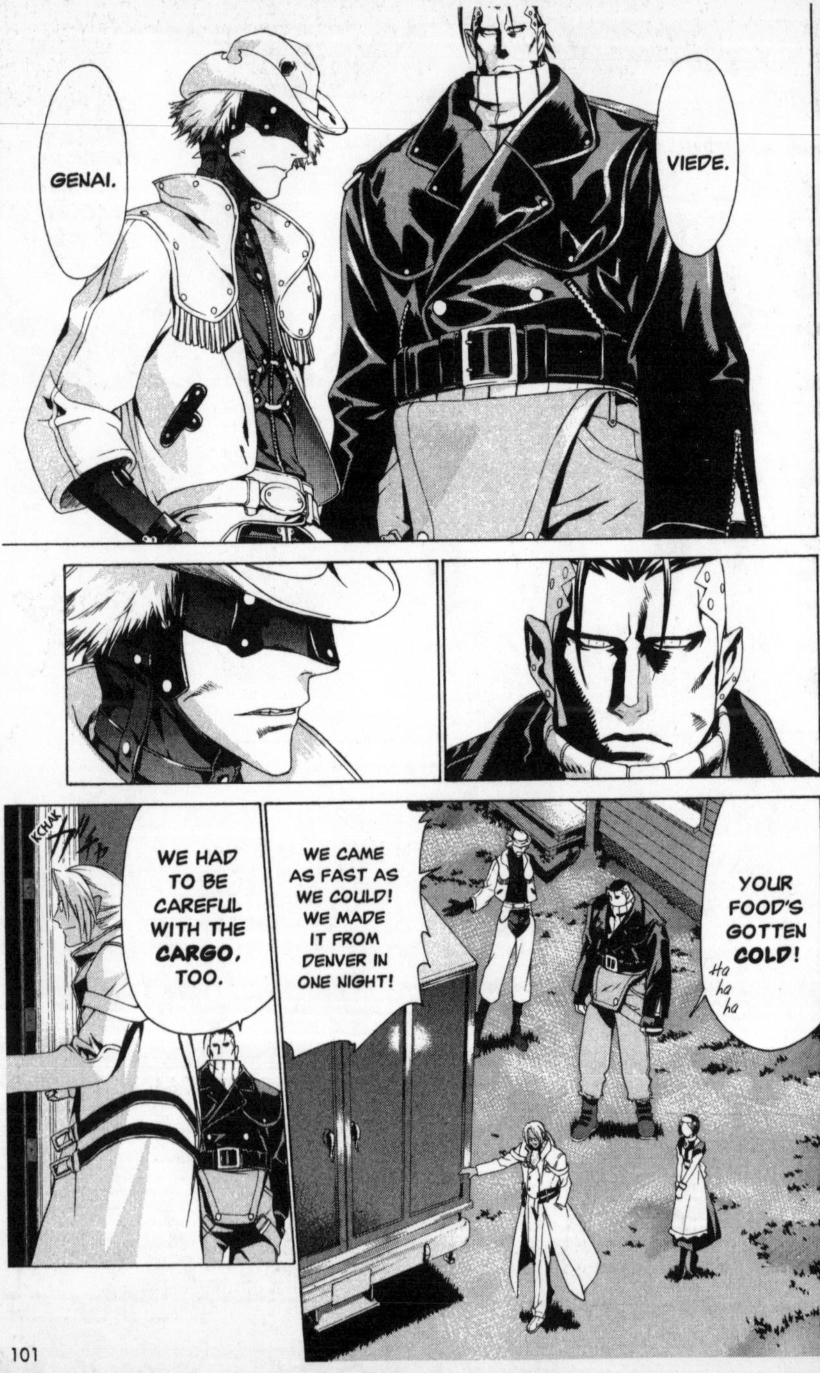
VIEDE.
GENAI.
YOUR FOOD'S GOTTEN COLD!
Ha ha ha
WE CAME AS FAST AS WE COULD! WE MADE IT FROM DENVER IN ONE NIGHT!
WE HAD TO BE CAREFUL WITH THE CARGO, TOO.
KCHAK

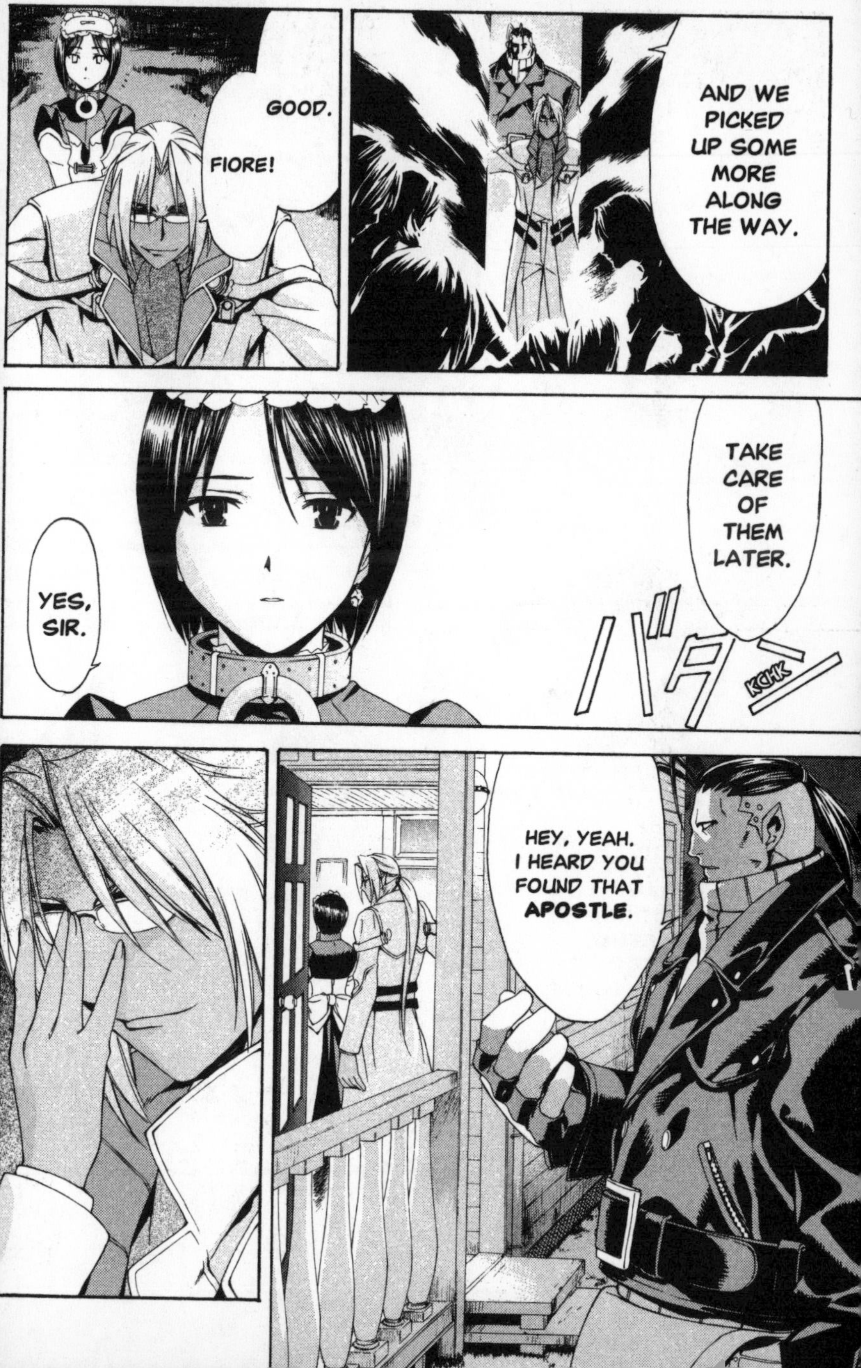
AND WE PICKED UP SOME MORE ALONG THE WAY.
GOOD.
FIORE!
TAKE CARE OF THEM LATER.
KCHK
YES, SIR.
HEY, YEAH. I HEARD YOU FOUND THAT **APOSTLE**.

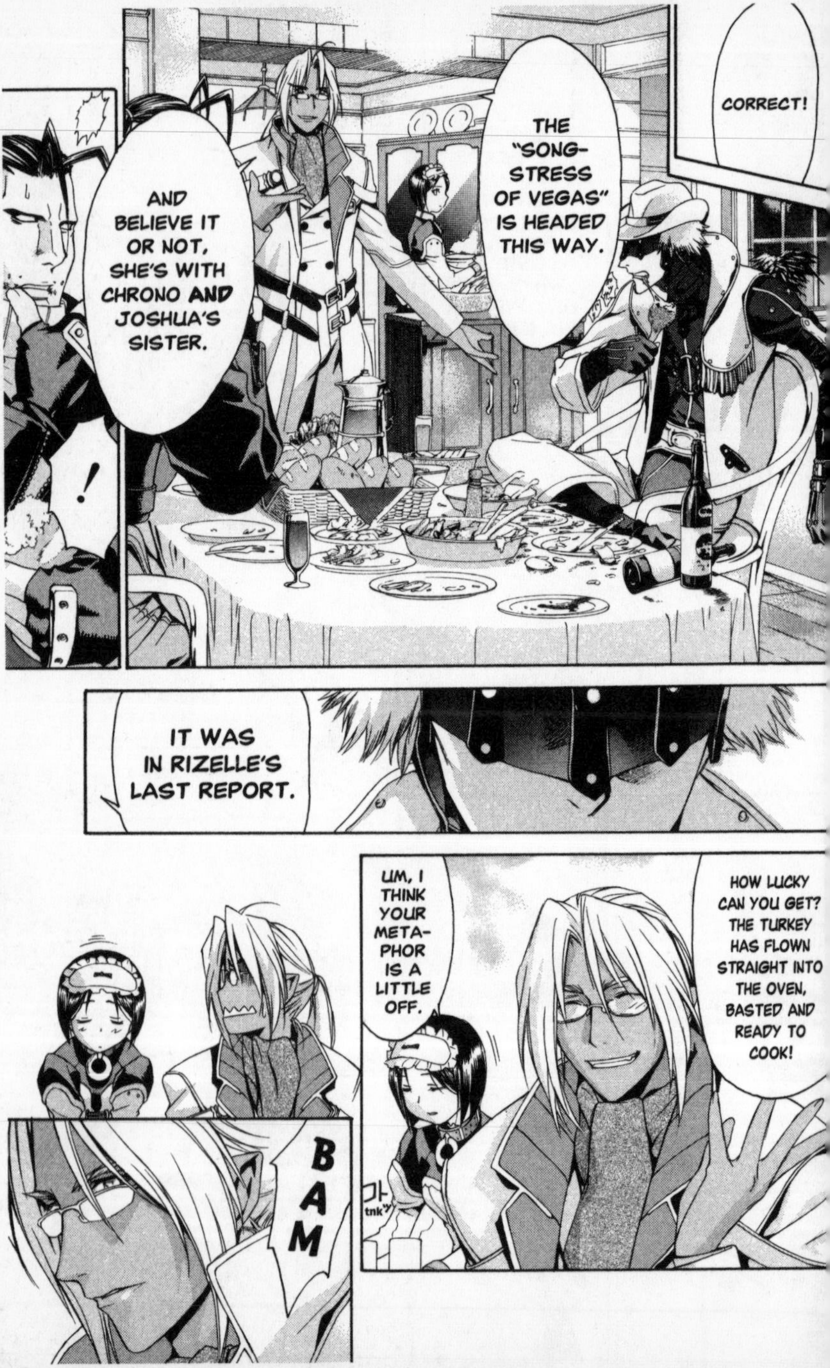
CORRECT!
THE "SONG-STRESS OF VEGAS" IS HEADED THIS WAY.
AND BELIEVE IT OR NOT, SHE'S WITH CHRONO AND JOSHUA'S SISTER.
!
IT WAS IN RIZELLE'S LAST REPORT.
HOW LUCKY CAN YOU GET? THE TURKEY HAS FLOWN STRAIGHT INTO THE OVEN, BASTED AND READY TO COOK!
UM, I THINK YOUR METAPHOR IS A LITTLE OFF.
tnk
BAM

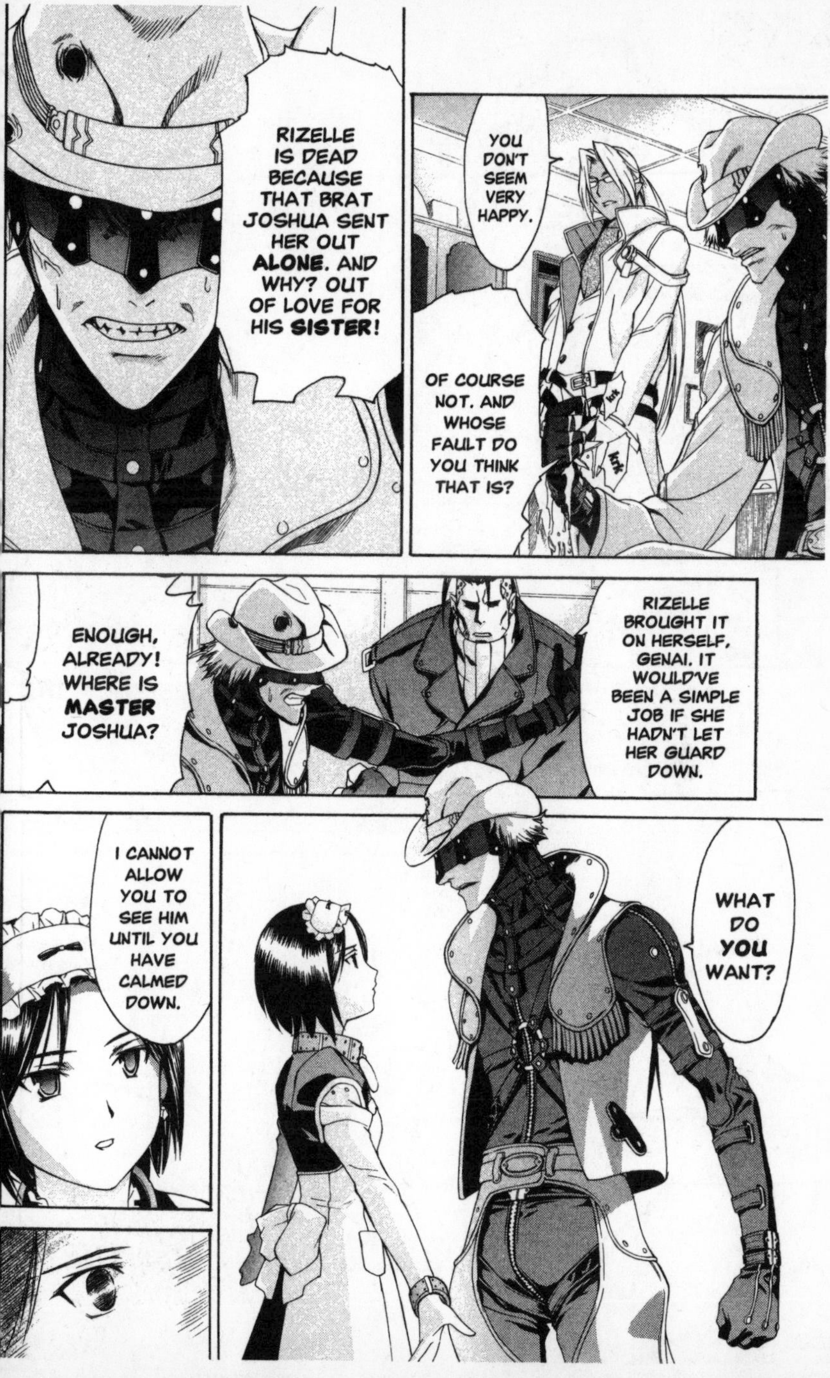
YOU DON'T SEEM VERY HAPPY.
krk
krk
OF COURSE NOT. AND WHOSE FAULT DO YOU THINK THAT IS?
RIZELLE IS DEAD BECAUSE THAT BRAT JOSHUA SENT HER OUT **ALONE**. AND WHY? OUT OF LOVE FOR HIS **SISTER**!
RIZELLE BROUGHT IT ON HERSELF, GENAI. IT WOULD'VE BEEN A SIMPLE JOB IF SHE HADN'T LET HER GUARD DOWN.
ENOUGH, ALREADY! WHERE IS **MASTER** JOSHUA?
WHAT DO **YOU** WANT?
I CANNOT ALLOW YOU TO SEE HIM UNTIL YOU HAVE CALMED DOWN.

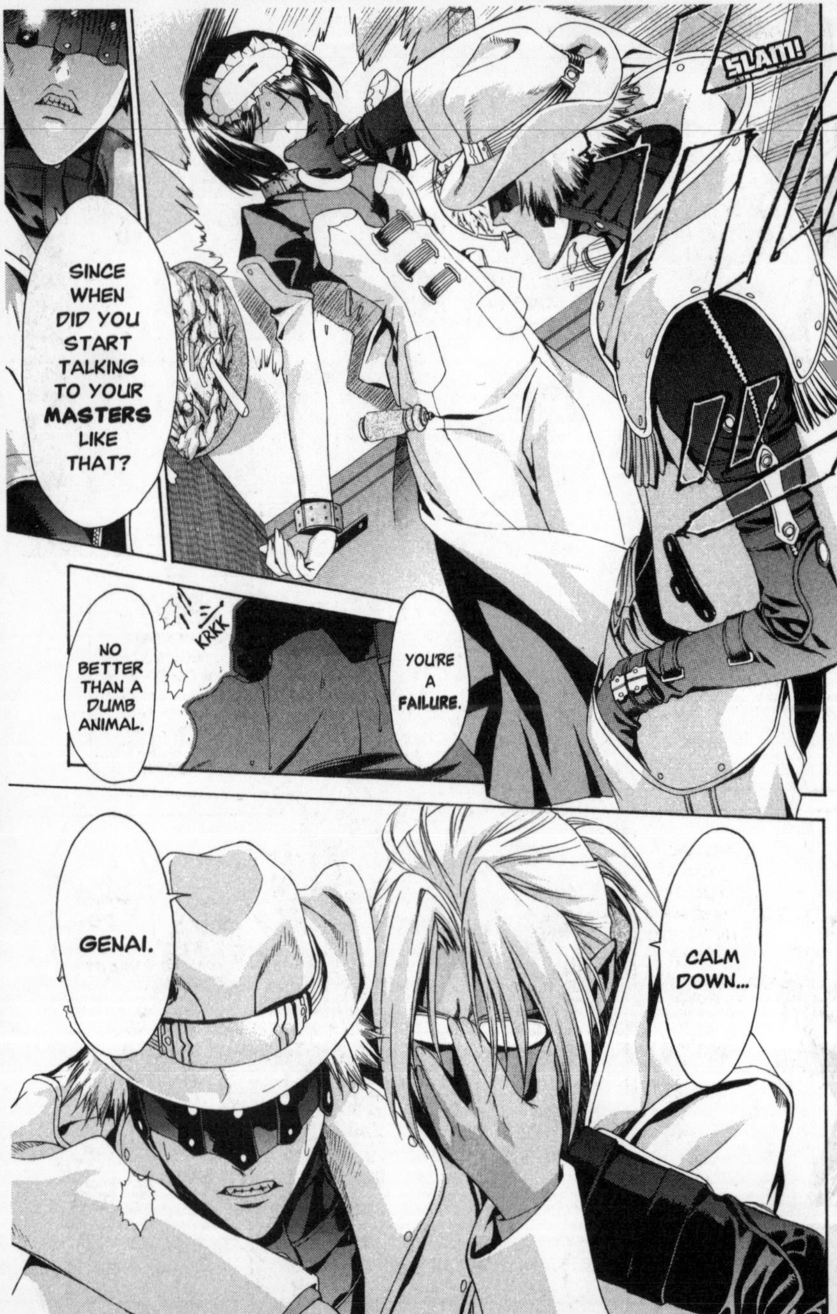
SLAM!
SINCE WHEN DID YOU START TALKING TO YOUR MASTERS LIKE THAT?
YOU'RE A FAILURE.
KRKK
NO BETTER THAN A DUMB ANIMAL.
CALM DOWN...
GENAI.

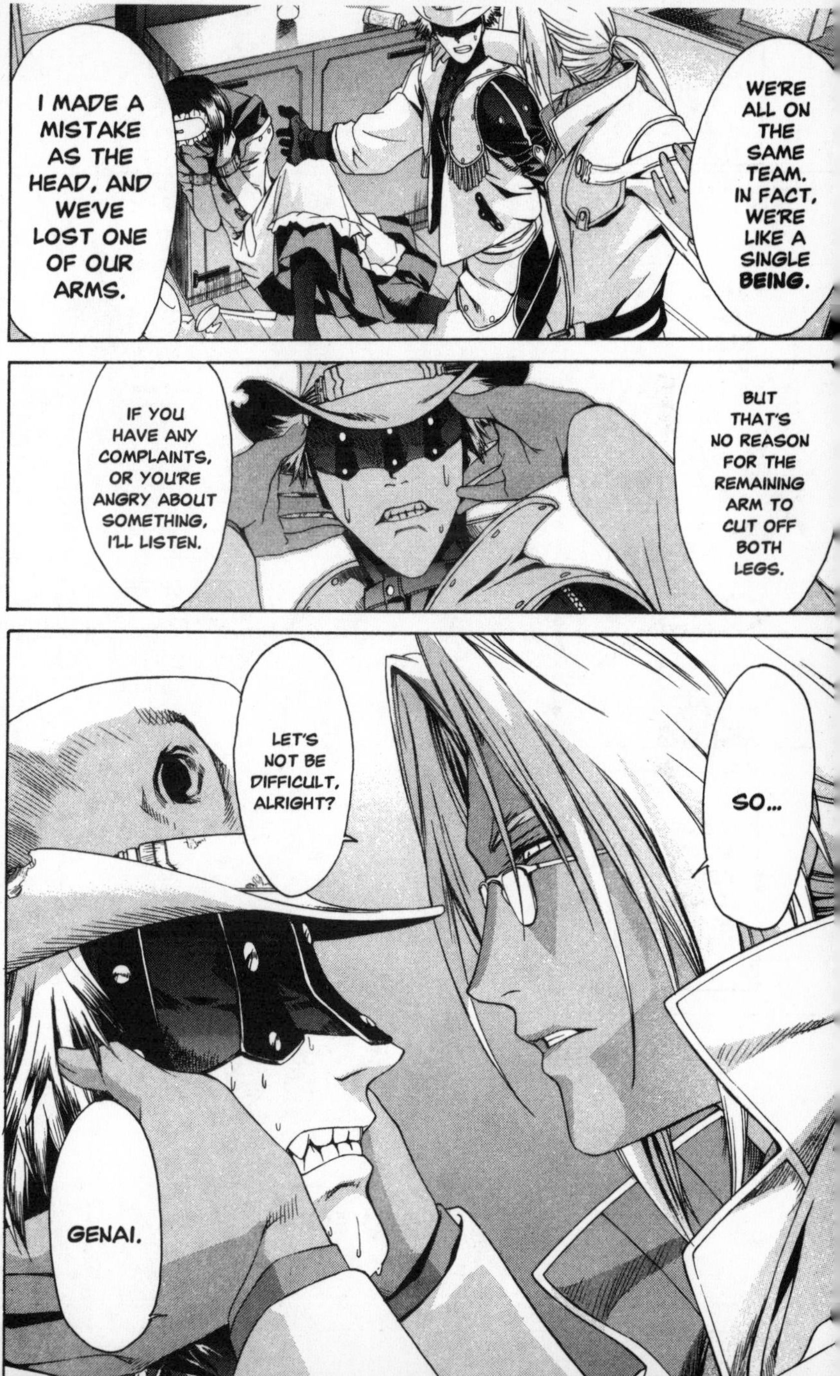
WE'RE ALL ON THE SAME TEAM. IN FACT, WE'RE LIKE A SINGLE **BEING.**
I MADE A MISTAKE AS THE HEAD, AND WE'VE LOST ONE OF OUR ARMS.
BUT THAT'S NO REASON FOR THE REMAINING ARM TO CUT OFF BOTH LEGS.
IF YOU HAVE ANY COMPLAINTS, OR YOU'RE ANGRY ABOUT SOMETHING, I'LL LISTEN.
SO...
LET'S NOT BE DIFFICULT, ALRIGHT?
GENAI.

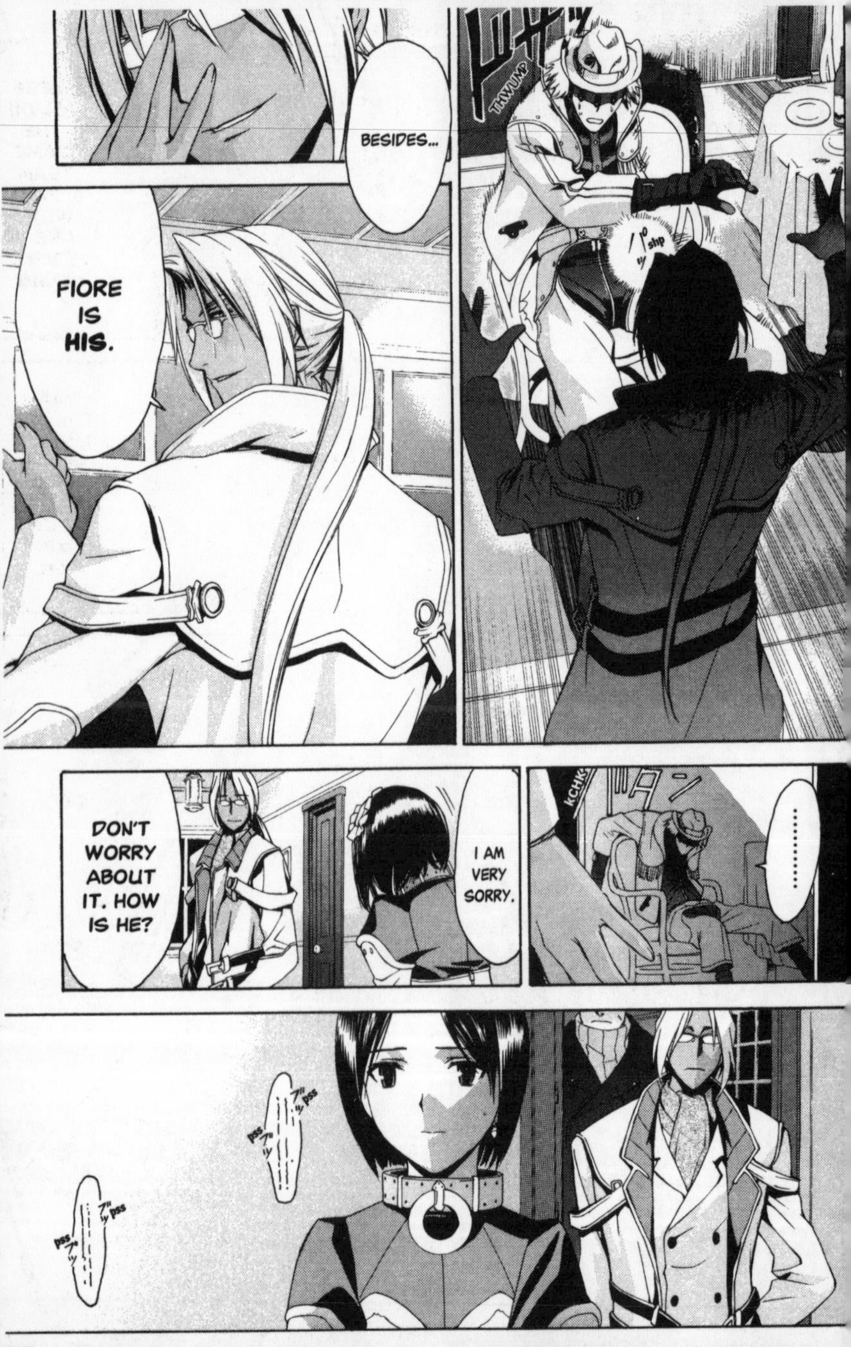
THWUMP
shp
BESIDES...
FIORE IS HIS.
KCHK
......
I AM VERY SORRY.
DON'T WORRY ABOUT IT. HOW IS HE?
pss
pss
pss
pss

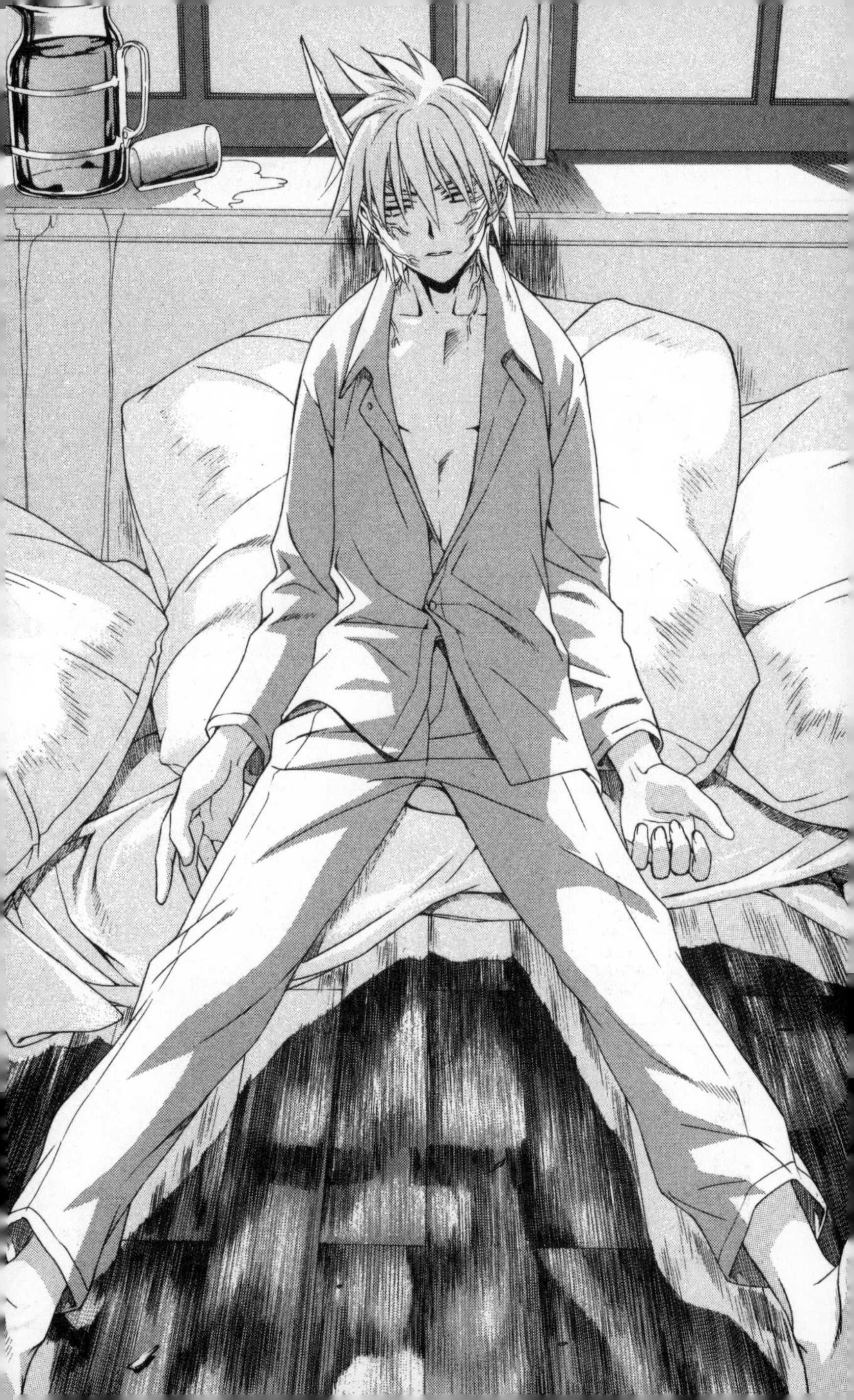

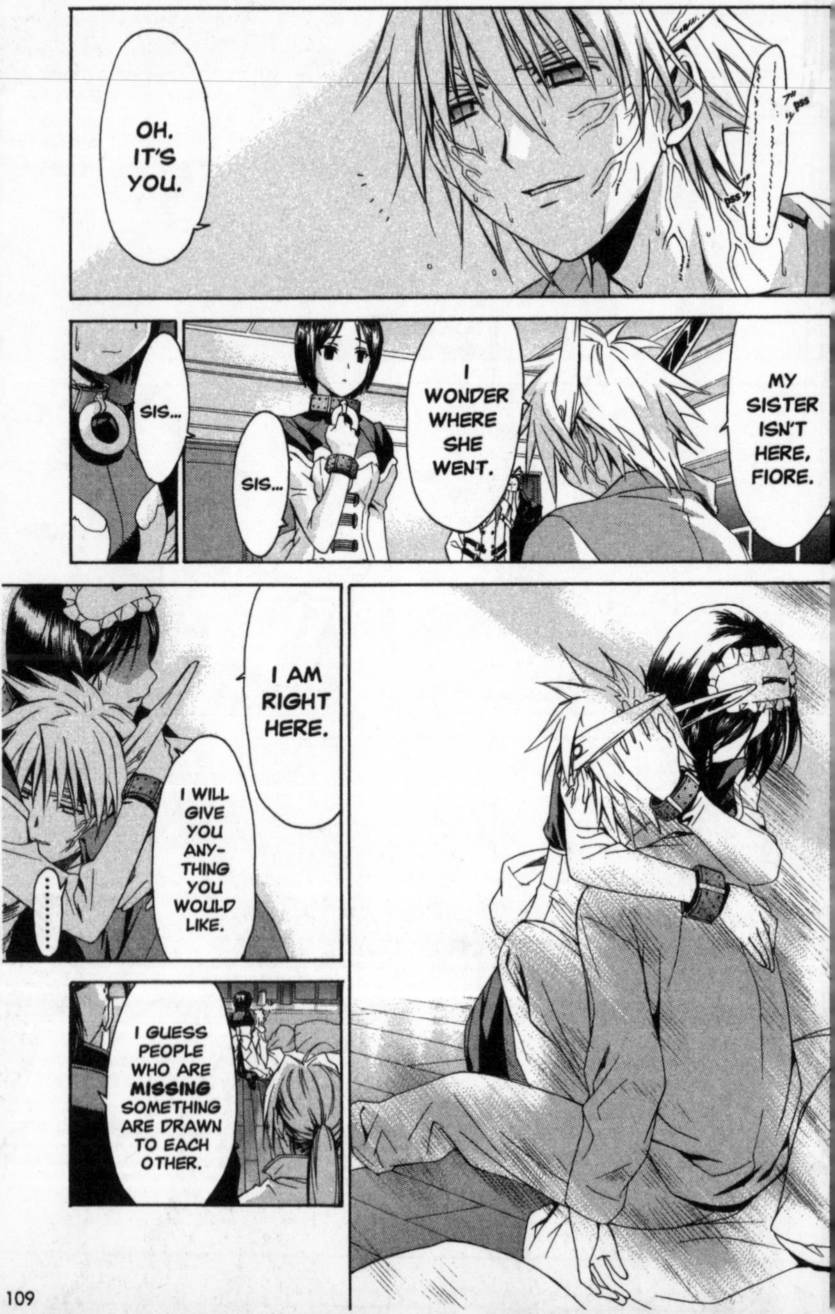
pss
pss
OH. IT'S YOU.
MY SISTER ISN'T HERE, FIORE.
I WONDER WHERE SHE WENT.
SIS...
SIS...
I AM RIGHT HERE.
I WILL GIVE YOU ANYTHING YOU WOULD LIKE.
....
I GUESS PEOPLE WHO ARE **MISSING** SOMETHING ARE DRAWN TO EACH OTHER.

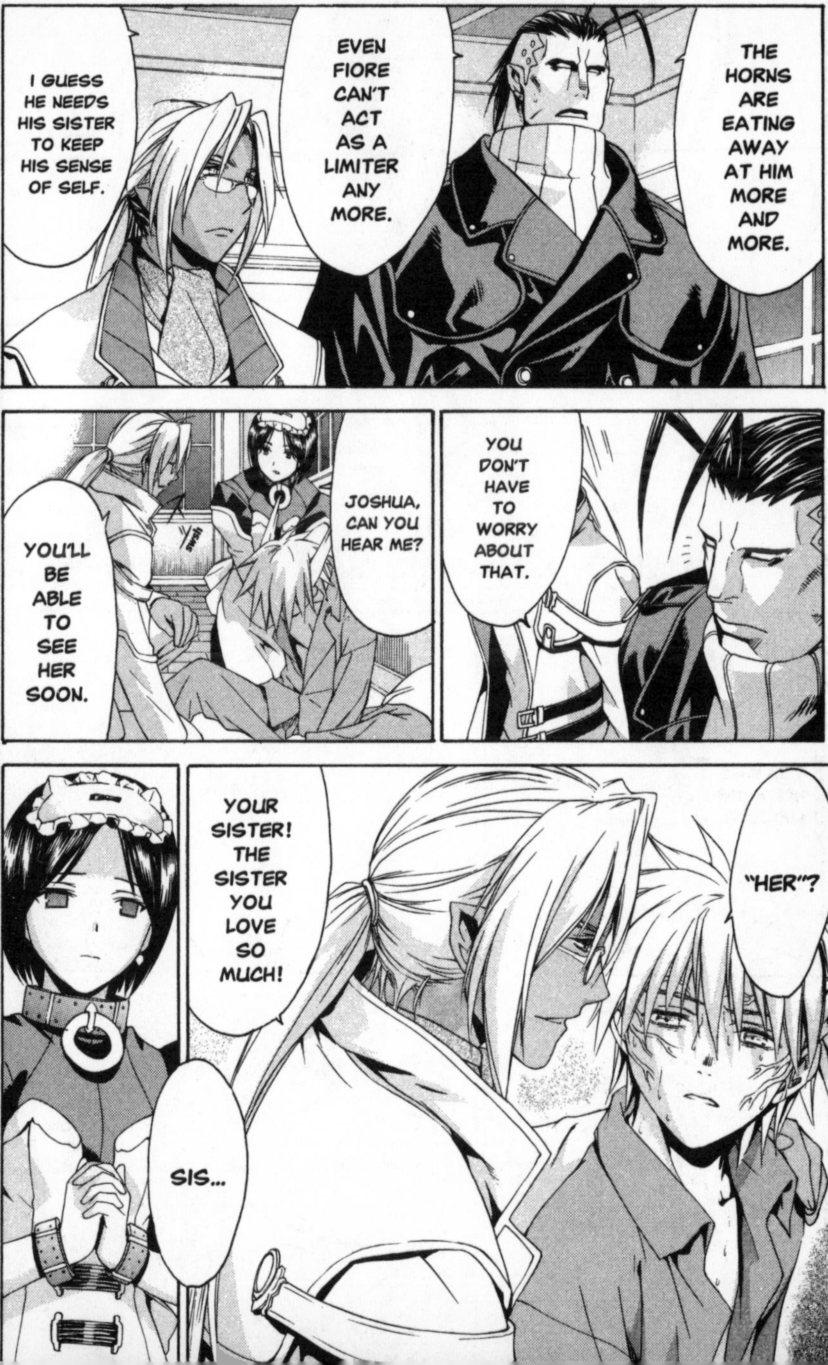
THE HORNS ARE EATING AWAY AT HIM MORE AND MORE.
EVEN FIORE CAN'T ACT AS A LIMITER ANY MORE.
I GUESS HE NEEDS HIS SISTER TO KEEP HIS SENSE OF SELF.
YOU DON'T HAVE TO WORRY ABOUT THAT.
JOSHUA, CAN YOU HEAR ME?
YOU'LL BE ABLE TO SEE HER SOON.
"HER"?
YOUR SISTER! THE SISTER YOU LOVE SO MUCH!
SIS...

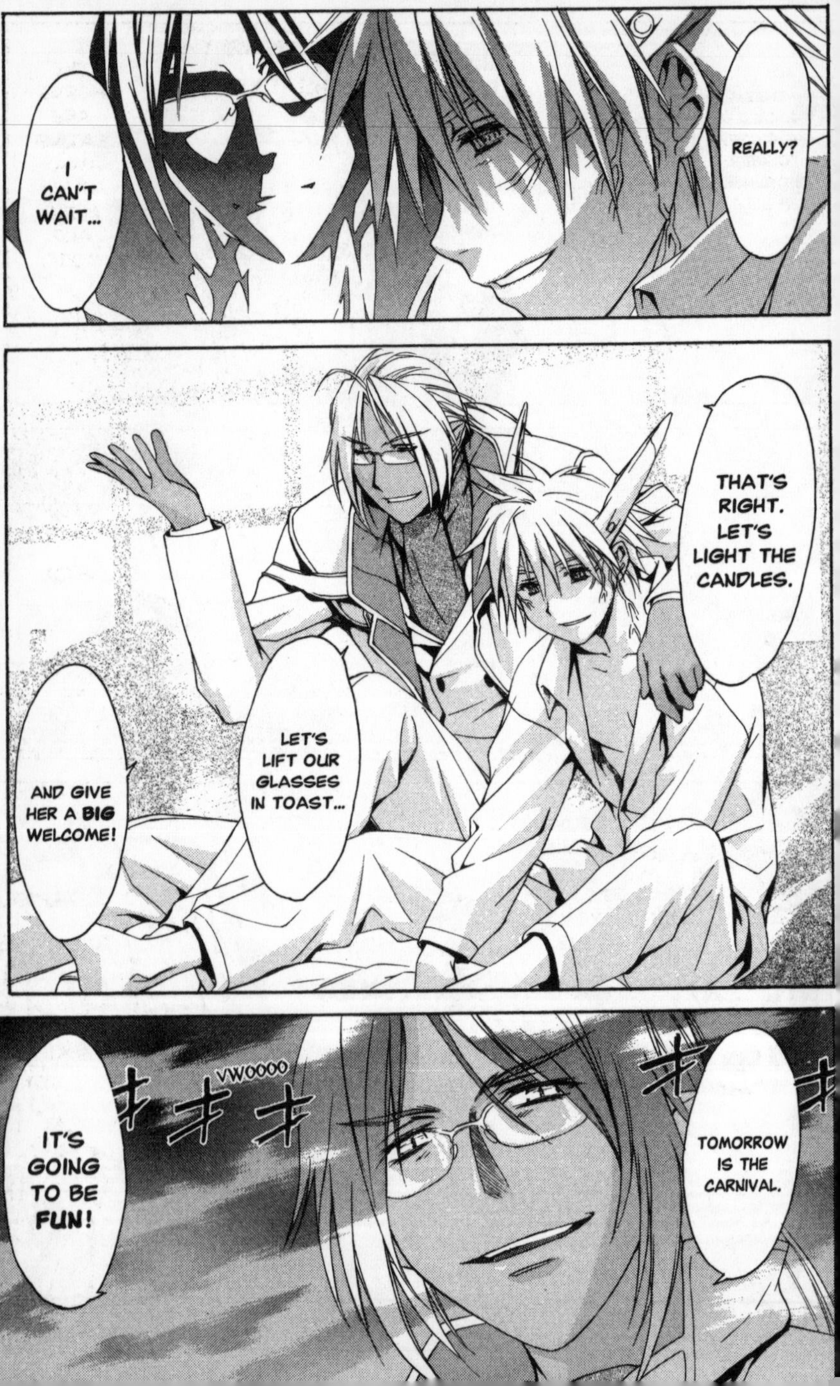
REALLY?
I CAN'T WAIT...
THAT'S RIGHT. LET'S LIGHT THE CANDLES.
LET'S LIFT OUR GLASSES IN TOAST...
AND GIVE HER A BIG WELCOME!
TOMORROW IS THE CARNIVAL.
VWOOOO
IT'S GOING TO BE FUN!

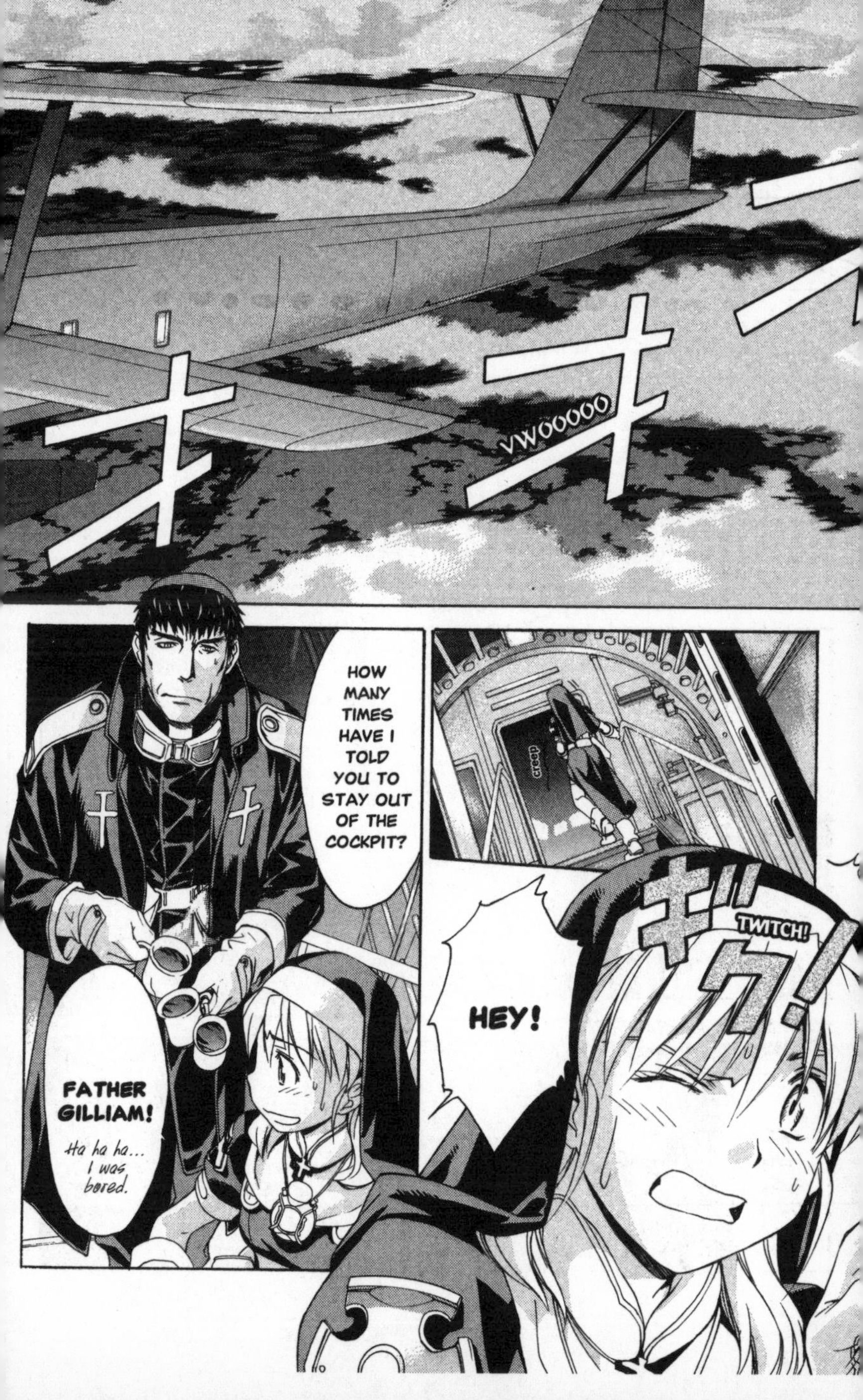
VWOOOOO
creep
HEY!
TWITCH!
HOW MANY TIMES HAVE I TOLD YOU TO STAY OUT OF THE COCKPIT?
FATHER GILLIAM!
Ha ha ha... I was bored.

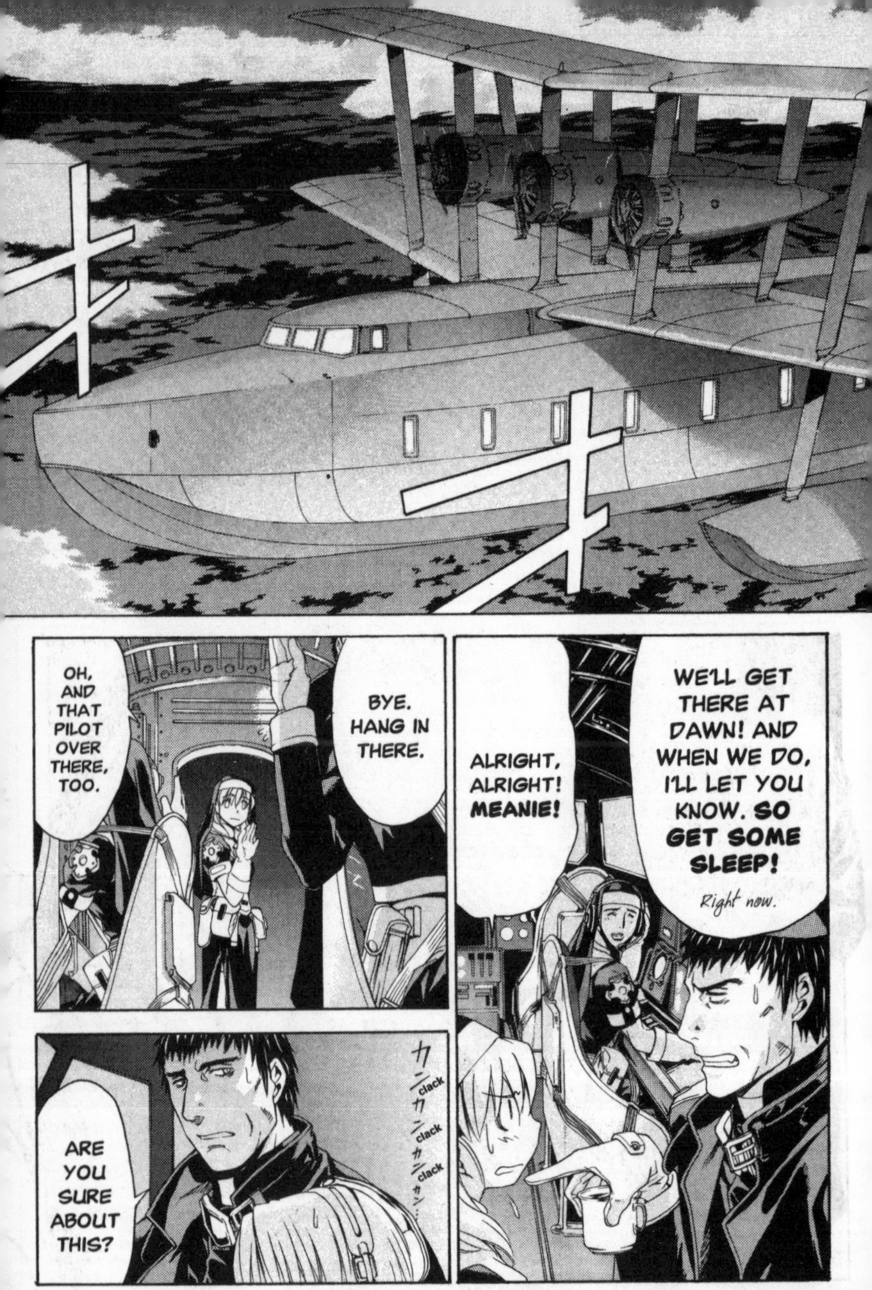
WE'LL GET THERE AT DAWN! AND WHEN WE DO, I'LL LET YOU KNOW. SO GET SOME SLEEP!
Right now.
ALRIGHT, ALRIGHT! MEANIE!
BYE. HANG IN THERE.
OH, AND THAT PILOT OVER THERE, TOO.
カンカンカン… clack clack clack
ARE YOU SURE ABOUT THIS?

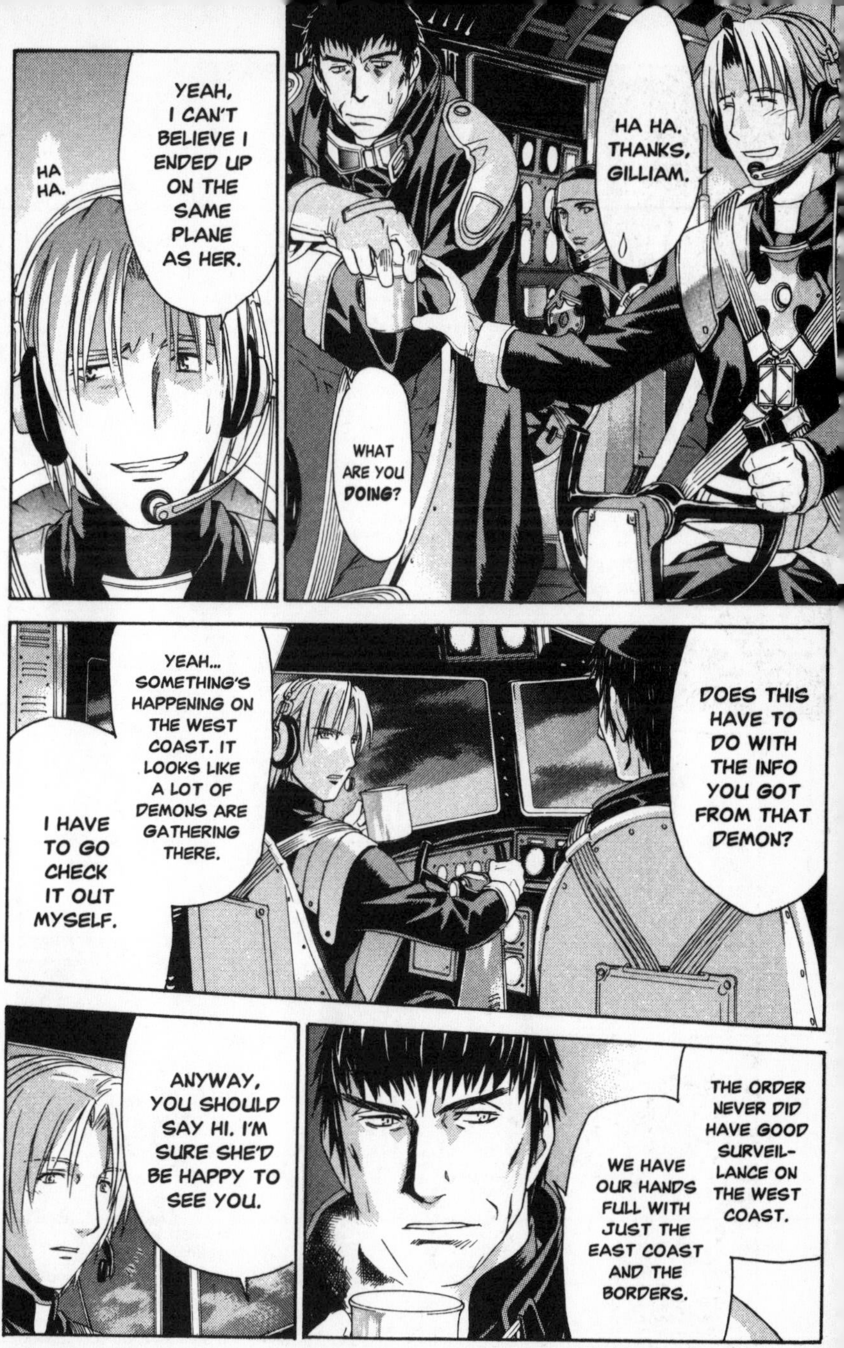
HA HA. THANKS, GILLIAM.
WHAT ARE YOU DOING?
YEAH, I CAN'T BELIEVE I ENDED UP ON THE SAME PLANE AS HER.
HA HA.
DOES THIS HAVE TO DO WITH THE INFO YOU GOT FROM THAT DEMON?
YEAH... SOMETHING'S HAPPENING ON THE WEST COAST. IT LOOKS LIKE A LOT OF DEMONS ARE GATHERING THERE.
I HAVE TO GO CHECK IT OUT MYSELF.
THE ORDER NEVER DID HAVE GOOD SURVEIL-LANCE ON THE WEST COAST.
WE HAVE OUR HANDS FULL WITH JUST THE EAST COAST AND THE BORDERS.
ANYWAY, YOU SHOULD SAY HI. I'M SURE SHE'D BE HAPPY TO SEE YOU.

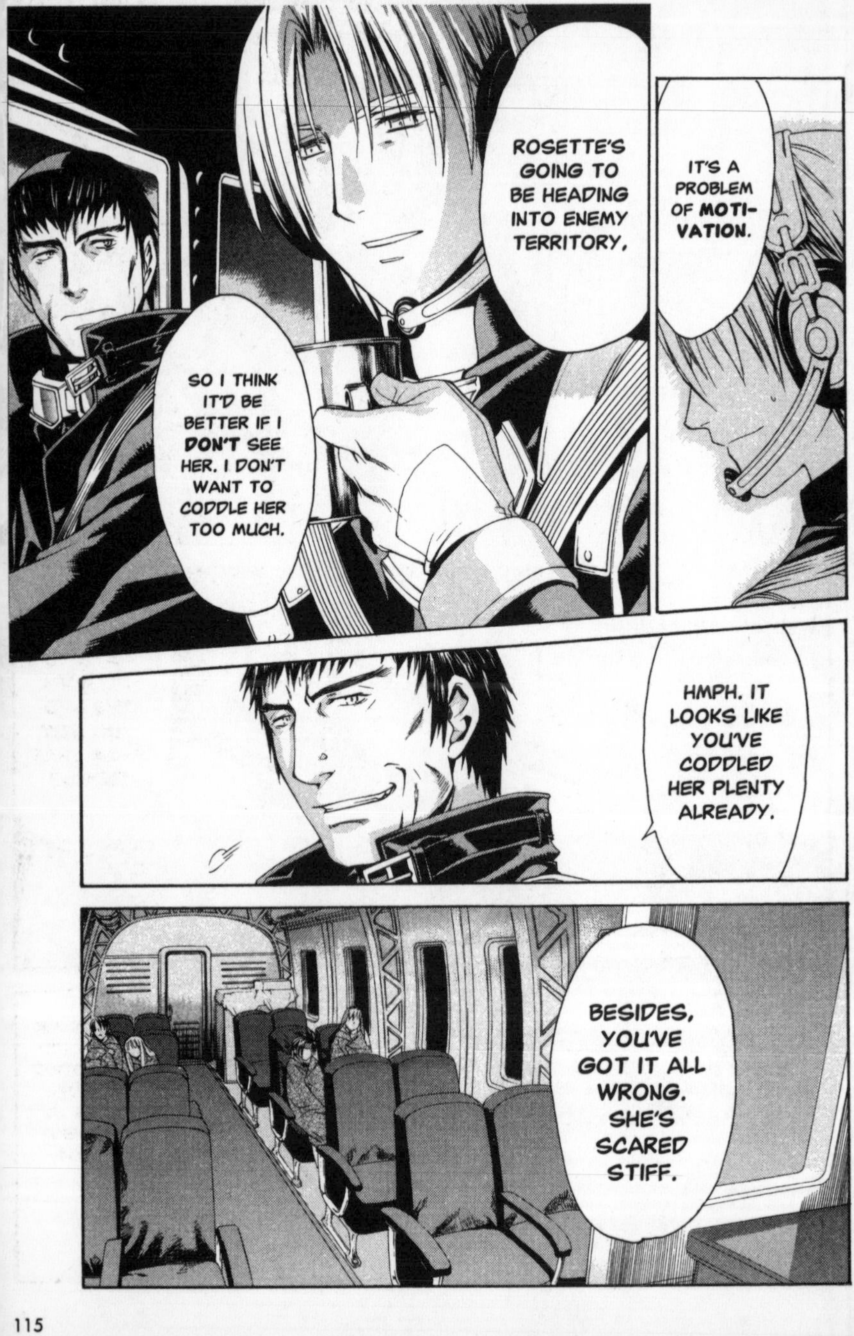
IT'S A PROBLEM OF MOTIVATION.
ROSETTE'S GOING TO BE HEADING INTO ENEMY TERRITORY,
SO I THINK IT'D BE BETTER IF I DON'T SEE HER. I DON'T WANT TO CODDLE HER TOO MUCH.
HMPH. IT LOOKS LIKE YOU'VE CODDLED HER PLENTY ALREADY.
BESIDES, YOU'VE GOT IT ALL WRONG. SHE'S SCARED STIFF.

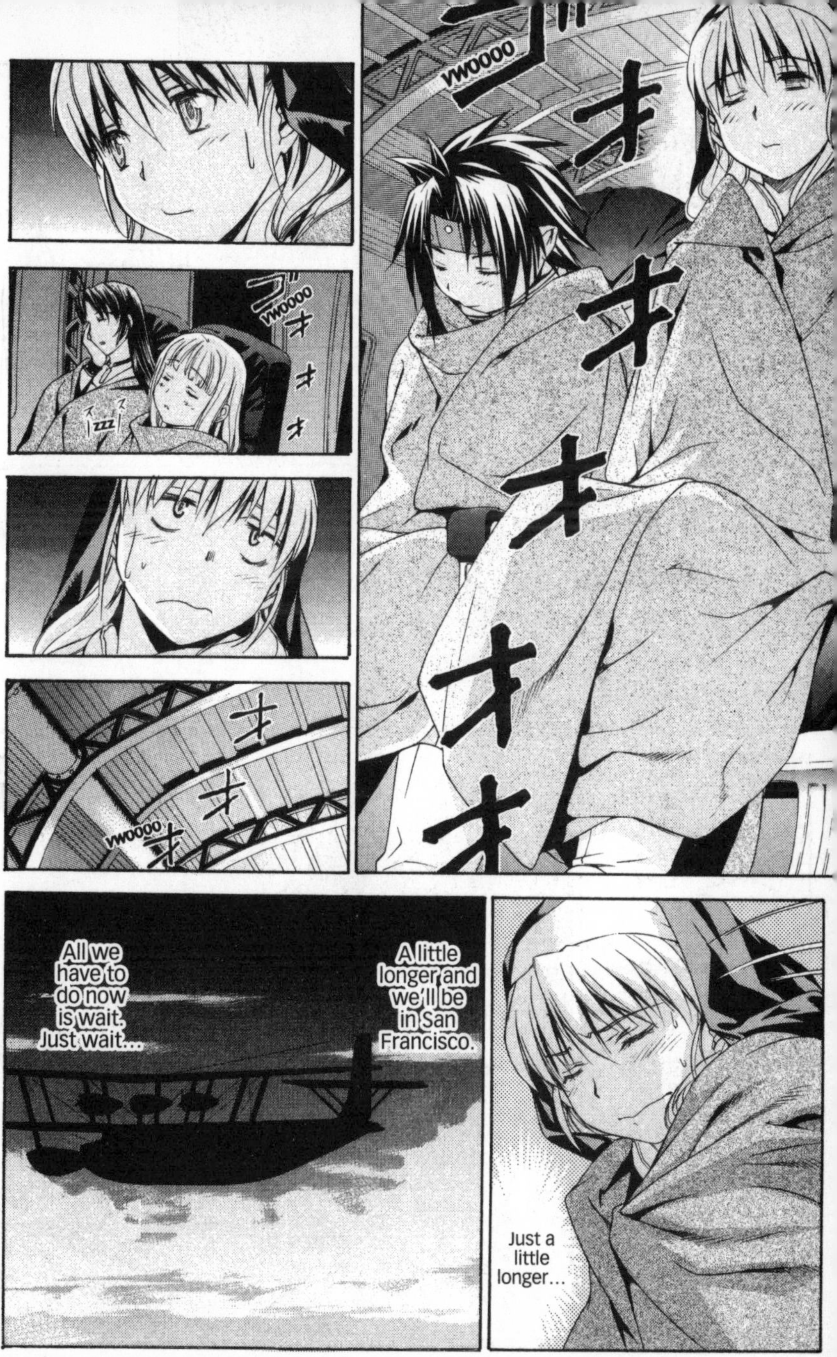
YWOOOO
YWOOOO
zzz
YWOOOO
Just a little longer...
A little longer and we'll be in San Francisco.
All we have to do now is wait. Just wait...

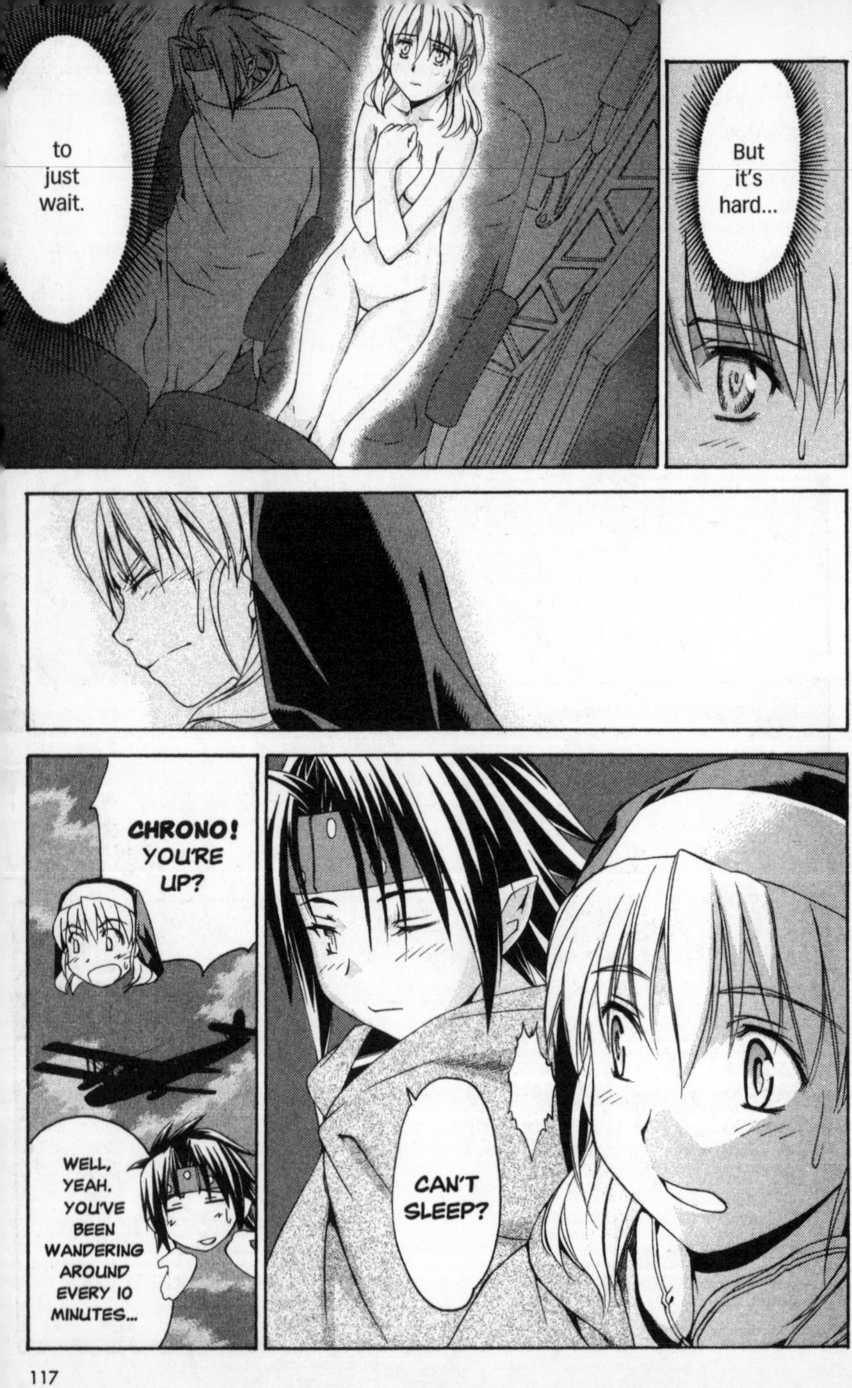
But it's hard...
to just wait.
CAN'T SLEEP?
CHRONO! YOU'RE UP?
WELL, YEAH. YOU'VE BEEN WANDERING AROUND EVERY 10 MINUTES...

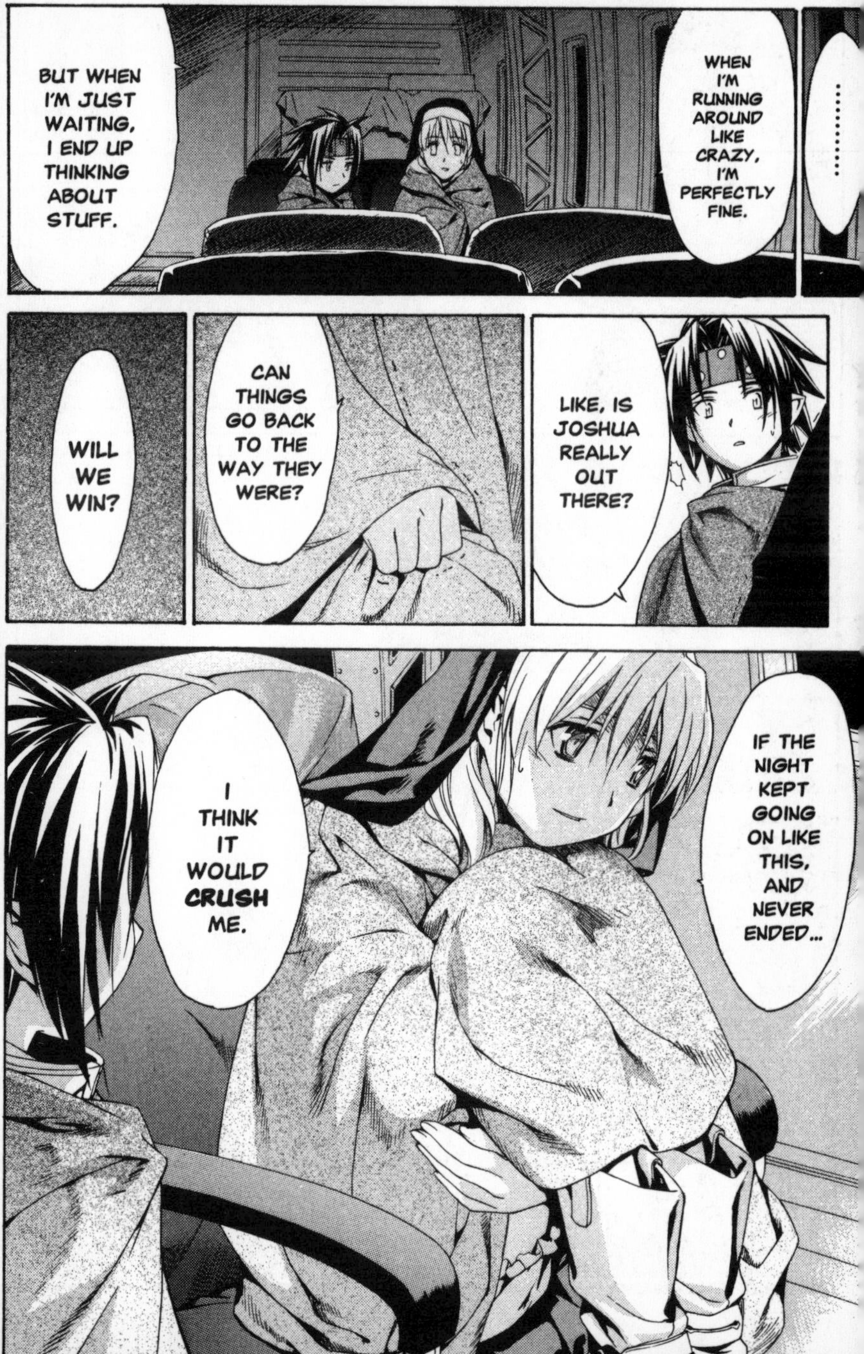
......
WHEN I'M RUNNING AROUND LIKE CRAZY, I'M PERFECTLY FINE.
BUT WHEN I'M JUST WAITING, I END UP THINKING ABOUT STUFF.
LIKE, IS JOSHUA REALLY OUT THERE?
CAN THINGS GO BACK TO THE WAY THEY WERE?
WILL WE WIN?
IF THE NIGHT KEPT GOING ON LIKE THIS, AND NEVER ENDED...
I THINK IT WOULD **CRUSH** ME.

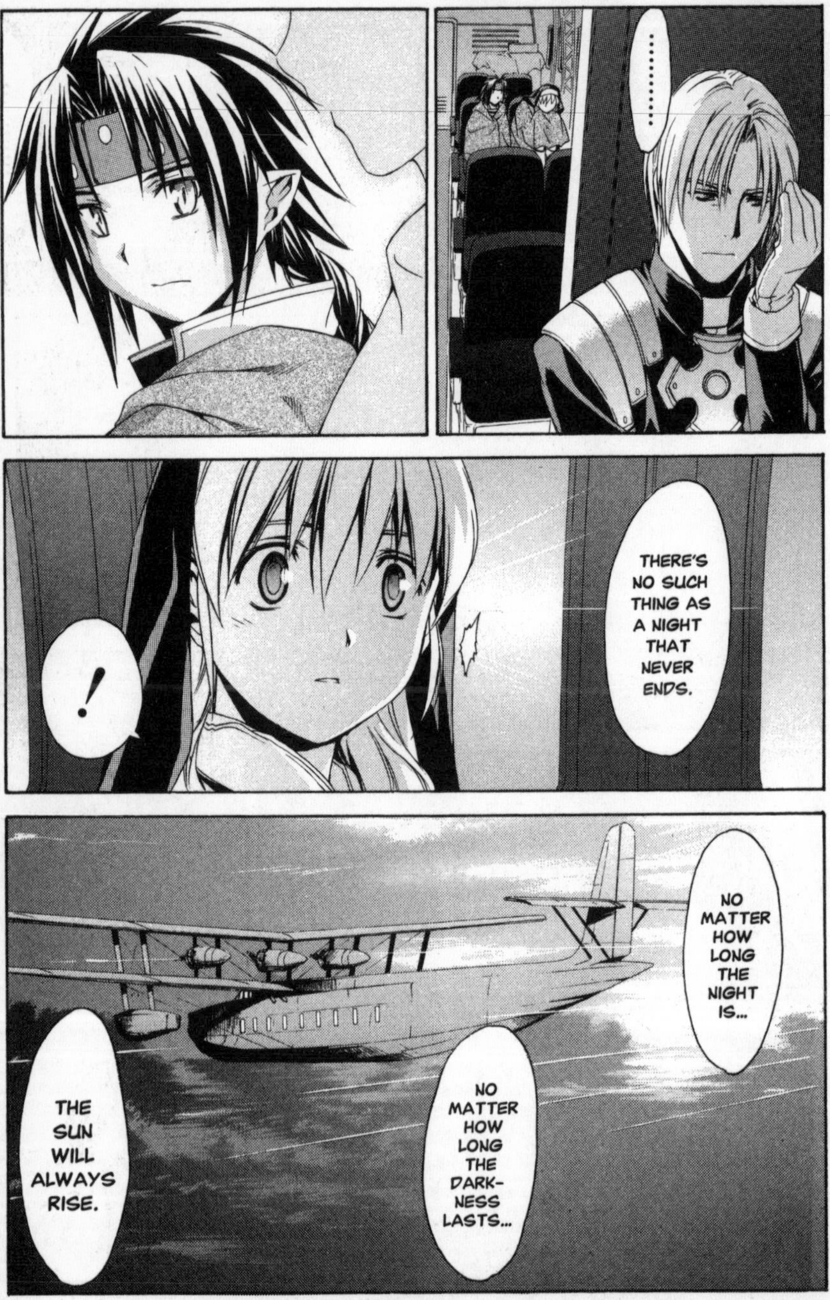
......
THERE'S NO SUCH THING AS A NIGHT THAT NEVER ENDS.
!
NO MATTER HOW LONG THE NIGHT IS...
NO MATTER HOW LONG THE DARK-NESS LASTS...
THE SUN WILL ALWAYS RISE.

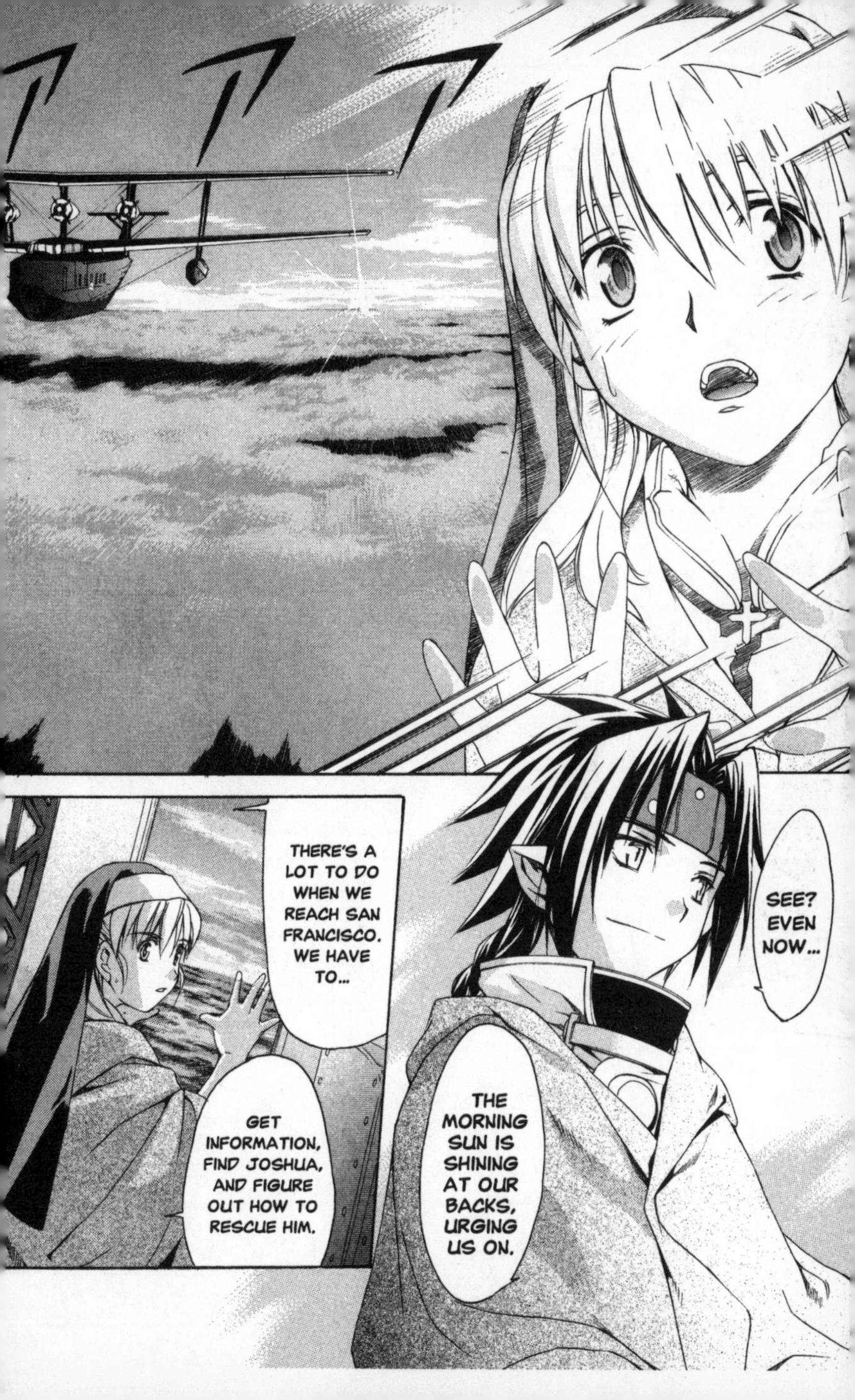
SEE? EVEN NOW...
THE MORNING SUN IS SHINING AT OUR BACKS, URGING US ON.
THERE'S A LOT TO DO WHEN WE REACH SAN FRANCISCO. WE HAVE TO...
GET INFORMATION, FIND JOSHUA, AND FIGURE OUT HOW TO RESCUE HIM.

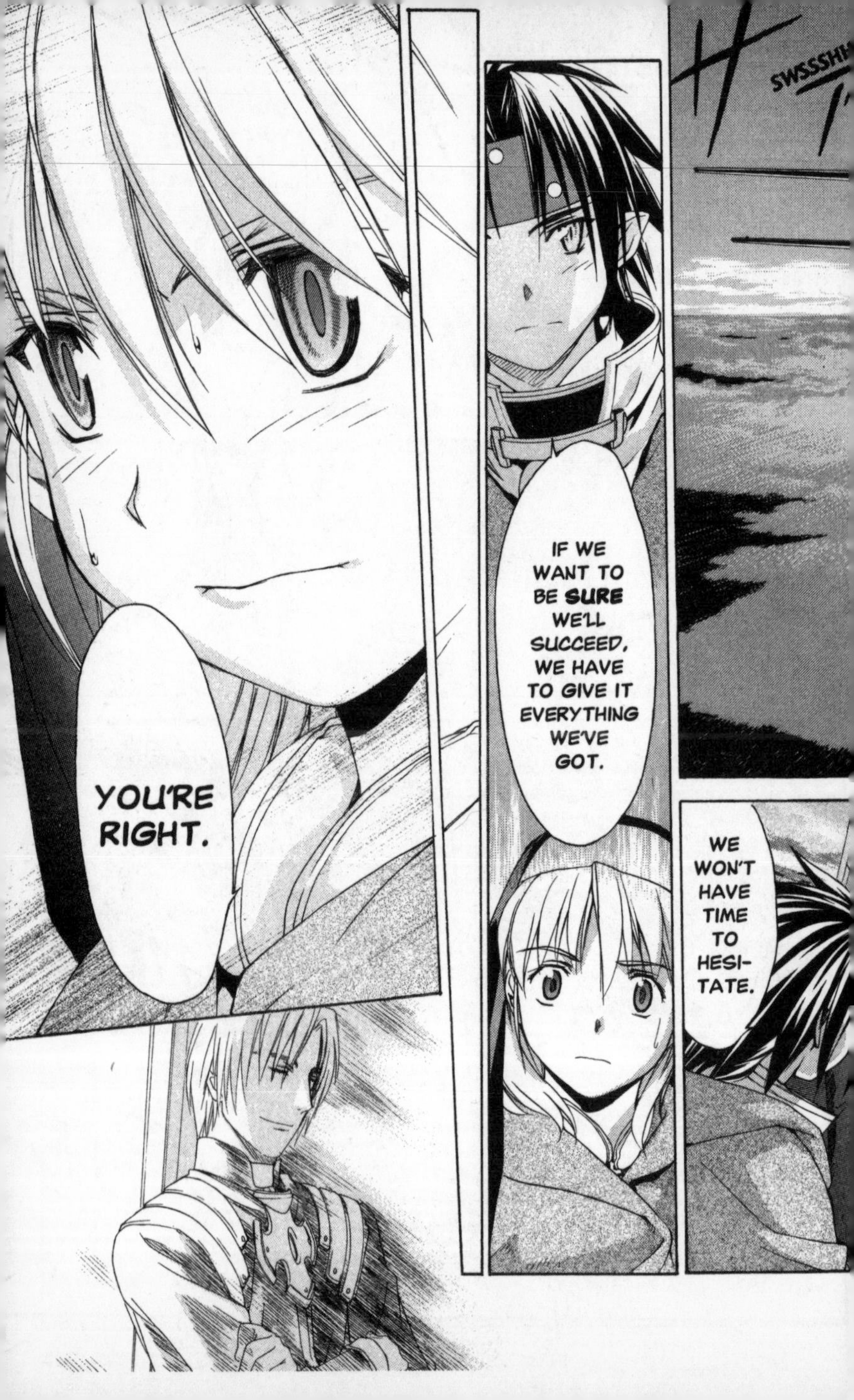
SWSSHH
IF WE WANT TO BE SURE WE'LL SUCCEED, WE HAVE TO GIVE IT EVERYTHING WE'VE GOT.
WE WON'T HAVE TIME TO HESI-TATE.
YOU'RE RIGHT.

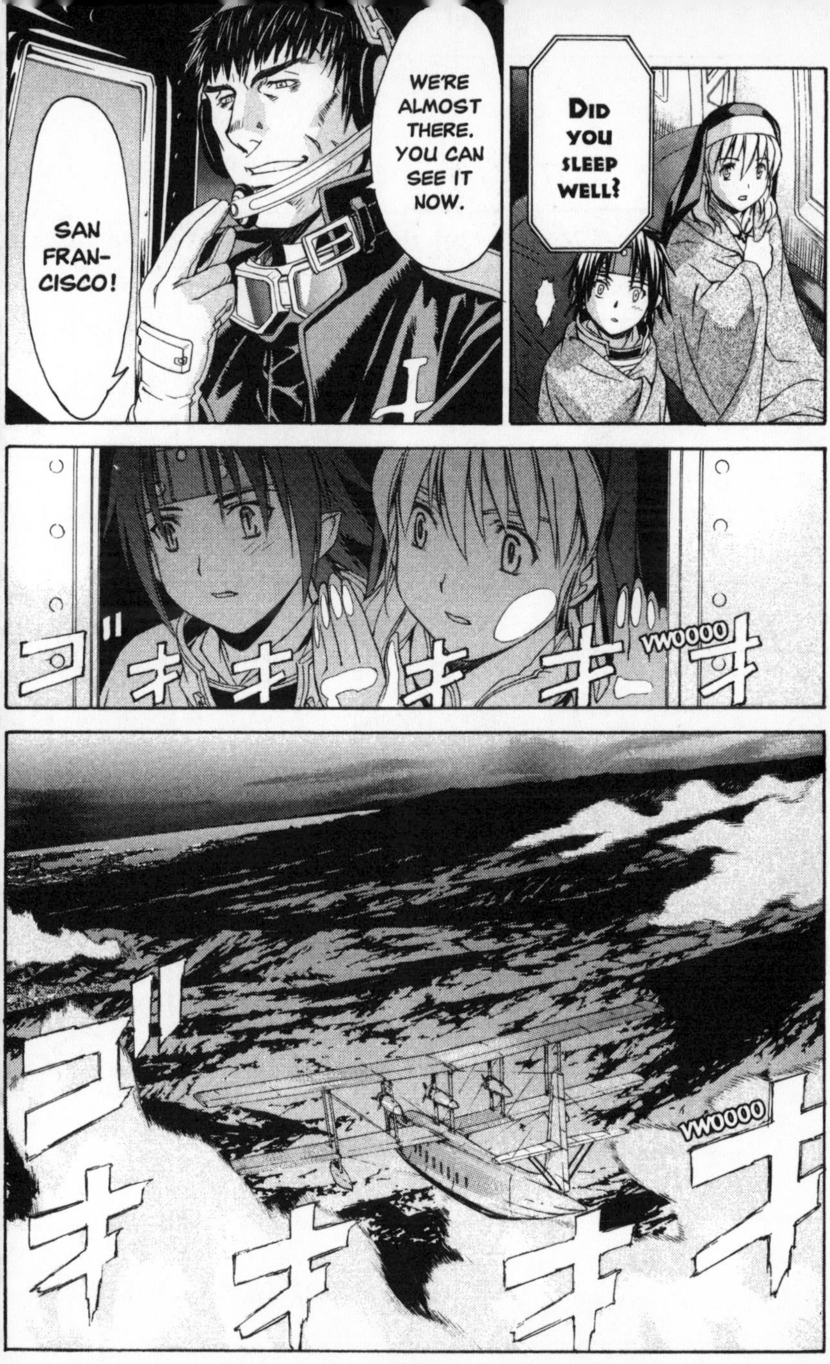
Did you sleep well?
We're almost there. You can see it now.
San Francisco!
VWOOOO
VWOOOO

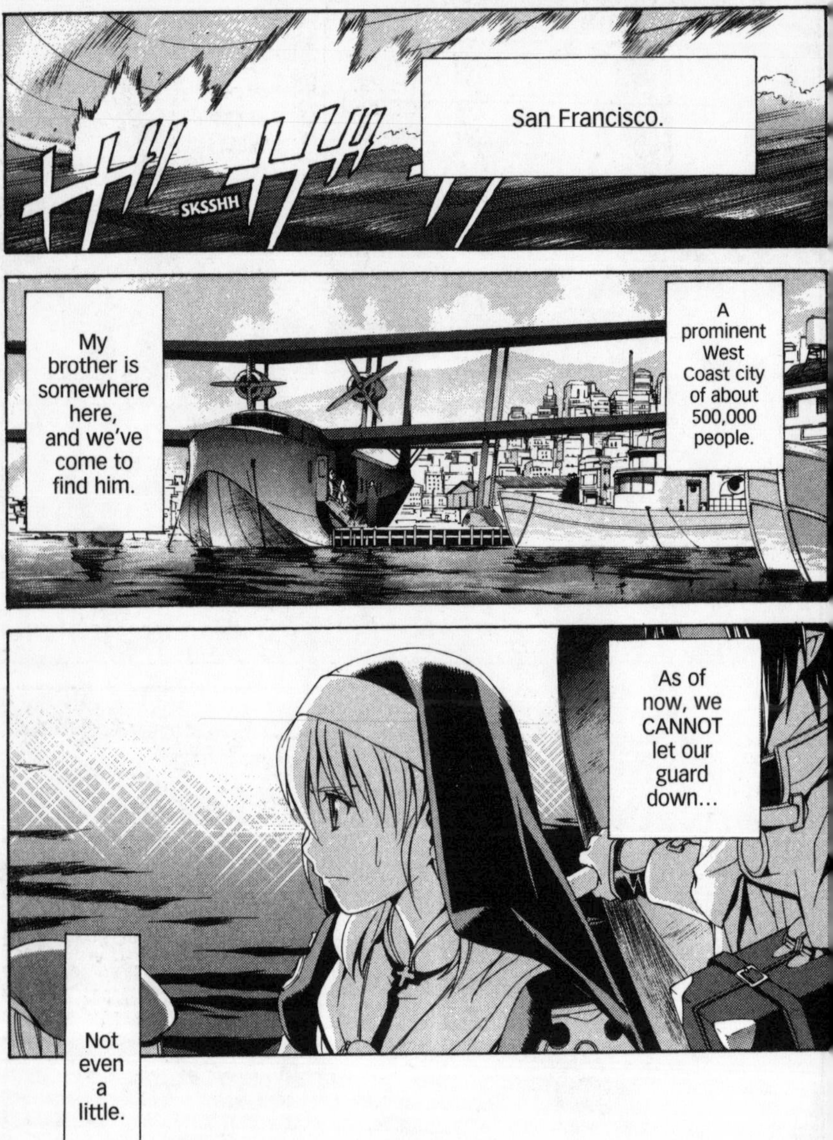
San Francisco.
SKSSHH
A prominent West Coast city of about 500,000 people.
My brother is somewhere here, and we've come to find him.
As of now, we CANNOT let our guard down...
Not even a little.

ACT 27
Night of the Carnival

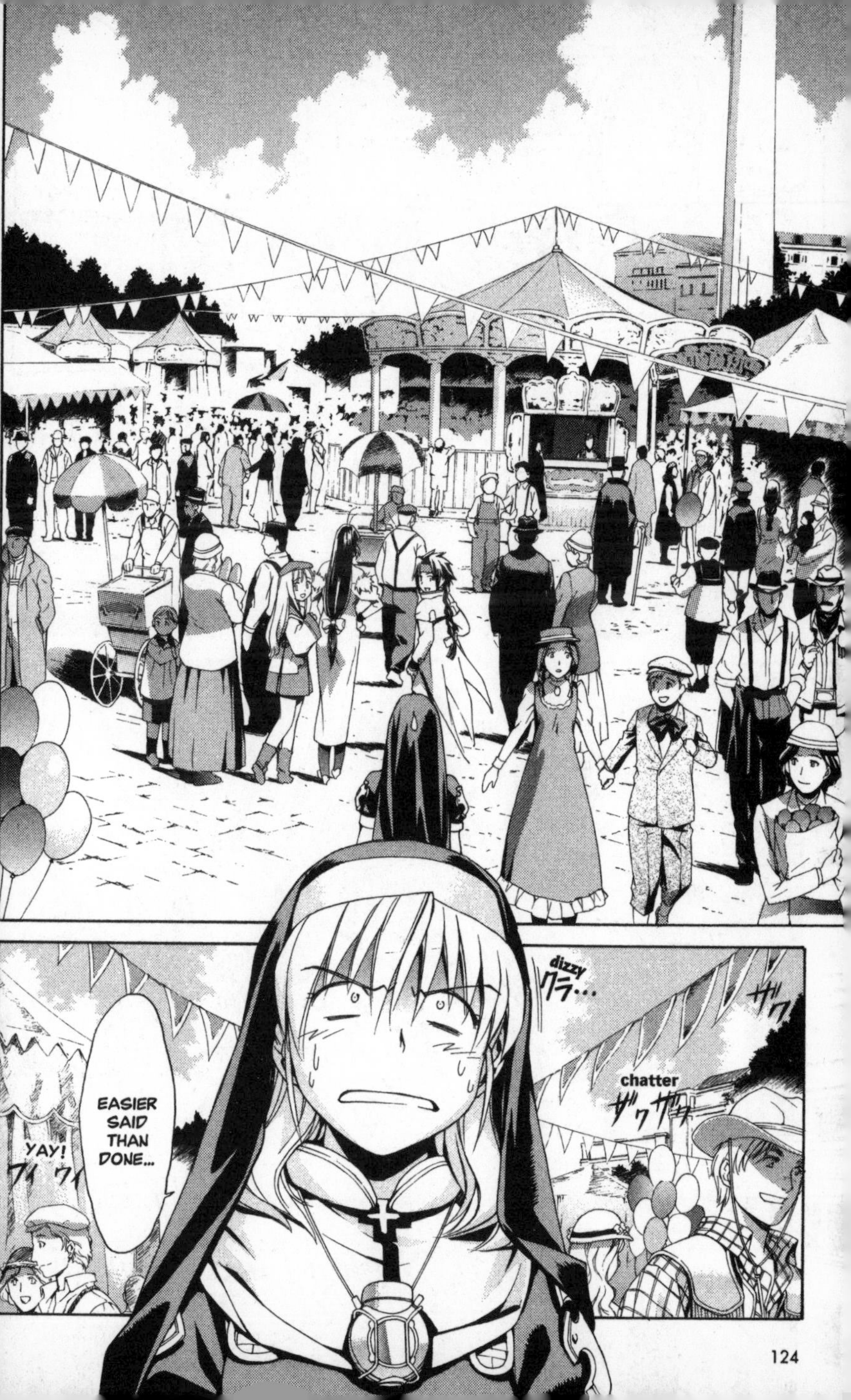
chatter
ザワザワ
ザワ
dizzy
クラ…
EASIER SAID THAN DONE...
YAY!
ワイ ワイ

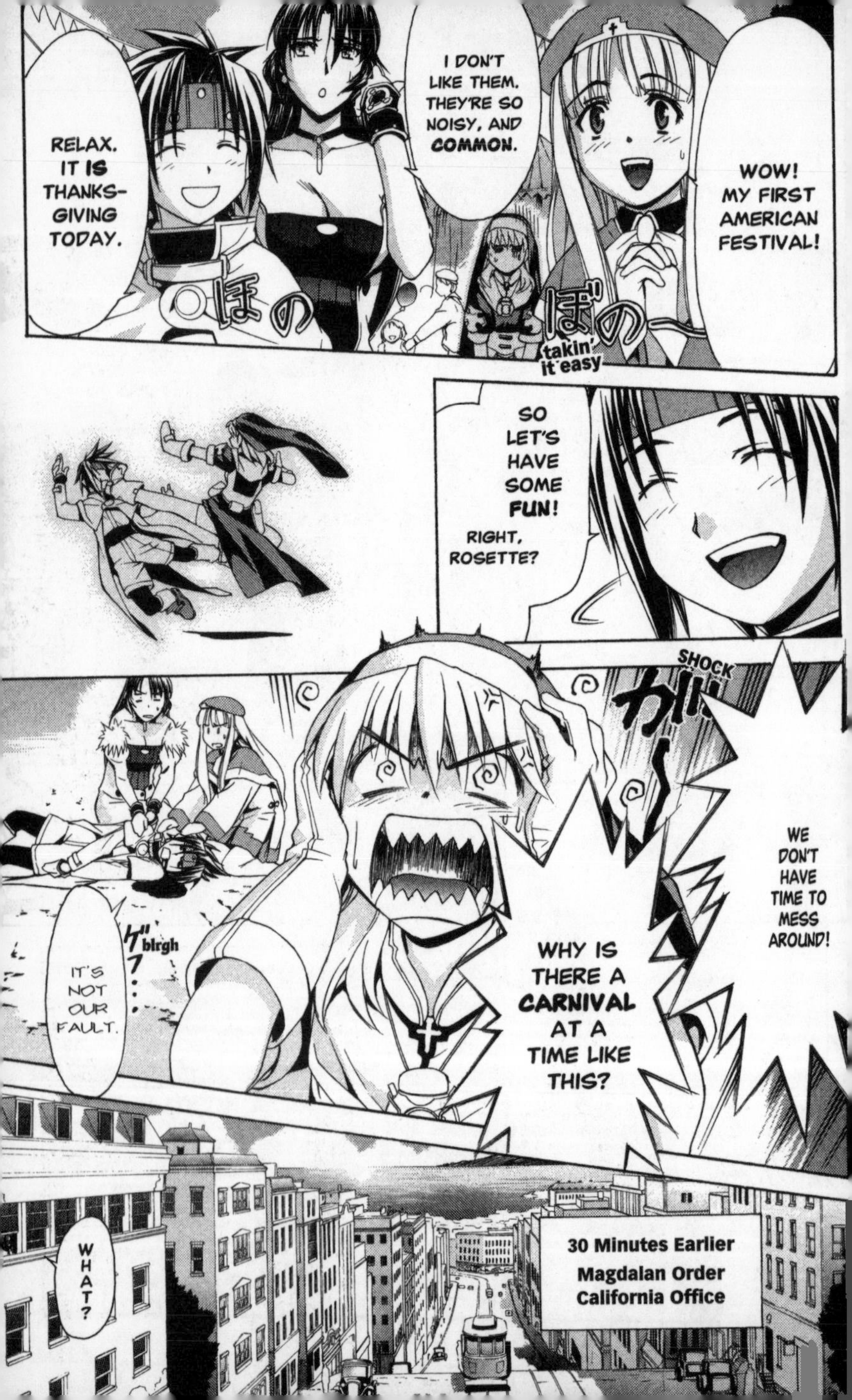
WOW! MY FIRST AMERICAN FESTIVAL!
I DON'T LIKE THEM. THEY'RE SO NOISY, AND COMMON.
RELAX. IT IS THANKS-GIVING TODAY.
ぽの
takin' it easy
ほの
SO LET'S HAVE SOME FUN!
RIGHT, ROSETTE?
SHOCK
WE DON'T HAVE TIME TO MESS AROUND!
WHY IS THERE A CARNIVAL AT A TIME LIKE THIS?
blrgh
IT'S NOT OUR FAULT.
30 Minutes Earlier
Magdalan Order California Office
WHAT?

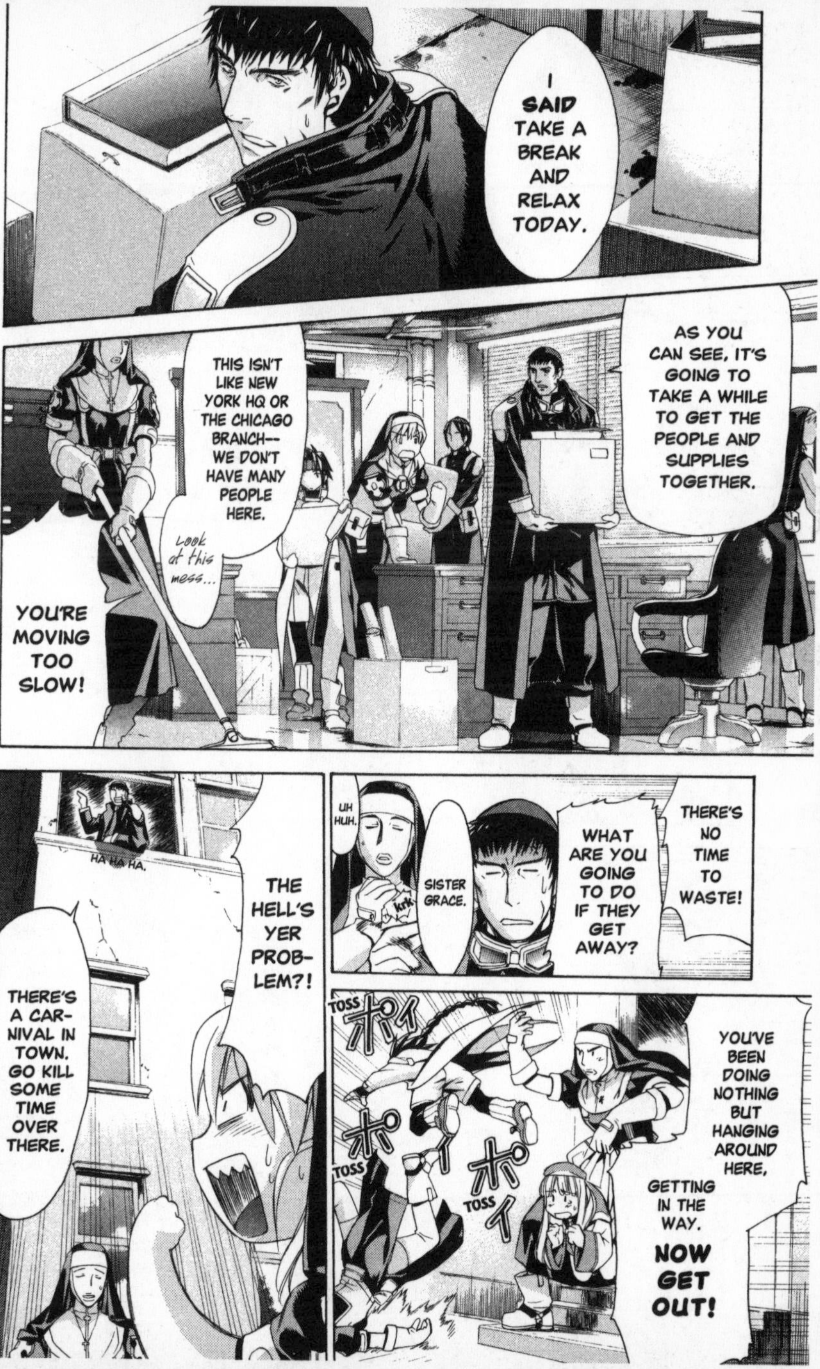
I SAID TAKE A BREAK AND RELAX TODAY.
AS YOU CAN SEE, IT'S GOING TO TAKE A WHILE TO GET THE PEOPLE AND SUPPLIES TOGETHER.
THIS ISN'T LIKE NEW YORK HQ OR THE CHICAGO BRANCH-- WE DON'T HAVE MANY PEOPLE HERE.
Look at this mess...
YOU'RE MOVING TOO SLOW!
THERE'S NO TIME TO WASTE!
WHAT ARE YOU GOING TO DO IF THEY GET AWAY?
SISTER GRACE.
UH HUH.
krk
YOU'VE BEEN DOING NOTHING BUT HANGING AROUND HERE,
GETTING IN THE WAY.
NOW GET OUT!
TOSS
ポイ
TOSS
ポイ
TOSS
ポイ
THE HELL'S YER PROBLEM?!
HA HA HA.
THERE'S A CARNIVAL IN TOWN. GO KILL SOME TIME OVER THERE.

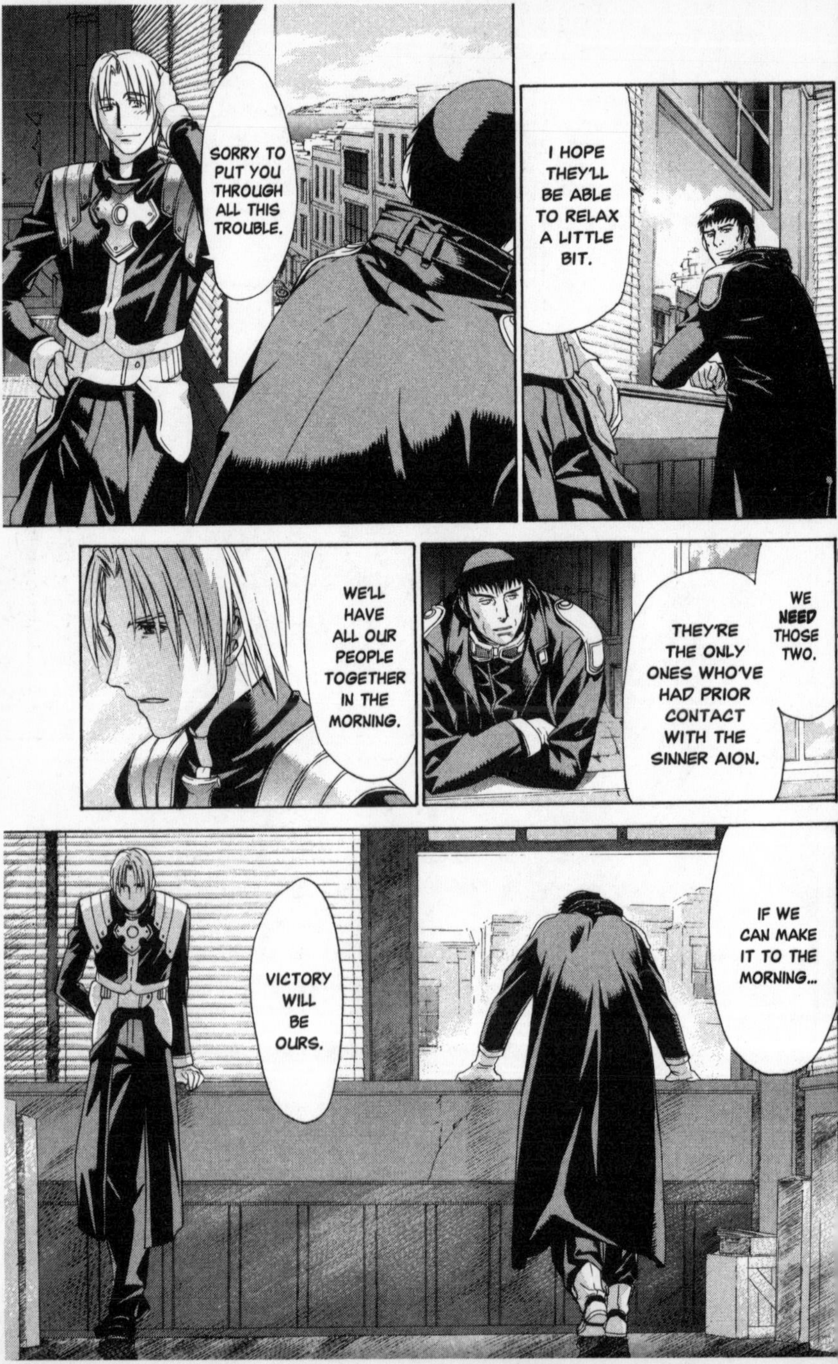
I HOPE THEY'LL BE ABLE TO RELAX A LITTLE BIT.
SORRY TO PUT YOU THROUGH ALL THIS TROUBLE.
WE **NEED** THOSE TWO.
THEY'RE THE ONLY ONES WHO'VE HAD PRIOR CONTACT WITH THE SINNER AION.
WE'LL HAVE ALL OUR PEOPLE TOGETHER IN THE MORNING.
IF WE CAN MAKE IT TO THE MORNING...
VICTORY WILL BE OURS.

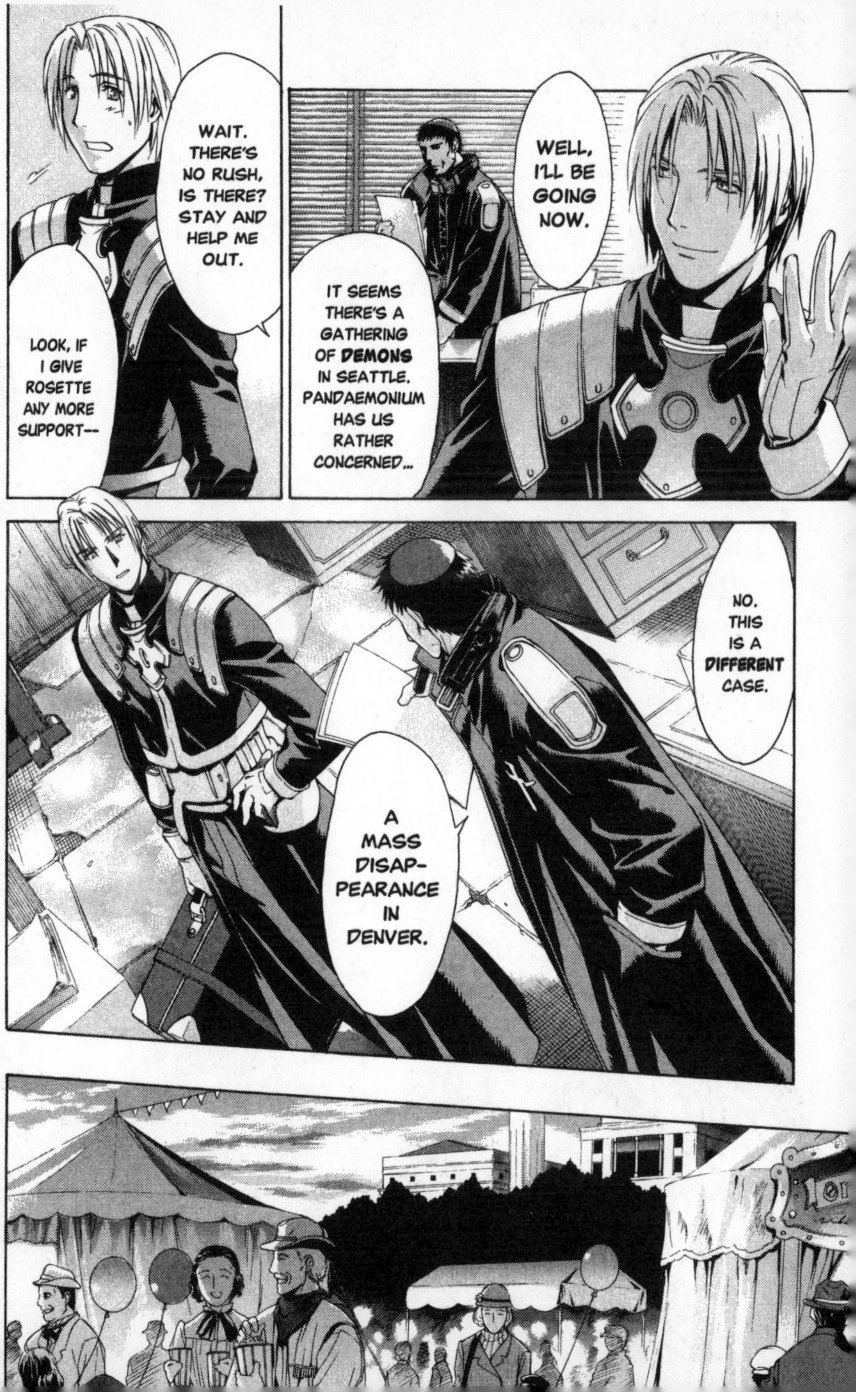
WELL, I'LL BE GOING NOW.
IT SEEMS THERE'S A GATHERING OF **DEMONS** IN SEATTLE. PANDAEMONIUM HAS US RATHER CONCERNED...
WAIT. THERE'S NO RUSH, IS THERE? STAY AND HELP ME OUT.
LOOK, IF I GIVE ROSETTE ANY MORE SUPPORT--
NO. THIS IS A **DIFFERENT** CASE.
A MASS DISAP-PEARANCE IN DENVER.

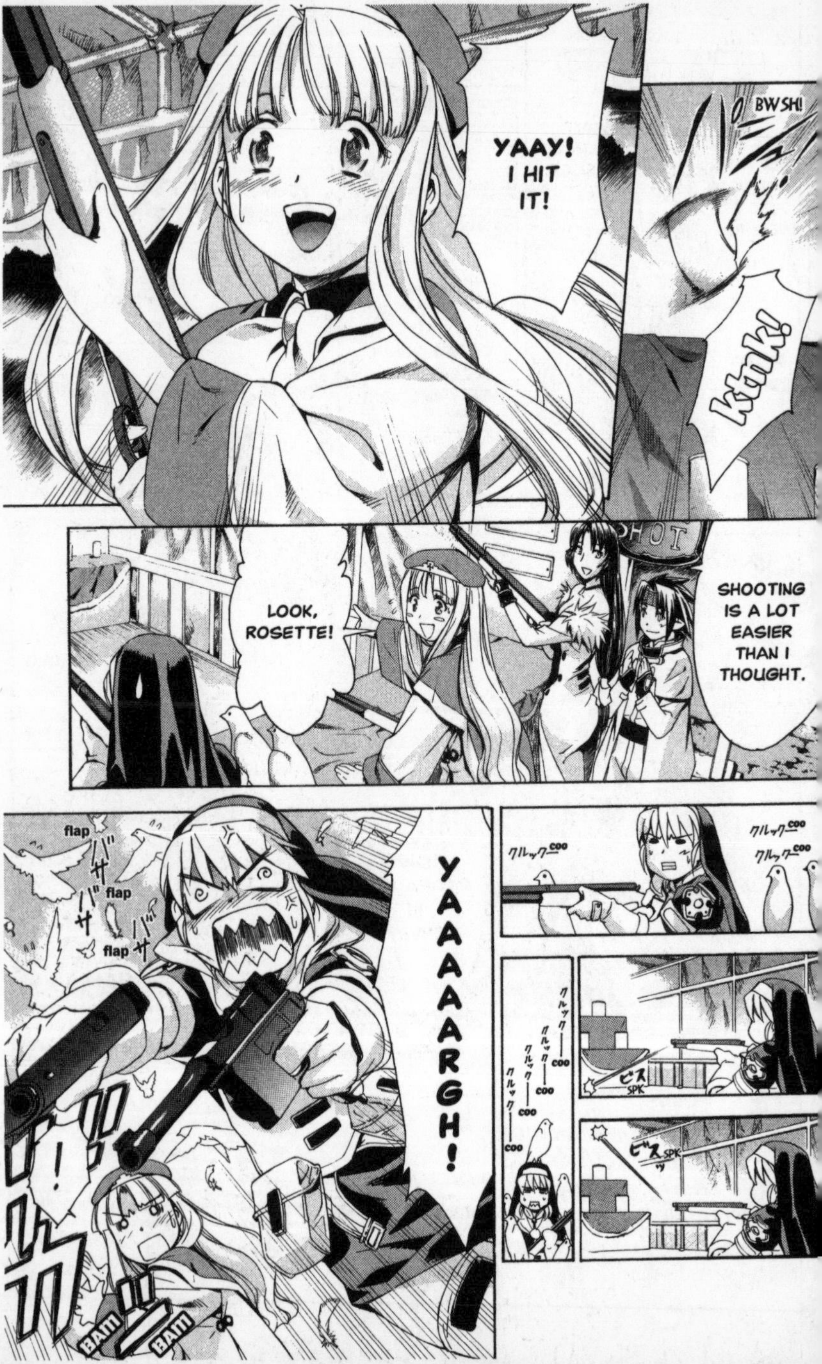

BWSH!
ktnk!
YAAY! I HIT IT!
SHOOTING IS A LOT EASIER THAN I THOUGHT.
LOOK, ROSETTE!
クルックー coo
クルックー coo
クルックー coo
ビス SPK
ビス SPK
クルックー coo
クルックー coo
クルックー coo
クルックー coo
YAAAAAARGH!
flap
flap
flap
BAM
BAM

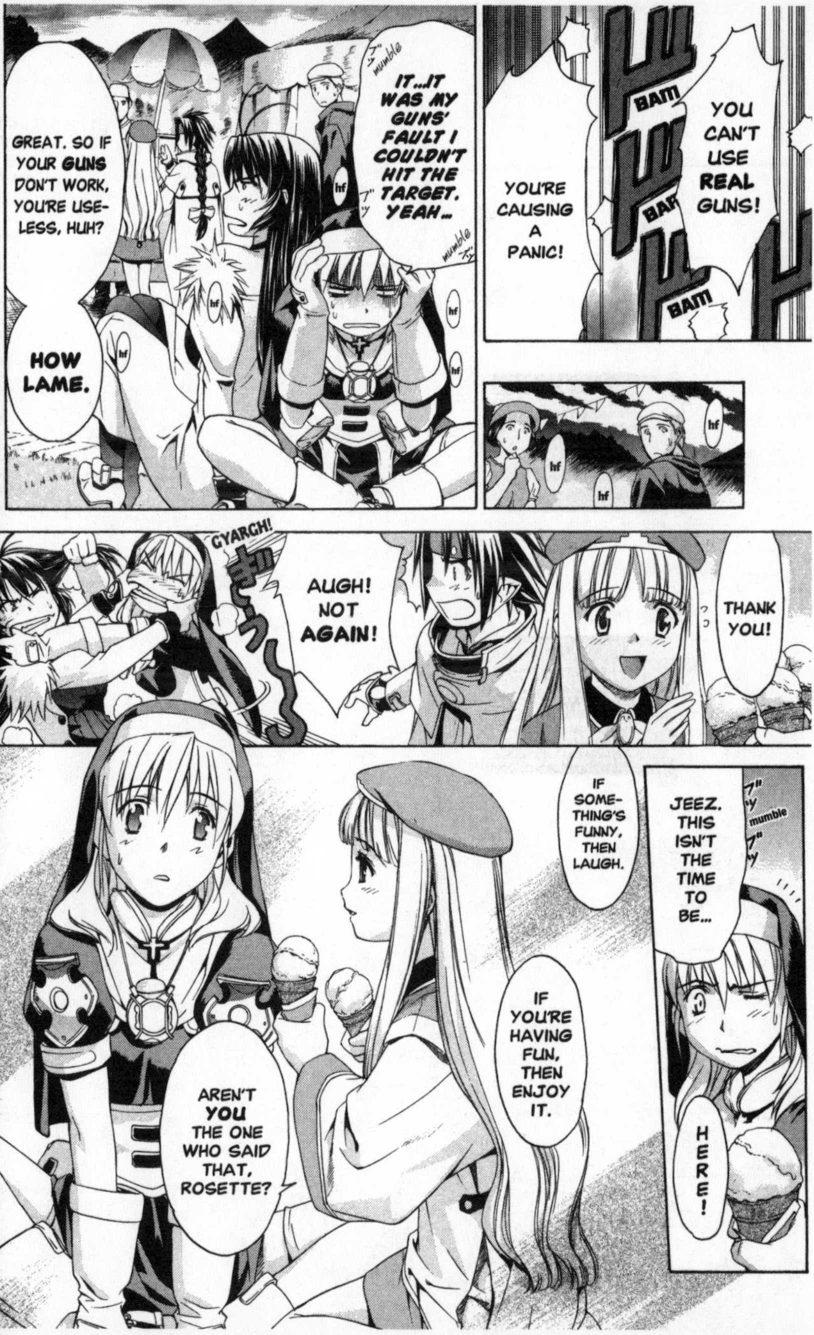
YOU CAN'T USE REAL GUNS!
BAM
BAM
BAM
YOU'RE CAUSING A PANIC!
hf
hf
hf
IT...IT WAS MY GUNS' FAULT I COULDN'T HIT THE TARGET. YEAH...
mumble
mumble
hf
GREAT. SO IF YOUR GUNS DON'T WORK, YOU'RE USE-LESS, HUH?
hf
hf
hf
hf
HOW LAME.
THANK YOU!
AUGH! NOT AGAIN!
GYARGH!
JEEZ. THIS ISN'T THE TIME TO BE...
mumble
HERE!
IF SOME-THING'S FUNNY, THEN LAUGH.
IF YOU'RE HAVING FUN, THEN ENJOY IT.
AREN'T YOU THE ONE WHO SAID THAT, ROSETTE?

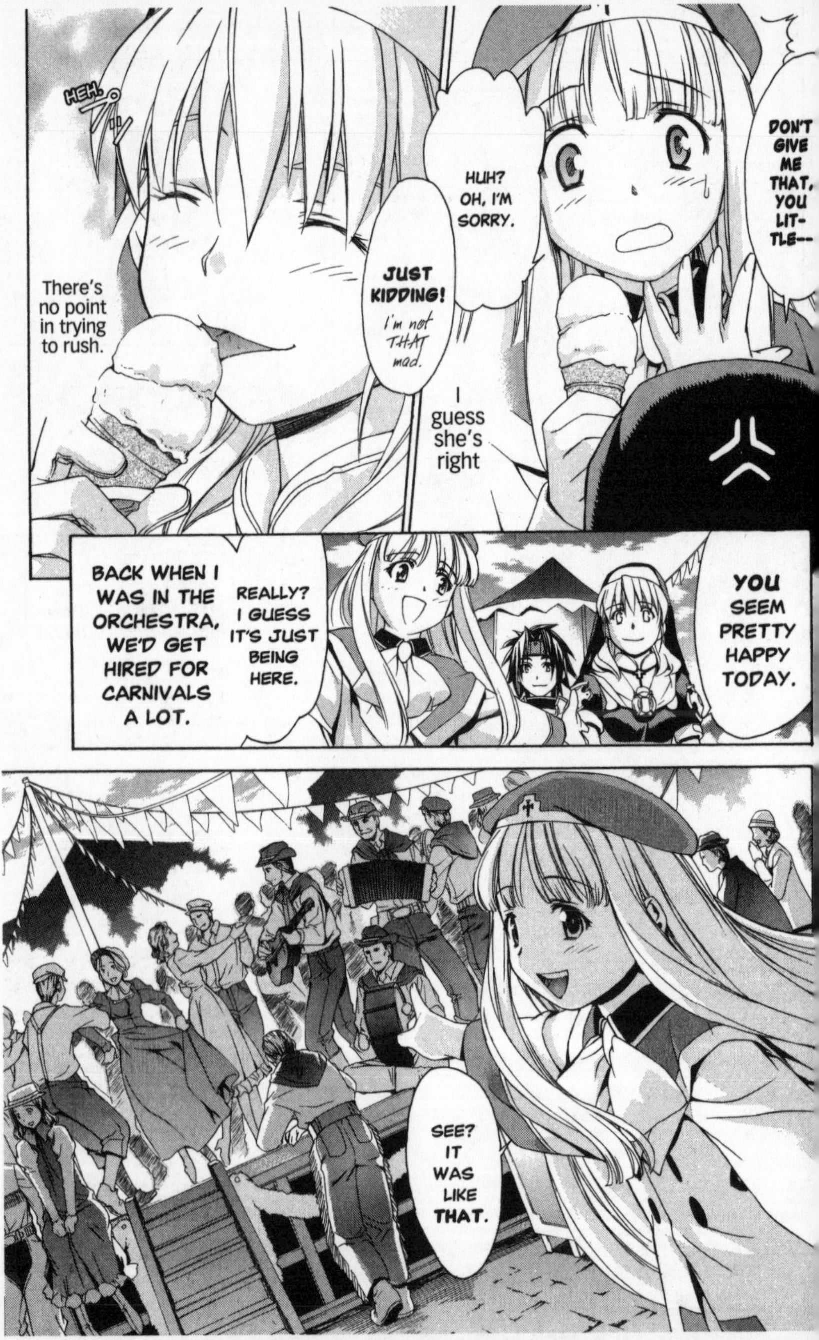
DON'T GIVE ME THAT, YOU LIT-TLE--
HUH? OH, I'M SORRY.
I guess she's right
HEH.
JUST KIDDING! I'm not THAT mad.
There's no point in trying to rush.
YOU SEEM PRETTY HAPPY TODAY.
REALLY? I GUESS IT'S JUST BEING HERE.
BACK WHEN I WAS IN THE ORCHESTRA, WE'D GET HIRED FOR CARNIVALS A LOT.
SEE? IT WAS LIKE THAT.

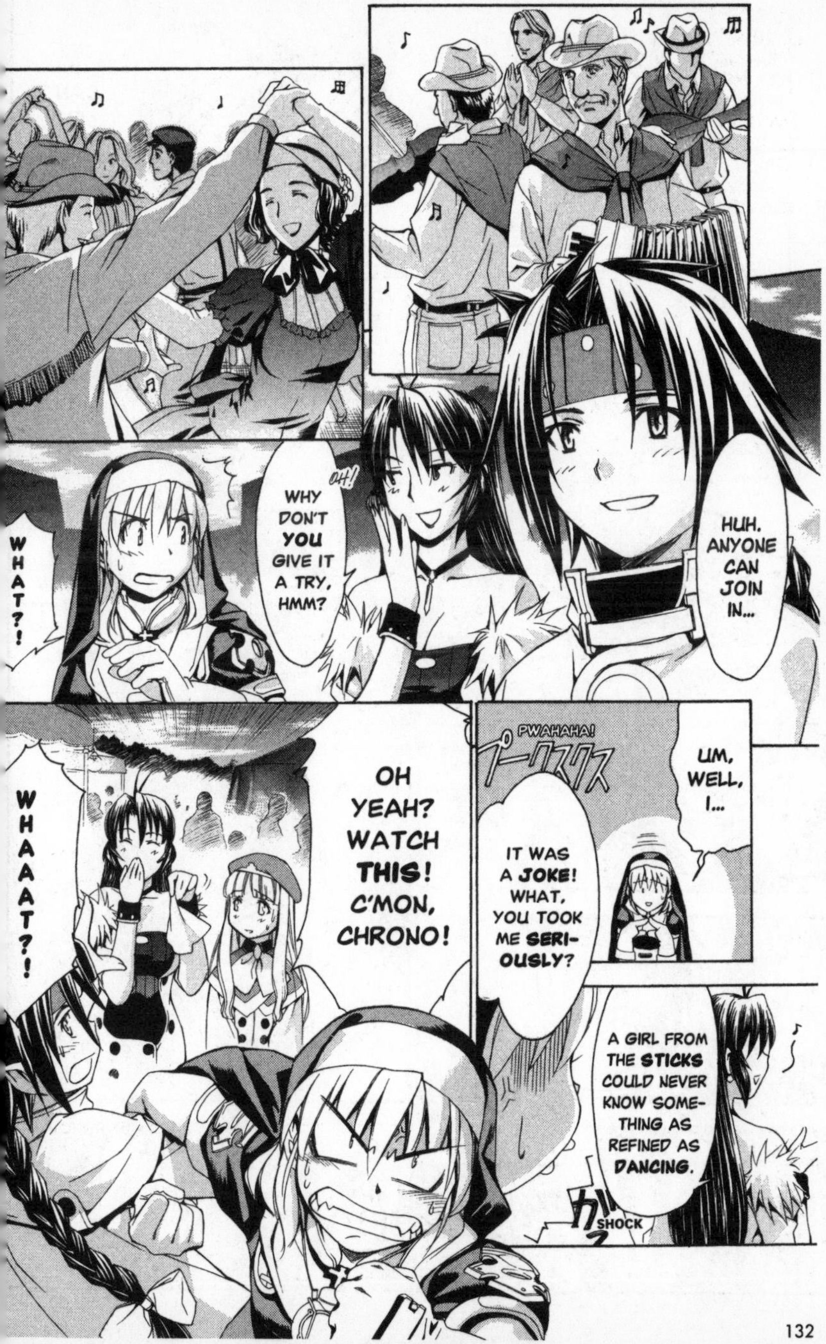
HUH. ANYONE CAN JOIN IN...
OH!
WHY DON'T **YOU** GIVE IT A TRY, HMM?
WHAT?!
UM, WELL, I...
PWAHAHA!
プークスクス
IT WAS A **JOKE**! WHAT, YOU TOOK ME **SERIOUSLY**?
A GIRL FROM THE **STICKS** COULD NEVER KNOW SOMETHING AS REFINED AS **DANCING**.
カッ
SHOCK
OH YEAH? WATCH **THIS**! C'MON, CHRONO!
WHAAAAT?!

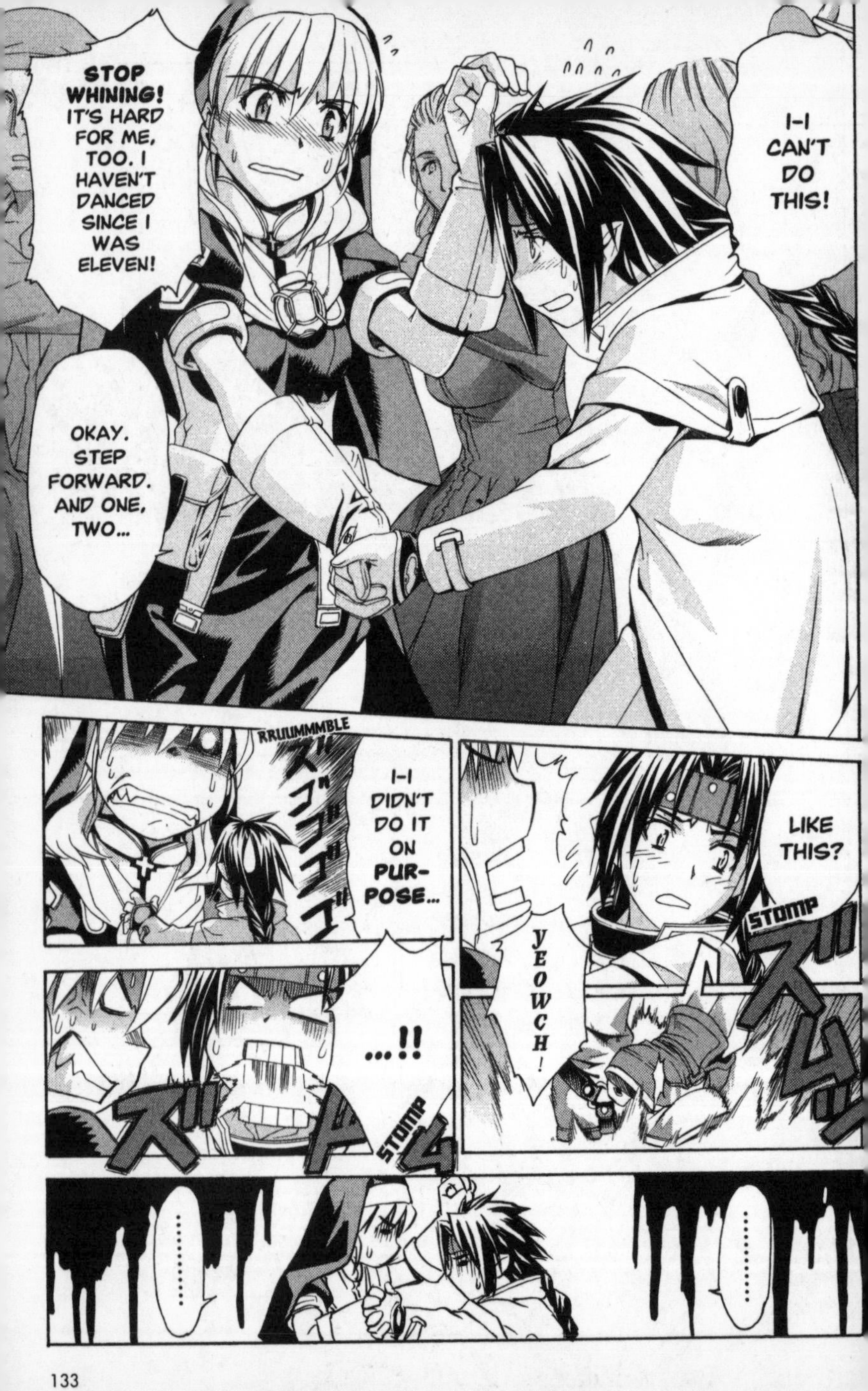
I-I CAN'T DO THIS!
STOP WHINING! IT'S HARD FOR ME, TOO. I HAVEN'T DANCED SINCE I WAS ELEVEN!
OKAY. STEP FORWARD. AND ONE, TWO...
LIKE THIS?
STOMP
RRUUMMMBLE
I-I DIDN'T DO IT ON PURPOSE...
YEOWCH!
...!!
STOMP
......
......

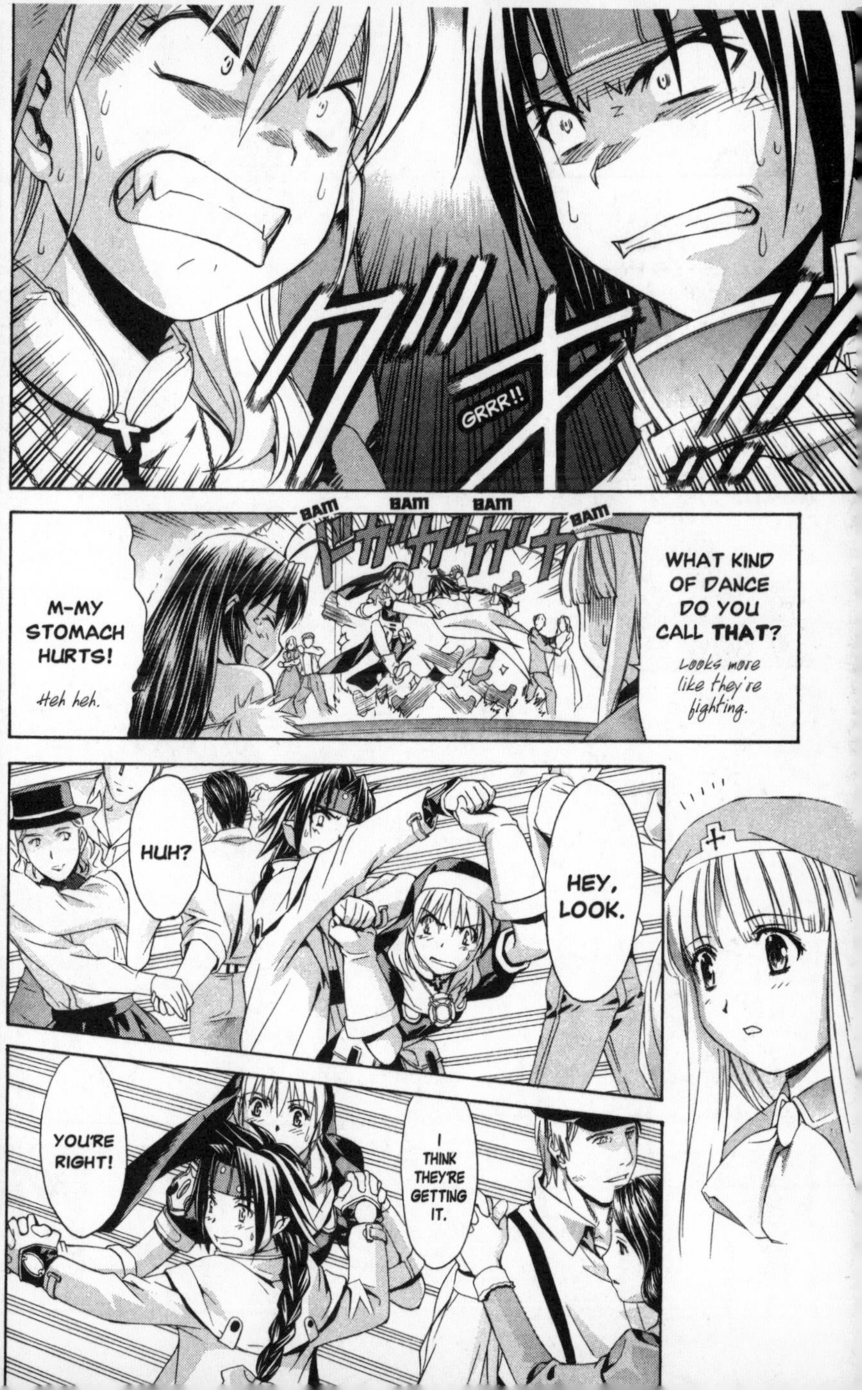
GRRR!!
BAM
BAM
BAM
BAM
WHAT KIND OF DANCE DO YOU CALL THAT?
Looks more like they're fighting.
M-MY STOMACH HURTS!
Heh heh.
HEY, LOOK.
HUH?
I THINK THEY'RE GETTING IT.
YOU'RE RIGHT!

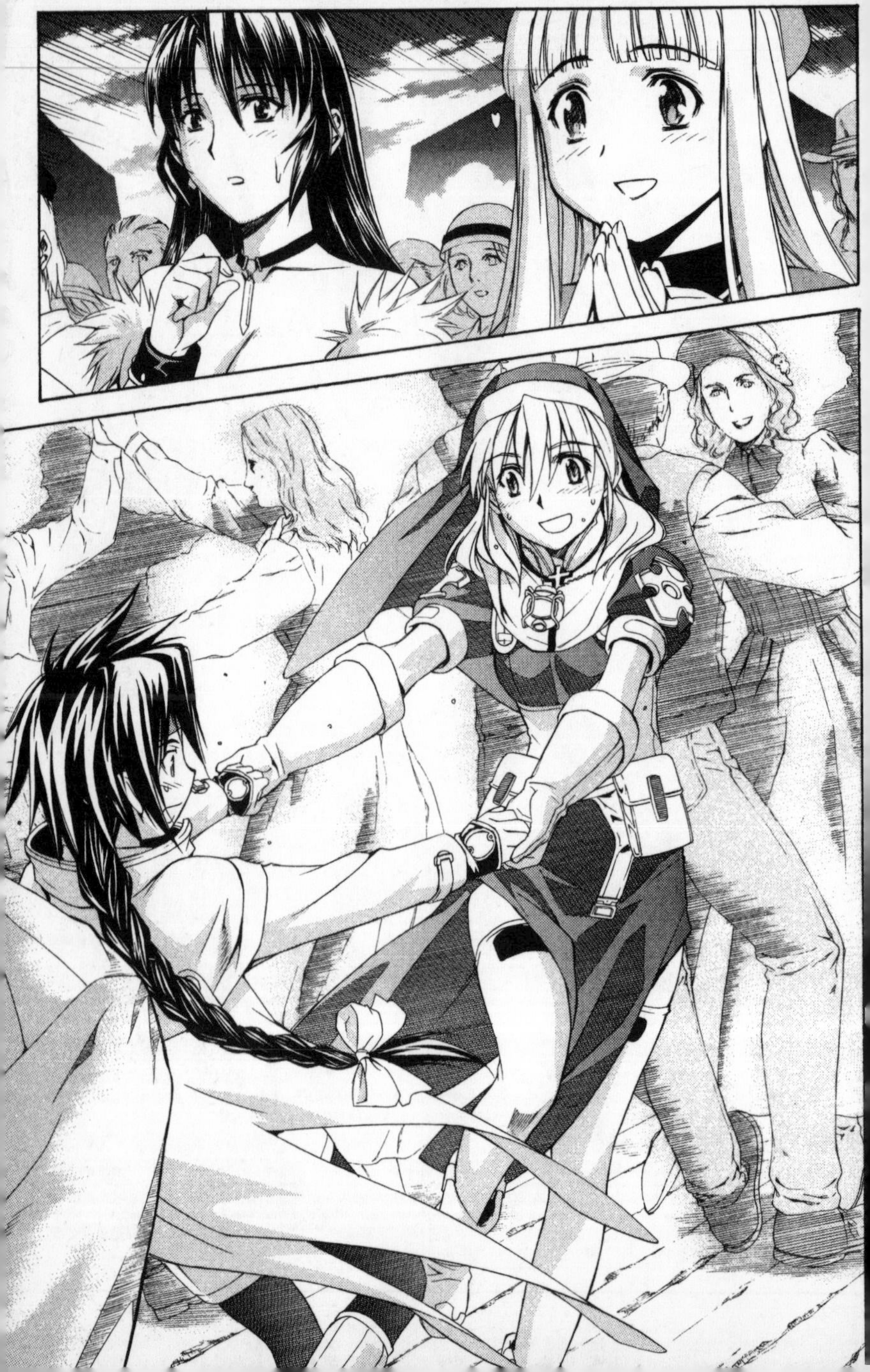

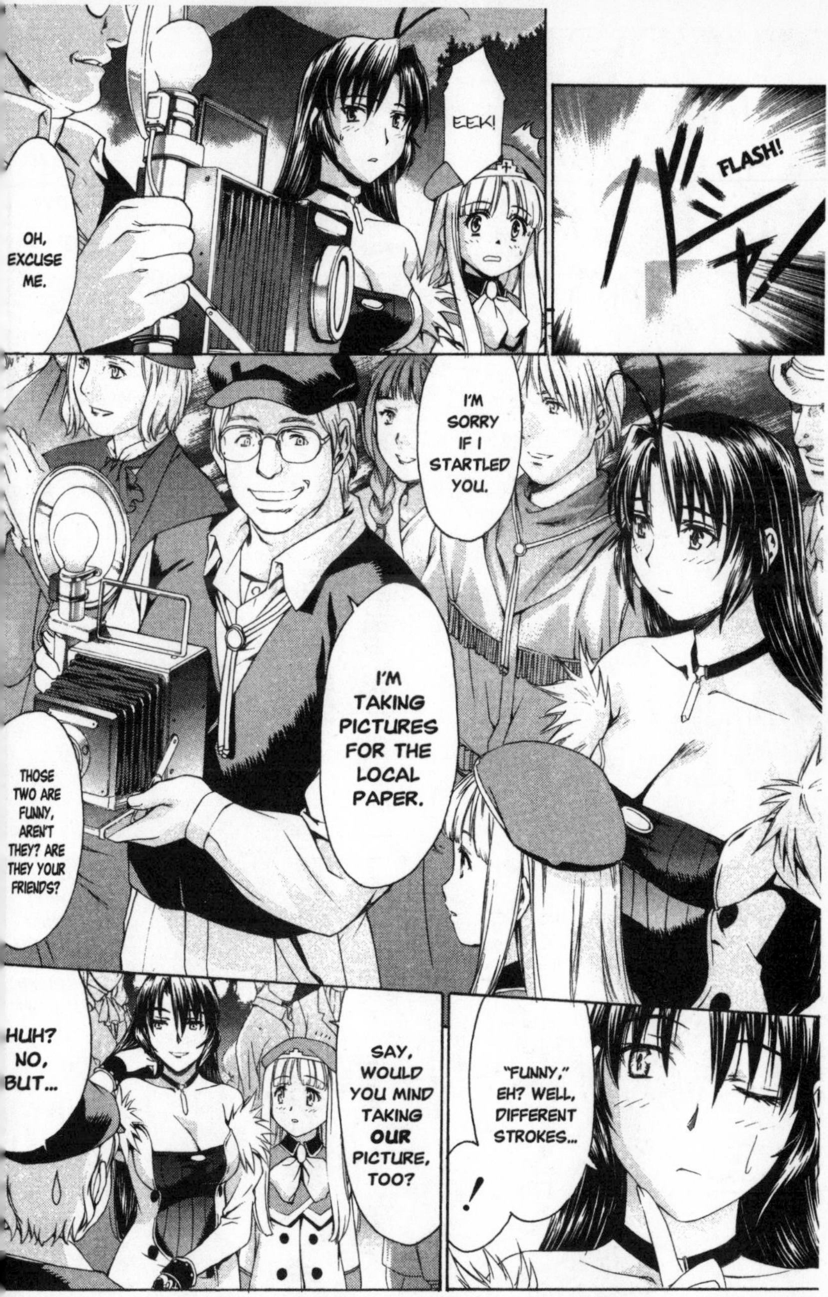
FLASH!
EEK!
OH, EXCUSE ME.
I'M SORRY IF I STARTLED YOU.
I'M TAKING PICTURES FOR THE LOCAL PAPER.
THOSE TWO ARE FUNNY, AREN'T THEY? ARE THEY YOUR FRIENDS?
"FUNNY," EH? WELL, DIFFERENT STROKES...
!
SAY, WOULD YOU MIND TAKING **OUR** PICTURE, TOO?
HUH? NO, BUT...

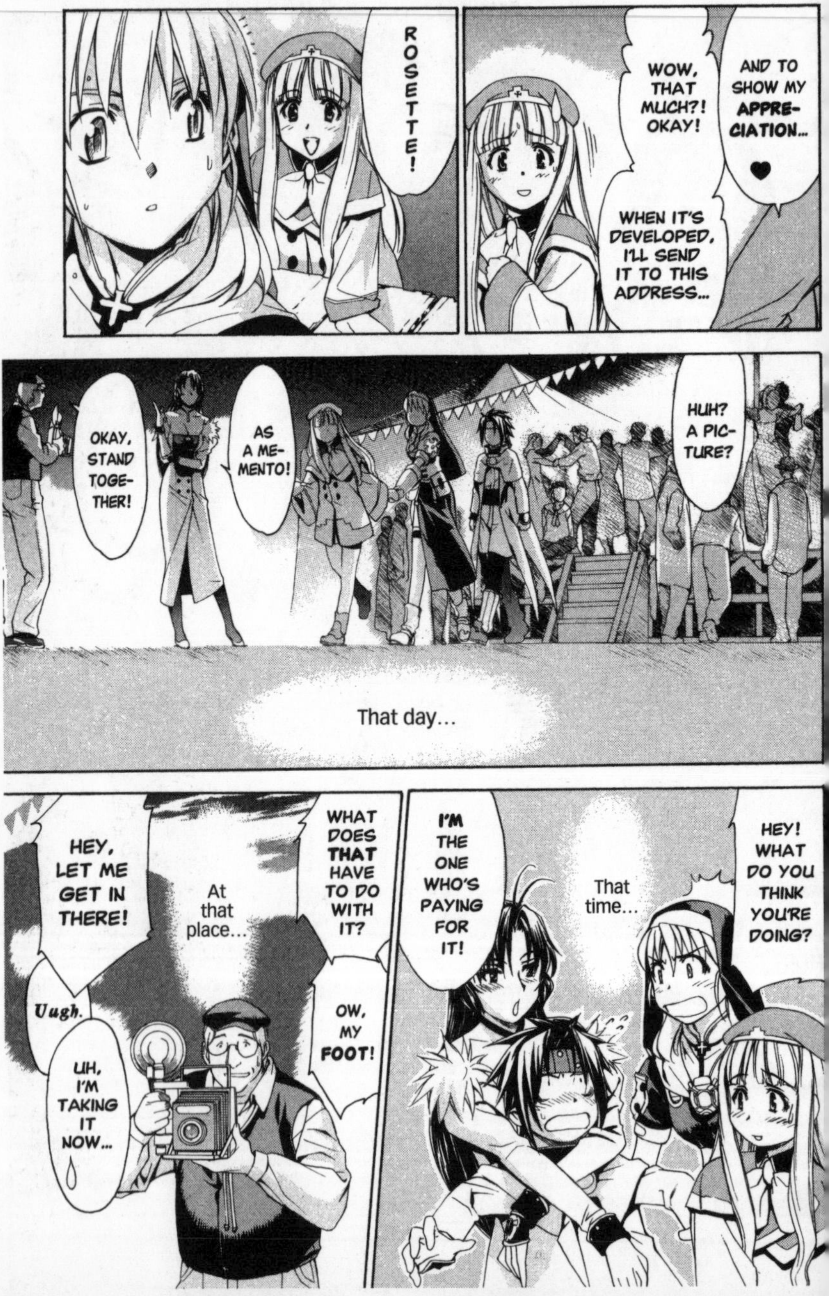
AND TO SHOW MY APPRECIATION... ♥
WOW, THAT MUCH?! OKAY!
WHEN IT'S DEVELOPED, I'LL SEND IT TO THIS ADDRESS...
ROSETTE!
HUH? A PICTURE?
AS A MEMENTO!
OKAY, STAND TOGETHER!
That day...
HEY! WHAT DO YOU THINK YOU'RE DOING?
That time...
I'M THE ONE WHO'S PAYING FOR IT!
WHAT DOES THAT HAVE TO DO WITH IT?
At that place...
HEY, LET ME GET IN THERE!
OW, MY FOOT!
Uugh.
UH, I'M TAKING IT NOW...

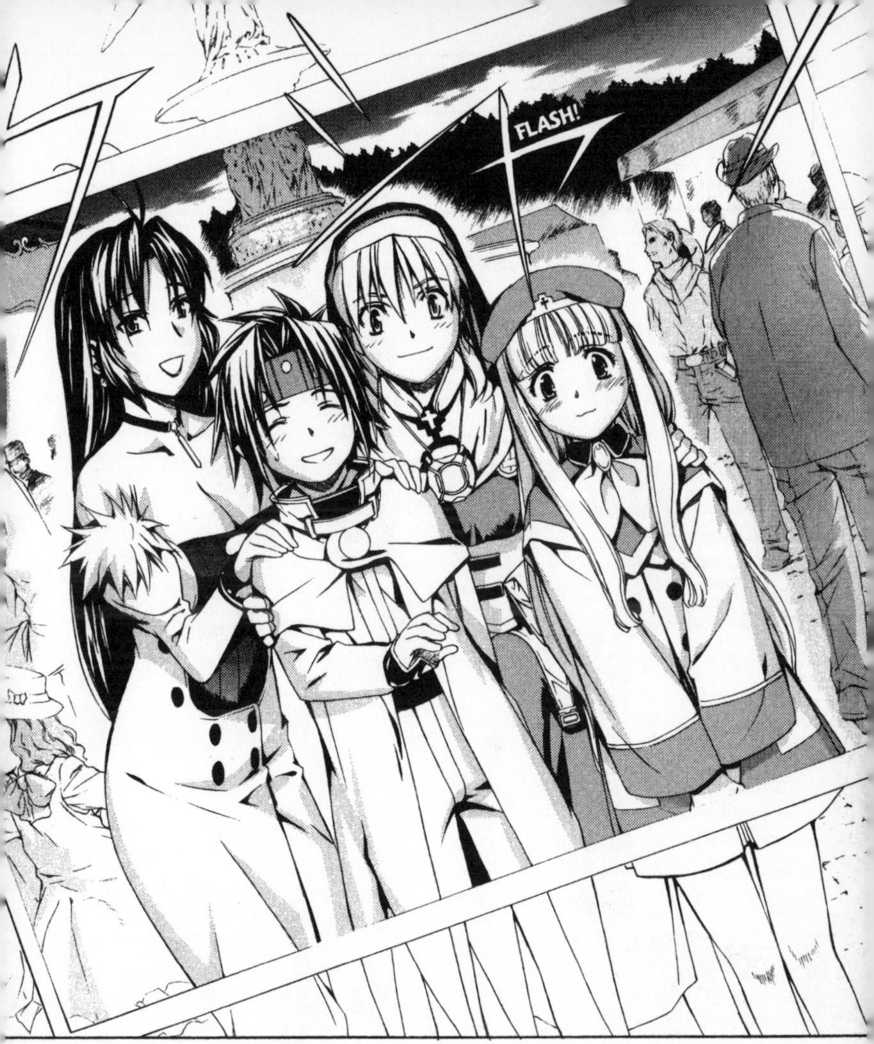
FLASH!

An irreplaceable moment was born.

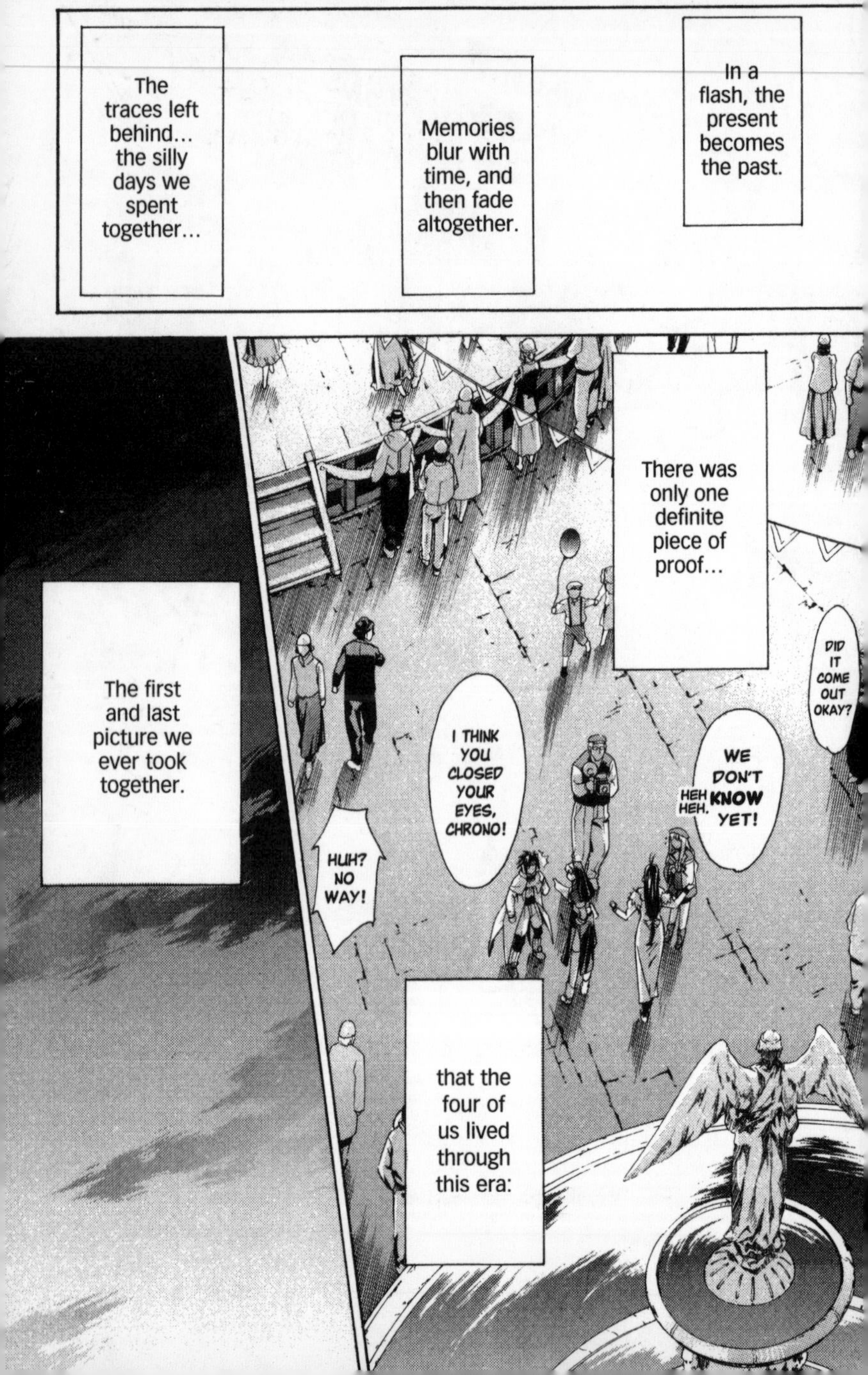
In a flash, the present becomes the past.
Memories blur with time, and then fade altogether.
The traces left behind... the silly days we spent together...
There was only one definite piece of proof...
DID IT COME OUT OKAY?
WE DON'T KNOW YET!
HEH HEH.
I THINK YOU CLOSED YOUR EYES, CHRONO!
HUH? NO WAY!
that the four of us lived through this era:
The first and last picture we ever took together.

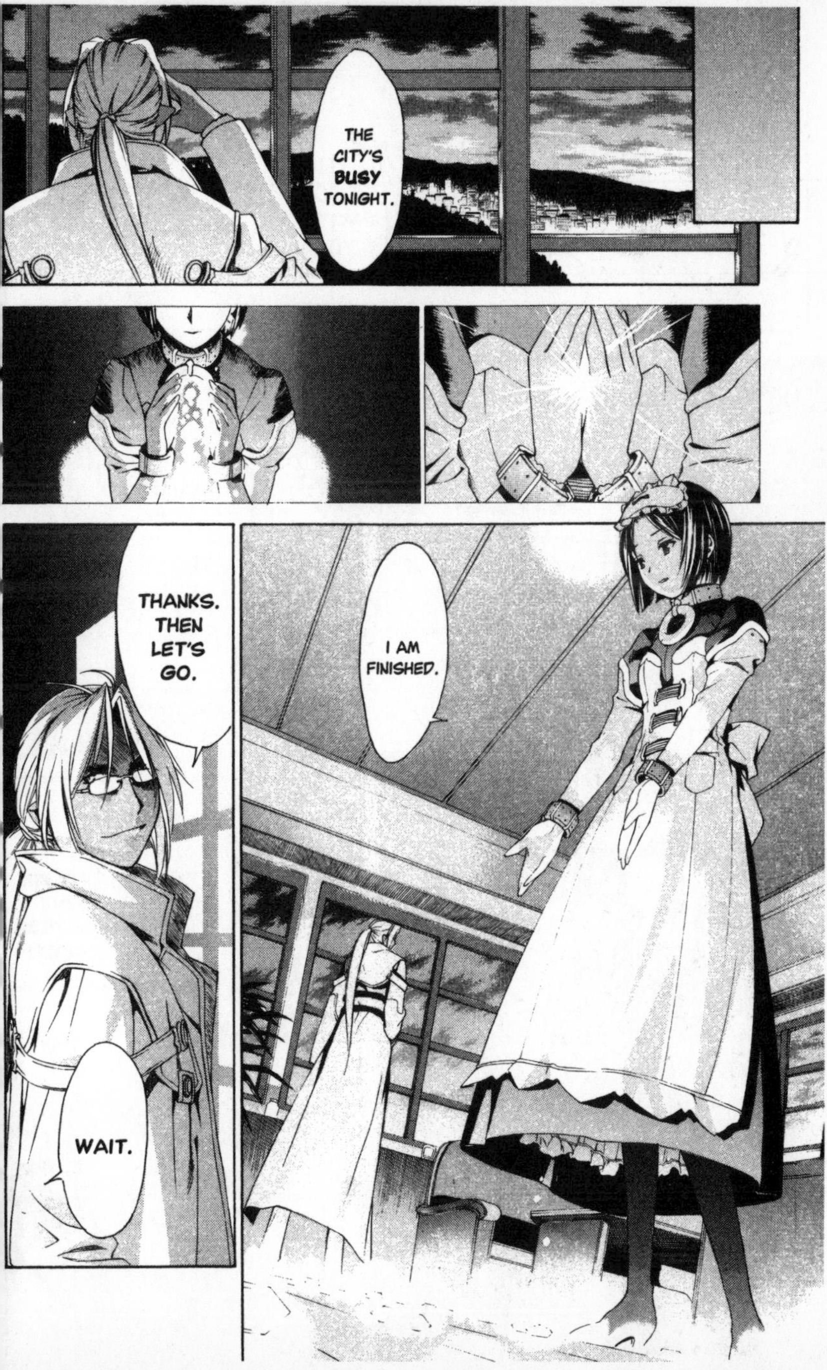
THE CITY'S BUSY TONIGHT.
I AM FINISHED.
THANKS. THEN LET'S GO.
WAIT.

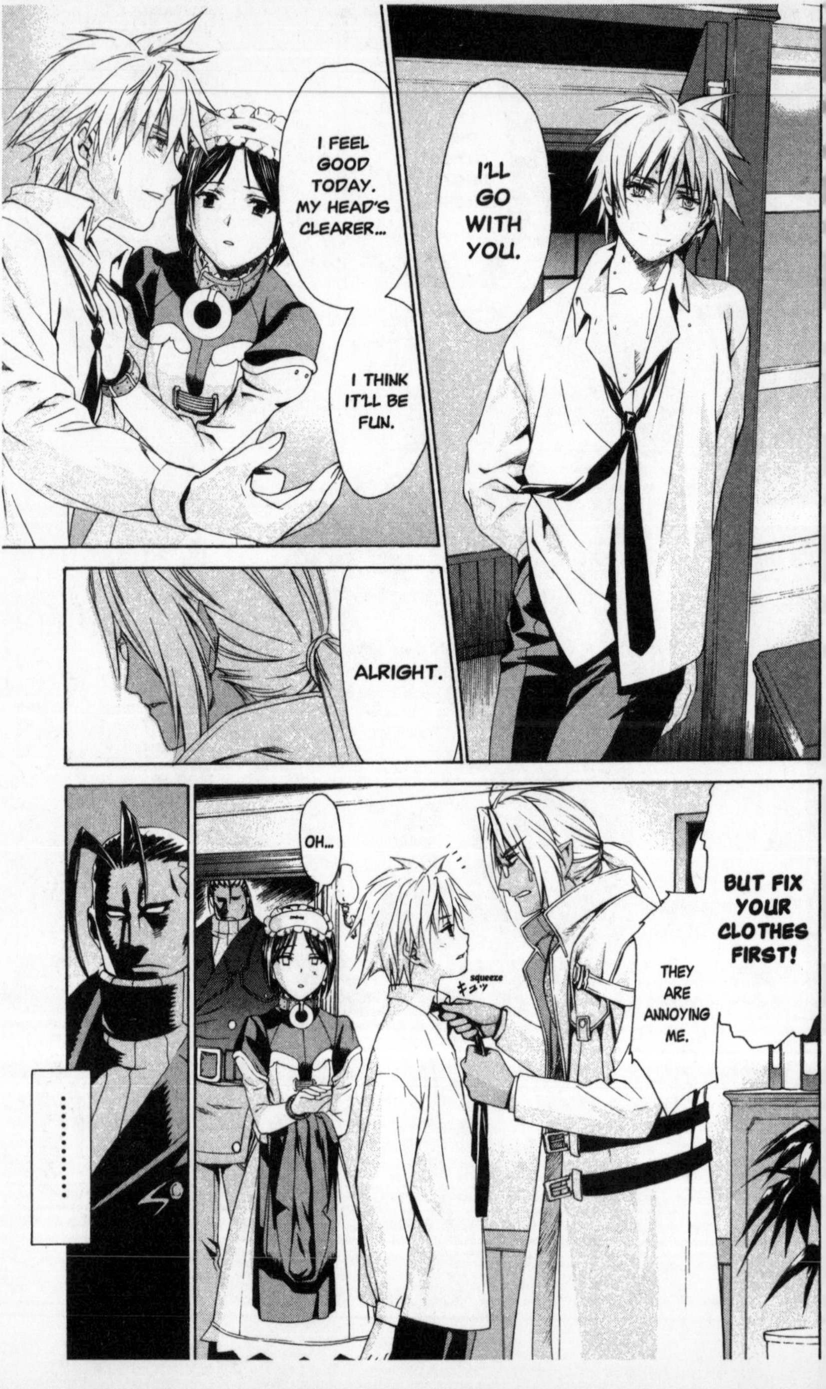
I'LL GO WITH YOU.
I FEEL GOOD TODAY. MY HEAD'S CLEARER...
I THINK IT'LL BE FUN.
ALRIGHT.
BUT FIX YOUR CLOTHES FIRST!
THEY ARE ANNOYING ME.
squeeze
キュッ
OH...
......

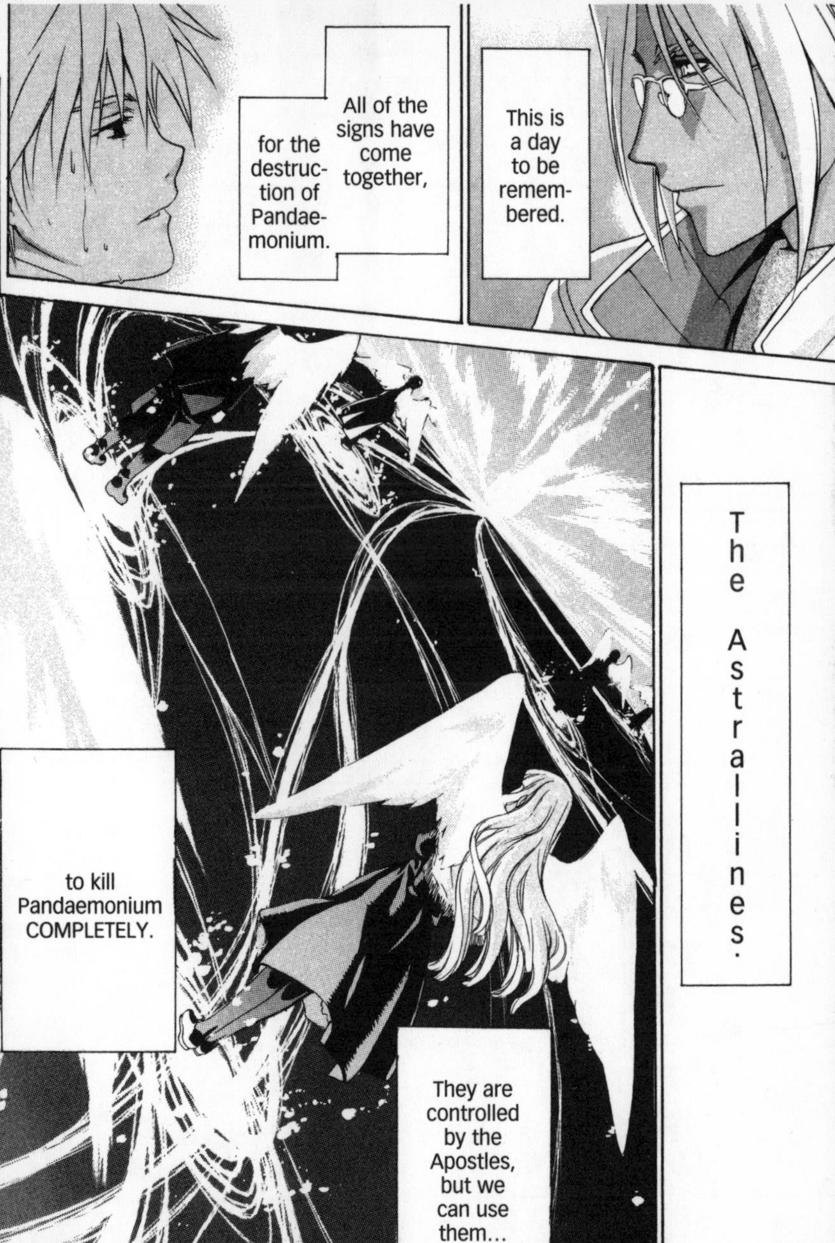
This is a day to be remembered.
All of the signs have come together,
for the destruction of Pandaemonium.
The Astrallines.
They are controlled by the Apostles, but we can use them...
to kill Pandaemonium COMPLETELY.

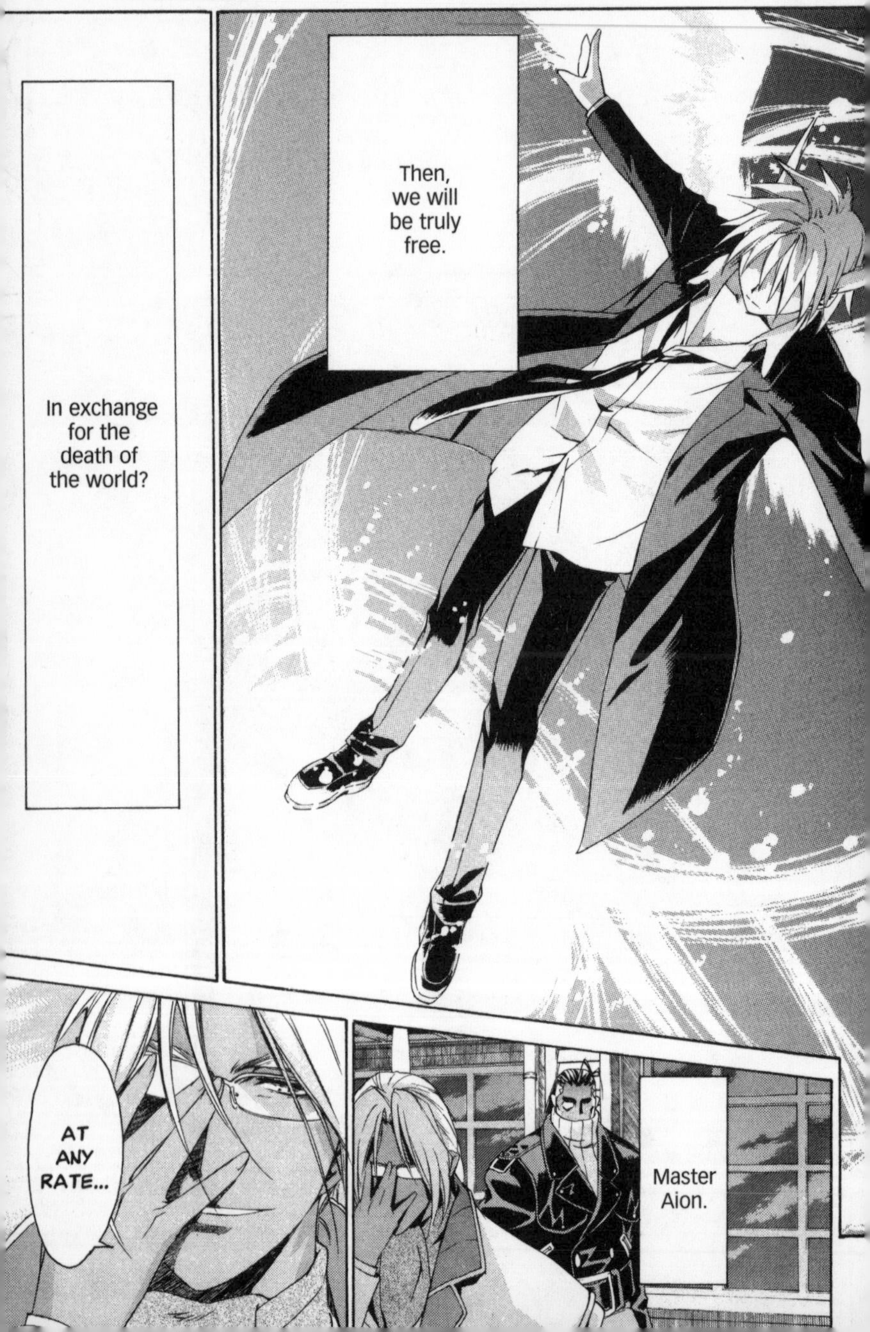
Then, we will be truly free.
In exchange for the death of the world?
Master Aion.
AT ANY RATE...

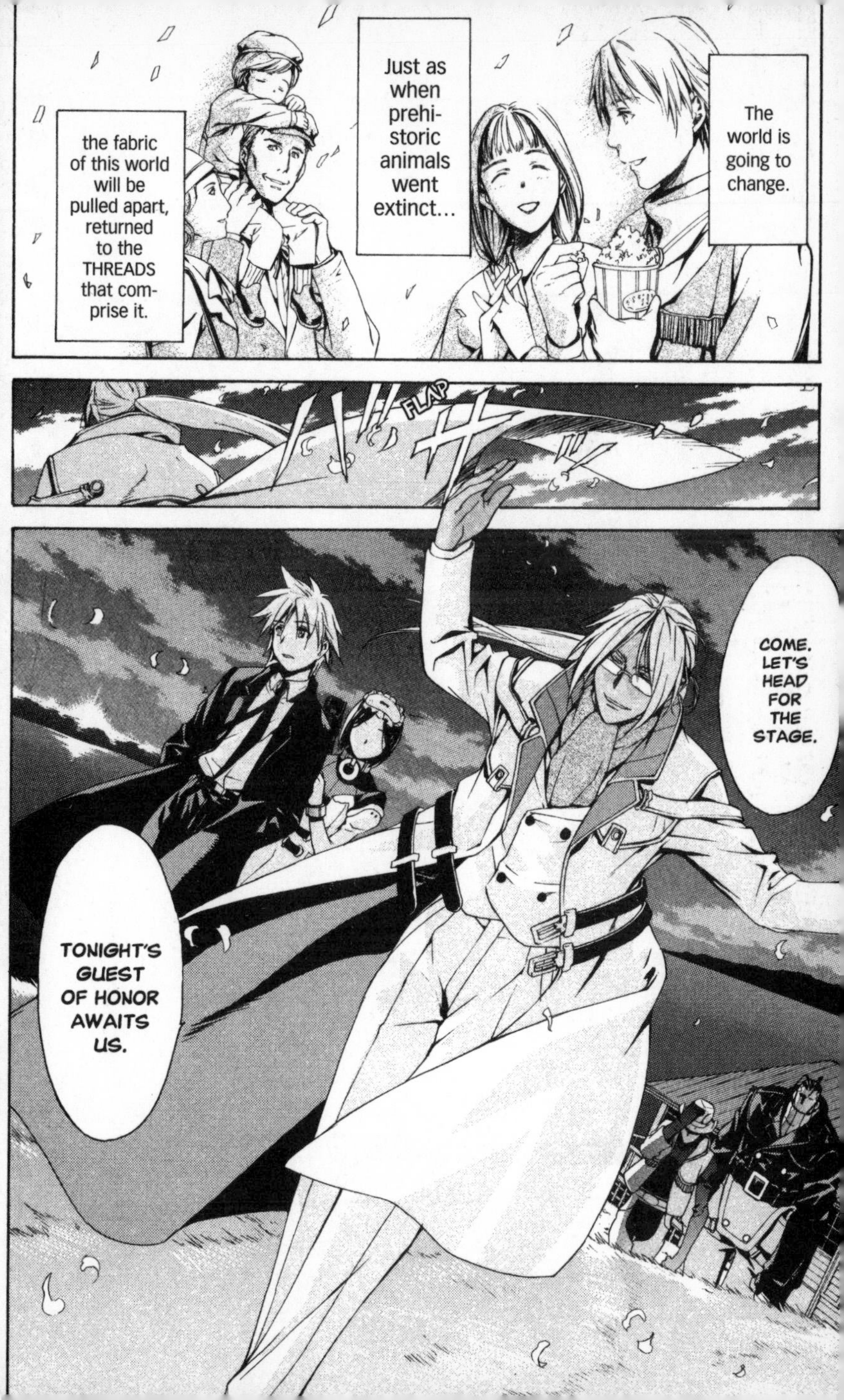
The world is going to change.
Just as when prehistoric animals went extinct…
the fabric of this world will be pulled apart, returned to the THREADS that comprise it.
FLAP
COME. LET'S HEAD FOR THE STAGE.
TONIGHT'S GUEST OF HONOR AWAITS US.

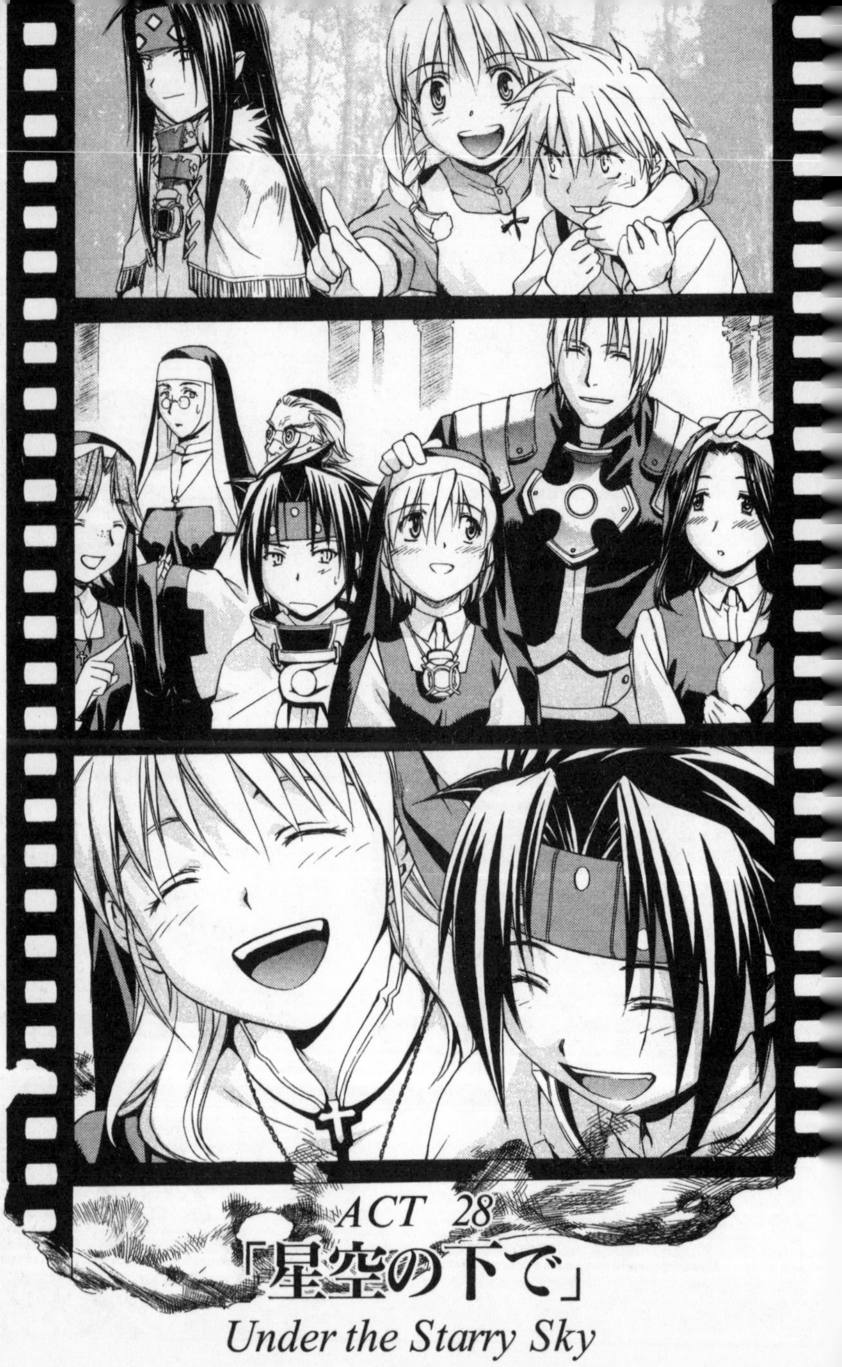

ACT 28
「星空の下で」
Under the Starry Sky

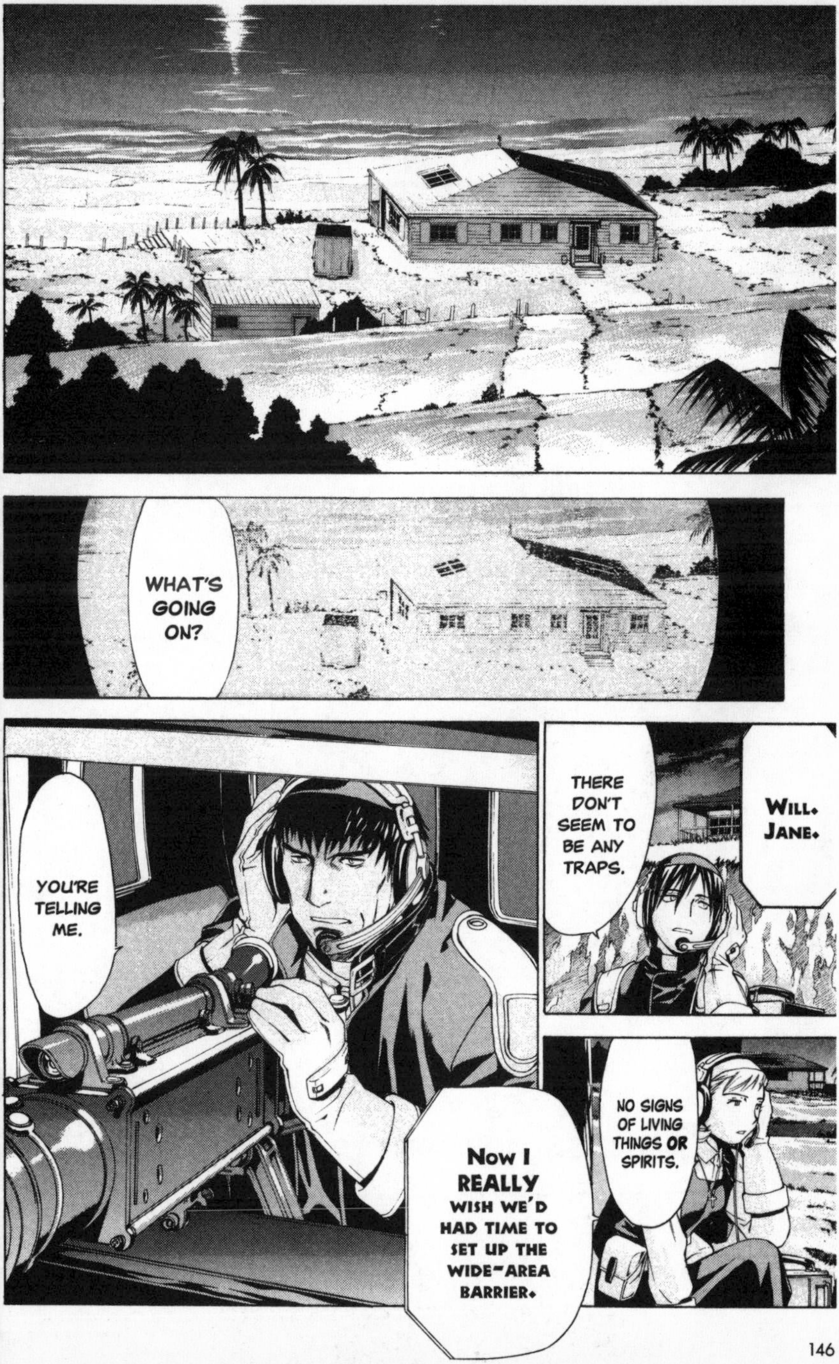
WHAT'S GOING ON?
WILL. JANE.
THERE DON'T SEEM TO BE ANY TRAPS.
NO SIGNS OF LIVING THINGS OR SPIRITS.
Now I REALLY WISH WE'D HAD TIME TO SET UP THE WIDE-AREA BARRIER.
YOU'RE TELLING ME.

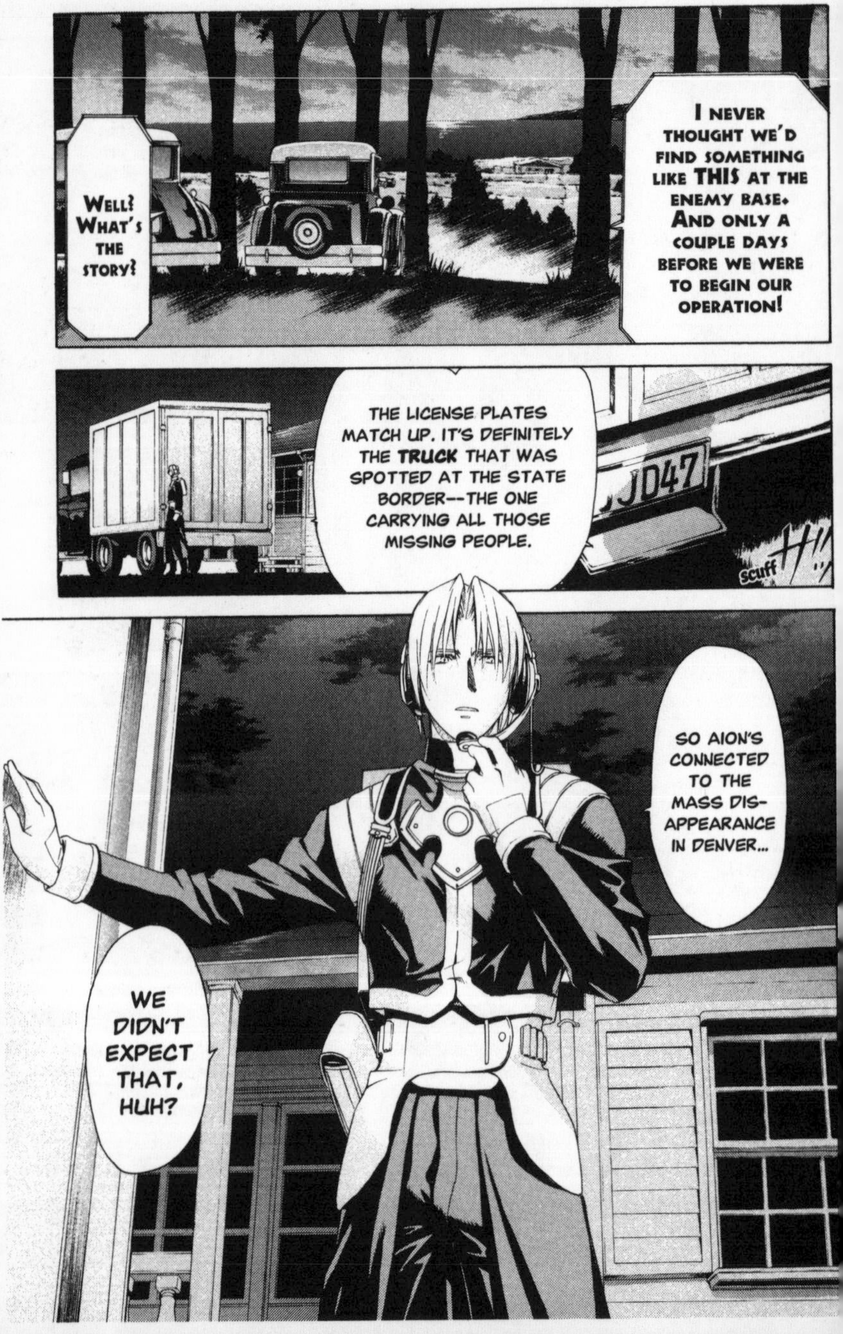
I NEVER THOUGHT WE'D FIND SOMETHING LIKE THIS AT THE ENEMY BASE. AND ONLY A COUPLE DAYS BEFORE WE WERE TO BEGIN OUR OPERATION!
WELL? WHAT'S THE STORY?
JD47
scuff
THE LICENSE PLATES MATCH UP. IT'S DEFINITELY THE TRUCK THAT WAS SPOTTED AT THE STATE BORDER--THE ONE CARRYING ALL THOSE MISSING PEOPLE.
SO AION'S CONNECTED TO THE MASS DIS-APPEARANCE IN DENVER...
WE DIDN'T EXPECT THAT, HUH?

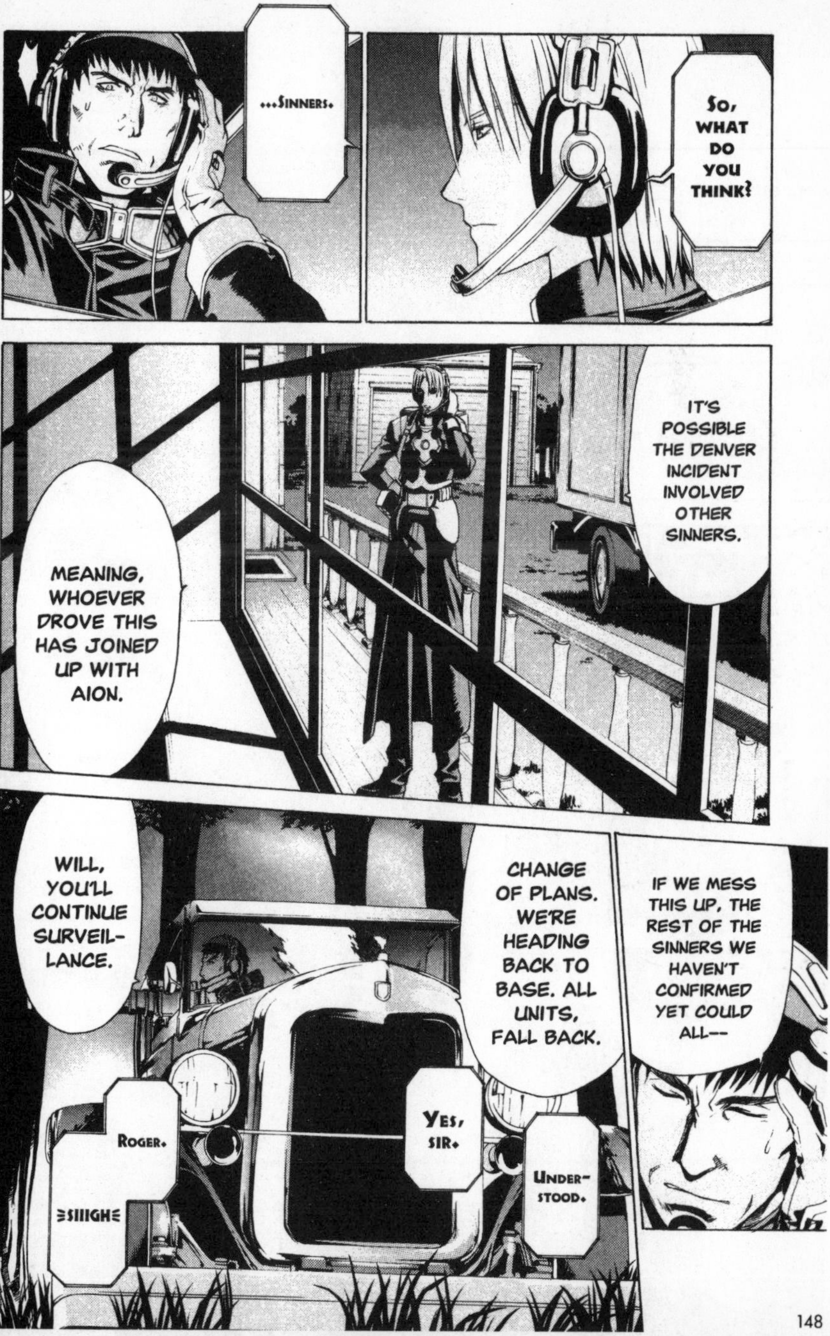
So, what do you think?
...Sinners.
It's possible the Denver incident involved other sinners.
Meaning, whoever drove this has joined up with Aion.
If we mess this up, the rest of the sinners we haven't confirmed yet could all--
Change of plans. We're heading back to base. All units, fall back.
Will, you'll continue surveil-lance.
Under-stood.
Yes, sir.
Roger.
≡SIIIGH≡

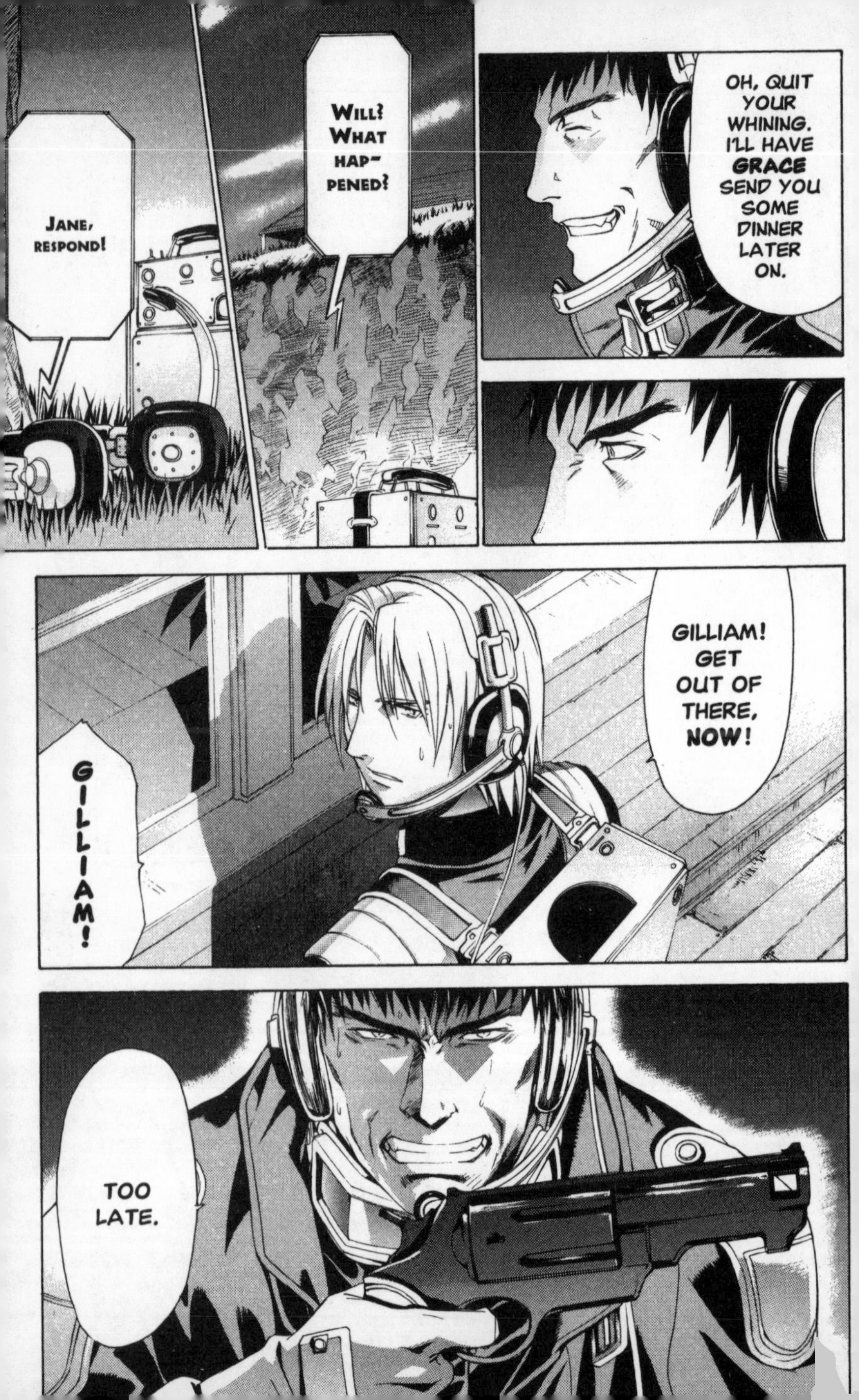
Oh, quit your whining. I'll have **Grace** send you some dinner later on.
Will? What hap-pened?
Jane, respond!
Gilliam! Get out of there, **now**!
Gilliam!
Too late.

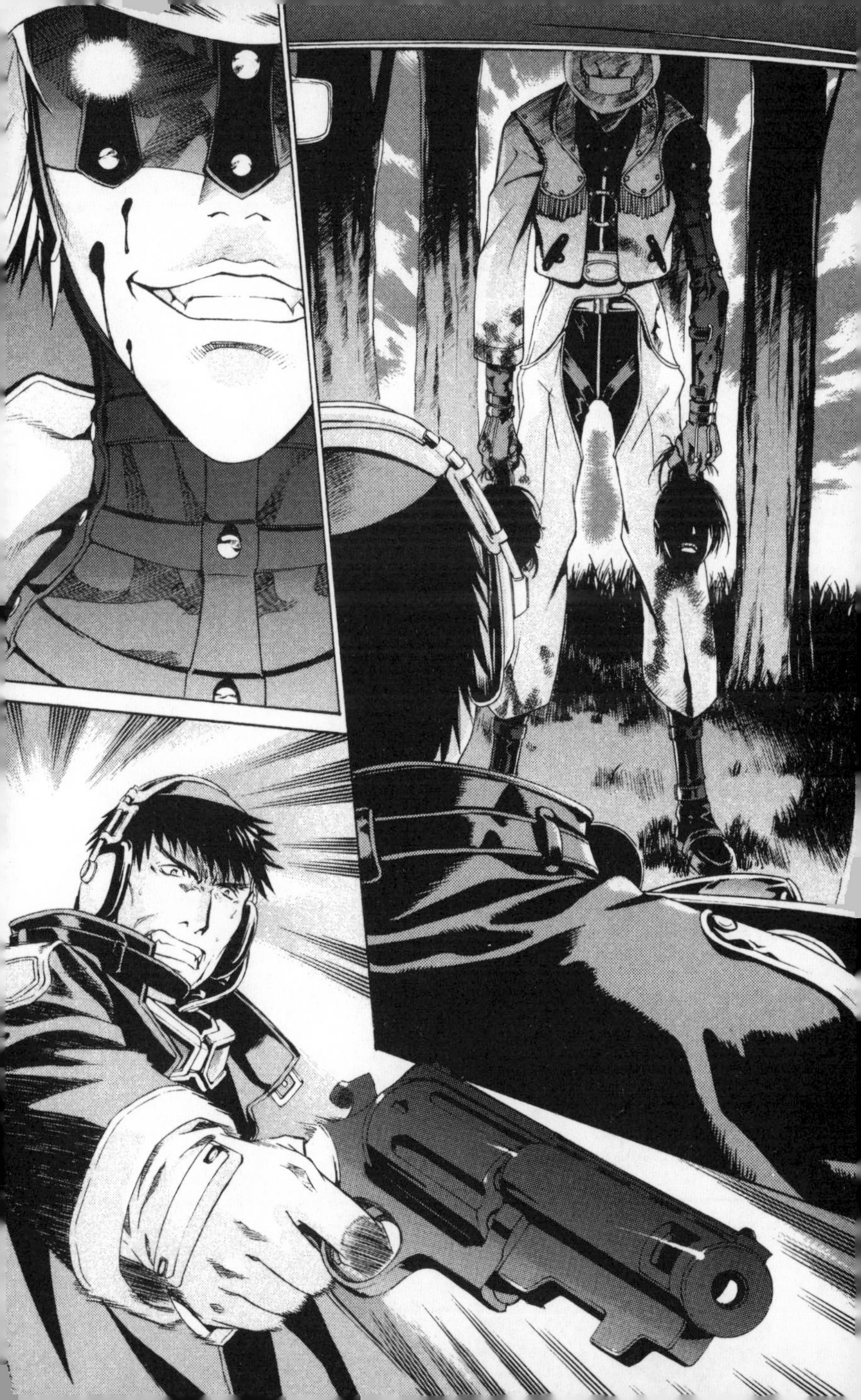

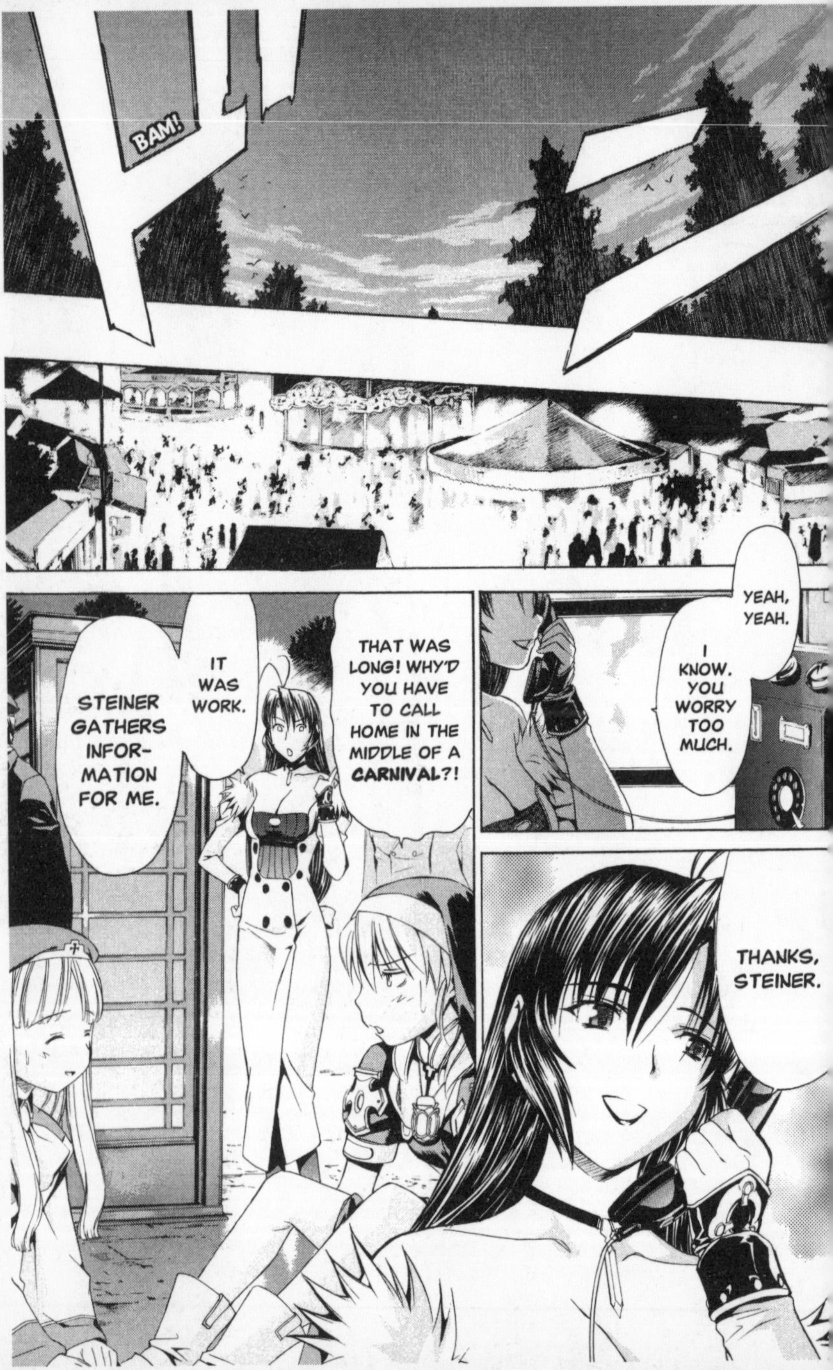
BAM!
YEAH, YEAH.
I KNOW. YOU WORRY TOO MUCH.
THANKS, STEINER.
THAT WAS LONG! WHY'D YOU HAVE TO CALL HOME IN THE MIDDLE OF A CARNIVAL?!
IT WAS WORK.
STEINER GATHERS INFORMATION FOR ME.

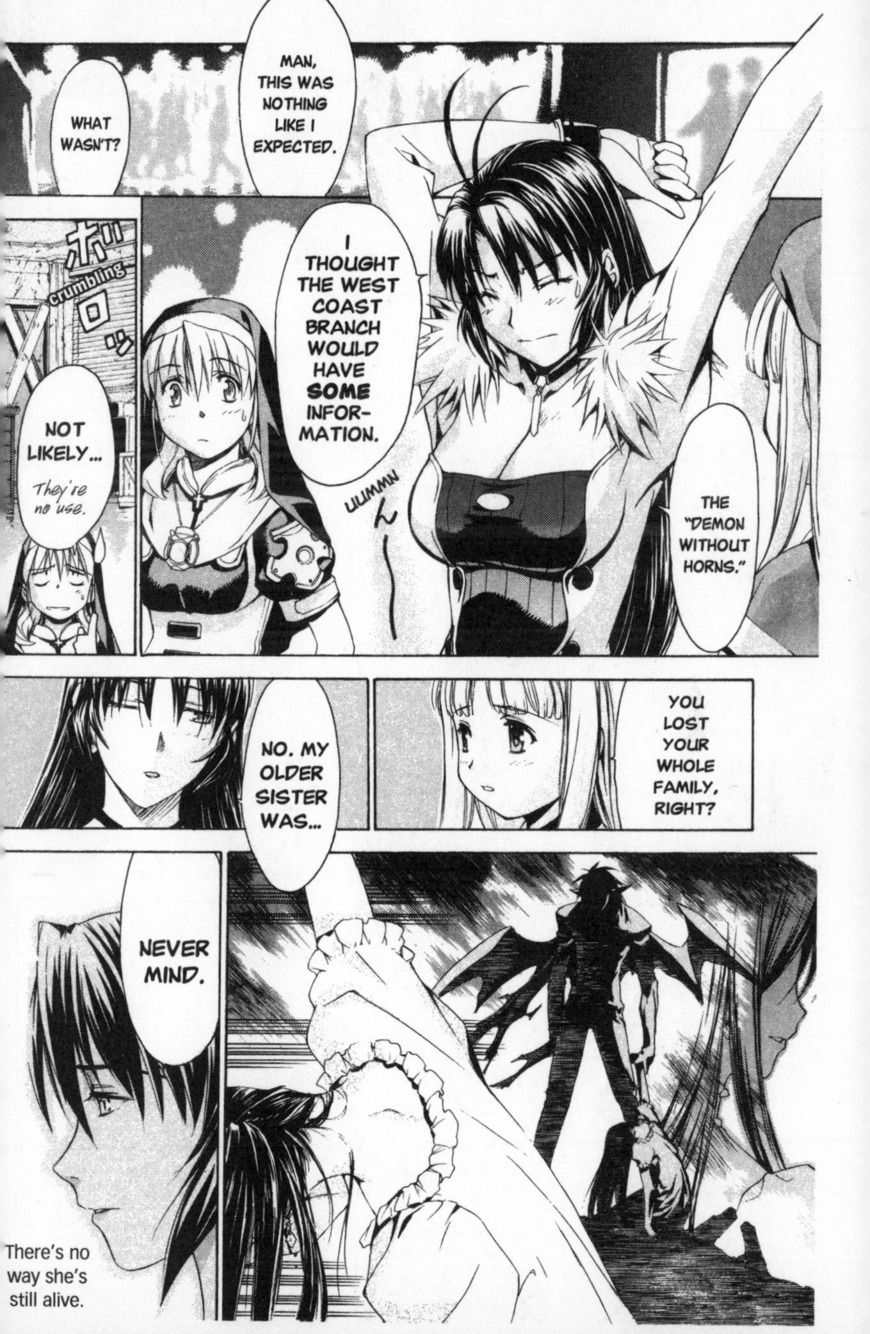

MAN, THIS WAS NOTHING LIKE I EXPECTED.
WHAT WASN'T?
I THOUGHT THE WEST COAST BRANCH WOULD HAVE **SOME** INFOR-MATION.
UUMMN
crumbling
NOT LIKELY...
They're no use.
THE "DEMON WITHOUT HORNS."
YOU LOST YOUR WHOLE FAMILY, RIGHT?
NO. MY OLDER SISTER WAS...
NEVER MIND.
There's no way she's still alive.

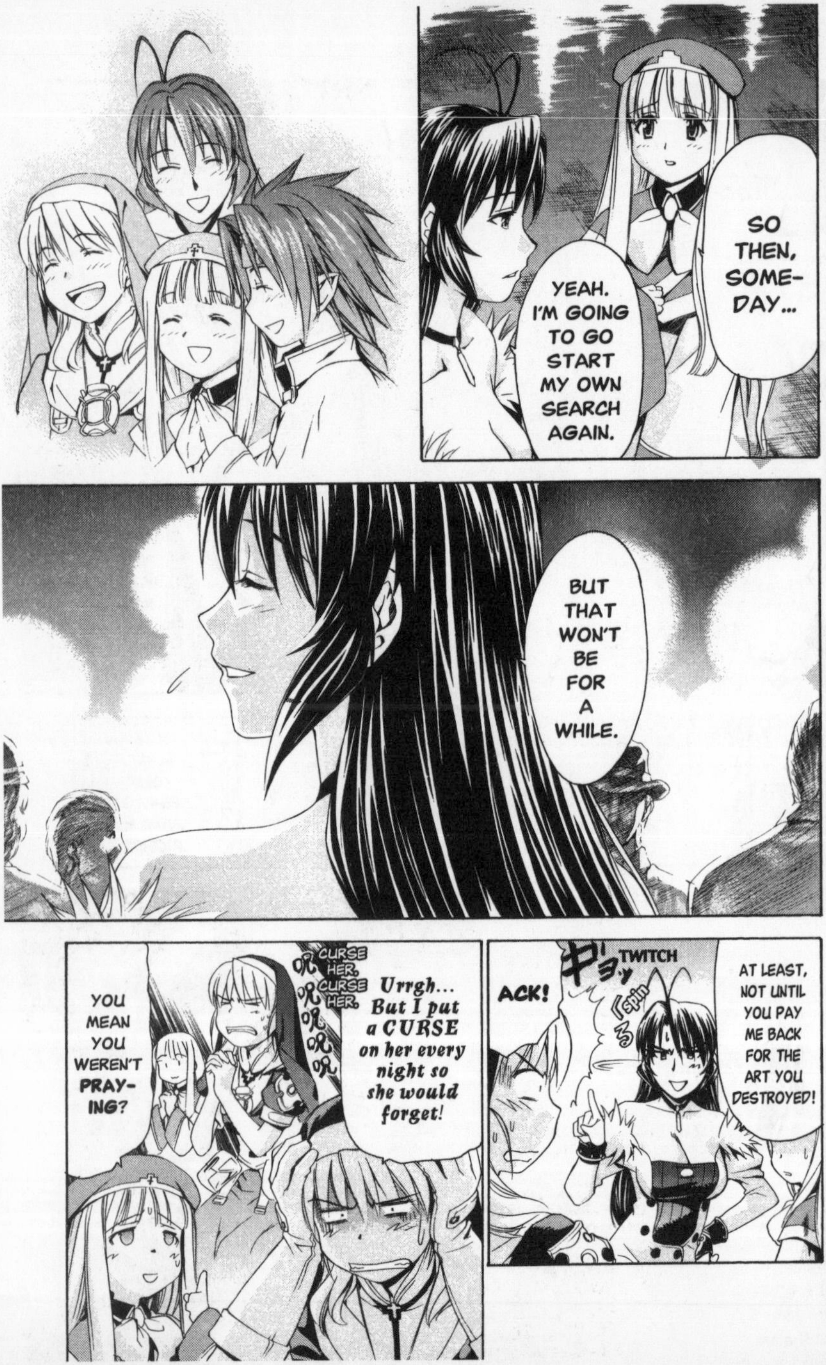
SO THEN, SOME-DAY...
YEAH. I'M GOING TO GO START MY OWN SEARCH AGAIN.
BUT THAT WON'T BE FOR A WHILE.
AT LEAST, NOT UNTIL YOU PAY ME BACK FOR THE ART YOU DESTROYED!
TWITCH
spin
ACK!
Urrgh... But I put a CURSE on her every night so she would forget!
CURSE HER, CURSE HER,
YOU MEAN YOU WEREN'T PRAY-ING?

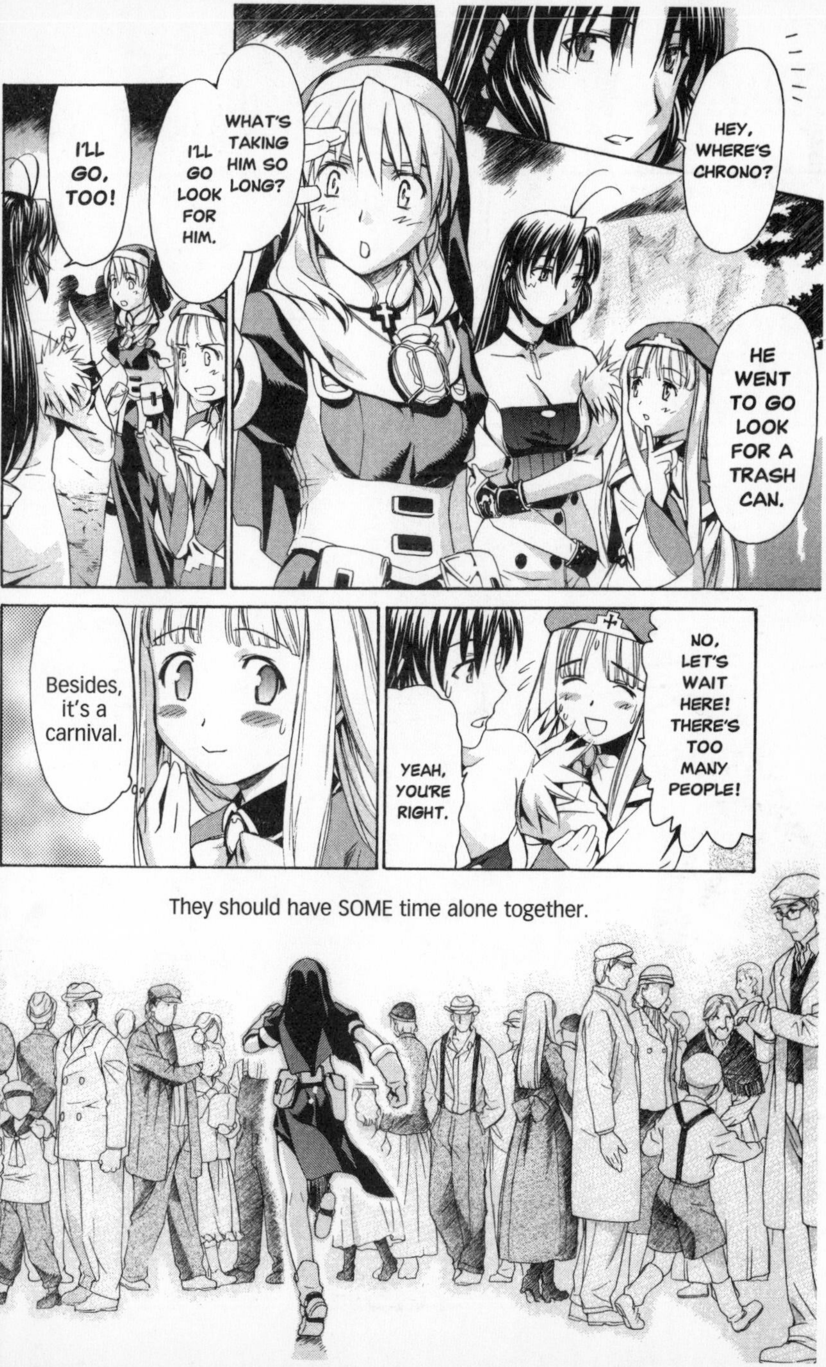
HEY, WHERE'S CHRONO?
HE WENT TO GO LOOK FOR A TRASH CAN.
WHAT'S TAKING HIM SO LONG?
I'LL GO LOOK FOR HIM.
I'LL GO, TOO!
NO, LET'S WAIT HERE! THERE'S TOO MANY PEOPLE!
YEAH, YOU'RE RIGHT.
Besides, it's a carnival.
They should have SOME time alone together.

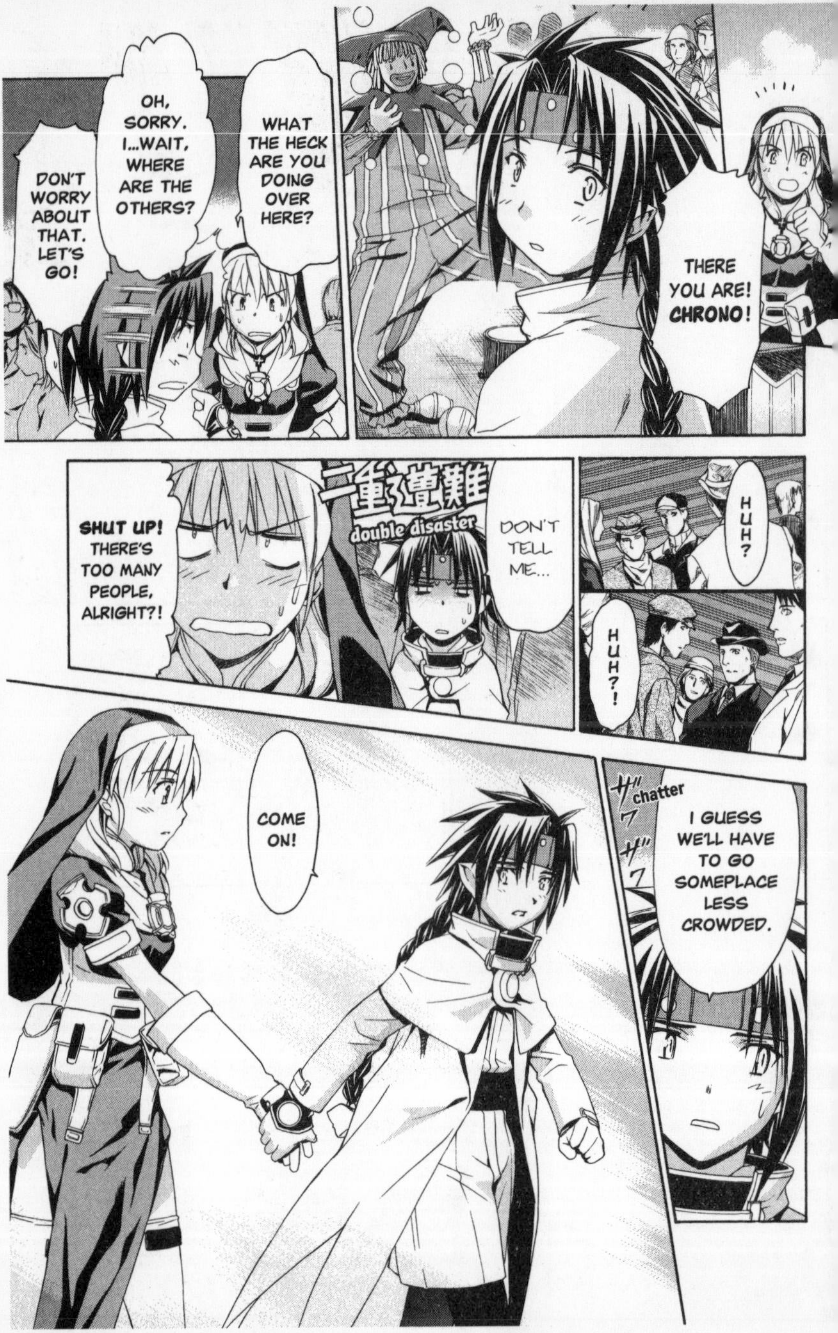
THERE YOU ARE! CHRONO!
WHAT THE HECK ARE YOU DOING OVER HERE?
OH, SORRY. I...WAIT, WHERE ARE THE OTHERS?
DON'T WORRY ABOUT THAT. LET'S GO!
HUH?
HUH?!
DON'T TELL ME...
二重遭難
double disaster
SHUT UP! THERE'S TOO MANY PEOPLE, ALRIGHT?!
ザワザワ
chatter
I GUESS WE'LL HAVE TO GO SOMEPLACE LESS CROWDED.
COME ON!

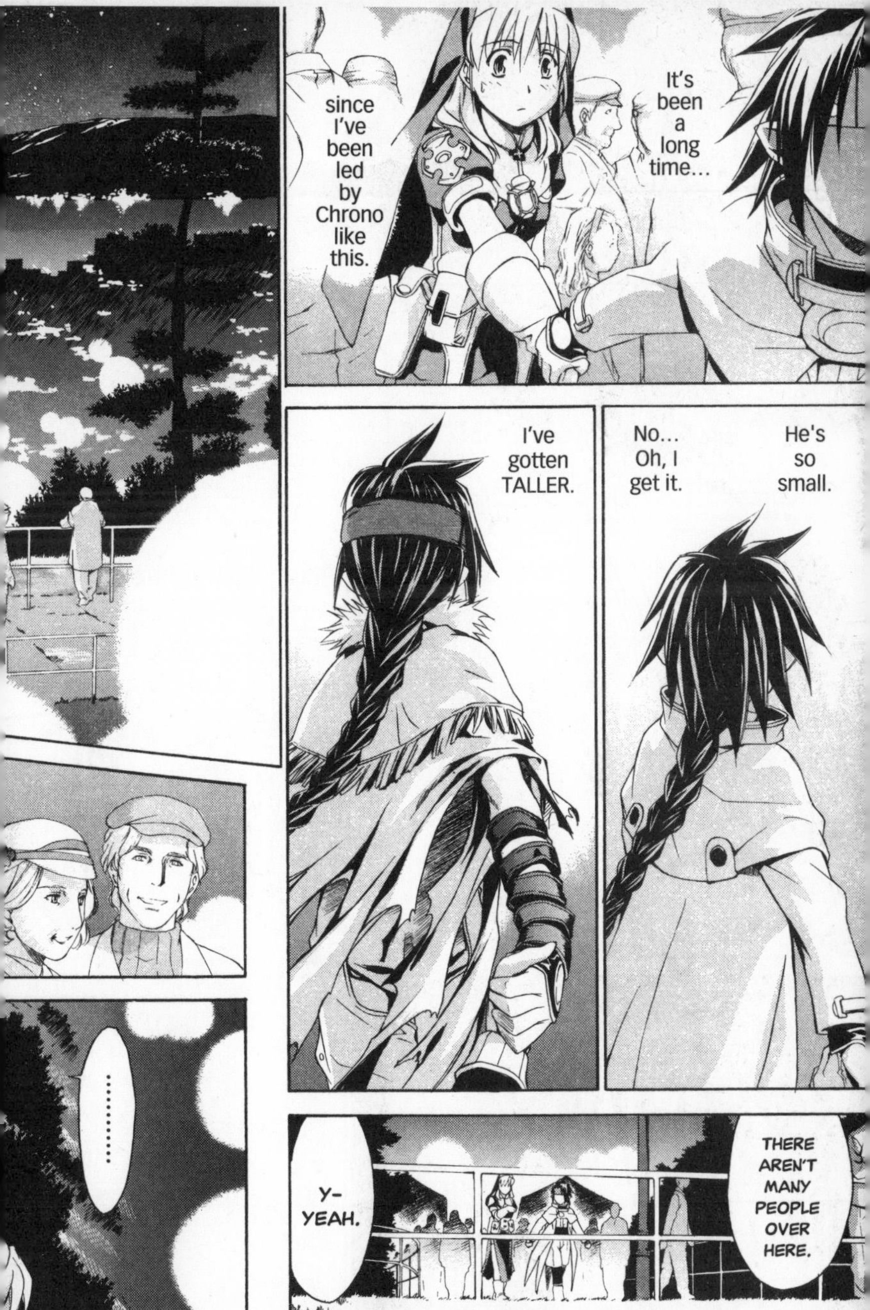
It's been a long time...
since I've been led by Chrono like this.
He's so small.
No... Oh, I get it.
I've gotten TALLER.
THERE AREN'T MANY PEOPLE OVER HERE.
Y-YEAH.
....

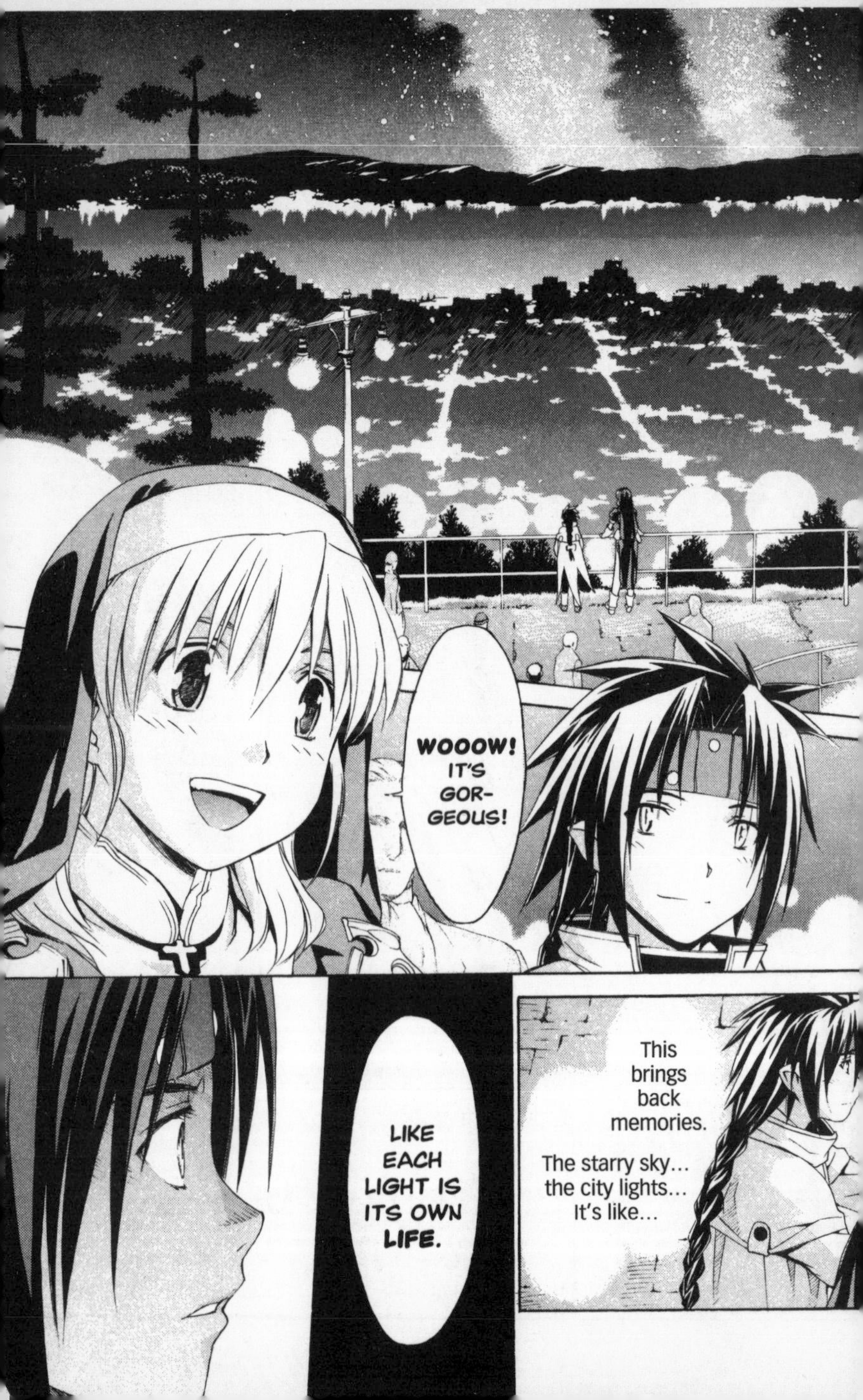
WOOOW! IT'S GOR-GEOUS!
This brings back memories.
The starry sky… the city lights… It's like…
LIKE EACH LIGHT IS ITS OWN LIFE.

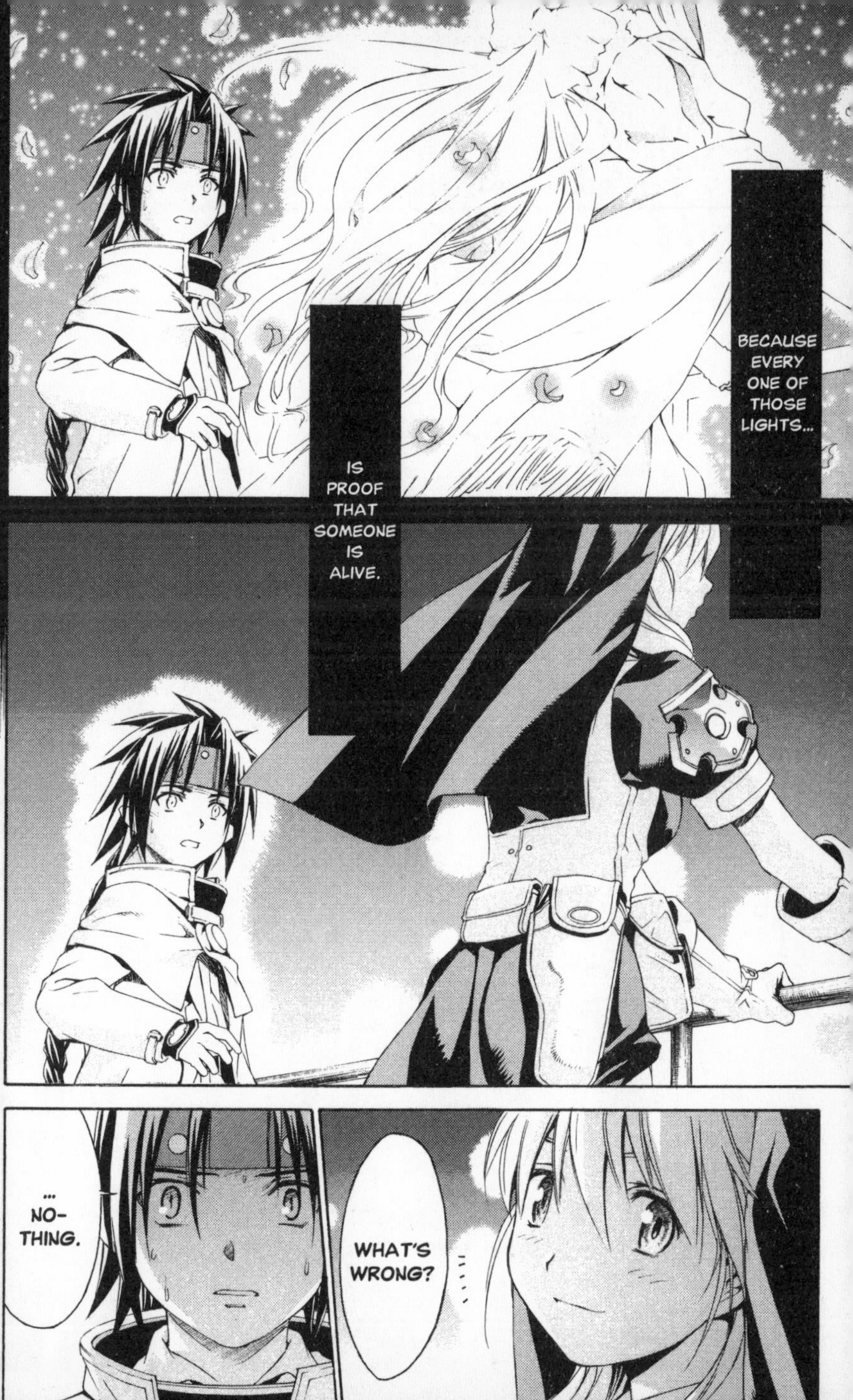
BECAUSE EVERY ONE OF THOSE LIGHTS...
IS PROOF THAT SOMEONE IS ALIVE.
WHAT'S WRONG?
... NO-THING.

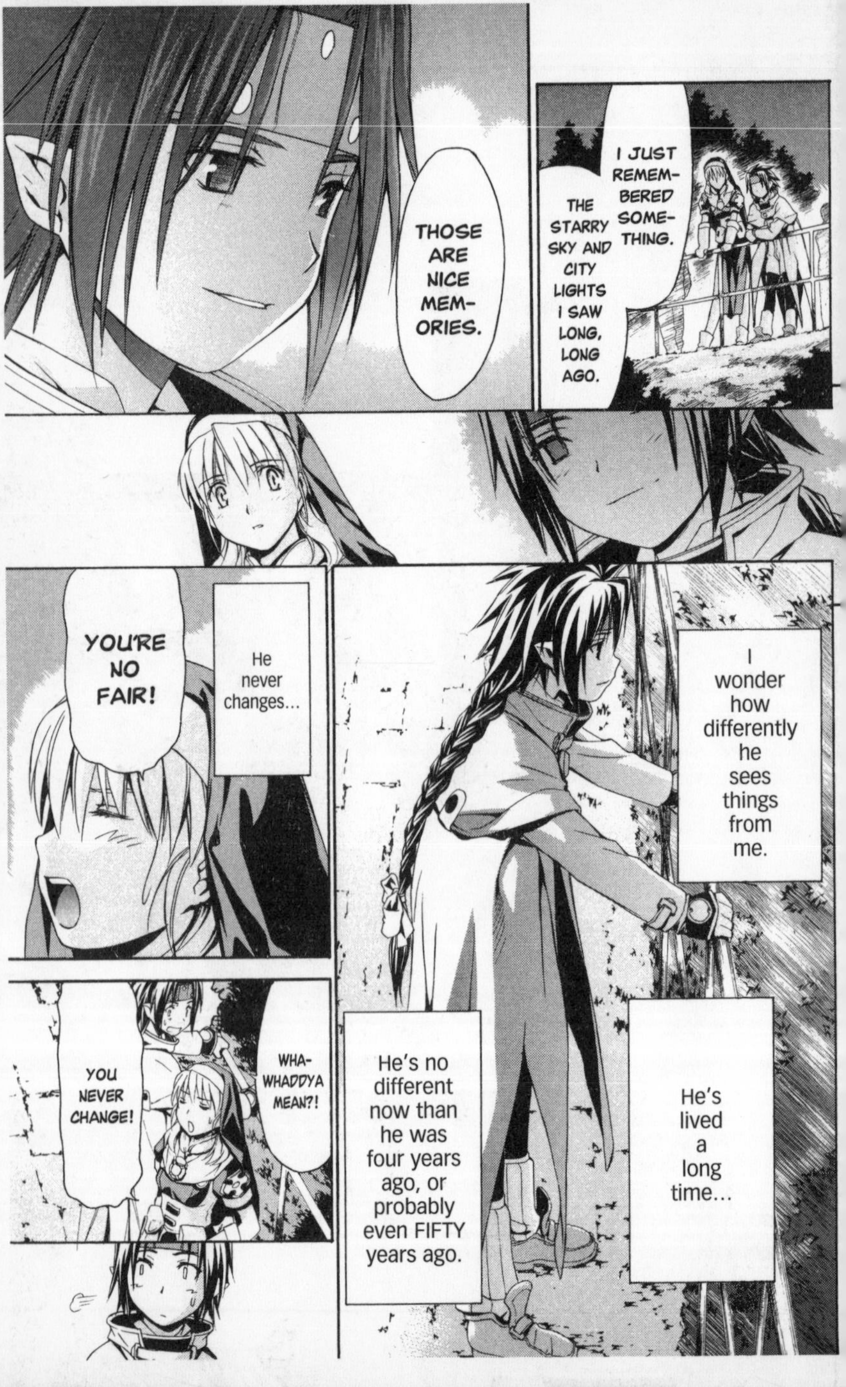
I JUST REMEMBERED SOMETHING.
THE STARRY SKY AND CITY LIGHTS I SAW LONG, LONG AGO.
THOSE ARE NICE MEMORIES.
I wonder how differently he sees things from me.
He's lived a long time...
He's no different now than he was four years ago, or probably even FIFTY years ago.
He never changes...
YOU'RE NO FAIR!
WHA-WHADDYA MEAN?!
YOU NEVER CHANGE!

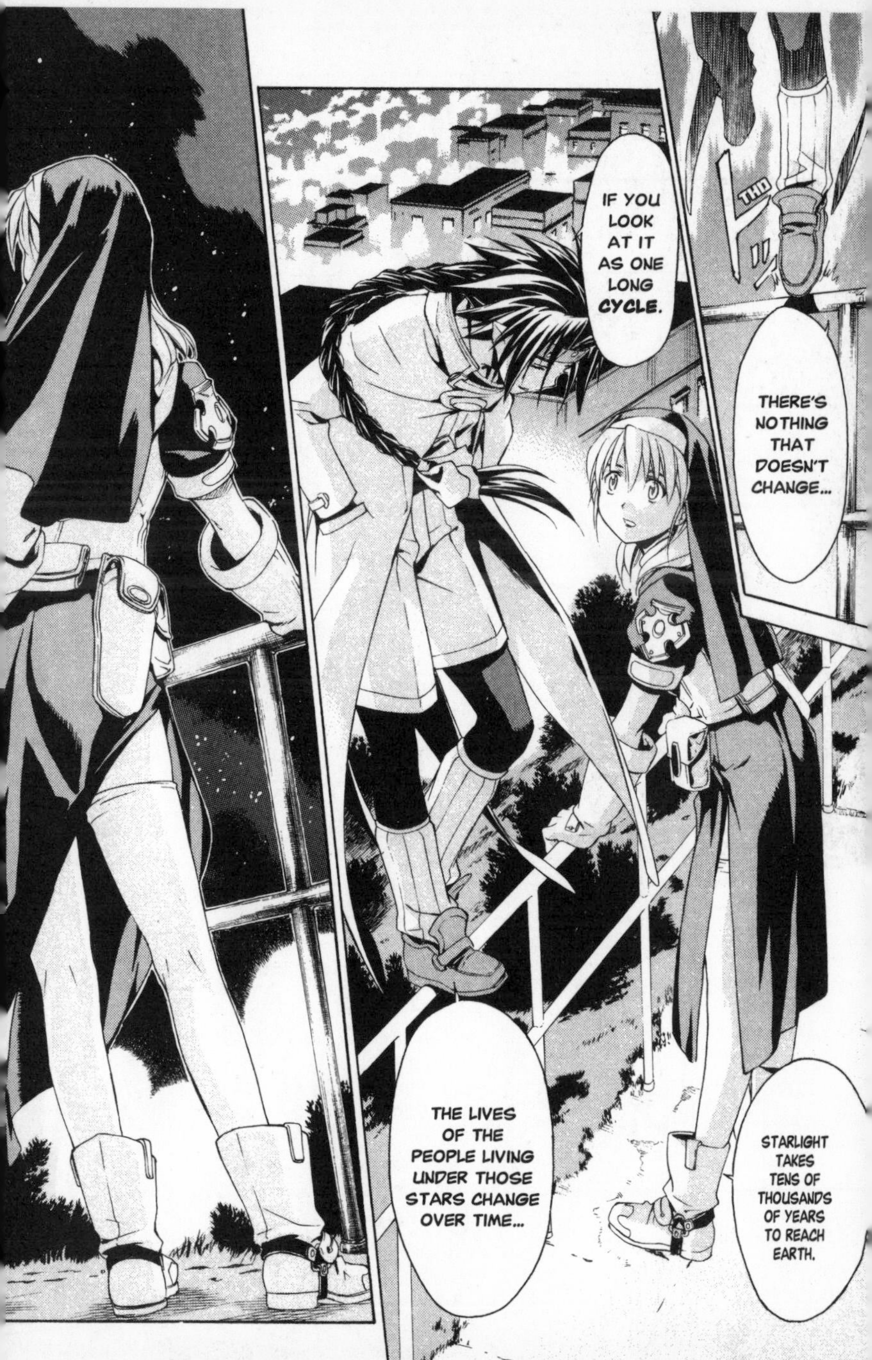
THD
THERE'S NOTHING THAT DOESN'T CHANGE...
IF YOU LOOK AT IT AS ONE LONG CYCLE.
STARLIGHT TAKES TENS OF THOUSANDS OF YEARS TO REACH EARTH.
THE LIVES OF THE PEOPLE LIVING UNDER THOSE STARS CHANGE OVER TIME...

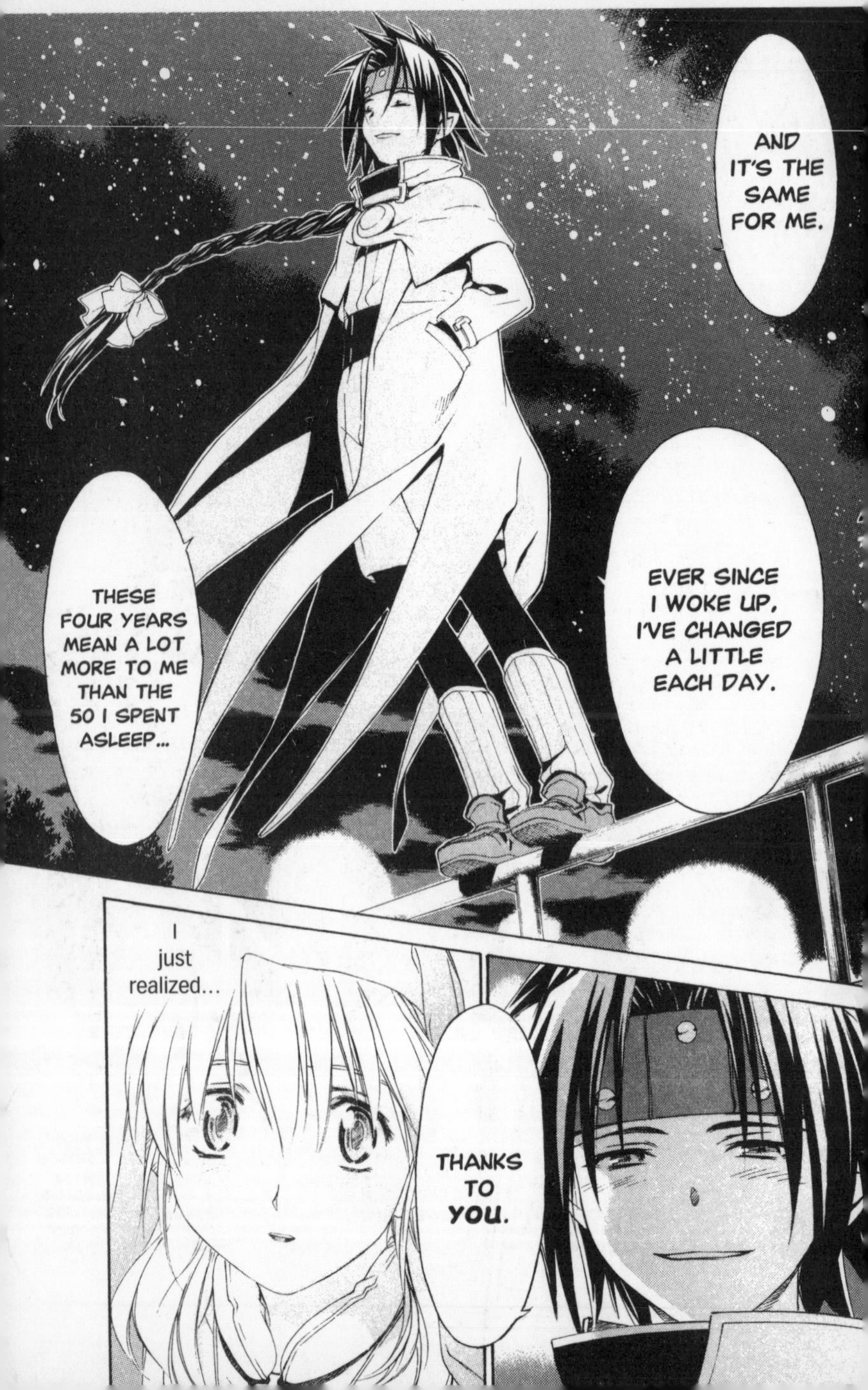
AND IT'S THE SAME FOR ME.
EVER SINCE I WOKE UP, I'VE CHANGED A LITTLE EACH DAY.
THESE FOUR YEARS MEAN A LOT MORE TO ME THAN THE 50 I SPENT ASLEEP...
THANKS TO YOU.
I just realized...

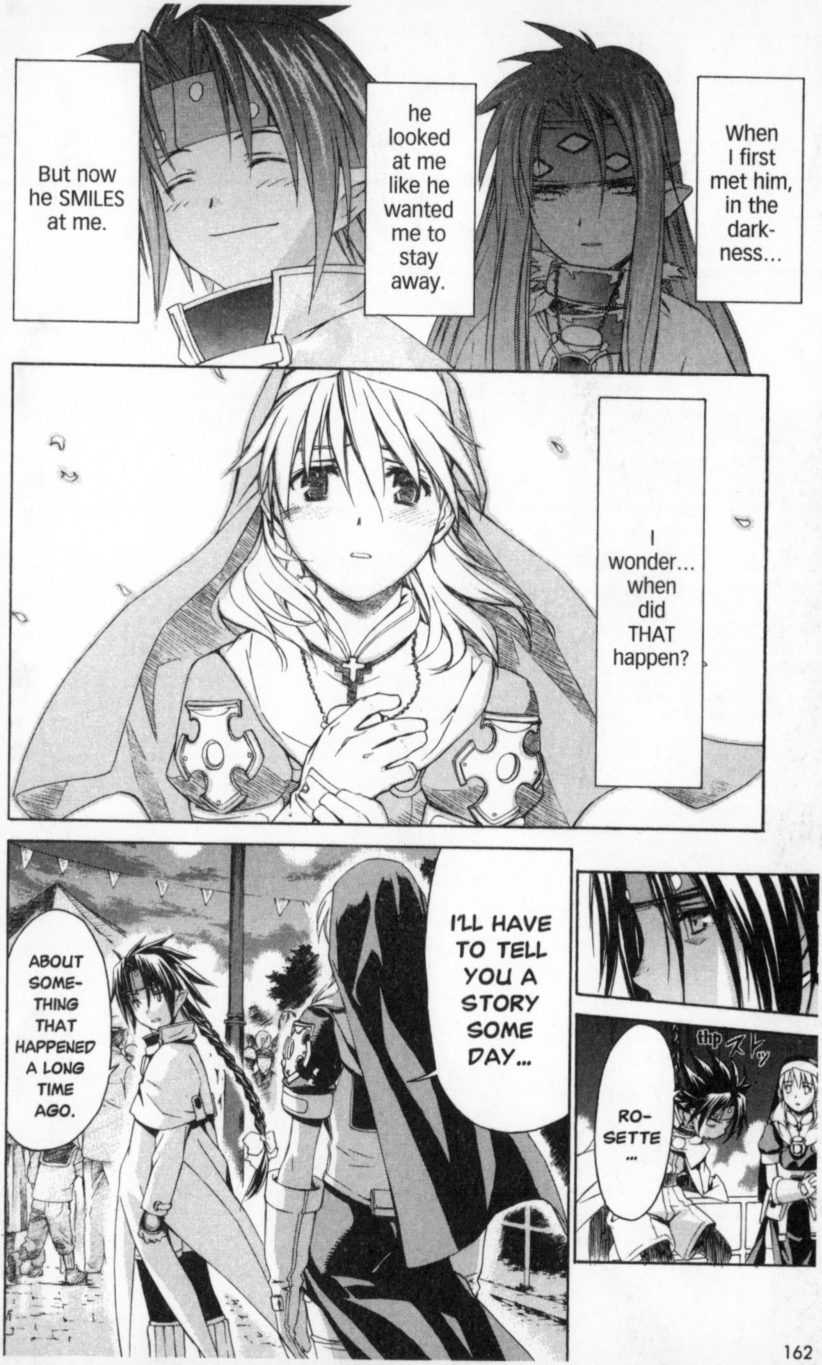
When I first met him, in the darkness...
he looked at me like he wanted me to stay away.
But now he SMILES at me.
I wonder... when did THAT happen?
thp
ストッ
ROSETTE...
I'LL HAVE TO TELL YOU A STORY SOME DAY...
ABOUT SOMETHING THAT HAPPENED A LONG TIME AGO.

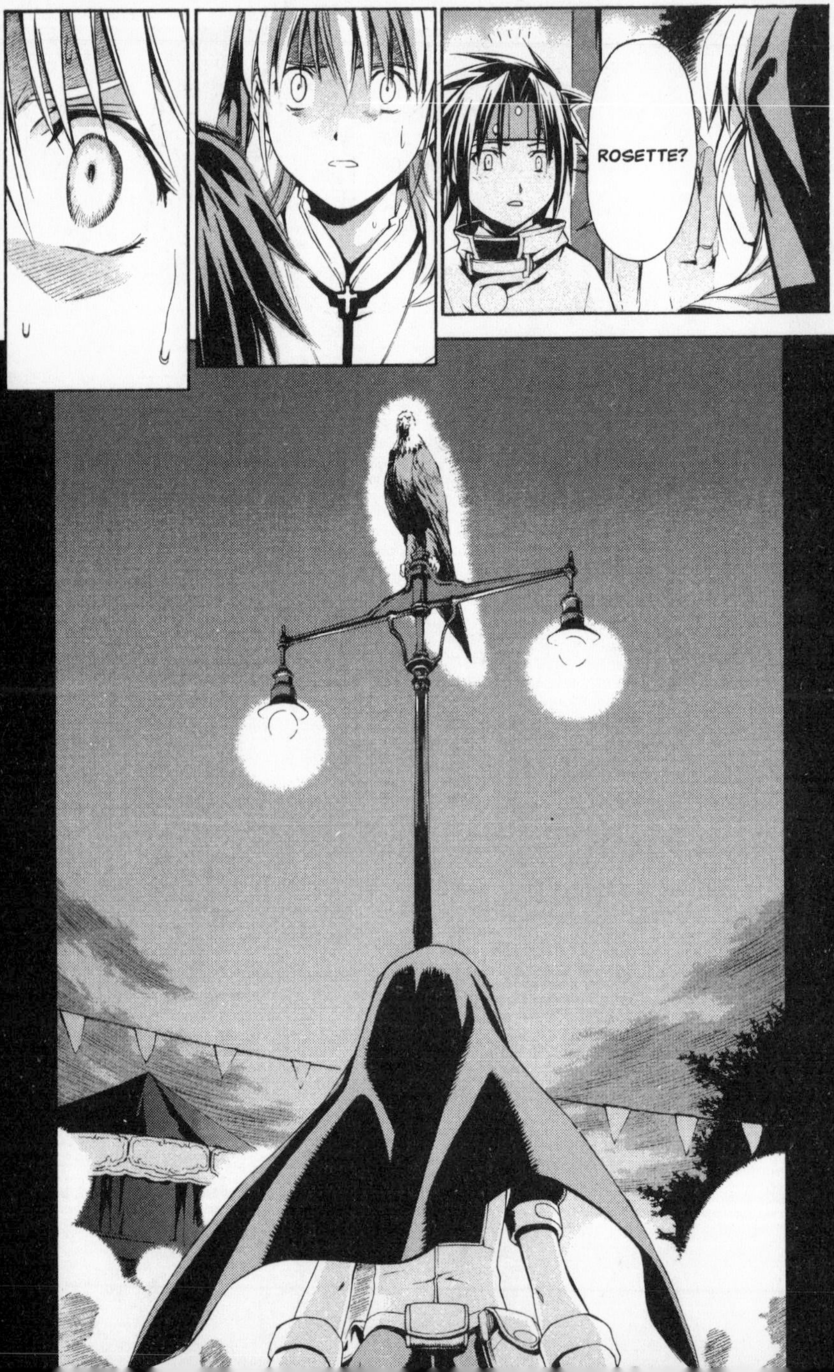
ROSETTE?

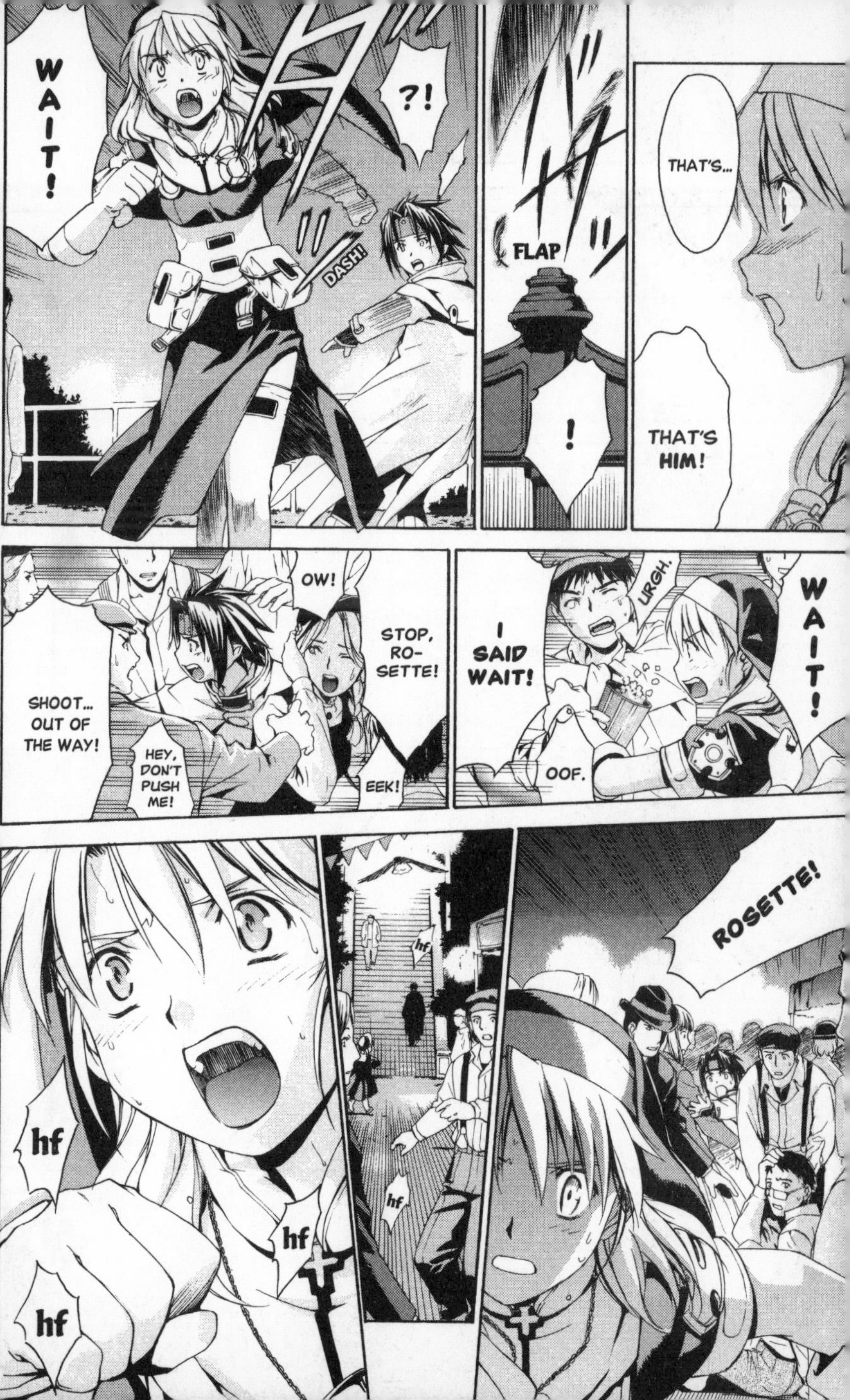

THAT'S...
THAT'S HIM!
FLAP
!
?!
WAIT!
DASH!
WAIT!
URGH.
I SAID WAIT!
OOF.
OW!
STOP, RO-SETTE!
SHOOT... OUT OF THE WAY!
HEY, DON'T PUSH ME!
EEK!
ROSETTE!
hf
hf
hf
hf
hf

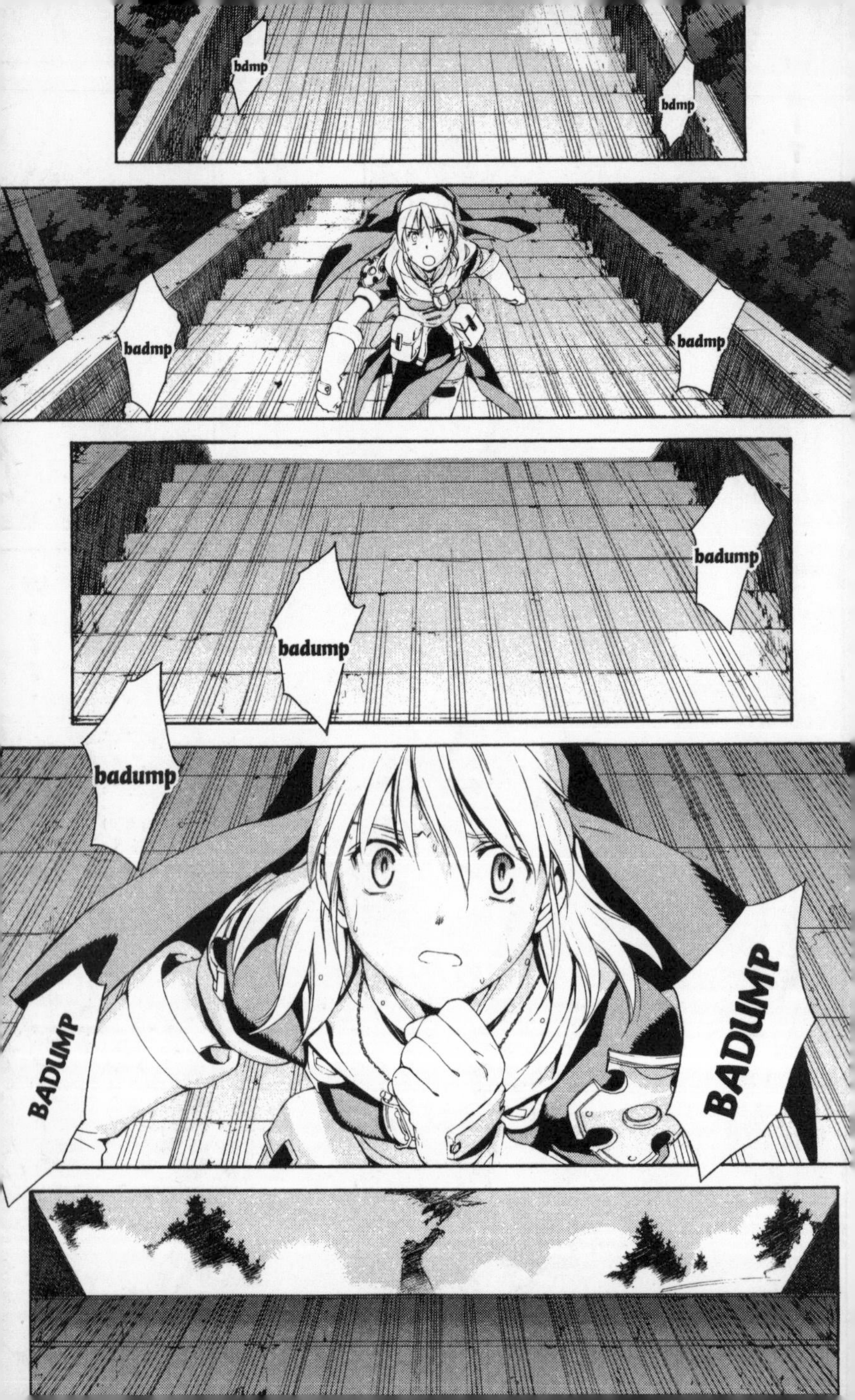
bdmp
bdmp
badmp
badmp
badump
badump
badump
BADUMP
BADUMP

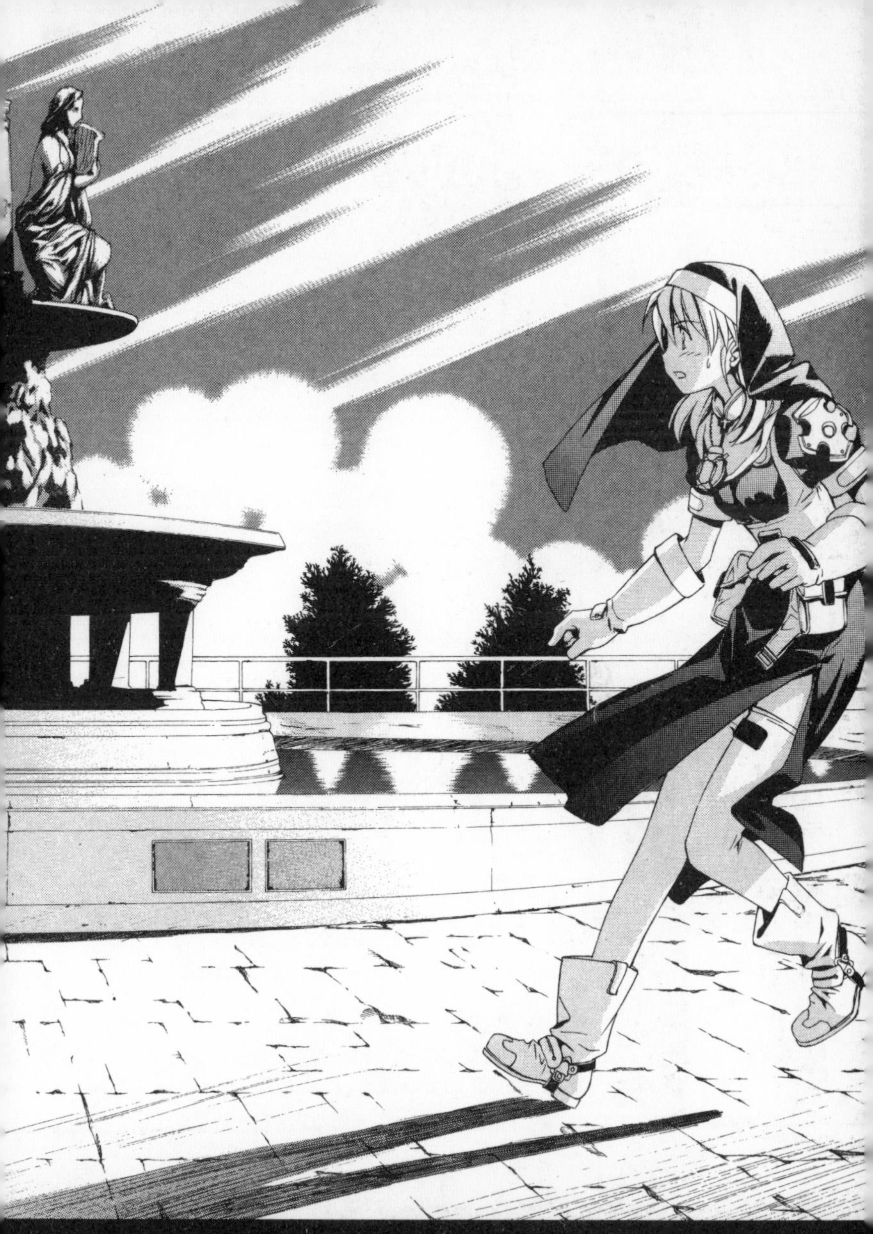

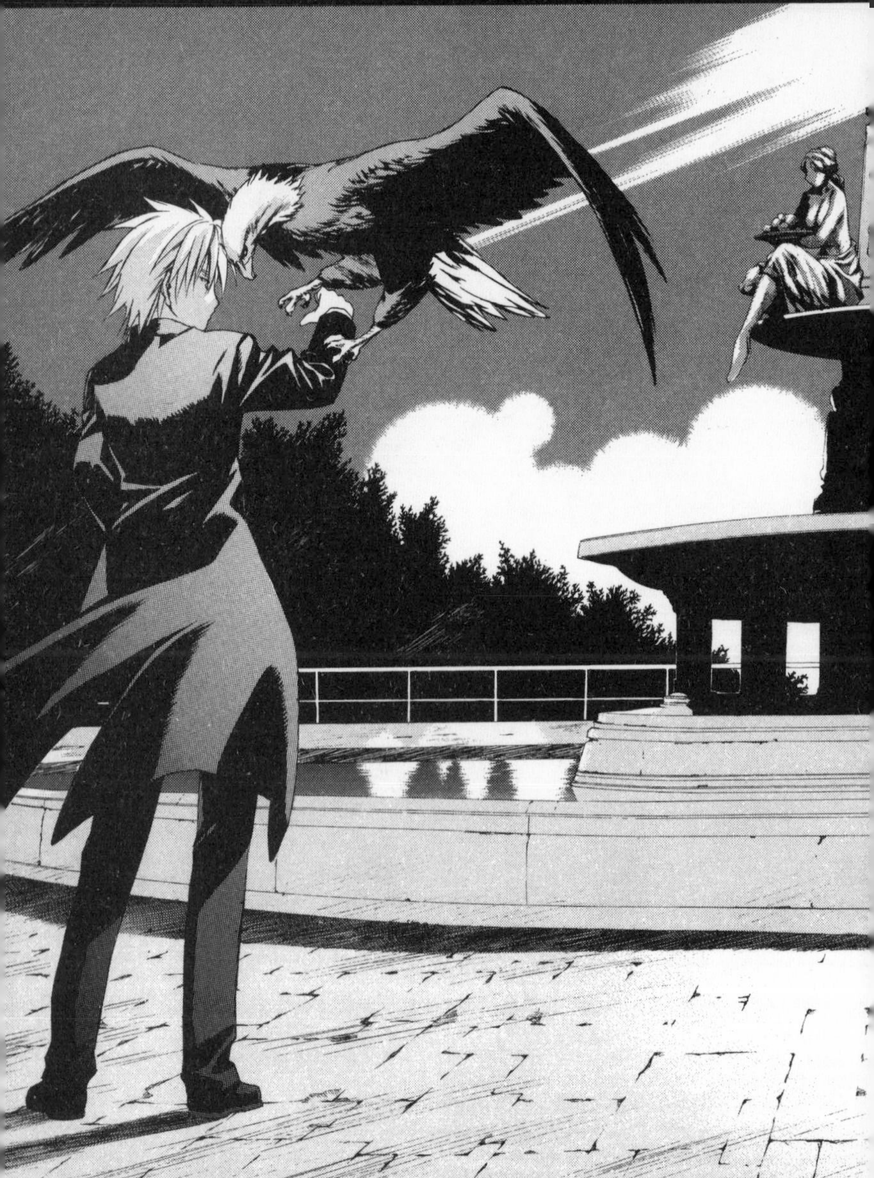

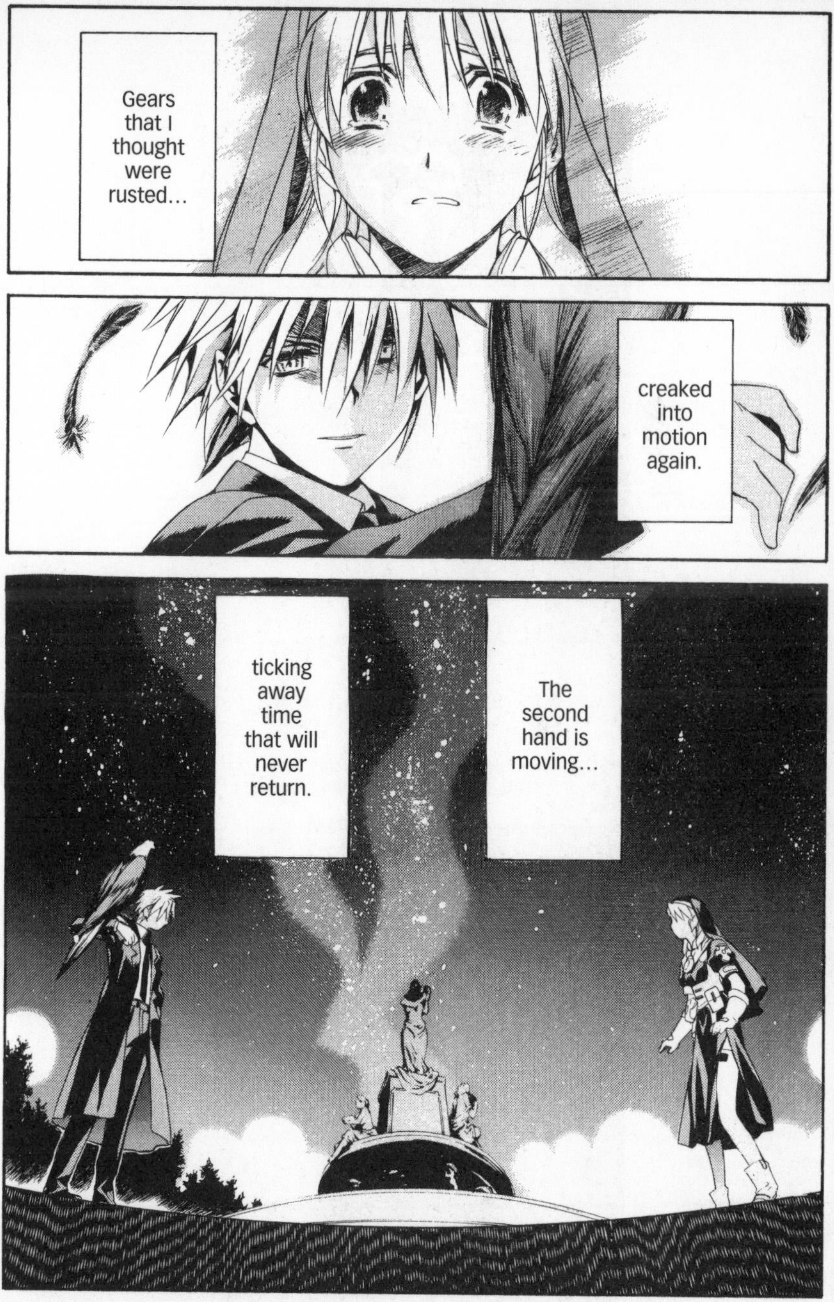
Gears that I thought were rusted…
creaked into motion again.
The second hand is moving…
ticking away time that will never return.

To be continued in Volume 5

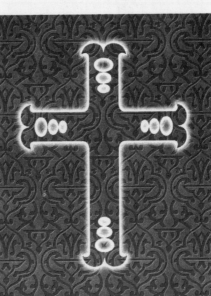

STAFF
DAISUKE MORIYAMA

TOKUNORI NAKANISHI
TETSUYA NAKATA
TSUGUO TAKIMOTO
TOMOYA ITOU
AYA KIGAWA
UI SUZUKI

RYO OGAHARA
HINATA TAKEDA

GUN DESIGN
SATOSHI ISONO

DESIGN
TADAO NAKAMURA (ARTEN)

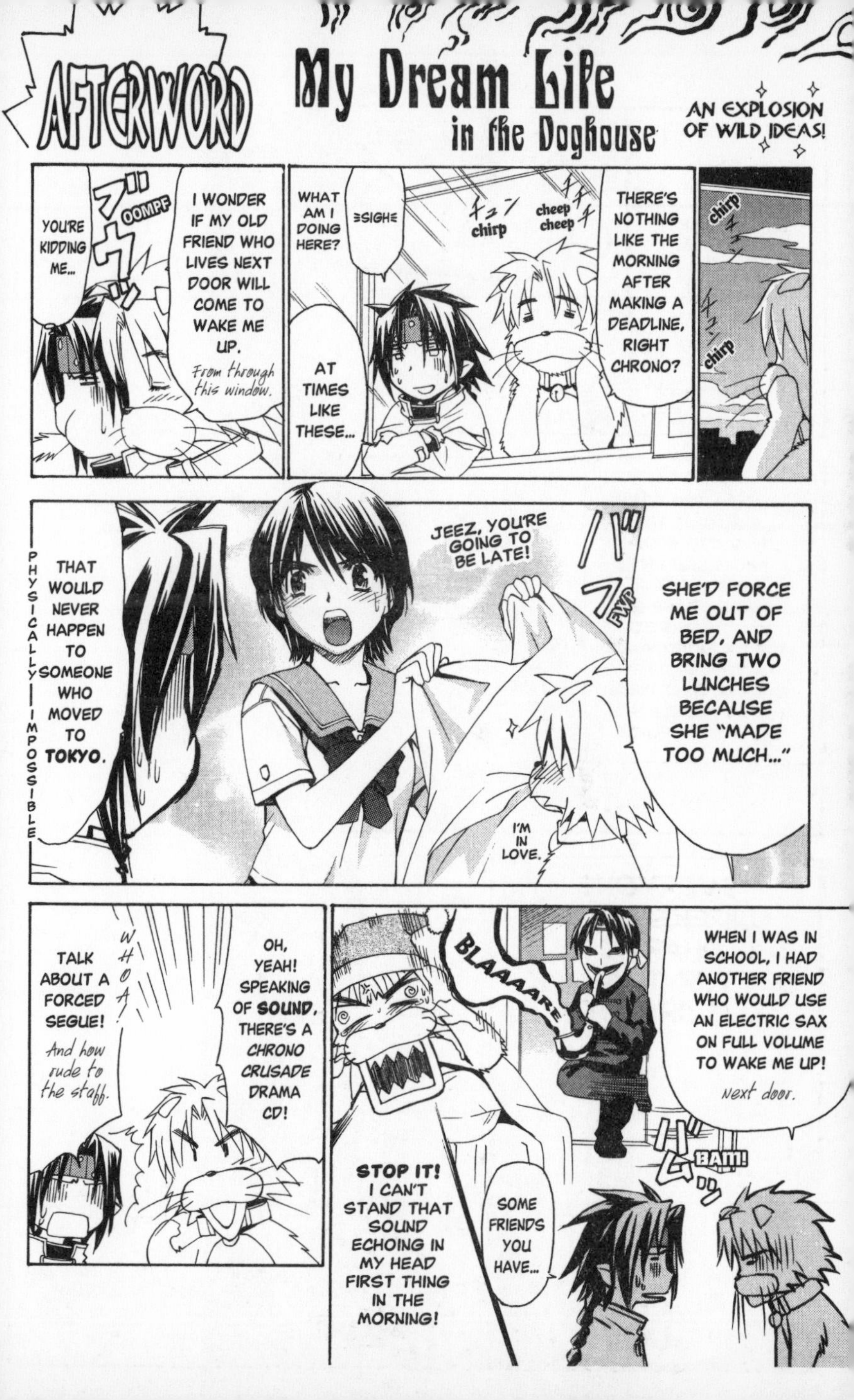
AFTERWORD
My Dream Life in the Doghouse
AN EXPLOSION OF WILD IDEAS!
chirp
chirp
THERE'S NOTHING LIKE THE MORNING AFTER MAKING A DEADLINE, RIGHT CHRONO?
cheep cheep
chirp
WHAT AM I DOING HERE?
≡SIGH≡
AT TIMES LIKE THESE...
I WONDER IF MY OLD FRIEND WHO LIVES NEXT DOOR WILL COME TO WAKE ME UP.
From through this window.
OOMPF
YOU'RE KIDDING ME...
SHE'D FORCE ME OUT OF BED, AND BRING TWO LUNCHES BECAUSE SHE "MADE TOO MUCH..."
FWP
JEEZ, YOU'RE GOING TO BE LATE!
I'M IN LOVE.
THAT WOULD NEVER HAPPEN TO SOMEONE WHO MOVED TO TOKYO.
PHYSICALLY IMPOSSIBLE
WHEN I WAS IN SCHOOL, I HAD ANOTHER FRIEND WHO WOULD USE AN ELECTRIC SAX ON FULL VOLUME TO WAKE ME UP!
Next door.
BLAAAAARE
BAM!
SOME FRIENDS YOU HAVE...
STOP IT! I CAN'T STAND THAT SOUND ECHOING IN MY HEAD FIRST THING IN THE MORNING!
OH, YEAH! SPEAKING OF SOUND, THERE'S A CHRONO CRUSADE DRAMA CD!
WHOA
TALK ABOUT A FORCED SEGUE!
And how rude to the staff.

TOTALLY FRICKIN' VAGUE

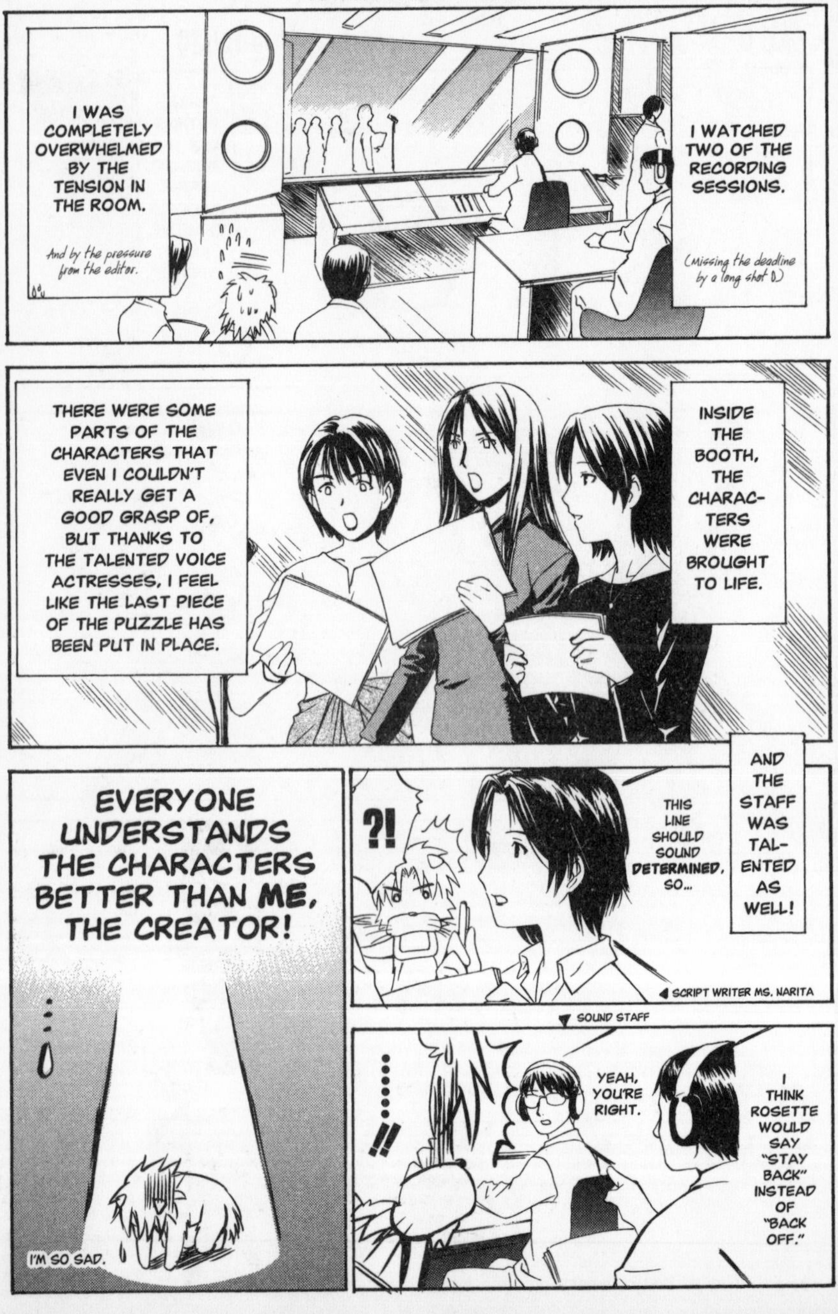
I WATCHED TWO OF THE RECORDING SESSIONS.
(Missing the deadline by a long shot)
I WAS COMPLETELY OVERWHELMED BY THE TENSION IN THE ROOM.
And by the pressure from the editor.
INSIDE THE BOOTH, THE CHARACTERS WERE BROUGHT TO LIFE.
THERE WERE SOME PARTS OF THE CHARACTERS THAT EVEN I COULDN'T REALLY GET A GOOD GRASP OF, BUT THANKS TO THE TALENTED VOICE ACTRESSES, I FEEL LIKE THE LAST PIECE OF THE PUZZLE HAS BEEN PUT IN PLACE.
AND THE STAFF WAS TALENTED AS WELL!
THIS LINE SHOULD SOUND DETERMINED, SO...
?!
SCRIPT WRITER MS. NARITA
SOUND STAFF
I THINK ROSETTE WOULD SAY "STAY BACK" INSTEAD OF "BACK OFF."
YEAH, YOU'RE RIGHT.
......!!
EVERYONE UNDERSTANDS THE CHARACTERS BETTER THAN ME, THE CREATOR!
...!
I'M SO SAD.

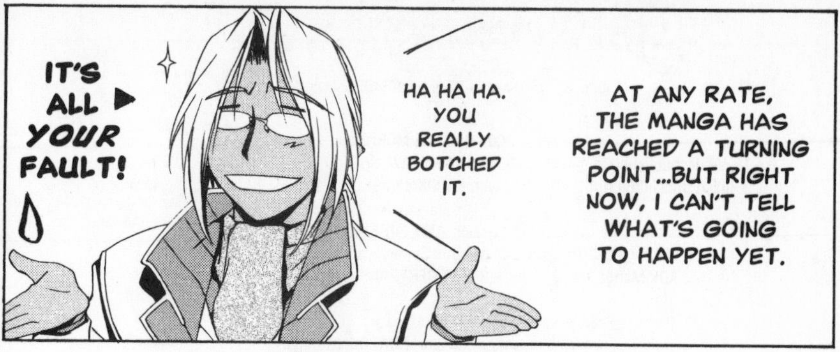
AT ANY RATE, THE MANGA HAS REACHED A TURNING POINT...BUT RIGHT NOW, I CAN'T TELL WHAT'S GOING TO HAPPEN YET.
HA HA HA. YOU REALLY BOTCHED IT.
IT'S ALL YOUR FAULT!

Preview of the next volume

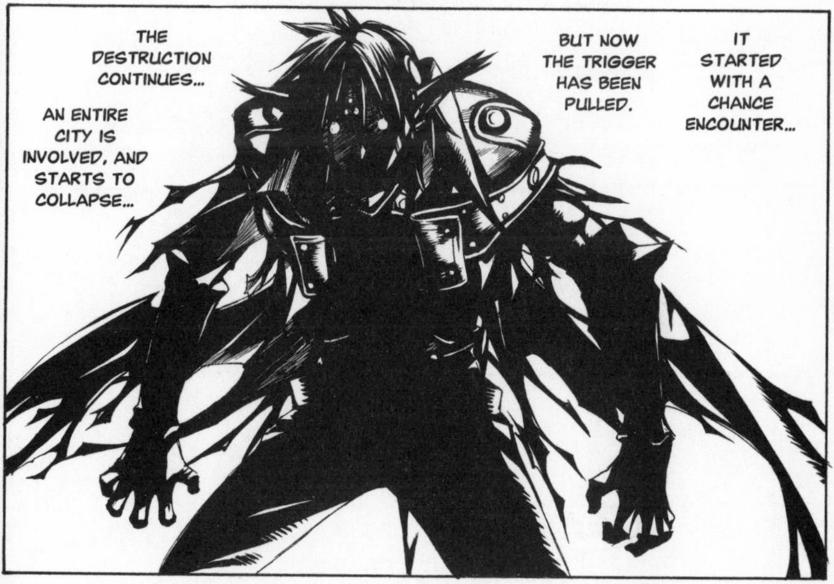
IT STARTED WITH A CHANCE ENCOUNTER...
BUT NOW THE TRIGGER HAS BEEN PULLED.
THE DESTRUCTION CONTINUES...
AN ENTIRE CITY IS INVOLVED, AND STARTS TO COLLAPSE...

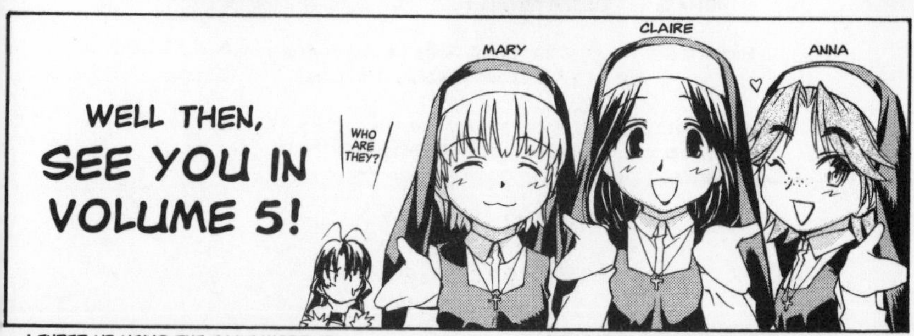
ANNA
CLAIRE
MARY
WHO ARE THEY?
WELL THEN, SEE YOU IN VOLUME 5!

ROSETTE'S FELLOW SISTERS

I ENDED UP USING THE SAME WORDING AS THE PREVIOUS VOLUME **AGAIN**...

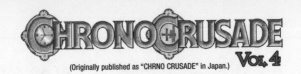

(Originally published as "CHRNO CRUSADE" in Japan.)

© 2001 DAISUKE MORIYAMA
Originally published in Japan in 2001 by KADOKAWA SHOTEN PUBLISHING CO., LTD., Tokyo.
English translation rights arranged with KADOKAWA SHOTEN PUBLISHING CO., LTD., Tokyo.

Translator **AMY FORSYTH**
Lead Translator/Translation Supervisor **JAVIER LOPEZ**
ADV Manga Translation Staff **KAY BERTRAND AND BRENDAN FRAYNE**

Print Production/Art Studio Manager **LISA PUCKETT**
Pre-press Manager **KLYS REEDYK**
Sr. Designer/Creative Manager **JORGE ALVARADO**
Graphic Designer/Group Leader **GEORGE REYNOLDS**
Graphic Artists **HEATHER GARY AND NATALIA MORALES**
Graphic Intern **MARK MEZA**

International Coordinators **TORU IWAKAMI, ATSUSHI KANBAYASHI
AND KYOKO DRUMHELLER**

Publishing Editor **SUSAN ITIN**
Assistant Editor **MARGARET SCHAROLD**
Editorial Assistant **SHERIDAN JACOBS**
Editorial Intern **MIKE ESSMYER**

Research/Traffic Coordinator **MARSHA ARNOLD**

Executive VP, CFO, COO **KEVIN CORCORAN**

President, CEO & Publisher **JOHN LEDFORD**

Email: editor@adv-manga.com
www.adv-manga.com
www.advfilms.com

For sales and distribution inquiries please call 1.800.282.7202

is a division of A.D. Vision, Inc.
10114 W. Sam Houston Parkway, Suite 200, Houston, Texas 77099

English text © 2005 published by A.D. Vision, Inc. under exclusive license.
ADV MANGA is a trademark of A.D. Vision, Inc.

ISBN: 1-4139-0239-1
First printing, March 2005
10 9 8 7 6 5 4 3 2 1
Printed in Canada

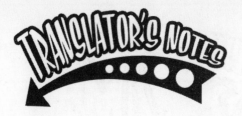

Chrono Crusade Vol. 04

PG. 25 **Laden!**
This is German for "to summon."

PG. 62 (1) **Stürmen!!**
This is German for "to attack" (or "storm").
(2) **Tief fischen!!**
The German here means "deep fishing." However, the Japanese translation given is "Deep March."

LETTER FROM THE ADV MANGA TRANSLATION STAFF

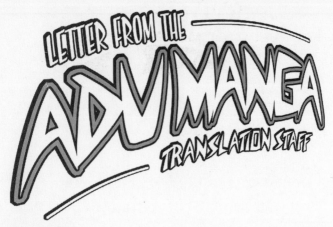

Dear Reader,

On behalf of the ADV Manga translation team, thank you for purchasing an ADV book. We are enthusiastic and committed to our work, and strive to carry our enthusiasm over into the book you hold in your hands.

Our goal is to retain the spirit of the original Japanese book. While great care has been taken to render a true and accurate translation, some cultural or readability issues may require a line to be adapted for greater accessibility to our readers. At times, manga titles that include culturally-specific concepts will feature a "Translator's Notes" section, which explains noteworthy references to the original text.

We hope our commitment to a faithful translation is evident in every ADV book you purchase.

Sincerely,

Javier Lopez
Lead Translator

Kay Bertrand

Brendan Frayne

Amy Forsyth

ADV Manga™

CHRONO CRUSADE
VOL. 5

Rosette has ventured out west to sunny
California in search of her estranged brother,
but this is no family reunion! Acting as a
puppet of the fearsome demon Aion, little
Joshua doesn't even remember his sister,
although Aion certainly remembers his
rival Chrono and their unfinished battle.
The reformed demon will shed his disguise
to even the playing field, but it could
lead Rosette to the pearly gates in
Chrono Crusade, **Volume 5!**

COMING 2005

EDITOR'S PICKS

If you liked *Chrono Crusade* Volume 4, then you'll love these!

PICK 1

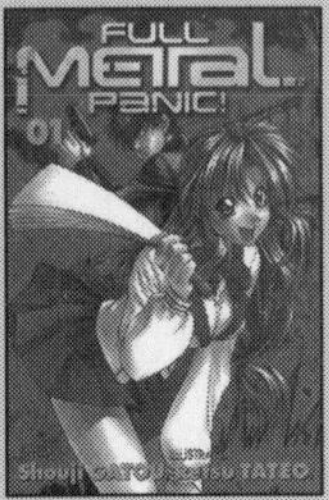

FULL METAL PANIC!

FULL METAL PANIC!

Kaname Chidori appears to be leading a normal life as a popular high school student, but unbeknownst to her, a group of terrorists believes she possesses the special powers of "The Whispered." When the terrorists' plan to kidnap Kaname reaches the ears of MITHRIL, a secret military organization, they send one of their own to pose as a student while acting as protector to the teenaged social butterfly. Sosuke Sagara, is gung-ho, war-crazed and completely obnoxious, finding his mission as a high school student to be sheer torture. It's an exciting blend of fully-loaded action and teenage romance in the thrilling tale of **Full Metal Panic!**

PICK 2

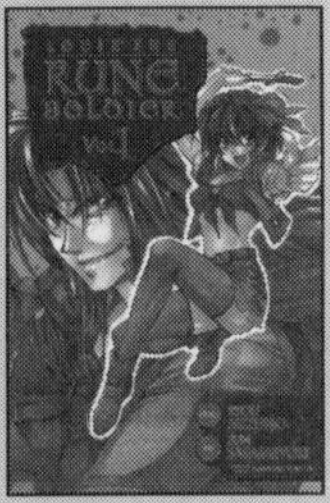

LOUIE THE RUNE SOLDIER

Louie is a careless sorcerer who has tossed aside his studies for the all-important booze, babes and brawls, only to tarnish an important family legacy. But all that will change when this womanizing flunky is chosen to lead a group of gorgeous female adventurers on a journey of sorcery, swordplay and some good ol' fistfights. His new bevy of babes are none to excited about their chosen guide, but when faced with showdown after bone-breaking showdown, Louie could ultimately prove himself to be the right man for the job. From street fights to sorcery spells, Louie tries to get a handle on the whole hero thing, and busts a few heads along the way!

PICK 3

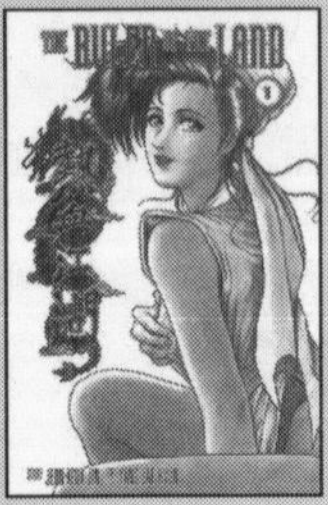

THE RULER OF THE LAND

Bi-Kwang Han is an immature, womanizing yellow-belly, but he might be the only man alive capable of helping the beautiful Hwa-Rin find her grandfather. Disguised as a man, she offers little enticement to girl-crazy Bi-Kwang, but with the empty promise of a passionate reward, he will join Hwa-Rin as she wields the coveted Sword of the Flowers on an action-packed and flat-out hilarious adventure. And with countless gangs of wretched and terrible enemies lusting after the Sword, Bi-Kwang might be forced to reach his potential and become the greatest fighter in the land.

THE HOLY-ROLLING ACTION CONTINUES IN CHRONO CRUSADE VOLUME 5! COMING SOON FROM ADV MANGA!

ADV Manga™

www.adv-manga.com

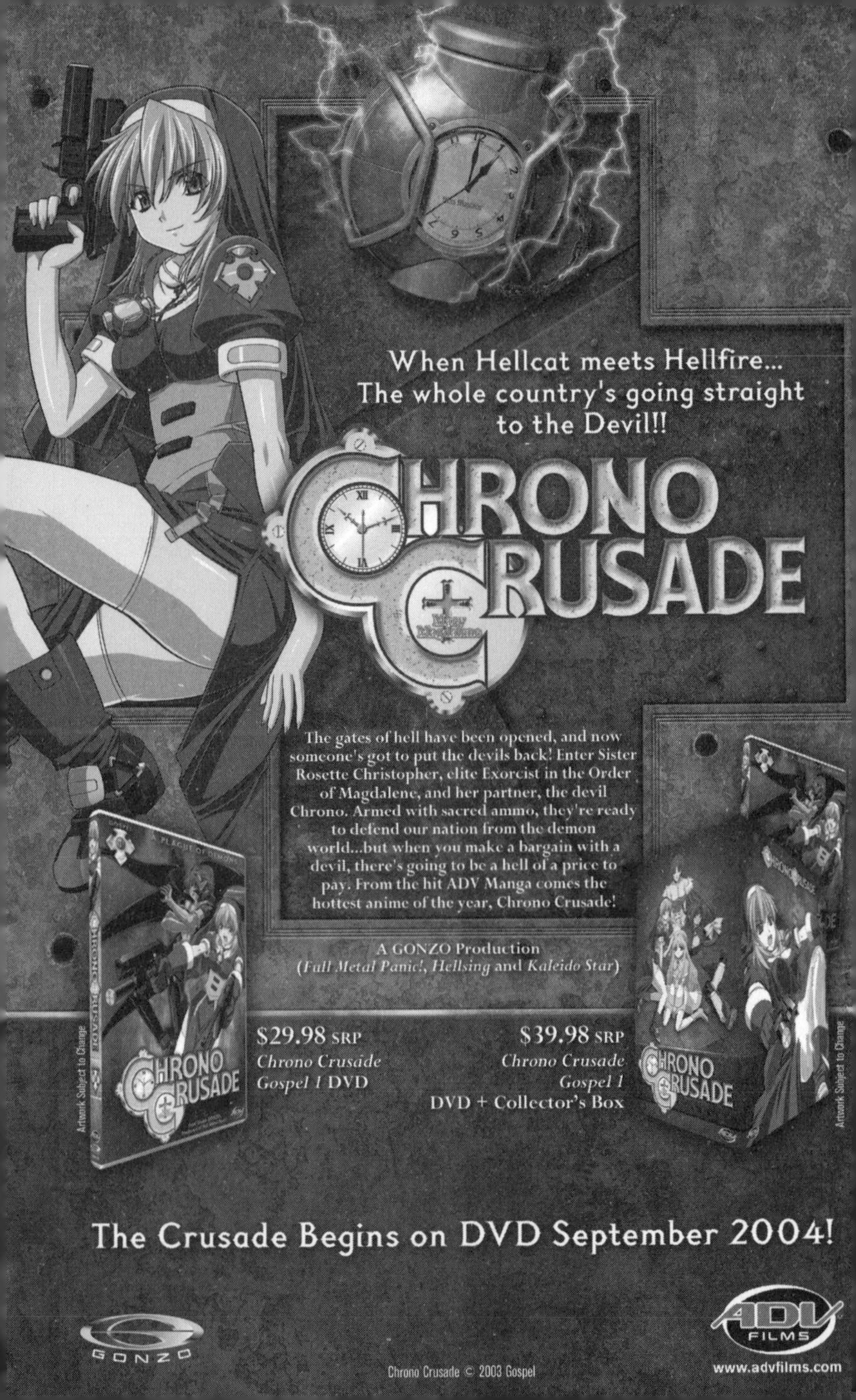
When Hellcat meets Hellfire...
The whole country's going straight to the Devil!!
CHRONO CRUSADE
The gates of hell have been opened, and now someone's got to put the devils back! Enter Sister Rosette Christopher, elite Exorcist in the Order of Magdalene, and her partner, the devil Chrono. Armed with sacred ammo, they're ready to defend our nation from the demon world...but when you make a bargain with a devil, there's going to be a hell of a price to pay. From the hit ADV Manga comes the hottest anime of the year, Chrono Crusade!
A GONZO Production
(Full Metal Panic!, Hellsing and Kaleido Star)
Artwork Subject to Change
CHRONO CRUSADE
$29.98 SRP
Chrono Crusade
Gospel 1 DVD
$39.98 SRP
Chrono Crusade
Gospel 1
DVD + Collector's Box
CHRONO CRUSADE
Artwork Subject to Change
The Crusade Begins on DVD September 2004!
GONZO
Chrono Crusade © 2003 Gospel
ADV FILMS
www.advfilms.com

SOMETHING MISSING
FROM YOUR TV?

ROBOT DESTRUCTION

SAMURAI VIOLENCE

KAWAII OVERDOSE

SKIMPY CLOTHES

NOSE BLEEDING

SUPER DEFORMED CHARACTERS

UPSKIRTS

EXTREME JIGGLING

HYPERACTIVE TEENS

MONSTER RAMPAGE

METROPOLITAN MELTDOWN

BLOOD & GUTS

Tired of networks that only dabble in anime? Tired of the same old cartoons?

Demand more from your cable or satellite operator. If they don't currently offer Anime Network as part of your channel lineup, then something is missing.

Your TV deserves better.

You deserve Anime Network.

Log on and demand anime in your home 24/7:
WWW.THEANIMENETWORK.COM

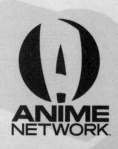

ANIME NETWORK

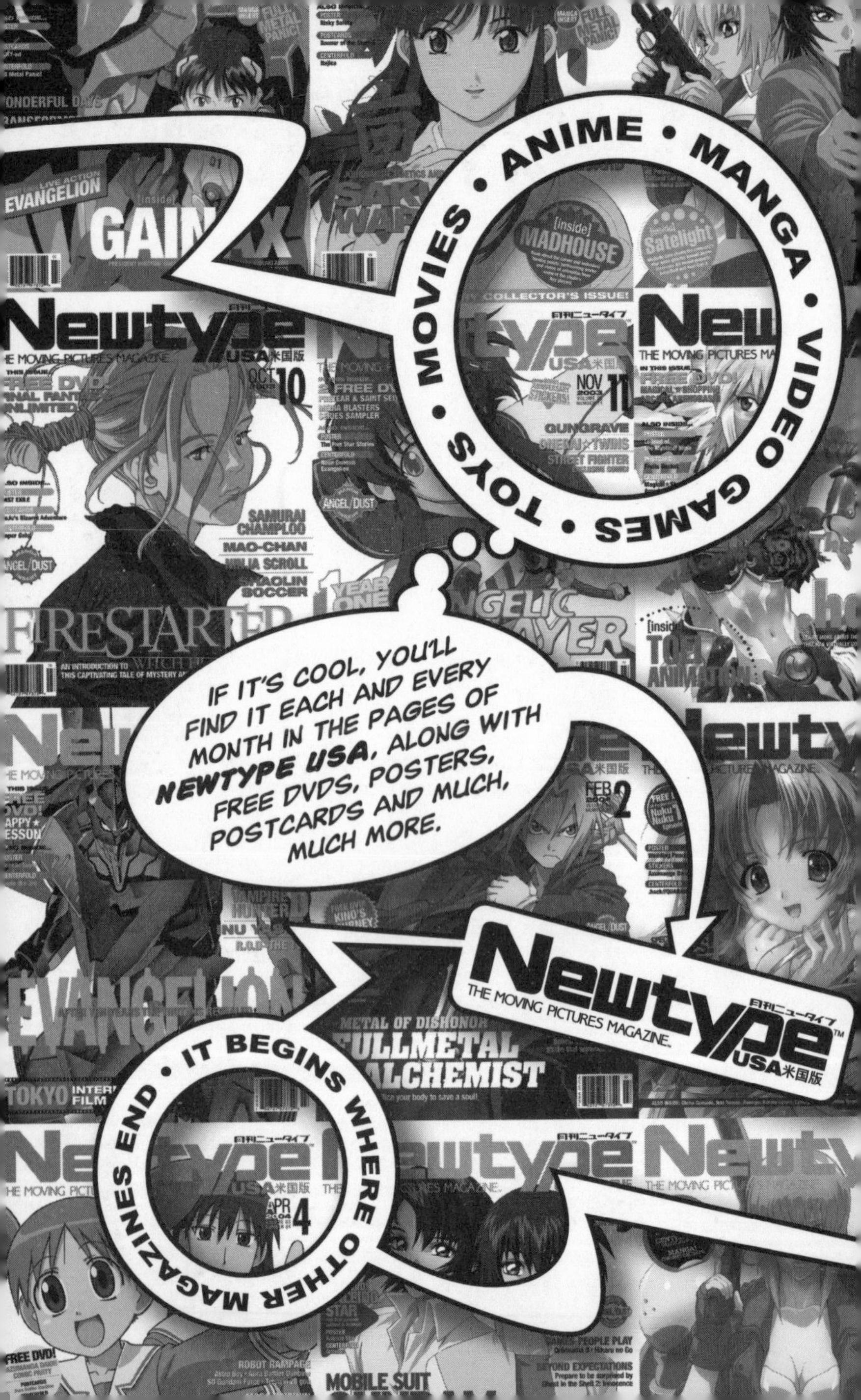
MOVIES • ANIME • MANGA • VIDEO GAMES • TOYS •
IF IT'S COOL, YOU'LL FIND IT EACH AND EVERY MONTH IN THE PAGES OF NEWTYPE USA, ALONG WITH FREE DVDS, POSTERS, POSTCARDS AND MUCH, MUCH MORE.
Newtype USA
THE MOVING PICTURES MAGAZINE.
月刊ニュータイプ 米国版
IT BEGINS WHERE OTHER MAGAZINES END •

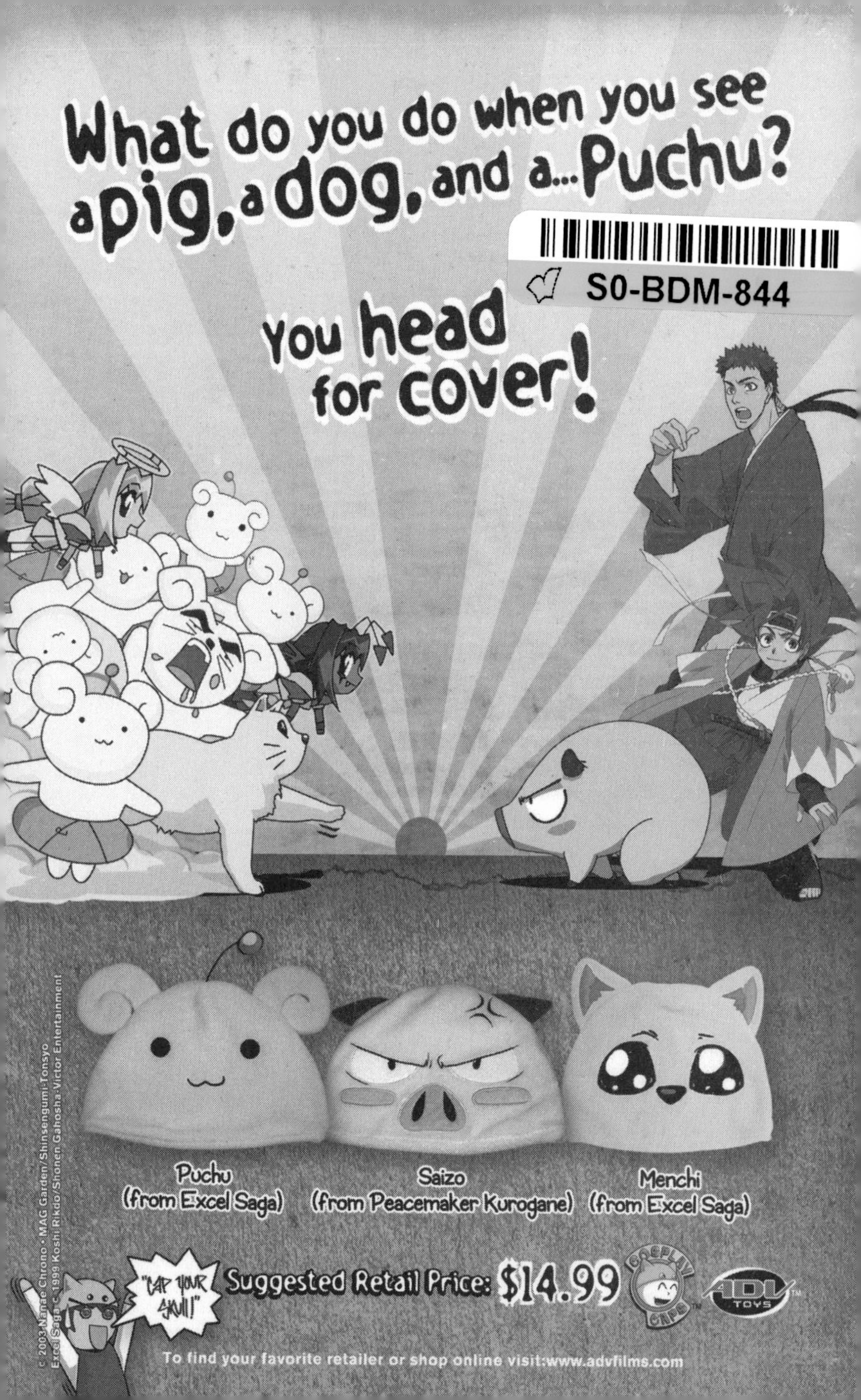
What do you do when you see a pig, a dog, and a...Puchu?
S0-BDM-844
You head for cover!
Puchu (from Excel Saga)
Saizo (from Peacemaker Kurogane)
Menchi (from Excel Saga)
"CAP YOUR SKULL!"
Suggested Retail Price: $14.99
COSPLAY CAPS
ADV TOYS
To find your favorite retailer or shop online visit:www.advfilms.com
c 2003 Nanae Chrono • MAG Garden/Shinsengumi-Tonsyo
Excel Saga c 1999 Koshi Rikdo/Shonen Gahosha•Victor Entertainment